BARH		MELB	
BASS		SAWST	
COMB		SWAV	
COTT	1/00	WATB	
FULB		WILL	
GAML			
GSHEL		CSMOB	
HIST		CTMOB	
LINT		SMOBC	

TWENTIETH CENTURY WAR MACHINES

CHRISTOPHER CHANT

ILLUSTRATIONS BY
JOHN BATCHELOR

TWENTIETH CENTURY WAR MACHINES

AIR

CHANCELLOR
PRESS

This edition published by Chancellor Press
an imprint of Bounty Books, a Division of the
Octopus Publishing Group Ltd,
2-4 Heron Quays, London, E14 4JP

© Graham Beehag Books

Printed in 1999
by Tat Wei Printing Packaging Singapore Pte Ltd

Contents

World War I: The Birth of Military Aviation

THE widespread use of aircraft in World War I (1914-18) altered both the nature of aviation and public opinion about flight and fliers. Although aircraft had seen extremely limited use as military weapons in the last few years before World War I, in 1914 most Europeans still considered flight to be the province of adventurous spirits who flew for sport and for excitement, without any real practical purpose. By the end of the conflict aviation was very big business, however, for many thousands of aircraft and engines had been built in a multitude of factories, most of which had no connection with aviation before the start of hostilities in August 1914. The air forces of the combatants, too, had grown into potent weapons of war, revealing to the far-sighted the potential that in World War II (1939-45) was to usher in the era of total war in which every man, woman and child, no matter how remote from the actual fighting front, was liable to attack.

Yet when World War I started few foresaw what was about to happen, for the role of aircraft was still uncertain. Although experiments with armament, principally light machine-guns and small bombs, had been carried out before the war, general military enthusiasm for the concept of armed aircraft had been lukewarm at best. This was understandable to a certain extent, for the already limited performance of most types of aircraft was seriously hampered by the addition of extra weight in the form of armament. Most generals could see little real scope for the employment of aircraft in war, nor could they see any purpose to be served by providing aircraft with armament to shoot at other aircraft serving in a similarly ill-defined role.

Despite military authorities' refusal to study the benefits and disadvantages of aircraft with any insight, enthusiasts called for aircraft to take their place in the nations' armed forces. This pressure, combined with a desire not to allow any one country to take a lead in building an air force, eventually led the French, German, British and other European governments to sanction the introduction of aircraft into their military forces. France and Germany soon led the field, and public indignation about this continental lead then forced the British government to spend more generously on their forces.

Thus the armed forces now had aircraft. But what were they to do with them, and how best were the services to exploit these expensive machines and the equally expensive force of men to fly and maintain them? The only possible solution in the years immediately preceding World War I seemed to be reconnaissance of two types: firstly tactical or strategic reconnaissance

6

Entering service in 1917 as an evolutionary development of the S.7, the SPAD S.13 was one of the finest fighters of World War I through its combination of excellent performance, adequate agility, considerable strength and great steadiness as a platform for its armament of two 0.303in (7.7mm) Vickers machine-guns installed in the upper part of the forward fuselage and fitted with synchronisation equipment so that they could fire through the disc swept by the propeller without hitting either of its two vital blades. Powered by a 235hp Hispano-Suiza 8Be water-cooled engine, the S.13 had a maximum level speed of 138mph (222km/h) at 6,560ft (2,000m), a ceiling of 21,800ft (6,645m), and an endurance of 2 hours. The fighter spanned 26ft 10.875in (9.84m) and was 20ft 8in (6.30m) long, and its weights included an empty figure of 1,257lb (570kg) and a maximum take-off figure of 1,808lb (820kg). During World War I, the S.13 equipped one Belgian, 81 French, 16 American and 11 Italian squadrons, and after the war was also escorted to Belgium, Czechoslovakia, Japan and Poland.

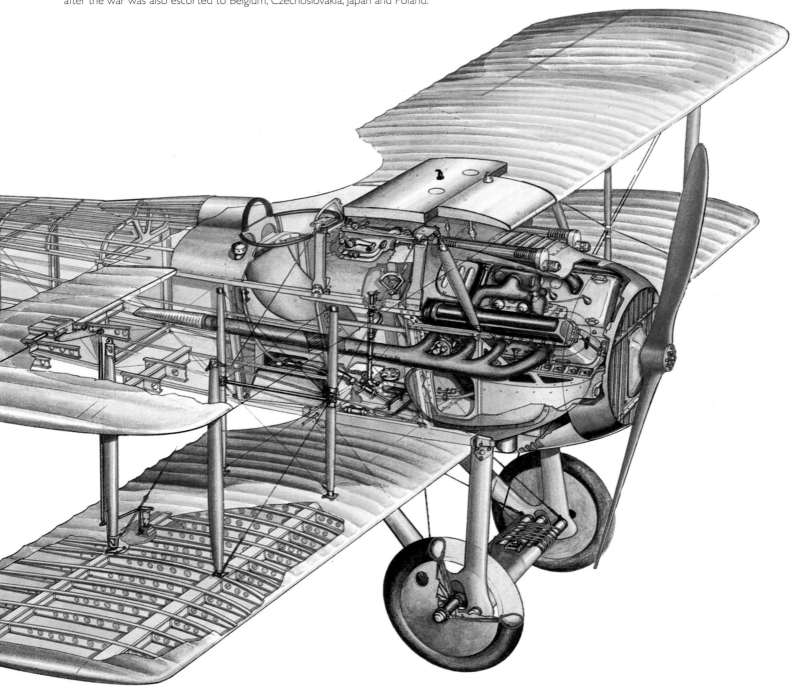

for commanders, and secondly spotting for the artillery. In the former, it was hoped, a trained officer would be able to use the vantage point the aircraft gave him to observe and note down enemy dispositions and movements and then report them to his command. In the latter an officer could spot the fall of his battery's shot, and then issue corrections which could be delivered in a weighted container, by signalling with manoeuvres or, it was hoped, by radio once a suitably light transmitter had been developed. France and Germany, both of whom placed great reliance on artillery, were quick to adopt the role of artillery spotting for their air forces. The United Kingdom, however, still lagged behind technically and theoretically, despite the efforts of many junior officers, and until 1914 its air forces were seen as an unwanted supplement to the cavalry in the latter's traditional capacity as light reconnoitring forces.

The various military aircraft competitions held in 1911 and 1912 had been intended to produce types that could be standardised for the squadrons, thus easing procurement and maintenance problems. Yet it was one thing to select what was considered a type suitable for widespread use, and another to get it into 'mass production' and thus into widespread service. The aviation industry of the period was just not geared to mass production: most factories had experience only in the building of 'one-off' types for designers or for very limited production. The result, in military terms, was that chosen designs could not as yet be built in sufficient quantity and there could be little standardisation of types within the squadrons.

In this respect the Germans and French were better off than the British. The Germans fielded a large number of Taube (dove) types derived from the experiments of Etrich and Wels, as well as units homogeneously equipped with tractor biplanes of Albatros and Aviatik design. The French had squadrons of Voisin bombers, and Blériots and Morane-Saulniers for reconnaissance work.

Above: The B.E.2a was a product of the Royal Aircraft Factory at Farnborough, and was in many ways an excellent aeroplane inasmuch as it was strong, possessed no handling vices, and was inherently stable. Experience in World War I soon showed, however, that while it promoted basic flight safety, inherent stability was a hindrance to effective operational use as it made rapid manoeuvring very difficult.

The British, almost inevitably, went to war with several French aircraft plus a large miscellany of British types, the best of which were the Royal Aircraft Factory's Blériot Experimental (B.E.) 2, the Sopwith Tabloid, the Bristol Scout D and various marks of Avro Type 504.

During the first stages of the war, the Allied powers operated 233 aircraft (160 French and 73 British in France) against the Germans' total of 246. At first the weather was superb, but the aircraft had not been designed for intensive operations and their serviceability was low, a factor compounded by the number of different types and engines in service at a time when the Allies were in full retreat and all logistical backing was run on an extemporised basis. Losses were tolerable, however, and the Royal Flying Corps (RFC) began to turn in useful reconnaissance reports. At first the high command was loath to heed the information received from this novel source, but when British reconnaissance aeroplanes brought in the first news of the Germans' great left wheel to sweep down past the west side of Paris, information which was subsequently confirmed by orthodox methods, the generals at last began to realise that in aircraft they had an important new aid. The art of camouflage against air reconnaissance was as yet unknown, and so the observers of the 'recce-jobs' had an easy time and could turn in useful information.

Although their primary tasks were reconnaissance and artillery spotting when the front was stable, the young and adventurous pilots of the day saw no reason why both sides should enjoy such benefits, when it might be possible to prevent the enemy from acquiring information by simply shooting at him and perhaps forcing him down. It was not long, therefore, before the first weapons made their appearance in the air. Initially these weapons consisted of personal equipment such as rifles and pistols. The resultant aerial duels stood little chance of inflicting mortal damage on the combatants. More hopeful, or perhaps just less realistic, innovators tried shotguns, hand grenades, bricks and even grappling hooks on the end of lengths of cord, the last of which it was hoped would hit and destroy the enemy's propeller. Others decided that flying close to the enemy might cause the pilot's nerve to fail and so cause him to come down. In fact, this last tactic was used against the first aeroplane verifiably forced down in combat, when a German two-seater was brought down by the aerial antics of three pilots from No. 2 Squadron, RFC, led by Lieutenant H. D. Harvey-Kelly on 25 August 1914.

The B classification was used by the Germans in the first part of World War I to signify their unarmed reconnaissance aircraft, and the mainstays of this force in the first part of the war were the Albatros B I and B II, here epitomised by the B II that was in essence a scaled-down version of the B I with the same arrangement of the pilot in the rear seat with the observer in the front seat. Operational experience soon revealed the inadequacy of this arrangement, for the observer had only very limited fields of vision from the front cockpit, and later aircraft reversed this arrangement to locate the observer in the rear cockpit, where he was also provided with a trainable machine-gun for defence of the aeroplane from rearward attack. The B II was powered by a 100hp Mercedes D.I water-cooled engine, and its performance included a maximum speed of 65mph (105km/h) at sea level, a ceiling of 9,845ft (3,000m) and endurance of 4 hours. The type had empty and maximum take-off weights of 1,591 and 2,361lb (722 and 1,070kg) respectively, and its dimensions included a span of 42ft 0in (12.80m) and length of 25ft 0.375in (7.63m).

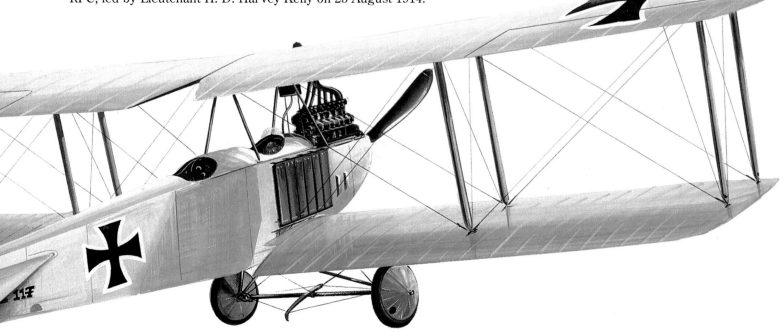

It was only a matter of time before effective aerial armament began to take effect, and on 5 October a French gunner, one Caporal Quénault, shot down an Aviatik two-seater with a Hotchkiss machine-gun mounted in the front of the nacelle of a Voisin bomber flown by Sergeant Joseph Frantz. From this time onwards the incidence of aerial combats, and also of aerial victories, began slowly to climb. But there remained one basic problem to be solved before air combat could be undertaken on a large scale, and this factor of interference between gun and propeller was not to be solved until 1915.

It had also occurred to various pilots that if one could fly over a target, then one could also drop missiles on it, and early in the war practical work began on the development of bombing. As early as June 1910 the indefatigable Glenn Curtiss had dropped dummy bombs on the outline of a battleship buoyed out on Lake Keuka, New York. Bombing competitions, using bags of flour, had even become a popular feature of pre-war flying meetings. The French and Germans, particularly the former, were concerned with bombing from the beginning of the war. On 14 August 1914, the French sent two Voisins to attack the Zeppelin sheds at Metz-Frascaty, and on 30 August a German Taube dropped five small bombs on Paris, killing one civilian and injuring another two.

The RFC was not at first especially interested in bombing, but its naval sister service, the Royal Naval Air Service (RNAS), showed more enterprise, launching its first, and in the event abortive, raid on the Zeppelin sheds at Düsseldorf with two aircraft from Antwerp on 22 September. Another raid on the same target was launched on 8 October, and this time the Zeppelin Z.IX was destroyed.

Early bombs were extemporised affairs, usually based on an artillery shell with fins attached, and bombing sights were nonexistent. Nevertheless the will was there, and in the autumn of 1914 the French decided to build up a major bombing force of Voisins, which were too slow and ponderous for air combat, but which had reasonable range and load-carrying capacity.

The problem that had hindered the development of true air fighting, that of the location of the machine-gun relative to the propeller, was easily solved on the older, pusher type of two-seaters. A light machine-gun, usually on a simple pillar mounting to allow easy traverse and elevation, was positioned at the front of the nacelle for the observer's use. Even on the newer tractor two-seaters, though the results were not particularly good, the observer could be provided with a light machine-gun capable of upward, rearward and lateral fire. The disadvantage of this system, however, was that the observer

This is the Voisin Type 3, otherwise known as the Voisin Type LA, in which the world's first air-to-air victory was gained on 5 October 1914. Although the aeroplane was a bomber and reconnaissance type, its size and weight-lifting ability made it feasible to install a 0.315in (8mm) Hotchkiss trainable machine-gun in the forward crew position, which was located in the extreme nose as the aeroplane was of the pusher configuration with the engine driving a pusher propeller at the rear of the central nacelle. On this history-making occasion, the Type 3 of Escadrille VB24 was being flown by Sergeant Joseph Frantz with Caporal Quénault as his observer/gunner, and near Reims encountered an Aviatik two-seater of the German air force. Quénault fired 47 rounds, and the Aviatik crashed in flames, killing its crew which comprised Schichting and von Zangen, the former an enlisted man flying the aeroplane and the latter an observer of commissioned rank. It was the German practice of the day to regard the pilot merely as the 'chauffeur' for the more important observer.

(who usually occupied the forward of the two seats so that the removal of his weight, on or near the aeroplane's centre of gravity, would not affect the trim of the machine on solo flights), was located between the wings, which seriously curtailed his field of vision and of fire, surrounded as he was by a mass of rigging and bracing wires, many of which would be cut by bullets. This problem was especially acute on early models of the B.E.2, the standard British two-seater in the first period of the war. The matter was later reconsidered and improved by reversing the positions of pilot and observer so that the observer had an improved field of fire over the aircraft's rear.

Although armament was fitted to two-seaters from the earliest days of the war, two-seaters were not really suited to conversion into fighters, or 'scouts' as such aircraft were then designated, as they were too big, too heavy, clumsy and slow. A single-seater fighter was required, but tractor types were almost universal by 1915 and the problem of the position of the gun relative to the propeller remained unsolved.

If the gun were fixed to fire forwards along the aeroplane's longitudinal axis and pilot's line of sight, some of the bullets fired would almost inevitably hit and damage one or more of the propeller blades. Various alternatives were tried, including the provision of guns angled out from the centreline of the aircraft by about 45 degrees, but the sighting of guns along such great deflection angles was so difficult as to make the expedient virtually useless.

The only practical solution to the sighting problem was to fix the gun along the aeroplane's centreline, so that basically all the pilot had to do was aim his whole machine at the target and press the trigger. What was needed was a method of stopping the occasional bullet from striking the propeller blades. Experiments carried out before the war by Franz Schneider of the German Luft-Verkehrs Gesellschaft (LVG) concern and by Raymond Saulnier of the French Morane-Saulnier company had paved the way, with the invention of primitive interrupter gears which halted the action of the gun when there was a propeller blade in front of the muzzle. But both experimenters' efforts had foundered on the problem of 'hang-fire' rounds. Here the fault lay with the manufacture of the primer and propellant for the ammunition: inconsistencies in the chemical compounds meant that bullets occasionally fired fractionally later than they should, obviating the work of the interrupter and shattering a blade. To preserve these expensive items, Saulnier had fitted experimental propellers with special steel deflectors, wedge-shaped

Early Bombs

THE bombs used by each side in the first part of World War I were small and extremely basic in design and operation. The standard German weapon was the Carbonit bomb, which was a pear-shaped device with a pointed nose, a propeller-activated arming pistol, and a tapered annular stabiliser connected to the body of the bomb by short struts. The Carbonit bomb was available in size ranging from 9.9lb (4.5kg) to 110lb (50kg).

On the other side of the front line, the British used the 20lb (9.1kg) Marten Hale bomb and the Woolwich Arsenal 100lb (45kg) bomb. The former carried 4.5lb (2kg) of Amatol (TNT and ammonium nitrate) explosive and was detonated by an impact fuse activated by a slipstream-driven propeller, but the latter was soon withdrawn from service as a result of its inadequate safety features. Also available to the British was a light incendiary bomb, which was a simple casing filled with 2 Imp gal (9.1 litres) of petrol that was ignited by an impact-fused cartridge.

The British also experimented with the so-called flechette, which was a dart-like weapon some 5in (127mm) long. These were carried in boxes of 500 and released from an altitude of 5,000ft (1,525m) to reach the velocity of a rifle bullet before reaching the ground, but proved generally ineffective even against infantry and cavalry concentrations.

The French bombs were based on the projectiles of their 75, 105 and 152mm (2.95, 4.13 and 5.98in) artillery pieces fitted with rudimentary fins for stabilisation in the air. The 75mm bomb weighed 20lb (9kg) and was a moderately effective anti-personnel weapon, the 105mm bomb was a more capable device weighing some 30lb (13.6kg), and the 152mm bomb was an altogether more devastating weapon weighing some 110lb (50kg).

French armourers bomb-up a flight of Breguet Bre.14 warplanes. Introduced in 1917, the Bre.14 was one of the finest warplanes of French design to emerge in World War I, and was a rugged, high-performance type that could function in the two-seat light bomber and two-seat tactical reconnaissance and army co-operation roles.

items bolted to the back of the propeller blades to deflect any bullet that was heading for a blade. The advent of war curtailed these experiments in favour of immediate production.

Early in 1915 the idea was resurrected by Saulnier and the great pre-war stunt pilot Roland Garros, now serving with the French Aviation Militaire. Probably at the instigation of the headstrong Garros, the two men decided that the actual interrupter gear should be omitted for the sake of lightness and simplicity, the few bullets that would hit a blade being warded off by the deflectors. Preliminary tests proved successful, and in March 1915 Garros returned to his unit with his modified Morane-Saulnier Type L parasol-wing scout. All was ready on 1 April 1915 and Garros set off in search of prey. He soon encountered four German Albatros two-seaters, which displayed no signs of fear or evasive action as the French scout closed in head-on, conventionally a safe angle of attack. A stream of bullets flew out from the nose of the Type L and an Albatros plummeted to the ground, its pilot dead at the controls. Before the astounded Germans could react, Garros had turned and fired at another Albatros, which immediately burst into flames and crashed. The remaining two Albatroses fled, taking with them the first news of the arrival of the 'era of the true fighter aeroplane'.

German pilots consequently avoided any Type L encountered, but in the next 17 days Garros managed to hit another three aircraft, thus becoming the world's first 'ace' fighter pilot. Although the Germans were mystified by this French success, the secret was soon to fall into their hands: on 19 April, Garros was forced down behind the German lines as the result of an inevitable engine failure. In the course of almost three weeks of combat, the propeller blades of his aeroplane had been shaken many times as the deflectors forced away bullets, the consequent vibration being transmitted via the crankshaft to the already highly stressed 80hp (59.6kW) rotary engine. Some form of engine failure had to happen, and Garros was unlucky that the prevailing westerly wind gave him no chance of gliding back over the lines. He was captured before he could set fire to his aeroplane, and was taken to a prisoner of war camp.

Seen here in the form of the aeroplane flown by Leutnant Werner Voss of Jagdstaffel 5 during the spring of 1917, the Albatros D III was the primary reason for the German tide of aerial success known to the British as 'Bloody April' 1917. Nicknamed by the British as the 'Vee-strutter' because of the configuration of the interplane struts connecting the larger upper and considerably smaller lower wings, the D III was an aerodynamically clean fighter with what, for the period was the heavy armament of two 7.92mm (0.312in) LMG08/15 machine-guns in the upper part of the forward fuselage and firing through the disc swept by the propeller blades with the aid of synchronisation equipment. The fuselage was a sturdy semi-monocoque structure of plywood construction, but the wing cellule had one major weakness in the tendency of its lower wing to twist and break away during high-velocity dives. The D III was powered by a 160hp Mercedes D.IIIa water-cooled engine for performance that included a maximum speed of 109mph (175km/h) at sea level, ceiling of 18,050ft (5,500m) and endurance of 2 hours. The D III had empty and maximum take-off weights of 1,454 and 1,953lb (660 and 885kg) respectively, and its dimensions included a span of 29ft 8.33in (9.05m) and length of 24ft 0.625in (9.16m). Voss was the fourth-ranking German ace of World War I, achieving 48 aerial victories before his death in September 1917.

Right: The standard reconnaissance and artillery spotting type used by the British between 1916 and 1918, the Royal Aircraft Factory R.E.8 suffered heavy losses while undertaking its exacting tasks. The type was armed with one 0.303in (7.7mm) Vickers fixed forward-firing machine-gun for the pilot and one or two 0.303in (7.7mm) Lewis trainable machine-guns in the rear cockpit for the observer/gunner, and could carry 260lb (118kg) of bombs. Known universally as the 'Harry Tate', the R.E.8 was powered by a 150hp RAF 4a water-cooled engine, and its performance included a maximum level speed of 102mph (164km/h) at 6,500ft (1,980m), ceiling of 13,500ft (6,125m) and endurance of 4 hours 15 minutes.

Below: The Breguet Bre.14 was the 'maid of all work' for the French air force in 1917 and 1918, but operated mainly in the light bomber and reconnaissance/artillery-spotting roles. In its Bre.14B.2 bomber form, the type was armed with one 0.303in (7.7mm) Vickers fixed forward-firing machine-gun for the pilot and two or three 0.303in (7.7mm) Lewis trainable machine-guns in the rear cockpit for the observer/gunner, and could carry 518lb (235kg) of bombs. The Bre.14 was powered by a 300hp Renault water-cooled engine, and its performance included a maximum level speed of 121mph (195km/h) at sea level, ceiling of 19,030ft (5,800m) and endurance of 2 hours 45 minutes.

The capture of this remarkable French aeroplane was a welcome surprise to the Germans, who immediately ordered Anthony Fokker, the enigmatic Dutch designer who was working for them, to copy the system on his recently introduced M 5 Eindecker monoplane. In just 48 hours, Fokker's team of talented designers and engineers produced not a copy of the primitive French system but an efficient interrupter gear for the 7.92mm (0.312in) Parabellum machine-gun then in widespread use as the standard German aerial gun. (Early in 1916, the 7.92mm/0.312in MG 08/15 machine-gun made at Spandau near Berlin superseded the Parabellum as the standard fixed gun, hence the popular Allied misnomer of the gun as the 'Spandau'.) The Fokker interrupter was tested on an M 5k monoplane and proved highly efficient, and the armed version of the M 5k was ordered into production as the E-I.

The new fighter entered service over the Western Front, and soon earned itself a fearsome reputation. Allied aircraft, which were mostly as agile and as fast as the German machine, could not cope with the technological advance of the interrupter-governed machine-gun, and for the first time in aerial

Left: The Airco (de Havilland) D.H.2 was one of the first true fighters to enter British service, an event that took place early in 1916. At this time the British lacked an effective synchronisation system, so the D.H.2 was designed as a pusher-type in which the engine was located at the rear of the central nacelle to drive a pusher propeller turning between the four narrow booms extending from the wing trailing edges to carry the tail unit. This configuration left the nose free for the armament of one 0.303in (7.7mm) Lewis machine gun, which could originally be moved in elevation but was later fixed to fire straight ahead.

Opposite top: These three views highlight the essential configuration of the Fokker E III, which was the definitive version of the world's first true fighter, the E I introduced by Fokker in 1915. The Fokker Eindecker (monoplane) aircraft secured their success solely through their incorporation for the first time in any production aeroplane of a fixed forward-firing machine-gun synchronised to fire through the propeller disc.

Opposite bottom: The Sopwith 1½ Strutter was a remarkable warplane that was built in large numbers and could be operated as a two-seat reconnaissance and fighter aeroplane with the observer/gunner manning a 0.303 in (7.7mm) Lewis trainable machine-gun, or alternatively as a single-seat light bomber with a bomb load of 224lb (102kg) in addition to the pilot's 0.303in (7.7mm) Vickers fixed forward-firing machine gun. The type was powered by a 110hp Le Clerget air-cooled rotary engine, and its performance included a maximum level speed of 106mph (171km/h) at sea level, ceiling of 15,000ft (4,570m) and endurance of 4 hours 30 minutes. The aeroplane had empty and maximum take-off weights of 1,259 and 2,149lb (571 and 975kg) respectively, and its primary dimensions included a span of 33ft 6in (10.21m) and length of 25ft 3in (7.70m).

warfare severe Allied casualties began to accrue. The press was quick to exploit the period as that of the 'Fokker Scourge', in which the prey were 'Fokker fodder'. The emotional controversy that resulted cast the first doubts on the way in which Allied aircraft were designed and procured, especially when no Allied counter to the Fokker was produced.

Over the Front, the 'Fokker Scourge' was at first limited in its effect because the Germans had not evolved a tactical system to make full use of the type's impact. The E-I, soon joined by the slightly larger and more powerful E-II and E-III, was issued to the *Fliegerabteilungen* (flight sections) on the basis of one or two machines to each unit. Luckily for the Germans, prescient officers in the Bavarian air force, one of the several semi-autonomous national forces that made up the Imperial German air service, realised that better results would be gained by grouping the presently scattered fighters into homogeneous units. Thus was born the *Kampfeinsitzerkommando* (single-seater fighter unit), of which three were formed in the late summer of 1915.

The Fokkers ruled supreme in the autumn and winter of 1915, with the Allies apparently loath to copy the German interrupter gear. Instead a variety of expedients were tried, with the result that the inferior German fighters continued to dominate the skies during the crucial early stages of the Battle of Verdun, that military and emotional bastion of France where the Germans had determined to 'bleed France white'.

In the spring of 1916, at last, the Allies began to make headway, albeit still without an interrupter gear. The French produced the delightful Nieuport Type 11 Bébé (baby) sesquiplane, with a Lewis gun firing over the top wing to clear the upper arc of the disc swept by the propeller. The British introduced the Airco (de Havilland) D.H.2, a neat pusher biplane with a Lewis gun mounted at the front of the one-man nacelle. The Bébé first achieved prominence over Verdun with Les Cigognes, an elite French formation that was basically an adaptation and expansion of Boelcke's ideas. The British considered it unwise to group all the best pilots into a few squadrons whilst leaving the majority of the squadrons to cope with mediocre and poor pilots, and instead tended to build up each fighter unit around a few pilots with excellent capabilities in the hope and expectation that their skills would be adopted by the other pilots. This system in fact proved the most satisfactory of all.

After an initial period in which he had allowed his inclinations towards squadrons equipped with homogeneous aircraft to be overruled by his subordinates' desire for a mixture of types, Major-General Sir David Henderson, the RFC's first commander in France, had witnessed the formation of the first homogeneous squadron in July 1915, when a squadron of Vickers F.B.5 'Gunbus' two-seat fighters entered combat. This policy was continued by his successor, Major-General Hugh Trenchard, and the first D.H.2 unit, No. 24 Squadron, arrived in France in February 1916.

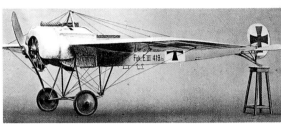

The early British objections to homogeneous squadrons had been based on the notion that the RFC's *raison d'etre* encompassed observation, reconnaissance and photographic duties, and so each squadron should be equipped with types suitable for such work. When the overwhelming desirability of fighter aircraft for protection became apparent, most junior commanders were of the opinion that each squadron should have a few fighters that could be sent out with the squadron's two-seaters. The high-intensity offensive operations demanded by Trenchard throughout the 'Fokker Scourge' had killed any lingering beliefs in this system, and the British were now wholehearted supporters of the homogeneous squadron.

Side-by-side, the Type 11s and D.H.2s gradually wrested command of the air from the Germans, taking the air war effectively to the Germans, driving the latters' observation machines virtually from the air. The 'Fokker Scourge' was defeated by April, and the Allies quickly exploited their command of the air by pushing several new types into action in the second half of 1916.

Interrupter gears were now in widespread use on the Allied side, on such types as the French Nieuport Type 17 and SPAD S.7, and the British Sopwith 1½-Strutter and Sopwith Pup. All four aircraft were fitted with a 0.303in (7.7mm) Vickers fixed forward-firing gun, and the 1½-Strutter, so named for

Great Aces of World War I

THE greatest aces of World War I were Manfred Freiherr von Richthofen, René Fonck and Edward 'Mick' Mannock with 80, 75 and 73 confirmed 'kills' respectively.

Von Richthofen first joined a cavalry regiment but later transferred to the flying service and he was at first a poor pilot who never became a truly great flier. This limitation was more than offset by von Richthofen's ability to find and stalk his prey. He was in essence a lone pilot, but possessed the leadership qualities to rise to Staffel (squadron) and then Geschwader (wing) commands, and became immensely popular in Germany for his aerial exploits and skill. Generally associated with the Albatros biplane fighters, von Richthofen finally became an exponent of the diminutive Fokker Dr I triple fighter, which was an extremely agile machine that could be used to good effect by skilled pilots. Von Richthofen was killed in April 1918, probably in air combat with a Canadian pilot, Captain Roy Brown, although it is possible that he was despatched from the ground by an Australian machine-gunner.

Although credited with 75 victories, Fonck was a 'loner' par excellence and often flew without even a wingman, so his victory tally was surely higher than this figure. Somewhat aloof and never very popular with his compatriots, Fonck was an excellent pilot and a truly superb shot, especially in deflection firing. An analytical thinker of considerable ability, Fonck spent much time in the analysis of air combat and its tactics, factoring in every consideration he could imagine, and was therefore well placed in the air to select precisely the ideal way in which to approach his target. So successful was this method that Fonck was often able to down an opponent with as few as five or six rounds: as Fonck said, '...je place mes balles au but comme avec la main' (I put my bullets into the target as if by hand). Fonck survived World War II and died in 1953.

Another whose victory tally is smaller than it should be is Mannock, whose approach to the Germans was marked by an intense hatred and ruthlessness. Unlike Fonck, however, Mannock was a firm believer in the use of several pilots acting together, and for this reason he must be reckoned the finest patrol leader of World War I. Often Mannock set up a 'kill' by crippling the target before entrusting the coup de grâce to a new pilot, who thus learned from the master and started his own victory tally. Mannock was killed in July 1918 after a German infantryman's bullet hit the petrol tank of the Royal Aircraft Factory S.E.5a fighter he was flying.

its single sets of interplane struts and 'half' struts supporting the centre section, also had a Lewis gun for the observer. Much to the annoyance of RFC officialdom, the Pup received its nickname from its scaled-down family likeness to the 1½-Strutter, and despite strenuous efforts to dissuade pilots from using the nickname, 'Pup' was so popular that the authorities were forced to accept it as official. The Pup was in many respects the first adequate fighter. Its performance was excellent, it had a fixed machine-gun with interrupter gear, and its agility was phenomenal.

Unlike many other aircraft, however, the Pup's manoeuvrability was not secured at the expense of other factors, and the type lives in the memory of those who have flown it as one of the most tractable and delightful aircraft ever built. Its control response was smooth, clean and swift, allowing the pilot to place his machine exactly as he wished.

Towards the end of 1916, however, the inexorable see-saw of technological advance over the Front had swung the balance in favour of Germany once again. Realising that the Allies would produce a counter to

The Bristol F.2B was without doubt the finest two-seat fighter of World War I. The type had an inauspicious combat debut as the F.2A with the 190hp Rolls-Royce Falcon water-cooled engine because its pilots regarded the new machine as a typical two-seater and flew it accordingly, with emphasis on defence by the gunner in the rear cockpit, but pilots soon learned to regard the more powerfully engined F.2B as a single-seater with extra capability provided by the gunner. Thereafter the type's success was assured, and the F.2B became a formidable warplane. The type was armed with one 0.303in (7.7mm) Vickers fixed forward-firing machine-gun for the pilot and one or two 0.303in (7.7mm) Lewis trainable machine-guns in the rear cockpit for the observer/gunner. Powered by the 275hp Falcon III engine, the F.2B possessed performance that included a maximum level speed of 125mph (201km/h) at sea level, ceiling of 20,000ft (6,095m) and endurance of 3 hours. The aeroplane had empty and maximum take-off weights of 1,930 and 2,779lb (875 and 1261kg) respectively, and its primary dimensions included a span of 39ft 3in (11.96m) and length of 25ft 10in (7.87m).

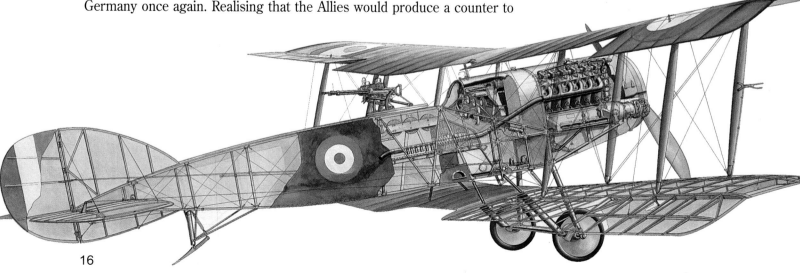

the Eindecker by the middle of 1916, the Germans had set about developing a new generation of aircraft late in 1915. By the last months of 1916 these were beginning to enter service with the Deutsche Luftstreitkräfte or German air force, formed in October 1916 from a variety of flying units. At the heart of this resurgence in German air superiority was the series of Albatros single-seat fighters, starting with the D-I, -II and -III, the last of which entered service early in 1917. These sleek, shark-like biplanes with their plywood fuselages and well-cowled engines were capable of very good performance. Most importantly of all, however, they were armed with two machine-guns, which gave them twice the firepower of Allied types.

The immediate consequence of the arrival of these new German fighters was total command of the air, and, in what became known in the RFC as 'Bloody April', the British suffered losses in aircrews and aircraft of some 30 per cent, their highest losses of the entire war. Most tragic of all, from the long-term point of view, was the loss of many survivors of the previous year's hard times. With these men went most of the practical experience in how to fight an air war, so crucial in helping the new pilots, who were shot down in droves by the 'Albatri' or 'Vee-strutters' as they were known in the slang of the RFC. The life expectancy of RFC subalterns on the Western Front in the 'Bloody April' period was between 11 days and three weeks. Bearing in mind that experienced pilots stood considerably more chance of survival, the life expectancy of new arrivals must have been a matter of hours, or at best, days. A high rate of losses was almost inevitable for the RFC as Trenchard still insisted on offensive patrols and aggressive work even by two-seaters, most of which were by now the newer Armstrong Whitworth F.K.8 and Royal Aircraft Factory R.E.8. Both of these were large biplanes, and the R.E.8 had acquired an unenviable and endeserved reputation as a 'deathtrap'. The fault really lay with the tactical employment of the type, in steady artillery-spotting work, where it was particularly vulnerable to German fighter attack.

Above: Entering service in February 1918, the Ansaldo SVA-5 was a single-seat strategic reconnaissance aeroplane that became one of Italy's best warplanes of World War I. Powered by a 220hp SPA 6A water-cooled engine, the SVA-5 was armed with two 0.303in (7.7mm) Vickers fixed forward-firing synchronised machine-guns, and could attain a maximum speed of 143mph (230km/h) at sea level.

Combined with the superiority of the new generation of German fighters, the RFC's offensive tactics served to take 'trade' to the Germans, who were quite content to wait on their own side of the lines. It was the Allies who were attempting to use their strategic initiative at the time, so the German tactics were quite correct. It can be argued that the aggressive British tactics, too, were basically correct despite the enormous losses entailed. Throughout the war, on the other hand, the French kept a much lower profile, and, like the Germans, restricted the amount of offensive work done by fighters. Instead they concentrated on offensive work by reconnaissance, spotter and bomber aircraft, which could more profitably take the war to the Germans. The fighters were used mainly to escort offensive machines, and to prevent incursions by German aircraft into French airspace.

There was also another way in which French tactics resembled those of the Germans. Whereas the British kept squadrons posted along the length of the Front, only reinforcing sectors under real threat or where a major offensive was planned, the French and Germans instead based their air defence on a smaller number of elite units.

On the German side, the *Jagdstaffeln* filled a similar, if smaller, position to that held by Les Cigognes in the first half of 1917. But in June of that year a reorganisation led to the formation of Jagdgeschwader Nr I (1st Fighter Wing). The Jagdgeschwader was made up of four Jastas, as the Jagdstaffeln were usually abbreviated.

Below: The Hannover CL II was one of Germany's best escort fighters and ground-attack warplanes of the later part of World War I. Intended as a lightweight partner to the C series of armed reconnaissance aircraft, the CL warplanes had a crew of two and a moderately high-powered engine, and in design were optimised for the combat role with compact dimensions, sturdy construction, and good fields of vision and fire for the pilot and observer/gunner. In the Hannover CL II, this last factor resulted in the location of the upper wing at the height of the pilot's eyes, and the adoption of a biplane tail unit to improve the observer/gunner's fields of fire.

By the 'Bloody April' of 1917 air combats had grown into massive affairs involving 100 aircraft or more, a far cry from the individual combats of 1915 and early 1916. The skies over the Western Front were now dominated by huge, swirling dogfights, impossible to follow from the ground except when a crippled machine staggered from the fray out of control, or when an aeroplane which had taken a bullet in the unprotected fuel system plunged down like a fiery comet, trailing flame and black oily smoke until it crashed into the ground and exploded.

The second quarter of 1917 found both sides exhausted by 'Bloody April', the only success of which had been, from the British point of view, the performance by the handful of Sopwith Triplanes, or 'Tripehounds' as they were nicknamed, operated by the RNAS. Although each was armed with only one machine-gun, these were clean aircraft that could combat the 'Albatri' by means of their remarkable rate of climb and their general agility, both functions of the large wing area contained within the small overall dimensions of a triplane layout. So impressed were the Germans that orders for triplane designs were immediately issued. The type ordered into production was the Fokker Dr I, the aeroplane flown by von Richthofen at the time of his death. Very manoeuvrable, the Dr I in fact appeared after the effective epoch of the triplane, and lacked the performance to make it a fighter suitable for any but the most experienced of pilots.

This painting highlights the Royal Aircraft Factory S.E.5a, one of the best British fighters of World War I. The type entered service in the spring of 1917 in its original S.E.5 form with a lower-powered engine, but reached definitive status with the S.E.5a powered by the 200hp Hispano-Suiza 8 water-cooled engine that was later replaced by 220 or 240hp versions of this unit, or most importantly the 200hp Wolseley Viper engine. The S.E.5a was not notable for its agility, which was no more than adequate, but was immensely strong, possessed very good performance, and was remarkably stable as a gun platform. The armament of two 0.303in (7.7mm) machine-guns was typical of the period, but was unusual in its configuration as one fixed forward-firing and synchronised Vickers gun in the forward fuselage, and one Lewis gun on a quadrant over the upper-wing centre section where it could be pulled back and down to rake the underside of any target above the S.E.5a.

Fokker Dr I

THE Fokker Dr I remains one of the best-known fighters of World War I although it was produced only in modest numbers and was at best obsolescent at the time of its introduction. The type was a response to the German enthusiasm for the triplane fighter (after the British had pioneered the type in the Sopwith Triplane in an effort to provide maximum wing area within minimum overall dimensions as a means of boosting agility), and was designed by Reinhold Platz with a welded steel tube fuselage and thick-section cantilever wings that were of fabric-covered wooden construction and fitted with I-type interplane struts only after pilots had expressed concern about the wings' vibration in manoeuvring flight. The Dr I appeared after the end of the 'triplane era', but found success with the more skilled of German pilots who could exploit the type's phenomenal agility in the type of defensive fighting imposed on the Germans from mid-1917. The Dr I was armed with two 0.312in (7.92mm) LMG08/15 fixed forward-firing and synchronised machine-guns in the upper part of the forward fuselage, and was powered by a 110hp Oberursel- or Thulin-built copy of a French air-cooled rotary piston engine, the Le Rhône 9. This gave the Dr I a maximum speed of 103mph (165km/h) at 13,125ft (4,000m), and its other performance figures included a ceiling of 20,000ft (6,095m) and endurance of 1 hour 30 minutes. The Dr I had empty and maximum take-off weights of 893 and 1,290lb (405 and 585kg) respectively, and its primary dimensions included a span of 23ft 7.625in (7.20m) and length of 18ft 11.125in (5.77m).

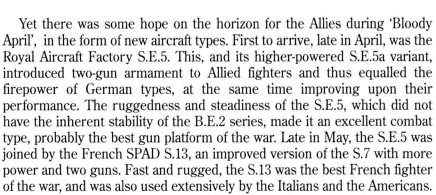

Yet there was some hope on the horizon for the Allies during 'Bloody April', in the form of new aircraft types. First to arrive, late in April, was the Royal Aircraft Factory S.E.5. This, and its higher-powered S.E.5a variant, introduced two-gun armament to Allied fighters and thus equalled the firepower of German types, at the same time improving upon their performance. The ruggedness and steadiness of the S.E.5, which did not have the inherent stability of the B.E.2 series, made it an excellent combat type, probably the best gun platform of the war. Late in May, the S.E.5 was joined by the French SPAD S.13, an improved version of the S.7 with more power and two guns. Fast and rugged, the S.13 was the best French fighter of the war, and was also used extensively by the Italians and the Americans.

Both the S.E.5 and S.13 were fitted with powerful inline engines, but the third new Allied fighter that brought about the eclipse of the German air

force in the middle of 1917 was the ultimate expression of the classic rotary-engined design philosophy. This was the Sopwith Camel, which appeared in July 1917. Bearing a strong resemblance to the Pup, the Camel lacked the earlier type's lightness of appearance, featuring instead a slightly squat, pugnacious belligerence emphasised by the 'hump' over the breeches of the twin Vickers guns that led to the type's nickname, later officially adopted. With the propeller, engine, fuel, oil, guns, ammunition and pilot all accommodated in the front 7ft (2.13m) of the fuselage, where their inertia would least interfere with manoeuvrability, the Camel was supremely agile, especially in right-hand turns, where the torque of the rotary action complemented the turning moment of rudder and ailerons. The Camel's only fault was the result of this compactness and the torque of the rotary action: pilots unused to the new fighter were liable to allow the turn to

become a spin, which at low altitudes was often a fatal mistake. In the hands of a skilled pilot, however, the Camel was a superlative fighter, and the type accounted for a credited 1,294 enemy aircraft before the end of the war, although later research revealed the real total to be considerably higher.

The fourth fighter to end German dominance of the air, a role it played for the rest of the war, was the Bristol F.2B Fighter which entered service in the summer of 1917. Originally intended as a standard two-seater to supplement the RFC's F.K.8s and R.E.8s, the F.2A version of the aircraft, which had entered service in April 1917, had sustained a rough baptism of fire at the hands of Richthofen's Jagdgeschwader Nr I, four of six F.2As failing to return. But pilots soon realised what a machine they had in the Fighter, with the performance and agility of a single-seater combined with the 'sting in the tail' of the two-seater. Once this lesson had been absorbed and the implications worked out, the Fighter became a formidable weapon.

The Germans were taken slightly unawares by the arrival of these latest Allied aircraft, and were slow to respond. Firstly a new version of the Albatros appeared, the D-V and D-Va, with improved aerodynamics and a more powerful engine, but this machine proved entirely incapable of wresting from the Allies the superiority they enjoyed by the summer of 1917. Urgent requests for improved types were sent out, and in January 1918 the Fokker D-VII was selected for quantity production. This was the war's best fighter, and the acme of the designs of Reinhold Platz, Fokker's chief designer. Originally employed as a welder in the factory, Platz had shown an intuitive flair for structures and aerodynamics, and had been appointed chief designer. Perhaps more important than these other qualifications for the job, Platz was a reticent man who would allow Fokker himself to claim credit for the designs. The hallmarks of Platz's designs were simplicity and strength: welded steel tube fuselages allied to wings of wooden construction but great depth, allowing massive box structures to be used for strength, at a time when other designers preferred very thin sections requiring masses of internal and external bracing by struts and wires. Platz's designs had the elegance of simplicity, and his three most celebrated designs, the Dr I triplane, the D-VII biplane and the D-VIII parasol monoplane which entered service only at the end of the war, were all excellent flying machines. The D-VII, in particular, was feared by Allied pilots, and was the only aeroplane to be singled out by name to be

Without doubt the most successful fighter of World War I in terms of air combat victories, the Sopwith F.1 Camel was optimised for the air combat role by the location of all the major masses (engine, fuel, lubricant, armament and pilot) in the forward 7ft (2.13m) of the fuselage around the centre of gravity. This combined with the fighter's low wing loading and compact overall dimensions to produce exceptional agility, and this was further enhanced under certain circumstances by the torque reaction of the air-cooled rotary engine, which made the Camel tricky for novices to fly but allowed more experienced pilots to effect extremely fast turns. The Camel, so nicknamed for the 'hump' covering the breeches of its two 0.303in (7.7mm) Vickers fixed forward-firing and synchronised machine-guns, was powered by any of several types of rotary engine in the power rating up to 150hp, and the most common units were the 130hp Clerget 9 and 150hp Bentley BR.1. With the Clerget engine the Camel had a maximum level speed of 115mph (185km/h) at 6,500ft (1,980m), a ceiling of 19,000ft (5,790m) and an endurance of 2 hours 30 minutes, its empty and maximum take-off weights were 929 and 1,453lb (421 and 659kg) respectively, and its primary dimensions included a span of 28ft 0in (8.53m) and length of 18ft 9in (5.715m).

surrendered in the armistice agreement of 1918. With an excellent BMW engine, the D-VII had outstanding high-altitude qualities, including the ability to hang on its propeller and fire upwards, a position in which Allied types would have stalled and spun.

Luckily for the Allies, the Germans were unable to rush these new types of fighter into service in sufficient numbers to prevent the British, French, American and Belgian fighter forces from exercising almost total command of the air from the spring of 1918, allowing the other elements of the Allied air forces to get on with their work almost unhampered.

The Western Front was not, of course, the only theatre of war to see air operations in World War I. Yet the activities and types of aircraft used over the Western Front set the style for other theatres including the Eastern Front, Italy, the Balkans and the various Middle Eastern areas in which the British and Turks faced each other. On all these fronts, with the possible exception of the Italian one, air operations followed the pattern set over the Western Front, using aircraft 'handed down' after reaching obsolescence in the West. But although the nature of air operations in other theatres followed the lead of the Western Front, each made its own demands on men and machines, principally for geographic reasons. Thus, while such operations may have lacked the intensity of air fighting over France, for those involved they were just as strenuous and dangerous.

On the Eastern Front, for example, the Russians, Germans and Austro-Hungarians had to contend with blazing summers and bitter winters, as well as having to cover vast areas. In the Balkans, airmen had to operate over very inhospitable and mountainous country from primitive airfields, and in climatic conditions similar to those of the Eastern Front. In the Middle East, where yet again it was the Germans who proved to be the Allies' most formidable adversaries, problems of dust, extreme heat and lack of water had to be overcome.

Unglamorous and unglamorized, it was in fact the work of machines other than the fighters which proved to be of primary importance in World War I. Artillery spotters and photo-reconnaissance aircraft shared all the dangers of the fighters, yet received little popular acclaim, the civilians at home preferring to read of the actions of dashing 'scout' pilots. Yet the fighters were there only to protect their own two-seaters and bombers, and to prevent the enemy's machines from acting freely.

Because they had to carry at least two men, armament and their specialised equipment, artillery spotter and reconnaissance aircraft were usually heavy and fairly clumsy. And because they needed to be able to fly

Introduced in the summer of 1917 as one of the new CL class of light two-seaters optimised for the escort and ground-attack roles, the Halberstadt CL II proved very successful and was built in moderately large numbers by Halberstadt and also be Bayerische Flugzeug-Werke. The CL II was armed with one or two 0.312in (7.92mm) LMG08/15 fixed forward-firing and synchronised machine-guns and one or two 0.312in (7.92mm) Parabellum trainable rearward-firing machine-guns on a ring mounting in the rear cockpit, and was powered by a 160hp Mercedes D.III water-cooled engine for a maximum level speed of 103mph (165km/h) at 16,405ft (5,000 m), a ceiling of 16,730ft (5,100m) and an endurance of 3 hours. The type had empty and maximum take-off weights of 1,701 and 2,498lb (772 and 1,133kg) respectively, and its primary dimensional data include a span of 35ft 4in (10.77m) and length of 23ft 11.375in (7.30m). Further development of the same basic airframe with the 185hp BMW water-cooled engine resulted in the CL IIa, but the definitive CL IV with the D.III engine had a somewhat different airframe with the biplane wing cellule re-sited on a shorter fuselage, the raising and lengthening of the horizontal tail surface, and the reshaping of the vertical tail surface.

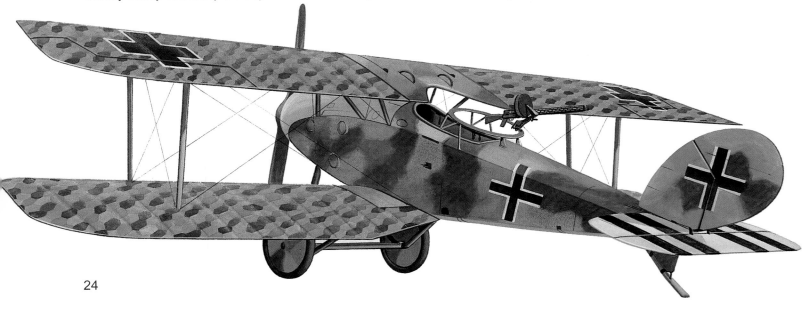

steadily for lengthy periods, a fair measure of inherent stability was called for. This quality had been too much in evidence in the B.E.2 series, but about the right measure was found in the frequently reviled R.E.8. These machines had to operate in all weathers, within reach of anti-aircraft fire and enemy fighters, and so anything which detracted from their manoeuvrability was a hindrance to survival. For all these reasons, the problems of designing a front-line two-seater were formidable, and it is remarkable how many good designs emerged in the second half of the war, usually resulting in the manufacture of aircraft as small as possible to ensure agility, whilst affording the observer a good field of fire for his flexible machine-gun. The Germans produced the Albatros C X and XII, Deutsche Flugzeugwerke (DFW) C IV and V, Halberstadt C V, Luft-Verkehrs Gesellschaft (LVG) C V and VI, and Rumpler C IV and VII. The French had the first-class Salmson 2, powered by an unusual water-cooled, rather than air-cooled, 260hp radial engine. The Italians produced the sleek Ansaldo SVA 10, and the Austro-Hungarians the useful Ufag C I. It is difficult to underestimate the heroic proportions of the work done with these unsung aircraft.

A less important role than that of spotter and reconnaissance machines was played by bomber and ground-attack aircraft, but it was a role which consistently grew in importance as the war progressed. The idea that one could drop a bomb on what could be seen from the air was as old or possibly older than flight itself. The first primitive efforts from aircraft had been made by the Italians in their war against the Turks in Libya during 1911 and 1912. So ineffective were early bombs, especially in the absence of any form of bombsight other than the dropper's eyes, and so small was the load that could be carried by early aircraft that bombing was initially of little use. The successes of a few men in raiding German Zeppelin sheds, however, and the success in terms of propaganda and morale attending the German bombing of Paris at the end of August 1914, made it clear that time and ingenuity would eventually lead to the development of bombing as a useful weapon of war.

Surprisingly, it was the Russians who led the way, despite the fact that the

The Bolshoi seen here was the precursor of the Sikorsky Ilya Muromets that entered Russian service in 1915 as the world's first four-engined bomber. Some 80 of these machines were eventually delivered to the Imperial Russian air service for service in the period up to November 1917, and these machines were completed to a number of differing standards depending largely on the precise nature of the installed powerplant. The Ilya Muromets Type B, for example, had a powerplant of four Salmson (Canton-Unné) water-cooled radial engines in the form of two 200hp and two 135hp units, and its armament comprised 1,124lb (510kg) of bombs and two trainable machine guns for defensive purposes.

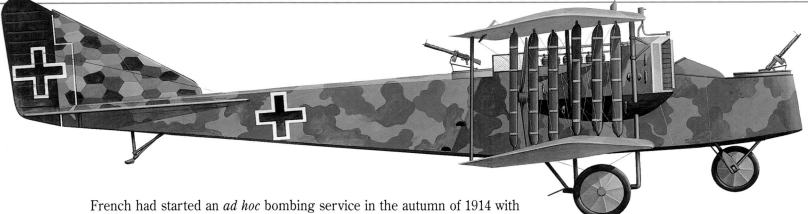

French had started an *ad hoc* bombing service in the autumn of 1914 with Voisin biplanes. The Russians realised that large aircraft would be needed to carry a significant quantity of bombs, and they already had such aircraft in the form of two four-engined machines, the Russkii Vitiaz and the Le Grand, both designed by Igor Sikorsky and built in 1913 by the Russo-Baltic Railway Car Factory in St Petersburg. These were the world's first four-engined aircraft. Early in 1914 the Russian technical bureau ordered 10 examples of an improved and enlarged version, the Ilya Muromets, for the Imperial Russian Air Service. Eventually some 80 of the type were built, but lack of suitable engines seriously hampered operational efforts. Nonetheless, over 400 sorties were flown with bomb loads of about 1,100lb (500kg). In reality, however, bombers of the size of the Ilya Muromets were inefficient even by the standards of the day.

Despite the efforts of the RNAS and the fledgling French bombing force, the Germans beat them to the first serious investigations in the possibilities of bombing. Here they had a head start, as a fair amount of preliminary work had been undertaken before the war during trials involving the use of Zeppelins as bombing craft. First into the field, during the summer of 1915, was the Allgemeine Electrizitäts Gesellschaft (AEG) G II, a large twin-engined biplane capable of delivering a 200kg (441lb) bomb load. This was joined in the autumn by the same company's G III, capable of lifting some 300kg (661lb) of bombs. A year later three other bombers had joined the German air service: the AEG G IV with a 400kg (882lb) bomb load, the Friedrichshafen G II with a 450kg (992lb) bomb load, and the Gotha G III, also with a 450kg (992lb) bomb load.

Though best known as the designer and manufacturer of twin-float seaplanes, Friedrichshafen also produced a number of land-based bombers that were used exclusively over the Western Front. The most important of these bombers was the type illustrated here, the G III with a powerplant of two 260hp Mercedes D.IVa water-cooled engines. This three-man machine could carry a bomb load of 3,307lb (1,500kg) and was fitted with a defensive armament of three 0.312in (7.92mm) Parabellum trainable machine-guns, and its performance included a maximum speed of 88mph (141km/h) at 3,280ft (1,000m), a ceiling of 14,765ft (4,500m) and an endurance of 5 hours. The type had empty and maximum take-off weights of 5,929 and 8,686lb (2,690 and 3,940kg) respectively, and its primary dimensional data included a span of 77ft 11in (23.75m) and length of 42ft 11.875in (13.10m).

The Rumpler C III two-seat reconnaissance aeroplane was a development of the earlier Rumpler C I with the more powerful Benz Bz.IV engine rated at 220hp and driving a two-blade propeller fitted with a slow-drag spinner, a comma-type rudder with nose-fixed fin, a shorter main landing gear arrangement, a revised wing cellule with pronounced stagger, and aerodynamically balanced ailerons and elevators. The type entered service in the early part of 1917, but all the surviving aircraft were withdrawn in April of that year, suggesting that the type had operational problems, in favour of the somewhat improved Rumpler C IV.

Bombers over Britain

In concert with the Imperial German navy air service's Zeppelin airship raids on targets in England, the Imperial German army air service started a campaign of attacks using land-based bombers. Even operating from bases in Belgium, these lacked the range to penetrate far beyond London, but as the losses of the airship forces began to mount, the importance placed on the bomber offensive increased. Such was the public fear of the raids, moreover, that the British war cabinet appointed one of its members, Lieutenant-General Sir Jan Smuts, to head a committee charged with the investigation of means to combat the 'Gotha menace'. Smuts reported the committee's finding to the cabinet in July 1917, and the single most important finding in the short term was the recommendation that the currently diffuse arrangement of defensive elements should be combined under a single commander. The cabinet approved the recommendation, and Major-General E.B. Ashdown was appointed to head the London Air Defence Area.

Three additional squadrons of modern fighters were soon allocated to the LADA, and in August a 'gun barrier' was established on the corridor overflown by the Gotha bombers as they approached London, and a new system of readiness and patrol routines was created for the defending fighter squadrons, which waited at readiness when a raid was reported as imminent but only took off to patrol a specific area when concrete information about a raid had been made available. The improvements soon made their effect felt, though the squadrons of the Royal Flying Corps patrolling over London had a lean time of it as most of the successes went to the gunners of the Royal Artillery and the Royal Naval Air Service squadrons operating over the coast.

Their increasing loss rate persuaded the Germans to switch from day to night attacks during September 1917, and among the new tactics evolved to meet this different threat was the creation of new 'aprons' of barrage balloons to cover the eastern and northern approaches to London. It was planned that 20 such 'aprons' should be created, each comprising three balloons flying at 7,500ft (2,285m) but later at 9,500ft (2895m) and linked to each other by 1,500ft (457m) wires each carrying twenty 1,000ft (305m) vertical wires, but only 10 of them had been established by the summer of 1918, when the threat of bomber attack virtually disappeared.

At the same time, the anti-aircraft gun defences of the London metropolitan area were divided into geographical squares under the control of a new overall system. The object of this change was that the attacking force would be tracked by sound locators and the information passed to the co-ordination centre, which would then order the concentration of the fire of the appropriate batteries in a 'curtain barrage' over the square through which the bomber force was reckoned to be passing.

The Germans lost 24 bombers to the British defences or crashes into the sea, the latter often as a result of damage inflicted by the fighters during the bombers' approach or later departure, and another 36 were destroyed in landing accidents. This clearly indicates that the perils of nocturnal flight operations were greater than those of the British defences at a time when the interception of bombers by night was still a matter of luck rather than skill.

These aircraft served a useful purpose in paving the way for later types, but were not in themselves very successful. With the arrival of the Gotha G IV early in 1917, however, the Germans had at last found a useful long-range bomber. since May 1915, Zeppelins had been launching sporadic attacks on targets in the southern half of Britain, principally on London, but by 1917 the British defences had been so strengthened, albeit by the removal of squadrons from France, that Zeppelin losses were no longer tolerable. The Germans therefore decided to use the Gotha G IV and V over England, and the first Gotha raids were launched in June 1917 to the total consternation of public and government alike. Although the Zeppelin raids were the first 'strategic bombing' operations ever attempted and had caused a great public shock, the aircraft raids proved a greater threat to life and property. There was an immediate demand for the British government to do something to curb the German daylight raids. The raids continued into 1918, causing a steady stream of casualties and damage.

Only with the deployment of aircraft such as the S.E.5a, which could climb fast enough to intercept the Gothas before they flew out of range, was the threat curtailed. The immediate result of these Germans raids, at first carried out with complete impunity, was the total reorganisation of the British air services. The most important reform was the unification, on 1 April 1918, of the RFC and the RNAS to become the Royal Air Force (RAF), the world's first independent air force.

In 1918, the Gothas were joined by a few Zeppelin (Staaken) R VI bombers, huge machines that could carry 2000kg (4,409lb) of bombs over short ranges. The Germans had a penchant for Riesenflugzeug (giant aircraft), and devoted great effort to the production of a number of types.

The importance, in terms of other factors of the German strategic bombing campaign, far outweighs its military success, which was minimal. The British people, who had imagined themselves immune from war in the personal sense, found themselves embroiled in the 'front line' for the first time. With the realisation that everyone could now be involved in the actual 'fighting', the era of 'total war' may be said to have begun.

The only one of the Allies to have devoted some effort to strategic bombing early in the war was Italy, and early designs by Gianni Caproni proved excellent starting points for the Ca 3, 4 and 5 series of three-engined heavy bombers. These entered service in the first months of 1917 with both the Italian and French air services, and in Italian hands they proved to be first-rate long-range aircraft.

The British also decided to use heavy bombers, at first under the impulsion of the Admiralty, whose Air Department head, Commodore

Below: Although the D.H.9 had been planned as an improved successor to the classic Airco (de Havilland) D.H.4 day bomber with the two-man crew located closer together for improved tactical communication, the type was let down by its indifferent 230hp Siddeley Puma engine. The promise of the D.H.9 was finally realised in the D.H.9A, illustrated here in post-war form. The D.H.9A was planned as the D.H.9 with the revised powerplant of one 400hp Liberty water-cooled engine and a biplane wing cellule of greater area, though problems with this Liberty meant that many early aircraft were completed with the 375hp Rolls-Royce Eagle water-cooled engine. The result was an altogether more successful warplane offering better performance than the D.H.9 despite a 45 per cent increase in the size of the bomb load.

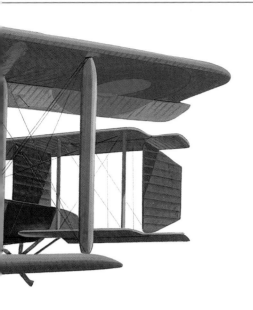

Above left: The Handley Page O/400 was the best British heavy bomber of World War I, and entered service in the late summer of 1918 as an evolutionary development of the O/100, itself designed to meet an Admiralty requirement for a 'bloody paralyser' of a bomber. The O/400 was protected by three 0.303in (7.7mm) Lewis trainable machine-guns and could carry a maximum bomb load of 2,000lb (907kg), and was powered by two 360hp Rolls-Royce Eagle VIII water-cooled engines for a maximum speed of 97.5mph (157km/h) at sea level, a ceiling of 8,500ft (2,590m) and an endurance of 8 hours. The bomber had empty and maximum take-off weights of 8,502 and 13,360lb (3,857 and 6,060kg) respectively, and its primary dimensional data included a span of 100ft 0in (30.48m) and length of 62ft 10.25in (19.16m).

Above right: The Caproni Ca 3 was one of Italy's most important heavy bombers of World War I, and was a four-man machine with a powerplant of three Isotta-Fraschini V.4B engines and an armament that included a defensive element of up to four 0.256in (6.5mm) Revelli trainable machine guns and a bomb load of 992lb (450kg).

Murray Sueter, called for a 'bloody paralyser' of an aeroplane early in 1915. This took the form of the Handley Page O/100, which entered service in September 1916 and proved an immediate success, being capable of carrying some 2,000lb (907kg) of bombs. A more powerful version was designated O/400, and entered service in 1918. This basic type was selected as the standard equipment of the world's first true strategic bomber force, the RAF's Independent Force, and 40 aircraft of the type took part in the largest 'strategic' raid of the war in September 1918, when the Saar area was bombed from bases near Nancy. Only three production models of Britain's first four-engined bomber, the Handley Page V/1500, had been built before the Armistice.

Although 'heavy' bombers pointed the way to the future, their military effect in World War I was minimal, and it was light bombers that played an important part in land operations during the closing stages of the war. Considering their importance, it is surprising that the Allies used only two basic types: the Airco (de Havilland) D.H.4 and its two derivatives, the D.H.9 and D.H.9a, and the French Breguet Bre.14.

The D.H.4 was in every respect one of the most remarkable aircraft of World War I. As well as being very agile and well armed, it had a speed of 143mph (230km/h) at a time when most fighters were capable only of speeds in the region of 130mph (209km/h), and was able to carry a bomb load of 460lb (209kg). The D.H.4 entered service in 1917, and was joined in squadron use during 1918 by the supposedly improved D.H.9, which had the pilot's and observer's cockpits close together to obviate the D.H.4's main tactical failing, the near impossibility of the pilot and observer being able to speak to each other as they were separated by the bomb bay. But reduced engine power meant that performance suffered badly, a factor only partially rectified by the development of the D.H.9a. The French equivalent of these de Havilland bombers was the Breguet 14, which began to enter service in September 1917. Sturdy and fairly fast, this bomber played an important part in harrying the retreating Germans in the second half of 1918, and also proved to be a very adequate reconnaissance aircraft.

While the Allies concentrated on light bombers, the Germans placed more faith in ground-attack machines to support their land forces, as the British had done in the Battle of the Somme in 1916. At first, such machines were modified reconnaissance aircraft used by *Schützstaffeln* (protection squadrons) and *Fliegerabteilungen-Infanterie* (infantry contact units), pending the arrival of more suitable, heavier armoured designs such as the all-metal Junkers J 1, designed by Dr Hugo Junkers, one of the pioneers of metal construction. In the autumn of 1917, however, the need for a lighter type which could fulfil both the ground-attack and reconnaissance roles became evident. This new type was to be operated by *Schlachtstaffeln*

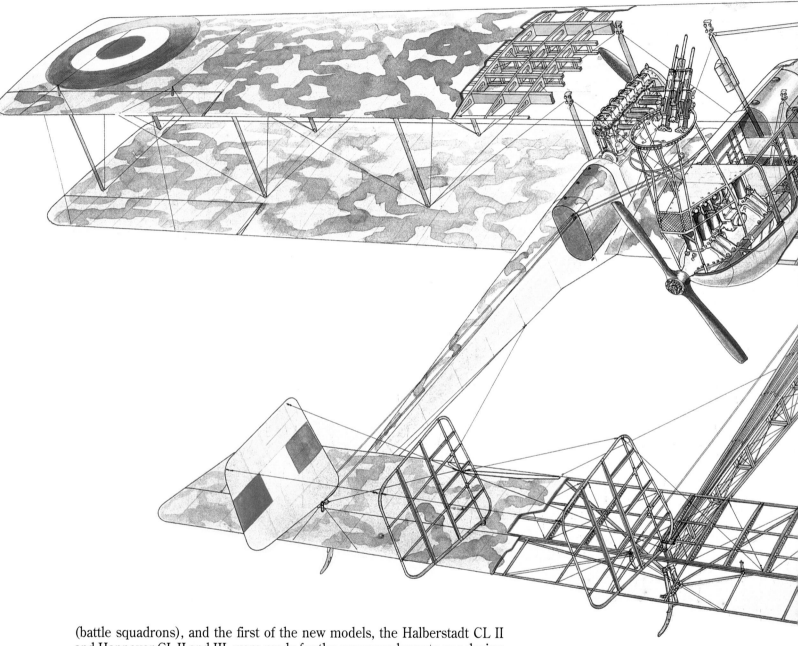

(battle squadrons), and the first of the new models, the Halberstadt CL II and Hannover CL II and III, were ready for the new squadrons to use during the final German offensives in the spring and early summer of 1918. But useful as these new machines were in anticipating one of the major uses of armoured aircraft in World War II, the novel tactics and aircraft deployed by the Germans in 1918 were unable to overcome the clear supremacy of the Allies.

Aircraft had entered World War I as unknown quantities, and their basic roles of reconnaissance and very light bombing were undertaken by aircraft of distinctly limited performance and reliability. Yet, by 1916, aircraft had evolved into durable, efficient fighting machines, capable of exerting some influence on the outcome of the decisive land operations. Two years later, towards the end of the war, aircraft had again advanced in overall performance, and were now to a certain extent the arbiters of the land battle.

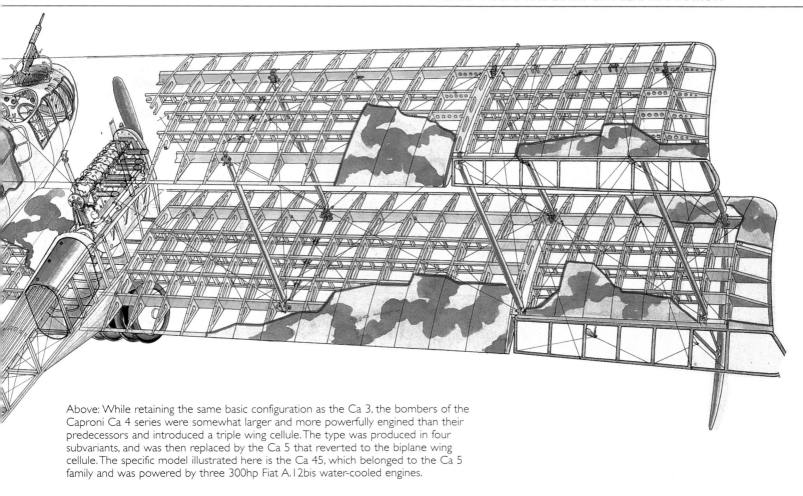

Above: While retaining the same basic configuration as the Ca 3, the bombers of the Caproni Ca 4 series were somewhat larger and more powerfully engined than their predecessors and introduced a triple wing cellule. The type was produced in four subvariants, and was then replaced by the Ca 5 that reverted to the biplane wing cellule. The specific model illustrated here is the Ca 45, which belonged to the Ca 5 family and was powered by three 300hp Fiat A.12bis water-cooled engines.

Below: Under development in the closing stages of World War I, the Farman F.60 was a capable bomber evolved from the F.50 and was the standard warplane of its type in French service during the first part of the 1920s.

Sad Years of Retrenchment

IF World War I had promoted aviation, the peace that followed almost broke it. For the terrible cost of the war, both emotional and financial, regressed aviation to where it had started in the last few years before 1914, at least from the constructors' and pilots' point of view. In those halcyon days there had been only a few hundred aircraft in the world (of perhaps 150 different types), with about three times that number of pilots. The war had brought vast and rapid growth: by the time of the Armistice in November 1918, France had built 68,000 aircraft, the United Kingdom 55,000, Germany 47,600, Italy 20,000, the United States 15,000 and Austria-Hungary 5,400. The scale of expansion may also be gauged by the number of pilots lost during the war, which was a relatively small proportion of the number actually trained: on the German side, for example, 5,853 had been killed, 7,302 wounded and 2,751 taken prisoner or listed as missing; on the British side 6,166 had been killed, 7,245 wounded and 3,212 taken prisoner or listed as missing.

With the war finally over, it was time to take stock of the consequences. Europe and the United States were dazed by the horrors of the war and the enormity of their losses; the people were all too ready to believe that World War I (or the Great War as it was known) had been the war to end all wars. After years of slaughter it was a natural reaction to turn away from all military machinery, including aviation; and the war's financial cost had an equally devastating impact on industry. Europe was almost bankrupt. France, the United Kingdom and Italy had spent all, or almost all, of their resources on the war and had then gone deep into debt with the United States to pay for the period 1917-18; Germany and Austro-Hungary were exhausted. There was no money in Europe for anything but essentials, and military spending was clearly not essential after the end of 'the war to end all wars'. With the run-down of the world's major air forces, there was no work for the aircraft industries that supplied them.

The drastic nature of the cutback was exemplified by the decline of the RAF in the immediate post-war period. At the time of the Armistice the RAF had 188 operational squadrons, with 291,000 men and women to fly, service and otherwise keep them in the air; by the end of 1919, less than 14 months later, the force had dropped to 12 operational squadrons, with manpower down to 31,500. Although the government soon realised that so small an air

Boeing F4B

ONE of the classic fighters of the period between the two world wars, the Boeing F4B was designed for the US Navy's carrierborne arm and was built in modest numbers for service between 1929 and 1938 as the initial F4B-1, of which 27 were built with provision for a 500lb (227kg) bomb carried on a ventral rack, the F4B-2 of which 46 were built with a through-axle main landing gear unit in place of the F4B-1's divided main units, the F4B-3 of which 21 were built with a semi-monocoque fuselage of light alloy construction, and the F4B-4 of which 92 were built with an uprated engine, a revised vertical tail surface, underwing racks for two 116lb (53kg) bombs, and stowage for an inflatable dinghy in an enlarged headrest. The aeroplane illustrated here is an F4B-4, which had a fixed forward-firing armament of one 0.5in (12.7mm) and one 0.3in (7.62mm) synchronised machine-guns and a powerplant of one 550hp Pratt & Whitney R-1340-16 Wasp air-cooled radial engine. The type's performance included a maximum speed of 188mph (302.5km/h) at 6,000ft (1,830m), a climb to 5,000ft (1,525m) in 2 minutes 42 seconds, a ceiling of 26,900ft (8200m) and a range of 370 miles (595km); its empty and maximum take-off weights were 2,354 and 2,750lb (1,068 and 1,638kg) respectively, and its primary dimensional data included a span of 30ft 0in (9.14m) and length of 20ft 1in (6.12m).

The Armstrong Siskin was one of the most important fighters equipping the Royal Air Force during the 1920s, and is seen here in the form of a Siskin Mk IIIA of which the RAF received 400 for service between March 1927 and late 1932. The type was entirely typical of the thinking of the period, and was a sesquiplane biplane armed with two 0.303in (7.7mm) Vickers fixed forward-firing and synchronised machine-guns and powered by a 450hp Armstrong Siddeley Jaguar IV air-cooled radial piston engine. The type had a maximum speed of 156mph (251km/h) at sea level, a climb to 5,000ft (1,525m) in 3 minutes 30 seconds, a ceiling of 27,000ft (8,230m), empty and maximum take-off weights of 2,061 and 3,012lb (935 and 1,366kg) respectively, and dimensions including a span of 33ft 2in (10.11m) and length of 25ft 4in (7.72m).

force was hardly worth having, expansion was limited to 25 squadrons by March 1920 and to 43 squadrons by October 1924.

More significant for aviation in general was the fact that a new generation of aircraft was just entering service at the time of the Armistice, and it was decided that these aircraft would be sufficient in number for peacetime. Thus the RAF's equipment immediately after the war consisted of the Bristol F.2B Fighter, the Sopwith Snipe, the de Havilland D.H.9a and Vickers Vimy. The first new bomber, the Fairey Fawn, did not enter service until 1923, and the first new fighters, in the forms of the Gloster Grebe and Armstrong Whitworth Siskin, were introduced a year later. Although severe, the British government's aviation cuts were matched throughout most of Europe as well as in the United States.

Aircraft builders found themselves in an extremely difficult position. No new orders could be expected for some time, and production capacity was being run down gradually as existing orders, heavily cut back after the Armistice, were filled. Without military interest, other work had to be found, but this was difficult while the market was glutted with ex-government machines being sold off at very low prices. The majority of aircraft firms went out of business. Those that survived, by forethought and careful planning, faced strict rationalisation. Companies that had bought their wartime premises were now able to sell them, using the capital wisely until business started to improve again in the early 1920s.

For the air forces of the world, survival in the face of political moves to axe military budgets was the most important matter, and the growing belief in the efficacy of bombing as a strategic weapon was a key factor. Invariably, for the bombing theorists, the most important consideration was the weight of bombs that could be dropped on a target. Aircraft speed at first played only a small part in their thinking: there was a firm conviction that 'the bomber will always get through'. British bombers such as the Vickers Virginia, Boulton & Paul Sidestrand and Handley Page Heyford were all slow biplanes, while the American Witteman-Lewis NBL-1 was a triplane.

Only in the early 1930s, therefore, did the need to combine a heavy bomb-carrying capability with high performance gain proper recognition. This led to the appearance of the first real heavy bombers in the United States: the Boeing B-9 and the Martin B-10 were both advanced monoplanes of metal construction, with performance equal or superior to that of contemporary biplane fighters.

Despite the disorganised nature of its air force and aircraft industry, France also adopted the concept of heavy bombing and produced a number of suitable aircraft in the late 1920s. Almost all were notable for their slab-sided, ungainly appearance and singular lack of streamlining. The twin-engined Amiot 143 and Bloch MB.200 bombers, together with the four-engined Farman F.221 bomber, entered service in the 1930s, and were the most notable examples of this aerodynamically unrefined tendency. Yet even these French machines appeared modern in comparison with a British contemporary, the Handley Page Heyford – a large biplane with the fuselage attached to the underside of the upper wing and the bomb load stowed in the thick centre section of the lower wing.

Meanwhile, fighters remained little more advanced in concept than World War I types. The first such machines to enter service with the RAF after the war were the Armstrong Whitworth Siskin and the Gloster Grebe, both of which made their service debuts in 1924. Several companies produced experimental monoplane fighters during the decade following the

The Martin B-10 was the American warplane that opened the era of the 'modern' monoplane bomber with features such as its metal structure, cantilever wing, enclosed accommodation, turreted nose armament, wing-mounted engines in stylish low-drag cowlings, and retractable main landing gear units. The B-10B was ordered in 1934, and its data include an offensive armament of 2,260lb (1,025kg) of bombs carried in the large ventral weapons bay, a defensive armament of three 0.3in (7.62mm) Browning trainable machine-guns, a powerplant of two 775hp Wright R-1820-33 air-cooled radial engines, a maximum speed of 213mph (343km/h) at optimum altitude, a ceiling of 24,200ft (7,375m), a range of 1,240 miles (1996km), empty and maximum take-off weights of 9,681 and 16,400lb (4391 and 7,439kg) respectively, span of 70ft 6in (21.49m) and length of 44ft 9in (13.64m).

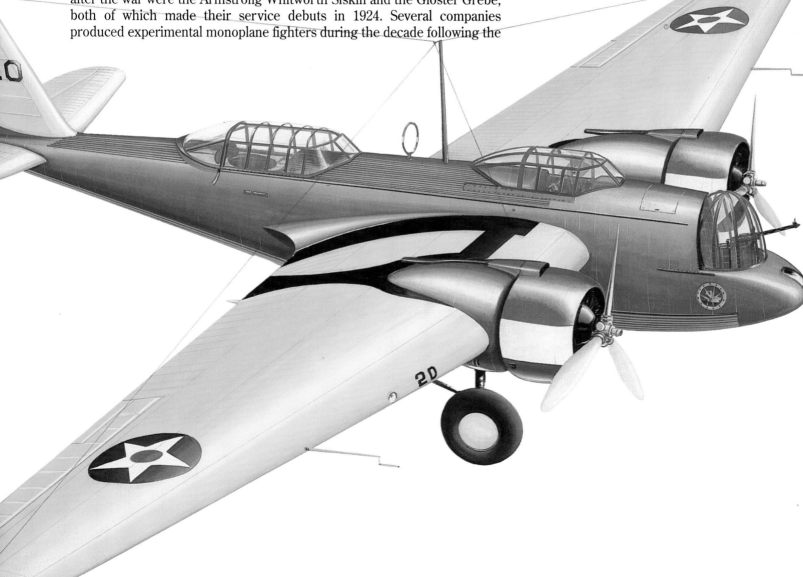

war, but the RAF rigidly adhered to the well-proved biplane formula, usually with a radial engine, for a period of some 15 years after World War I. Later types such as the Bristol Bulldog, Gloster Gauntlet and Gloster Gladiator continued this tradition, and the only notable exception was the Hawker Fury. Powered by a Rolls-Royce Kestrel inline piston engine, this was the first British fighter to exceed 200mph (320km/h) in level flight.

Keynotes of the design philosophy that created these fighters were the strong yet light biplane layout, the excellent manoeuvrability, and the armament of two rifle-calibre machine-guns located with their breeches within easy reach of the pilot, who could thus solve the problem of jammed rounds. British light bombers followed the same basic formula, but carried a gunner behind the pilot and a small bomb load under the lower wings. Classic examples were the Fairey Fox, Hawker Hart and Hawker Hind. The major difference between all these aircraft and their counterparts in World War I was the widespread use of metal in the structures of the later machines. This use of metal became Air Ministry policy after 1924, to avoid the problems encountered in World War I through shortage of suitably seasoned timber for airframes, and gradually became more common in other parts of British military aircraft, but as the basic design philosophy remained unaltered, the aircraft were essentially wooden types rendered in metal.

Although often condemned for being 'behind the times' in the 1920s and 1930s, the French were well up with the leaders in the field of fighters. Several advanced monoplane designs were evolved during the 1920s, with heavily braced parasol or gull wings. These offered strength, relatively low drag and a good field of vision for the pilot. Unlike the British, many of whose aircraft companies had disappeared in the troubled times after the war, the French could rely on long-established firms such as Morane-Saulnier, Nieuport and SPAD, as well as more recent companies such as Dewoitine, Loire and Wibault. The 1920s, therefore, saw a large number of interesting fighters, and a smaller number of reconnaissance and light bomber machines, which were being offered both for the home market and for export sale.

In the late 1920s and early 1930s, the French aircraft industry revealed a strong penchant for extraordinarily slab-sided bombers with angular flying surfaces, massive fixed landing gear units, and excrescences such as balconied gun/bombing positions and observation gondolas. The result was aircraft that were comparatively easy to make, but possessed so high a drag factor that their performance was severely compromised even with moderately powerful engines. A good example of this tendency is the Bloch MB.200 heavy bomber that entered service in 1934 and was still in limited service in the first stages of World War II. This could carry a bomb load of 5,511lb (2,500kg) and was defended by three 0.295in (7.5mm) trainable machines guns and, with a powerplant of two 870hp Gnome-Rhône 14Kirs/Kjrs air-cooled radial engines, could attain a maximum speed of 143mph (230km/h), a ceiling of 26,245ft (8,000m) and a normal range of 621 miles (1,000km). The MB.200 had a maximum take-off weight of 16,050lb (7,280kg), and its dimensions included a span of 73ft 7.67in (22.45m) and length of 52ft 6in (16.00m).

Fighter Armament

DURING World War I, the standard fixed forward-firing armament for fighters had started in 1915 as one rifle-calibre machine-gun synchronised to fire through the propeller disc, and by 1917 had been standardised as two such weapons. This weight of fire was adequate during the time and through most of the 1920s, and the weapons were usually located in the fuselage so that the pilot could reach the breeches and clear the jammed rounds that were common with the ammunition of the period. The sole major exception to this tendency were the Americans, who made provision for one of the two rifle-calibre weapons to be replaced by a heavy machine-gun of 0.5in (12.7mm) calibre for heavier weight of fire to a longer range.

During the later 1920s, however, the performance of warplanes started to improve so rapidly as a result of the adoption of more powerful engines, improved aerodynamics and more advanced structural practices, that many air forces began to query the continued efficacy of the two machine-guns as the armament of fighters designed to tackle larger and more sturdily constructed bombers whose high performance meant that they could be kept in the sights of intercepting fighters for only fleeting moments. This suggested not only the development of more advanced fighters (leading to the introduction of the 'modern' fighter with a cantilever low-set wing, enclosed cockpit and retractable main landing gear units) but to consideration of heavier armament.

By the mid-1930s, this heavier armament was seen as taking the form of the same number of larger-calibre weapons or alternatively a larger number of weapons of the same calibre. The former offered greater striking power per round (including explosive shells if the 20mm cannon was adopted) but a smaller number of rounds as the larger-calibre weapons could not match the firing rate of rifle-calibre machine-guns), while the latter offered the possibility of swamping the target with a mass of relatively light rounds. Most European air forces opted for a mixed battery of cannon and rifle-calibre machine-guns (typically one 20mm cannon and two or four rifle-calibre machine-guns), the British decided to increase the number of rifle-calibre machine-guns to four and then eight pending the development of the cannon to a more capable standard, and the Americans opted generally for a battery of two heavy and four rifle-calibre machines guns evolving rapidly to six or even eight heavy machine-guns for a combination of a high volume of fire with a round that offered considerably greater striking power than the rifle-calibre round. Of the other major aeronautical powers, the USSR opted for the combination of one 20mm cannon and a mixed machine-gun battery and then for a larger number of cannon, while Japan was divided, the Imperial Japanese army air force remained a believer in relatively light armament (just two rifle-calibre or heavy machine-guns) up to a fairly late date, and the Imperial Japanese army air force was an early adherent to the concept of heavier firepower in the form of two 20mm cannon and a number of rifle-calibre or heavy machine-guns.

At the end of the 1920s, the French air force was equipped with the parasol-winged Nieuport-Delage NiD.62 series, the Loire/Gourdou-Leseurre 32 and the Wibault 72, all capable of a maximum speed in the order of 260km/h (160mph). In 1930, however, the French realised that all its fighters were approaching obsolescence, and so issued specifications for a new standard fighter. The best response came from the Dewoitine company, which had experimented with a number of sturdy parasol types in the 1920's and had won a good export record. For its D.500 series Dewoitine adopted a new layout: a cantilever low-wing monoplane powered by a closely cowled Hispano-Suiza 12Y inline piston engine (soon to become the most important French aero engine of the decade), and supported on the ground by wide-track fixed landing gear. The new fighter had a top speed of 360km/h (225mph), which was far higher than the maximum speeds of current first-line French fighters.

The United States, on the other hand, was at last beginning to emerge from the aeronautical wilderness into which it had fallen during the middle of the 1920s. The gradual development of the fledgling commercial airlines was partially responsible for this renaissance, but equally significant was the amalgamation of a number of small builders into a few large and increasingly well-organised concerns, each operating in a custom-built, modern factory accommodating design staff, experimental workshops and production lines. Pratt & Whitney and Wright had become the two most important and competitive aero engine manufacturers, and these two major companies were producing reliable air-cooled radials such as the Pratt & Whitney Wasp and its derivatives, and the Wright Whirlwind and

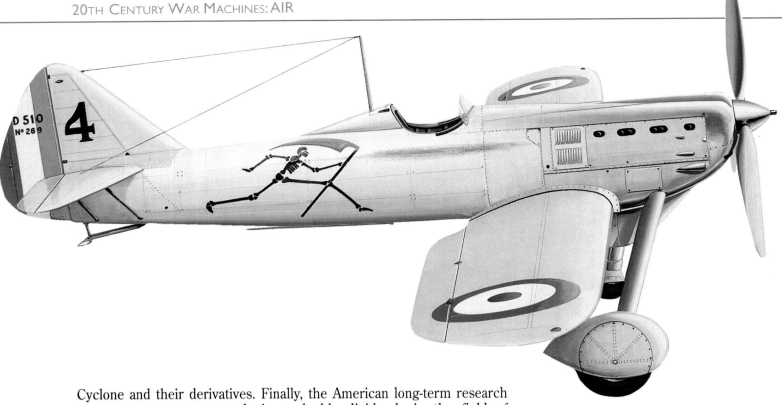

Cyclone and their derivatives. Finally, the American long-term research programme was now producing valuable dividends in the field of structures and aerodynamics.

The American revival became fully evident with the advent of a number of new and formidable aircraft produced in the late 1920s and early 1930s. The Boeing B-9 and Martin B-10 bombers mentioned above were two clear examples of advanced aerodynamic theory allied to advanced military concepts, but the fighter equipment of the two American air forces also revealed that the American aeronautical machine now possessed strength in depth. The US Army and the US Navy each had its own air force, with the US Marine Corps operating further air formations flying basically the same types of aircraft as the US Navy.

Authorities in most countries with aspirations of naval air power, principally the United Kingdom, felt that the complex requirements of carrierborne operations meant that naval aircraft had to embody a compromise between several design factors, and therefore could not be a match for land-based aircraft. The US Navy, on the other hand, realised that its carriers would play a dominant part in any future war, principally because of the geographical isolation of the United States between the Pacific and Atlantic oceans. It was therefore crucial that the aircraft-carrier arm's aircraft were capable of combating land-based aircraft. The early realisation of this fact proved highly significant in America's struggle with Japan from 1941 onwards.

The most important carrierborne fighters of the US Navy were the Curtiss Hawk and Boeing F2B, each possessing a maximum speed of 155mph (250km/h), later supplanted by the Boeing F4B, which was capable of 190mph (305km/h). The US Army Air Corps' fighters of the period were the Boeing PW-9 and Curtiss P-6, capable of 155 and 180mph (250 and 318km/h) respectively, later joined by the Boeing P-12 (the land plane equivalent of the F4B), and in 1933 by the Boeing P-26 'Peashooter', the first American monoplane fighter, which was capable of 235mph (380km/h). Of these only the P-26 represented an extraordinary advance on its predecessors, but all these fighters were workmanlike aircraft notable for their sturdy construction, high manoeuvrability and good performance.

Despite its belief (or perhaps suspension of disbelief) in angularity for its larger warplanes during the later 1920s and early 1930s, France was considerably more adventurous in the design of fighters, and as such was a pioneer of the monoplane fighter in a number of different configurations. One of the most important of these, which entered service in 1935 and was still in limited service at the time of France's defeat by Germany in June 1940, was the Dewoitine D.500. This was of all-metal construction with a cantilever low-set wing, but cannot be regarded as truly modern as it retained an open pilot's cockpit and fixed landing gear. The D.500 was powered by one 600hp Hispano-Suiza 12Xbrs water-cooled engine, and the armament comprised one 20mm cannon (located between the engine's two cylinder banks to fire through the hollow propeller shaft) and two 0.295in (7.5mm) machine-guns installed in the wing leading edges. The D.500 could attain a maximum speed of 224mph (360km/h) at optimum altitude, and its other primary performance data included a ceiling of 34,450ft (10,500m) and a range of 528 miles (850km). The type had a maximum take-off weight of 3,770lb (1,710kg), and its dimensional data included a span of 39ft 8in (12.10m) and length of 25ft 4.75in (7.74m).

Although they had no long pedigree, therefore, they were in most respects the equals of contemporary British and French fighters.

The development of aircraft had not yet become prohibitively expensive, so it was normal for all but the very poorest countries to try their hand at the design and production of fighters and other small aircraft. Most notable of these was the Polish PZL P.7 fighter of 1932. An inverted gull-wing monoplane clearly inspired by French design thinking, the P.7 was powered by a licence-built Bristol Jupiter radial, and capable of 200mph (320km/h). Further development led to the P.11 and P.24, both of which performed well in the hands of Polish and Greek pilots against the Luftwaffe in 1939 and 1941.

Yugoslavia and Czechoslovakia were also building fighters in this period, and some mention must also be made of Italy. Although not a poor country, Italy had gone into an aeronautical slump in the late 1920s, despite her excellent seaplanes and heroic efforts in the Schneider Trophy races. Not until 1933, with the development of the Fiat CR.32, did all Italian combat aircraft reach world standards. Designed by the illustrious Celestino Rosatelli, the CR.32 was very strong and manoeuvrable, and it was fast for its time, with a top speed of 370km/h (230mph). The very capabilities of the CR.32 led to unfortunate consequences for the Italians, however: so good was the CR.32 that little notice was taken of the rapidly advancing theory of air warfare, and accordingly no priority was given to the development of an advanced successor.

By 1933, therefore, the design philosophies of World War I had been completely revised. There were still believers in the biplane formula, including the Italians, but this design concept's practical limits had been reached by fighters such as the Gloster Gladiator from the United Kingdom, the Fiat CR.42 from Italy, and the Polikarpov I-153 from the USSR.

Even before this, however, the nature and shape of the biplane's inevitable successor had been demonstrated by the Boeing and Martin bombers, the French monoplane fighters, and the racing aircraft developed by the United Kingdom, Italy and the United States. The high-drag biplane with fixed landing gear was to be supplanted by the low-drag monoplane with retractable landing gear. This change had already begun when the

The main rival to Boeing and Douglas for the supply of warplanes to the US services in the late 1920s and early 1930s was Curtiss, which designed and manufactured a number of classic warplane types. One of the most important of these, which has perhaps never received the full credit that is due to it, is the Falcon series of biplanes that was produced in three basic forms for service from 1927 as the A-3 for the land-based attack role, F8C for the carrierborne fighter and fighter-bomber roles, and the O-1 and O-11 for the land-based observation and reconnaissance roles. The aeroplane seen here is an O-1, and the data for the two-seat O-1E may be taken as typical for the type: powered by one 435hp Curtiss V-1150-5 Conqueror liquid-cooled engine and armed with four 0.3in (7.62mm) Browning machine-guns (two fixed and two trainable), this model attained a maximum speed of 141mph (227km/h) at optimum altitude, an initial climb rate of 980ft (299m) per minute, and a ceiling of 15,300ft (4,665m); the type had empty and maximum take-off weights of 2,922 and 4,347lb (1,325 and ,1972kg) respectively, and its primary dimensional data included a span of 38ft 0in (11.58m) and length of 27ft 2in (8.28m).

process was boosted by the reappearance of Germany on the military scene.

With the connivance of Sweden and the USSR, Germany had circumvented the clauses of the Treaty of Versailles which prohibited its development of advanced offensive weapons. In both these countries German designers had been free to plan and build military aircraft and tanks, and in Germany itself fighters and bombers had appeared in the guise of sporting planes and airliners. A clandestine air force had been prepared under cover of the air ministry, the national airline and various flying clubs that had been formed all over Germany.

In 1935, Adolf Hitler announced Germany's renunciation of the military terms of the Treaty of Versailles, and a fully fledged Luftwaffe was unveiled overnight. This force possessed a large number of aircraft and also enjoyed the backing of a powerful aircraft industry together with a large number of well-planned and well-staffed military airfields.

At first the Luftwaffe was not equipped with particularly advanced aircraft, the standard fighter and bomber being the Heinkel He 51 biplane and Junkers Ju 52/3m monoplane respectively. Knowing that military operations were still probably some distance in the future, the Luftwaffe

An odd and angular little aeroplane, but one possessing beautiful handling characteristics and excellent agility, the Fairey Flycatcher was the most important carrierborne fighter operated by the British from 1923 into the early 1930s before finally disappearing from service in 1935. The Flycatcher was powered by one 400hp Armstrong Siddeley Jaguar II or IV air-cooled radial engine and was armed with two 0.303in (7.7mm) Vickers fixed forward-firing and synchronised machine-guns. The type's performance included a maximum speed of 134mph (216km/h) at 5,000ft (1,525m), a ceiling of 20,600ft (6,280m) and a range of 310 miles (499km), its maximum take-off weight was 2,979lb (1,351kg), and its dimensional data included a span of 29ft 0in (8.84m) and length of 23ft 0in (7.01m).

high command was satisfied with these aircraft as 'operational' trainers which, in the period before the advent of more advanced aircraft, could suffice as 'front-line' machines. Newer types were already being designed or placed in production, and it was these aircraft that would establish the Luftwaffe as an extraordinarily potent exponent of tactical air power in the first campaigns of World War II.

Exaggerated claims for the Luftwaffe have helped to obscure the great advances made by the USSR in the late 1920s and early 1930s. After experimenting with strategic heavy bombing from aircraft such as the Tupolev ANT-6, and causing a number of aeronautical eyebrows to be raised as a result of its long-distance record breaking aircraft, the USSR decided that the most important role for air power was tactical support of ground forces. A new generation of tactical aircraft was developed, based on the latest advances in aeronautical techniques. The Soviets also built competitive aircraft, pressing the limits of current experimental concepts so that the widest spectrum of aeronautical and structural notions could be tested.

One of the earliest and most important results of this Soviet programme was the 1934 appearance of the Polikarpov I-16, which has the distinction of being the world's first cantilever low-wing monoplane fighter with retractable landing gear. The first examples of this epoch-making type also possessed another advanced feature in the form of an enclosed cockpit, but pilots did not like this enclosure and it was eliminated from later variants. The 700hp (522kW) radial engine was mounted in a very bluff, high-drag nose, but this notwithstanding, the I-16 could attain 280mph (450km/h), comparing very favourably with the maximum speed of 223mph (359km/h) attained by the Gloster Gauntlet which appeared in the following year. The Soviet programme then seemed to relax, and the German invasion six years later found the Soviet fighter arm still equipped mainly with later models of the I-16, and even large numbers of the I-15bis and I-153 biplane fighters.

The country which then took the practical lead in introducing advanced combat aircraft was Germany. After lengthy evaluation, the Messerschmitt Bf 109 was selected as the Luftwaffe's primary fighter, the Dornier Do 17 and Heinkel He 111 as its standard medium bombers, and the Junkers Ju 87 Stuka (abbreviated from *Sturzkampfflugzeug*, or dive-bomber) as its basic tactical support aeroplane.

The last of the Luftwaffe's mainstay aircraft to appear before World War II was the Junkers Ju 88 medium bomber, which entered service in 1939. The Ju 88 was originally intended as a fast medium bomber with limited dive-bombing capability, but served with great distinction in a variety of roles throughout World War II. In terms of versatility, the Ju 88 was rivalled only by the remarkable British de Havilland D.H.98 Mosquito.

The Germans tested the standard European concept of air power during the Spanish Civil War (1936-39). German aircraft were involved from the beginning, when Ju 52/3m transports were used to ferry General Francisco Franco's Nationalist troops from Spanish Morocco into southern Spain. As a bomber, however, the Ju 52/3m proved a failure, as did the Heinkel He 51 fighter when opposed by the formidable Soviet I-15 and I-16 fighters.

As the latest German combat aircraft emerged from their production lines they were sent to Spain in small numbers for operational evaluation. It was here that most of Germany's early World War II aircraft first saw combat and pilots learned how to get the best out of their aircraft. The problems with German aircraft in combat were experienced and cured, and as a result the Luftwaffe was a confident and experienced air force by the start of World War II in 1939.

Lessons of the Spanish Civil War

FOUGHT between 1936 and 1939, the Spanish Civil War pitted the Nationalist insurgent movement against the Republican government, the former with the active aid of the Germans and Italians, and the latter with the support of the USSR. Though these three countries backed the ideological aims of the Spanish side they supported, they also had a number of less altruistic reasons for their involvement in this bitter war, which was eventually won by the Nationalists. These reasons included the operational evaluation of modern weapons under harsh combat conditions, and the testing of their latest tactical and operational thinking.

The USSR sent examples of its most modern warplanes to Spain, including the Polikarpov I-15 and I-16 fighters and the Tupolev SB-2 bomber, and in the light of experience in this theatre decided that there was continued viability in a two-handed approach to fighter design (the monoplane for high-speed interception and the more agile biplane for air combat), but that considerations of strategic air power should be forsaken for complete concentration on tactical air power for the support of the ground forces, which were deemed to be the decisive element of the Soviet armed forces. The Italian experience was basically similar to that of the USSR, certainly as far as the two-handed approach to fighter design was concerned.

Germany also decided that the most important lesson of the Spanish Civil War was the creation of an air force optimised for tactical operations, and as a result effectively ceased development of long-range heavy warplanes in place of attack aircraft and multi-role medium bombers. Contrary to the Soviet and Italian conclusion, however, Germany decided that the day of the biplane fighter was clearly over, and henceforward concentrated its fighter developments on the modern monoplane fighter.

The results of this thinking became evident in World War II (1939-45), when German tactical air power was a decisive element in the success of German arms up to 1942, but was thereafter revealed as wholly inadequate to stem the tide of Allied and Soviet air power once earlier misconceptions had been set aside and more advanced aircraft were being produced in an ever swelling tide.

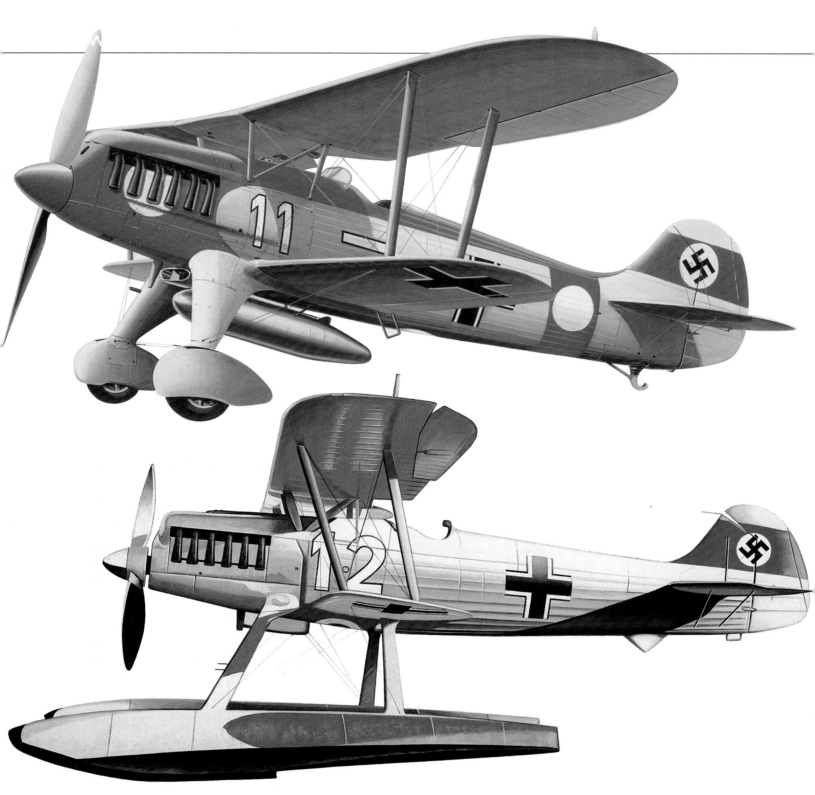

The Germans entered the Spanish Civil War with a firm belief in using their aircraft in a strategic role, but soon discovered the vulnerability of their bombers when these were forced to operate without long-range fighter escort. After the death in a 1936 flying accident of Lieutenant-General Walther Wever, the Luftwaffe's first chief-of-staff and Germany's primary protagonist of strategic air power, the Germans effectively turned their backs on the concept of strategic bombing and devoted virtually their full attention to the development of tactical air power to be used as 'flying artillery' in support of the German army's new fast-moving, hard-hitting armoured divisions. Thus the Luftwaffe became a tactical air force in terms

Above: Of all-metal construction with a skinning of corrugated Dural alloy, the Tupolev ANT-5 entered service in 1928 as the I-4 single-seat fighter, and for its time was a very advanced type with a sesquiplane wing cellule. The I-4 was powered by one 460hp M-22 (licence-built Bristol Jupiter) air-cooled radial engine, and was armed with two 0.3in (7.62mm) fixed forward-firing and synchronised machine-guns. The type's performance included a maximum speed of 160mph (258km/h) at optimum altitude and a ceiling of 25,100ft (7,650m), its maximum take-off weight was 3,000lb (1,360kg), and its dimensions included a span of 37ft 5in (11.40m) and length of 23ft 10.5in (7.28m).

Opposite: Produced in both landplane and floatplane forms (above and below respectively), the Heinkel He 51 was one of Germany's last single-seat biplane fighters, and as such marked one of the high points in the design of such warplanes even though it was obsolescent as it entered service in 1934. The definitive He 51B-1 was powered by one 750hp BMW VI water-cooled engine and armed with two 0.312in (7.92mm) MG17 fixed forward-firing and synchronised machine-guns, and its performance included a maximum speed of 205mph (330km/h) at optimum altitude, a ceiling of 25,350ft (7725m) and a range of 431 miles (695km). The type had a maximum take-off weight of 4,189lb (1,900kg), and its dimensional data included a span of 36ft 1.5in (11.00m) and a length of 27ft 6.75in (8.40m).

of its equipment, practical experience, training and operational philosophy.

The initial successes enjoyed by the Axis powers (Germany, Italy and Japan) were partially due to the fact that all three nations had gained experience before the outbreak of World War II. Italy had not only supported the Nationalists in Spain, but had also been able to test her forces in the conquest of Abyssinia, which began in 1935. The Italian bombers, principally the Savoia-Marchetti S.M.79 tri-motor monoplane, distinguished themselves in Spain, but the CR.32 and CR.42 fighters appeared better than they were, due to their phenomenal agility.

The Italian Regia Aeronautica therefore emerged from these two campaigns overestimating the operational utility of its first-line fighters. Three very promising designs for monoplane fighters, the Fiat G.50 Freccia, Macchi MC.200 Saetta and Reggiane Re.2000 Sagittario, were developed just before World War II, but the Italians had failed to keep up with the development of high-powered inline engines. All three of these potentially good fighters were therefore fitted with low-powered radials: furthermore, speed and rate of climb were also sacrificed to the pilots' expressed preference for manoeuvrability. Armament was poor, especially compared with the standards set in German fighters, which had 20mm cannon firing explosive shells.

Like Germany, Japan came late to modern aviation, and developed a good air force almost from the beginning. Although the army and navy had possessed their own air arms since 1911, Japan began to develop her aircraft industries and air forces only in the 1930s. Content at first to build Western types under licence, so absorbing the latest production and design techniques, Japan began a major expansion of her air forces in the mid-1930s, using her own designs.

The Western nations were only too glad to condemn these Japanese aircraft as inferior copies and adaptations of Western designs. In fact, they were skilfully designed to take advantage of Japan's capacity for producing lightweight structures with heavy armament, superior agility and good

performance especially in speed, climb rate and range. The Mitsubishi A5M and Nakajima Ki-27 low-wing monoplane fighters had very good performance despite their retention of fixed landing gear arrangements, and the next generation of fighters was even better. The Mitsubishi A6M Reisen (zero fighter), later known as the 'Zeke', received a glowing assessment from Americans flying against them in China, as did the Mitsubishi G3M 'Nell' and G4M 'Betty' bombers. All such warnings were disregarded, and this was to cost the Allies dearly in 1941 and 1942.

By 1936 the United Kingdom and France had become thoroughly alarmed by the nature and rate of German military expansion, and decided to institute major rearmament programmes in which aircraft had a high priority. The nationalised French aircraft groups created during 1936 in the north, centre, west, south-west and south-east of the country had produced some excellent designs by the beginning of the war, but these were not ready in time for the French campaign of 1940. The main burden fell instead on aircraft designed by the few successful private firms: Dewoitine's petite D.520 fighter, Morane-Saulnier's angular M.S.406 fighter, Bloch's stubby but powerful MB.151 fighter, Breguet's promising Bre.690 twin-engined fighter and Potez's useful Type 63 twin-engined fighter-bomber. Other excellent machines that could have played an important role had more of them been delivered in time were the Bloch MB.175 light bomber, the elegant Lioré-et-Olivier LeO 451 medium bomber and the useful Amiot 350 series bomber.

By the middle of the 1930s the British aircraft industry was well advanced in the production of important new fighters: the RAF abandoned the biplane formula after the Gloster Gladiator and turned to the low-wing monoplane. The best-known of these were the Hawker Hurricane and the Supermarine

A Fairey Flycatcher fighter flies past the British aircraft-carrier HMS Eagle during the 1930s. This was a time of great and rapid change in the nature of maritime air capabilities as the more important naval powers replaced their early-generation carrierborne warplanes with more advanced monoplanes offering considerably higher performance.

44

Spitfire, each powered by the magnificent Rolls-Royce Merlin engine and armed with eight rifle-calibre machine-guns. Both these interceptors had top speeds in the order of 350mph (565km/h), about 100mph (160km/h) faster than the Gladiator. With their retractable landing gear, trailing-edge flaps and enclosed cockpits, the aircraft caused problems at first in operational units, but as soon as pilots had mastered the necessary techniques the Hurricane and Spitfire won great popularity.

The British bomber force was also given completely new equipment in the shape of the Armstrong Whitworth Whitley, the Handley Page Hampden and the Vickers Wellington, each of these being cantilever low-wing monoplane bombers with twin engines and retractable landing gear. There was also the Fairey Battle single-engined light bomber, which was to prove almost worthless in combat, and the twin-engined Bristol Blenheim light bomber, an advanced and speedy aeroplane for its time, although somewhat flimsy and under-armed.

The Americans were producing some very advanced aircraft, including the first Boeing B-17 Flying Fortress four-engined heavy bomber in 1935, but they still lagged behind the Europeans in the theory and practice of air warfare. American aircraft had good performance, and allowed the pilot to perform his tasks in some comfort, but they lacked the 'edge' of their European counterparts. Nonetheless, American production was considerable, and the European powers were happy to order large quantities of aircraft such as the Curtiss P-36 and P-40 fighters, the Douglas DB-7 and Martin Maryland bombers, and a number of other types. Meanwhile, the Americans were hard at work on a new generation of aircraft that would make great and enduring reputations for themselves in World War II.

The Supermarine Spitfire may be regarded as the UK's first truly 'modern' fighter of the 1930s, for it was of metal construction with a stressed-skin metal covering and incorporated 'modern' features such as an enclosed cockpit, a cantilever low-set wing, retractable main landing gear units, trailing-edge flaps and, in the definitive models, a propeller of the variable-pitch type. The slightly earlier Hawker Hurricane, on the other hand, was not truly a 'modern' fighter as it had an earlier-generation structure based on steel tube covered with fabric.

During this period, both British and German scientists had been working on a new type of powerplant that would revolutionise aircraft design and operation. This was the turbojet engine, which was intended to thrust the aeroplane forward by the reaction of a stream of gases flowing backwards. Frank Whittle's early prototype ran for the first time in April 1937, and Hans von Ohain's model a month later. These British and German pioneers were working entirely independently of each other and evolved radically different types of engine. In fact, the Germans soon overtook the British, and scored a considerable success when in August 1939, less than one week before the outbreak of World War II, the Heinkel He 178 became the world's first jet-powered aeroplane to fly. Yet the authorities in both Germany and the United Kingdom were slow to appreciate the possibilities of such engines, and operational jet aircraft did not appear until late in World War II.

World War II in the Air

OF all the combatants in World War II, only Germany had evolved a practical method of tactical air support for its ground forces in the period leading up to hostilities. Careful evaluation of their performance in the Spanish Civil War had led the Germans to work out a new system of warfare in which the main striking elements were the armoured forces and their tactical air support formations. Contrary to popular belief, the German armed forces at the start of World War II did not comprise vast formations of tanks and infantry, mechanised and homogeneous, supported by masses of aircraft. In reality, the German formations were on the whole rather old-fashioned, relying heavily on horse transport and cumbersome artillery. The strength of the German army for offensive operations, however, lay in the relatively small but well-trained *Panzer* (tank) divisions.

The role of the Panzer formations was to strike swiftly and deeply into the enemy's defences, isolating his main operational groupings both from each other and the high command, and as a result destroying his cohesion in military, political and economic terms. As the Panzer forces bit deep into hostile territory, relying on mobility to keep them out of trouble, the infantry would follow up more slowly, completing the isolation of enemy groups, 'mopping up' and consolidating in the wake of the Panzer formations.

In theory this was a neat and economical solution to the question of how best to avoid the type of static warfare that had become the norm during World War I. As the Germans had discovered in Spain, however, the practical reality was that the Panzer formations could not fulfil their task on their own as they lacked the heavy fire support so frequently needed. Artillery would have been the conventional answer, but the German artillery was neither modern nor mobile enough to keep up with the Panzer formations. The solution was found in deployment of the Luftwaffe

Douglas SBD Dauntless

THE Douglas SBD Dauntless was the most important dive-bomber operated by the US Navy and US Marine Corps in the first half of World War II. Although it was at best obsolescent by 1944 in terms of its primary anti-ship role, the type was retained in service because of the limitations of its successor, the Curtiss SB2C Helldiver, and operated from the smaller escort (or 'jeep') carriers for the support of amphibious landings in the later stages of World War II. Rugged and reliable, the Dauntless was well liked by its crews for these primary features as well as its adequate performance and considerable agility. Total production was 5,937 aircraft in a number of variants characterised by heavier armament, increased fuel capacity, enhanced defensive features (improved armour protection and self-sealing fuel tanks), and an uprated engine. The Dauntless was used by France, New Zealand, Mexico and the UK in addition to the USA, although the British aircraft were used for training rather than combat, and the Mexican aircraft were limited in operational terms to anti-submarine patrols in the Gulf of Mexico.

With 3,025 built, the SBD-5 was the last major production version and may be taken as a good representative of the type. The SBD had a crew of two (pilot and observer/gunner), was powered by one Wright R-1820-60 Cyclone air-cooled radial piston engine rated at 1,200hp, and carried a disposable armament of 2,250lb (1,021kg) in the form of a 1,600lb (726kg) or smaller bomb on the underfuselage crutch used to swing the bomb clear of the propeller before release, and 650lb (295kg) of smaller bombs under the wings; the gun armament comprised two 0.5in (12.7mm) fixed forward-firing machine guns operated by the pilot, and two 0.3in (7.62mm) trainable rearward-firing machine guns operated buy the observer/gunner. The SBD-5's other primary details included a span of 41ft 6.25in (12,65m), length of 33ft 0in (1,0.06m), empty weight of 6,533lb (2,963kg), maximum take-off weight of 10,700lb (4,855kg), maximum speed of 245mph (394km/h) at 15,800ft (4,815m), initial climb rate of 1,190ft (363m) per minute, service ceiling of 24,300ft (7,405m), and range of 1,100 miles (1,770km).

for this task. Under the command of Hermann Göring, a World War I air ace, the Luftwaffe quickly evolved as a highly mobile and efficient tactical support force.

Effective co-operation between the ground and air forces was essential for the success of the new *Blitzkrieg* (lightning war) tactics, and this co-operation was wholly dependent on radio communications, which were assured by allocating a number of air controllers in specially equipped half-track vehicles to all the major combat units as well as to senior commanders. If a Panzer battalion ran into stiff resistance, it could call for air support without suffering the inevitable delay of going through a higher command echelon. The value of these forward controllers, able to speak directly to the air units, played a significant part in Germany's successes in 1939 and 1940.

Tactical support for the army appeared complex because of the large number of different types of aircraft involved. It was in fact a smooth and relatively simple affair, with each type of aeroplane playing an individual and specific role. Far forward of the actual fighting, for instance, operational reconnaissance aircraft, usually converted bombers carrying a number of cameras, kept constant watch for any signs of enemy activity that might have an important long-term effect on the campaign.

Over the battlefield itself, and just forward of it, tactical reconnaissance machines such as the Fieseler Fi 156 Storch kept a watchful eye on short-term developments. Providing short-range cover for these aircraft, and also supporting the ground forces with machine-gun and cannon fire, were the single-engined Messerschmitt Bf 109 fighters. Also available in comparatively large numbers was the twin-engined Messerschmitt Bf 110

The Fieseler Fi 156 Storch was Germany's most important battlefield liaison aeroplane of World War II, and was also operated in the battlefield observation role. The type's most important characteristic was its phenomenally good low-speed handling as a result of its low wing loading and the high-lift devices on the leading and trailing edges of its wing. This produced exceptionally good field performance of the short take-off and landing (STOL) type, and also allowed the aeroplane virtually to hover in only modest winds.

Zerstörer (destroyer) heavy fighter, whose primary function was to hunt down enemy bombers, but which could also support the ground forces with machine-gun and cannon fire. A dedicated ground-attack aeroplane, the single-engined Henschel Hs 123 biplane, with fixed landing gear, was used only in the war's early campaigns: its offensive complement of machine-guns and light bombs, brought to bear accurately by the aeroplane's steadiness and considerable low-level agility, made it very useful against enemy infantry.

The dread of most enemy infantry, however, was the Junkers Ju 87 Stuka dive-bomber, which was used to provide the Panzer units with extremely accurate support at close ranges, thus replacing conventional horse- and tractor-drawn artillery. The Stukas were armed with bombs up to 500kg (1,102lb) in weight, and were capable of dealing with most of the enemy's defensive positions and tanks. Finally, support of a more general nature was provided by Dornier Do 17, Heinkel He 111 and Junkers Ju 88 medium bombers, which could operate at low level, and therefore with greater accuracy, once the Bf 109s had eliminated the enemy's air cover.

Battlefield support of this type was the Luftwaffe's main task, but it depended first on the destruction of the enemy's air power, usually by attacks on the enemy's main airfields at the start of hostilities. Undertaken

In numerical terms the Messerschmitt Bf 109 was Germany's most important fighter of World War II, and in 1939 and 1940 was in real terms her only single-engined fighter until supplemented by the superlative Focke-Wulf Fw 190 multi-role fighter. Illustrated here is an example of the Bf 109E-3, one of the standard fighters used by the Luftwaffe in the Battle of Britain. Powered by a Daimler-Benz DB 601Aa liquid-cooled inverted-Vee piston engine, the Bf 109E-3 was armed with two 20mm MG FF fixed forward-firing cannon in the wing leading edges, two 0.312in (7.92mm) MG 17 fixed forward-firing machine guns in the upper part of the forward fuselage and, on some aircraft, one 20 mm MG FF/M fixed forward-firing cannon located between the engine cylinder banks to fire through the hollow propeller shaft. The Bf 109E-3 had a maximum speed of 348mph (560km/h) at 14,560ft (4,440m), and among its attributes was the ability to nose straight down into a dive without the fuel-injected engine cutting out.

49

on a large scale by the medium bombers, such raids were truly devastating and generally caused such destruction that airfields were rendered inoperative, with comparatively few combat aircraft likely to have survived the bombers' attentions. While the bombers roamed deep into the enemy's rear areas to destroy airfields, turning their attentions to targets such as transport and communications centres, the German fighters attacked their counterparts in the air during the first few days of the campaign. The success of this operational method is attested by the fact that in their first campaigns, the Germans encountered virtually no significant air opposition

First tested with considerable success in the Spanish Civil War, the Junkers Ju 87 dive-bomber was universally known as the 'Stuka' and in the first campaigns of World War II proved an invaluable asset for the Germans in the course of their campaigns of conquest in Poland, North-West Europe, and the Balkans. Here the Ju 87 was not faced by significant fighter or anti-aircraft artillery opposition, and was therefore able to operate effectively in its role of 'flying artillery' for the Panzer divisions, blasting any defensive feature that might have hindered the rapid progress of these armoured formations. The Battle of Britain highlighted the tactical limitations of the Ju 87 against a high-grade defence, however, and the Ju 87 was then translated into a potent if limited anti-tank type such as this Ju 87G with a pair of 37mm cannon under the wings

after the first few hours or days of any campaign, and this allowed the bulk of their tactical air strength to be allocated to the direct support of the ground forces.

The Ju 87 was central to the German concept of tactical support. A very sturdy aeroplane with wide-track fixed landing gear, the Stuka could operate from rough airstrips close behind the front line, allowing it to make frequent sorties and to respond rapidly to calls for close support. The aeroplane's performance was adequate and its offensive load quite good by the standards of the day, making it an effective combat type.

Yet a large part of the Stuka's success was due to its psychological effect. The angular Ju 87 had a belligerent and aggressive aspect, most impressive as it dived under full control – assisted by the powerful and effective dive-brakes under its wings, and this aspect was enhanced by the screaming of the pair of 'Jericho trumpets' installed as single units in each landing gear fairing. These emitted a banshee howl of increasing pitch as the Stuka swooped down to release its bombs only a few hundred feet above the target. The combination of the Stuka's appearance and sound, and later its reputation, did much to demoralise opposing ground forces during 1939 and 1940.

The Polish campaign which opened World War II began on 1 September 1939, and the Luftwaffe soon proved its worth. The Polish air force fought back, using combat aircraft such as the single-engined P.11

Junkers Ju 87 'Stuka'

BUILT to a total of 5,709 aircraft up to 1944, when it was finally phased out of production despite the fact that it had no successor, the Ju 87 was an extremely sturdy aeroplane able to undertake nearly vertical attacks for the delivery of its bomb load with pinpoint accuracy. The speed in the dive was controlled by powerful air brakes under the wings, and recovery from the dive was made under control of an automatic system as the high g loadings of the recovery tended to cause the pilot to black out. The fear of the Ju 87's accurate attack was further enhanced by the 'Jericho trumpets' in the main landing gear legs: the increasing pitch of these sirens as the Ju 87 dived became a potent morale-shattering weapon in its own right against poorly trained troops.

The Ju 87B-1 may be taken as typical of the 'Stuka' in its primary dive-bomber form. The type was manned by a pilot and a radio operator/gunner in tandem under a 'glasshouse' canopy, and its powerplant was one Junkers Jumo 211Da liquid-cooled Vee piston engine rated at 1,200hp. The type's dimensions included a span of 45ft 3.33in (13.80m) and length of 36ft 5in (11.10m), and its weights comprised an empty figure of 5,980lb (2,710 g) and a maximum take-off figure of 9,560lb (4340kg). The Ju 87B-1 had a maximum speed of 238mph (383km/h) at 13,410ft (4090 m), a climb to 6,560ft (2000 m) in 4 minutes 18 seconds, a service ceiling of 26,150ft (8,000m), and a range of 490 miles (790km). The inbuilt armament comprised two 0.312in (7.92mm) MG 17 fixed forward-firing machine guns in the wing leading edges and one 0.312in (7.9 mm) MG 15 trainable rearward-firing machine gun in the rear of the cockpit, and the disposable armament was 1,102lb (500kg), generally carried in the form of one 1,102lb SC-500 bomb on the underfuselage crutch that swung this weapon clear of the propeller before releasing it.

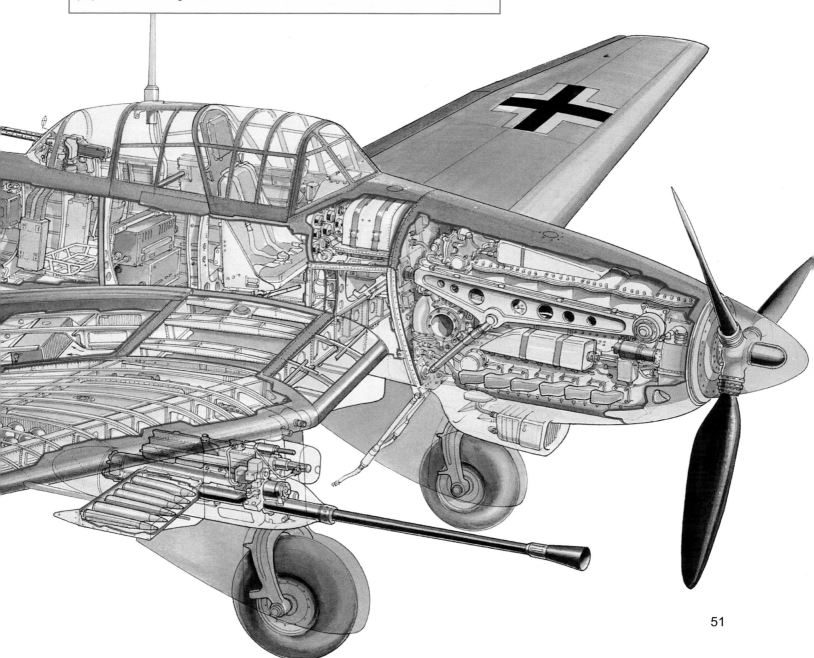

gull-winged fighter, single-engined P.23 Karás light bomber and twin-engined P.37 Lós medium bomber, all produced by PZL, the state aircraft company, and in the initial stages of the fighting inflicted some severe losses on their attackers. But the weight and experience of the Luftwaffe was bound to succeed in the end. After a few days the Poles could offer no large-scale aerial resistance, and the main weight of the Luftwaffe was switched to tactical support of the Panzer divisions, whose pincer movements were biting deep into Poland. German aircraft losses to ground fire were moderately heavy, but Luftwaffe aircraft continued to support the advancing Panzer formations.

If any doubts remained about the efficiency of the German armed forces, they were soon dispelled by the capture of Denmark and the most important strategic points in Norway by airborne and seaborne landings on 9 April 1940. The subsequent Luftwaffe operations in Norway followed the pattern set for them in Poland. The Norwegian air force was negligible, and the only major air support sent by the Allies was a number of British aircraft, most of them obsolete compared with the German opposition. It is interesting to note, however, that the Gloster Gladiator biplane fighter did achieve some success against the German bombers, although its use stood no chance of altering the course of the campaign, and this success is a useful reflection of the British pilots' high level of training and the relatively small qualitative

Above: With production exceeding 7,300 aircraft of all marks, the Heinkel He 111 was Germany's standard twin-engined medium bomber throughout World War II. The type was a useful warplane at the beginning of the war, but was forced to soldier on into obsolescence for lack of an adequate successor and, although the Germans achieved near miracles of upgrading the type and maintaining its operational capabilities, losses in the later stages of the war were inevitably high.

Right: The PZL P.37 Lós medium bomber was entering service at the beginning of World War II and was the best tactical warplane available to the Polish air force. Only a few aircraft had been delivered, however, and these were unable to change the course of the Polish campaign.

superiority of first-generation monoplane bombers over last-generation biplane fighters.

While the Germans were clearing up the last Allied pockets in central and northern Norway, momentous events were taking place in western Europe. On 10 May 1940, Hitler unleashed a huge offensive against the Netherlands, Belgium and France, which were defended by their own forces as well as by elements of the British services. The German attacks followed the Polish pattern, and were therefore centred on breakthrough and deep exploitation by the Panzer formations. These struck through the 'impassable' Ardennes to reach the Channel coast, splitting the Allied armies in two. The Germans then concentrated on eliminating the two halves in detail. With the Dutch, Belgians and French defeated to the north of the 'Panzer corridor', and the British and a number of their allies escaping from Dunkirk, the Germans turned their full weight upon the remnants of the French army holding that portion of France south of the corridor. The last elements of the French army surrendered towards the end of June.

Germany's next move was to attack the United Kingdom. Hitler had been amazed by the British declaration of war after the German invasion of Poland, and now urged the United Kingdom to make an honourable peace on the basis of the status quo. When this offer was refused, Hitler had no option but to plan the conquest of the United Kingdom, to be accomplished by an invasion codenamed Seelöwe (sealion). The German navy had suffered moderately heavy losses in the Norwegian campaign, and plans for the landings progressed only spasmodically. But Göring, promoted to the unique rank of Reichsmarschall for his part in the Luftwaffe's triumph over France, now declared that his air forces could render invasion unnecessary through the aerial destruction of the United Kingdom's ability and will to resist. This boastful claim led to the Battle of Britain, which was the world's first strategic all-air battle.

The Battle of Britain fell into three main phases: firstly, the attacks on convoys and coastal installations; secondly, the assault on Fighter Command's bases and fighter production centres; and thirdly, the campaign against urban areas. The coastal shipping phase began as France fell, and was typified by raids, usually by a few bombers with a heavy fighter escort, against British coastal convoys and the ports and naval installations on the English south and east coasts. With the aid of radar, the RAF was able to meet the Germans on equal terms and inflicted fairly heavy losses.

Since this coastal phase proved relatively ineffectual, the Luftwaffe high command decided at the beginning of August to attack British fighter bases and radar stations. The bombers would be used to lure the British fighters

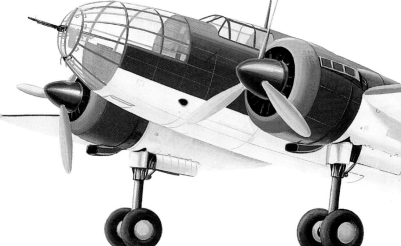

aloft, and could also cause considerable damage to industrial areas and air bases, but again it was the fighters that were expected to inflict the main damage as the British fighters clawed for altitude on their bomber-interception missions.

This second phase of the battle exposed major flaws in the German air machine. The coastal phase had already proved the Stuka to be useless wherever the enemy had parity, let alone air superiority: the Ju 87 was hopelessly vulnerable at the bottom of its dive, where it lacked the energy for any kind of effective defensive manoeuvring. The fighter phase now revealed that the Bf 110, much favoured by the German propaganda machine and the Luftwaffe high command, was comparatively easy prey for the faster and nimbler British fighters. Losses were severe on both sides, but with the slower Hurricanes taking on the bombers and Bf 110s, and the Spitfires holding off the Bf 109s, the RAF slowly but inexorably gained ascendancy over the Luftwaffe, especially along the Channel coast.

On 7 September 1940, the Germans switched the focus of their offensive from Fighter Command to the great conurbations of London and the other great industrial cities of the United Kingdom. This change was demanded by Hitler, who was furious that Bomber Command had made air raids (as a result of navigational error) on Berlin. The German fighters were now ordered to abandon their roving (and therefore fuel-economical and tactically advantageous) loose escort of the bombers; instead they were to concentrate on close escort of the bombers. This denied the fighters advantageous use of their speed and agility, and also forced them into a

Above left: Conceived as an interceptor fighter to supplant the Hawker Hurricane, the Hawker Typhoon proved an abject failure in its planned role as its climb rate and high-altitude performance were inadequate, but then became one of the classic attack fighters of World War II. Operating at low level with its inbuilt armament of four 20mm Hispano cannon supplemented by two 500lb (227kg) bombs or eight unguided rockets each carrying a 60lb (27kg) warhead, the Typhoon Mk IB was one of the decisive weapons of the Normandy campaign in the summer of 1944, and wrought enormous destruction both on the German armoured forces as well as the logistical infrastructure on which the Germans were reliant for a sustained defence.

The Fairey Albacore was planned as successor to the legendary Fairey Swordfish in the carrierborne torpedo-bomber role, and offered such improvements as better performance and enclosed crew accommodation. Yet the type was never quite as 'right' as the Swordfish, which therefore remained not only in production but also in highly profitable service well after the Albacore had been phased out of first-line operation.

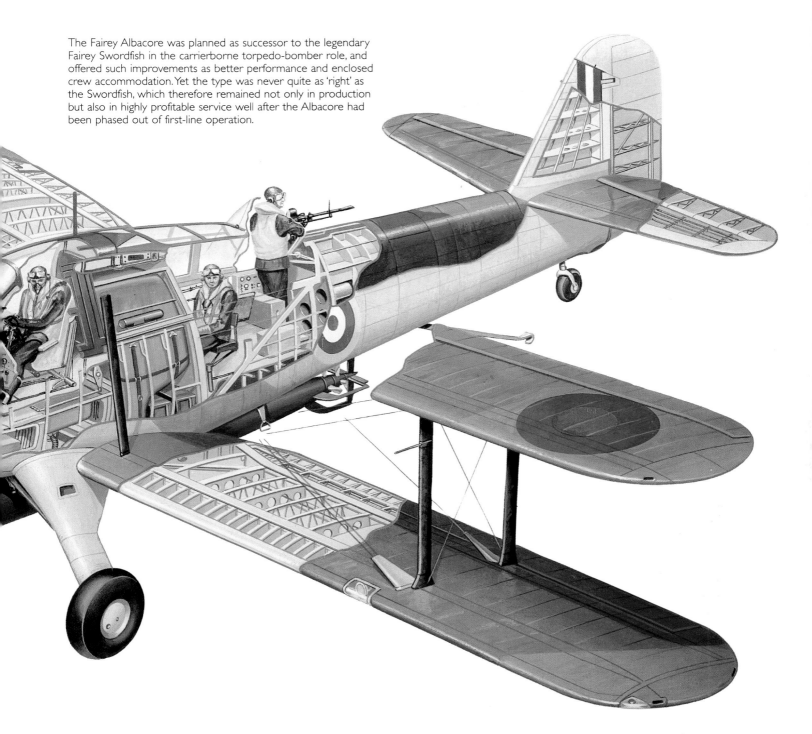

flight regime that was distinctly wasteful of their already strained range capabilities. In effect, the fighters had sufficient fuel for about 10 minutes of combat over London, after which time the bombers were left mostly unprotected, providing easier prey for the British fighters, which began to inflict increasingly heavy losses.

The Luftwaffe maintained its night attacks on British cities until the end of the spring of 1941, and RAF Bomber Command began a campaign of nocturnal raids on German cities. While the German bombers found it relatively easy to locate London and other major British cities from their

Seen here in the form of a Spitfire Mk I of No. 610 Squadron during 1940, the Supermarine Spitfire remains the most celebrated British fighter of all time. The type was already in full service on the outbreak of World War II, and was still in development at the end of the war in 1945, the intervening period of almost six years having seen a transformation of the type with double the horsepower (including a switch from the Rolls-Royce Merlin to the Rolls-Royce Griffon engine) for vastly improved performance, considerably increased fixed firepower now supplemented by a useful disposable load in the type's secondary fighter-bomber role, diversification into other roles such as photo-reconnaissance and carrierborne fighter, and a number of important aerodynamic enhancements.

bases in northern France and the Low Countries, British bombers found it far more difficult to find German cities. An operational research report at the end of 1940 showed that only a very small percentage of British bombs was falling anywhere near the intended targets. Yet this night bombing campaign was the only means available to the United Kingdom for direct attack on Germany, and the effort was therefore continued, gradually increasing in strength if not initially in accuracy.

The Blitz came to an eventual end in May 1941 for two reasons. Firstly, the twin-engined Bristol Beaufighter night-fighter, fitted with the new AI (airborne interception) radar, was taking an increasingly heavy toll of the raiders; secondly, German air formations were being transferred east for the invasion of the USSR. By June 1941 the United Kingdom was faced by only two fighter squadrons, but these managed to check British offensive operations over north-west Europe with the aid of the latest German fighter, the Focke-Wulf Fw 190. Powered by a closely cowled radial piston engine, this structurally sturdy fighter was highly manoeuvrable, carried very heavy armament, and enjoyed the advantage of performance generally superior to that of any British fighter.

The German plans for the conquest of the USSR were postponed for a short, but fatal, time by Hitler's decision to invade Yugoslavia and Greece in April. Belgrade was subjected to the now customary 'terror' bombing on 6 April 1941, the day on which the Germans crossed the borders. Despite the presence of British ground and air forces, the Germans swept all before them, although the Greeks and British managed to inflict relatively severe losses on the Luftwaffe. The Blitzkrieg combination of armoured and aerial power prevailed, and by the end of April both Greece and Yugoslavia were in German hands.

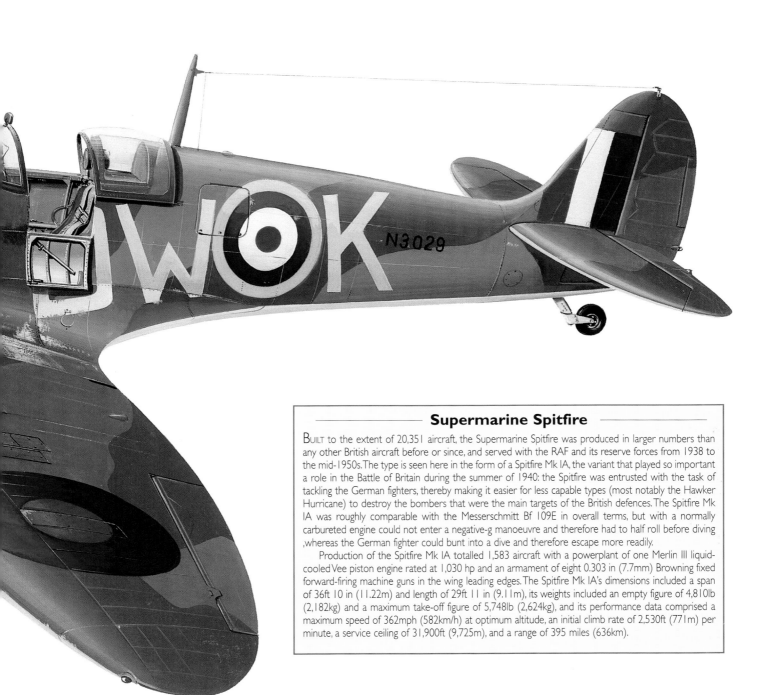

Supermarine Spitfire

Built to the extent of 20,351 aircraft, the Supermarine Spitfire was produced in larger numbers than any other British aircraft before or since, and served with the RAF and its reserve forces from 1938 to the mid-1950s. The type is seen here in the form of a Spitfire Mk IA, the variant that played so important a role in the Battle of Britain during the summer of 1940: the Spitfire was entrusted with the task of tackling the German fighters, thereby making it easier for less capable types (most notably the Hawker Hurricane) to destroy the bombers that were the main targets of the British defences. The Spitfire Mk IA was roughly comparable with the Messerschmitt Bf 109E in overall terms, but with a normally carbureted engine could not enter a negative-g manoeuvre and therefore had to half roll before diving ,whereas the German fighter could bunt into a dive and therefore escape more readily.

Production of the Spitfire Mk IA totalled 1,583 aircraft with a powerplant of one Merlin III liquid-cooled Vee piston engine rated at 1,030 hp and an armament of eight 0.303 in (7.7mm) Browning fixed forward-firing machine guns in the wing leading edges. The Spitfire Mk IA's dimensions included a span of 36ft 10 in (11.22m) and length of 29ft 11 in (9.11m), its weights included an empty figure of 4,810lb (2,182kg) and a maximum take-off figure of 5,748lb (2,624kg), and its performance data comprised a maximum speed of 362mph (582km/h) at optimum altitude, an initial climb rate of 2,530ft (771m) per minute, a service ceiling of 31,900ft (9,725m), and a range of 395 miles (636km).

By mid-June 1941, most of Germany's offensive strength gathered along the Soviet frontier. Hitler planned to destroy the USSR as a political entity within four months, and a major tactical role was allocated to the Luftwaffe in the Germans' overall plan for the operation, codenamed 'Barbarossa'. The invasion began on 22 June, and from the first hours of the campaign the Germans secured total air superiority along the front. Tactical surprise was complete and most of the forward-based Soviet aircraft were destroyed on the ground, in the process constituting the majority of the thousands of Soviet aircraft knocked out or captured in the fighting's first few days.

By the type of paradox typical in war, this German success proved to be of enormous benefit to the Soviets in the longer term. Standards had declined radically during Stalin's purges of the Soviet armed forces during 1937 and 1938, and the Red air force was only just emerging from the shock of its mauling by the tiny Finnish air force in the 'Winter War'. In addition, at the time of the start of hostilities with Germany, the Red air force was saddled with vast numbers of obsolete aircraft that the government was unwilling to scrap. The Luftwaffe's action forced the communist leadership to accelerate the design, development and production of new aircraft.

The Soviets were already producing one of the war's finest ground-attack types, the single-engined Ilyushin Il-2 Shturmovik, and this was soon joined by the excellent twin-engined Petlyakov Pe-2 tactical medium bomber and the improving series of single-engined fighters designed by Lavochkin and Yakovlev. With just these four types at the core of their operational inventory between 1942 and 1945, the Soviets were able to produce vast numbers of aircraft that were austerely equipped by Western standards, but which were nonetheless ideally suited to the USSR's climatic extremes and

Left: The Hawker Hurricane was not as advanced a fighter as the Supermarine Spitfire, but was nonetheless a very worthy type that was available in larger numbers during the crucial Battle of Britain period, when it was responsible for the destruction of more German aircraft than all the other British defences combined. Of 'modern' aerodynamic design but with a somewhat dated structure, which did however ease production and repair, the Hurricane was obsolescent as a fighter by 1941 and was thereafter developed as a highly capable fighter-bomber for service mainly in North Africa and Burma.

Below: The Hawker Fury was one of the last British fighters to be developed in World War II, but appeared when the thrust of advanced fighter development was switching to turbojet-powered fighters. The type nevertheless entered limited production in its original landplane form and in somewhat larger numbers in its Sea Fury carrierborne form.

simple military tactics. Other types used were the Mikoyan-Gurevich fighter and the Ilyushin Il-4 bomber.

Although Germany's main interests from June 1941 lay in the east, the departure of most German air units did not lead to a halt of air operations in the west. Throughout 1941, fighter-bombers kept up a constant series of nuisance raids on targets in southern England, but the year was notable especially for the gradual emergence of the RAF as an offensive force, and for the increasing importance of air power in the Mediterranean theatre.

The most fascinating RAF aircraft to enter widespread service in 1941 was the de Havilland Mosquito which, with the possible exception of the Ju 88, may be judged to have been the war's most versatile aeroplane. It was almost certainly the most effective combat aeroplane of the war in terms of successes and achievements against losses. Conceived as a private venture, the Mosquito was planned as a high-speed bomber, using the same type of wooden sandwich-material structure pioneered in the pre-war Albatross airliner, and among the features demanded by the design team was a maximum speed so high that the Mosquito would need no defensive armament. Initially, the Air Ministry was sceptical, but when the prototype appeared in November 1940, its exquisite lines, extraordinary high speed and superb handling characteristics immediately revealed that the basic design was right.

Although the United Kingdom had accepted the philosophy of strategic bombing for some considerable time, the RAF entered World War II with no true heavy bomber. The Armstrong Whitworth Whitley had a useful maximum bomb load of 7,000lb (3,175kg) but possessed a range of only 470 miles (756km) with this load; the Handley Page Hampden could carry 4,000lb (1,814kg) of bombs for 1,200 miles (1,931km); and the Vickers Wellington Mk III had a range of 1,540 miles (2,478km) with 4,500lb (2,041kg) of bombs. These were all twin-engined machines, and the RAF

First Turbojet-Powered Fighters

THE world's first two turbojet-powered fighters entered service almost simultaneously in the summer of 1944, and were the British Gloster Meteor and the German Messerschmitt Me 262. The former was decidedly the inferior type in terms of short-term overall capability and long-term 'developability'.

The Meteor may be characterized as the piston-engined fighter merely translated into a turbojet-powered type by the replacement of the nose-mounted piston engine by a pair of bulky Rolls-Royce Welland (soon replaced by Rolls-Royce Derwent) centrifugal-flow turbojets in large wing-mounted nacelles, it had a fixed forward-firing armament of four 20mm Hispano cannon. The Me 262, on the other hand, had been more adventurously designed with cleaner lines, slightly swept flying surfaces, a powerplant of two slim Junkers Jumo 004 axial-flow turbojets in smaller nacelles attached to the undersurfaces of the wings, and a fixed forward-firing armament of four 30mm MK 108 cannon.

Development of the Me 262 ended with the conclusion of World War II while the Meteor remained in development and production into the mid-1950s, but this cannot disguise the fact that the Me 262 was basically the better fighter and, as such, the real precursor of later turbojet-powered fighters.

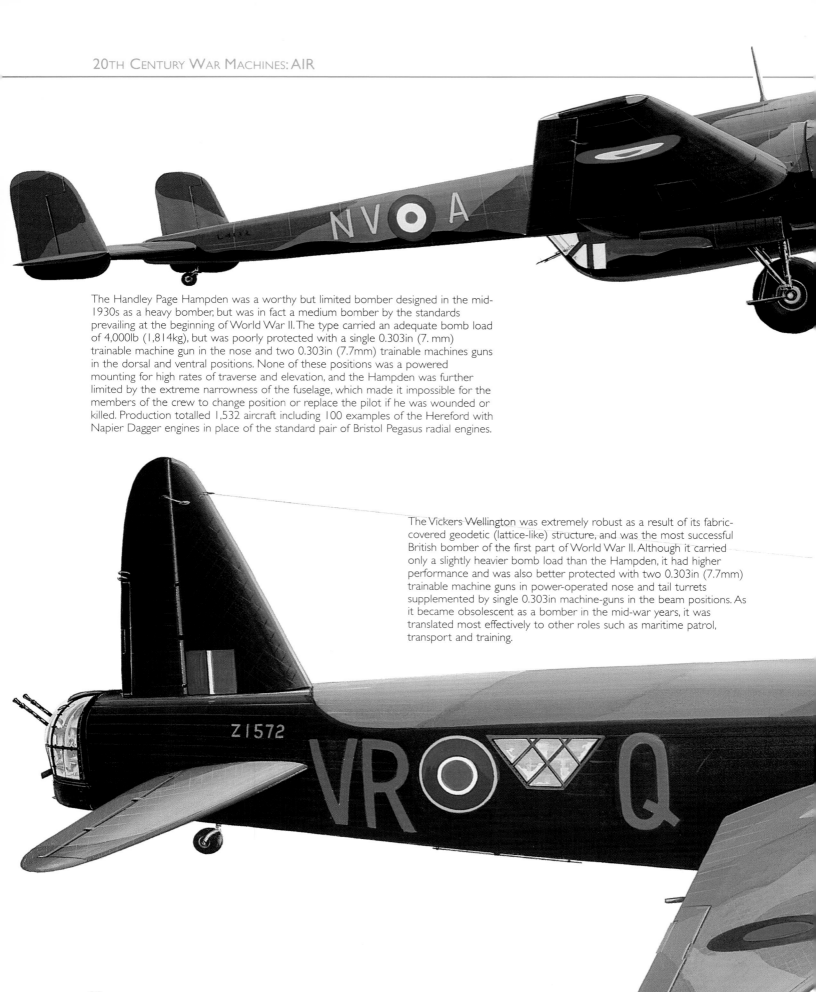

The Handley Page Hampden was a worthy but limited bomber designed in the mid-1930s as a heavy bomber, but was in fact a medium bomber by the standards prevailing at the beginning of World War II. The type carried an adequate bomb load of 4,000lb (1,814kg), but was poorly protected with a single 0.303in (7. mm) trainable machine gun in the nose and two 0.303in (7.7mm) trainable machines guns in the dorsal and ventral positions. None of these positions was a powered mounting for high rates of traverse and elevation, and the Hampden was further limited by the extreme narrowness of the fuselage, which made it impossible for the members of the crew to change position or replace the pilot if he was wounded or killed. Production totalled 1,532 aircraft including 100 examples of the Hereford with Napier Dagger engines in place of the standard pair of Bristol Pegasus radial engines.

The Vickers Wellington was extremely robust as a result of its fabric-covered geodetic (lattice-like) structure, and was the most successful British bomber of the first part of World War II. Although it carried only a slightly heavier bomb load than the Hampden, it had higher performance and was also better protected with two 0.303in (7.7mm) trainable machine guns in power-operated nose and tail turrets supplemented by single 0.303in machine-guns in the beam positions. As it became obsolescent as a bomber in the mid-war years, it was translated most effectively to other roles such as maritime patrol, transport and training.

Night Bombing

At the beginning of World War II, the British hoped to avoid the need for any bombing of targets on German soil but planned that any such attacks would be undertaken by day so that the bomber force could navigate more easily and attack with greater accuracy. Events soon dictated that bombing should be undertaken, but early experience revealed the hopeless vulnerability of British bombers to German fighter interception. The RAF therefore switched to night bombing.

The RAF had virtually no experience of long-range navigation by night, and no experience at all of undertaking such flying in formation. The result was a major decline in accuracy: although many crews reported in good faith that they had reached and bombed the target, subsequent reconnaissance revealed that only a very small percentage of the bomb load had in fact been delivered to the vicinity of the target, and virtually none at all on the target itself.

Growing experience and better training did result in an increase of navigational and bombing accuracies, but it remained impossible to strike at point targets such as particular shipyards or railway marshalling yards, and it became the British practice to bomb area targets, such as major industrial areas. The theory behind this system was that some of the bombs would almost certainly hit targets of direct military value, and that the rest of the bombs would hit and destroy the urban areas populated by the military targets' workforce, thereby reducing production as workers were killed, wounded, or merely had their sleep patterns destroyed by the need to take shelter, as they moved away from the area.

Throughout 1941 and 1942 the scale and effect of the British bombing increased as four-engined heavy bombers replaced the earlier twin-engined types and as navigational and bombing accuracies improved. These were never sufficient in themselves, however, and attacks of adequate accuracy could only result from the use of massive forces that might suffer very heavy losses. The right blend of force and accuracy was finally created by the establishment of the Path-Finder Force, which comprised highly skilled crews in aircraft often fitted with special navigational aids: these crews reached the target area shortly before the Main Force bombers, sought out the right target areas and then marked these with special pyrotechnic markers, providing a clear and unmistakable target for the Main Force bombers to attack.

The twin-engined Vickers Wellington has been overshadowed since the end of World War II by the four-engined heavy bombers that bore the bulk of the nocturnal raids on Germany from 1942, but was nevertheless of vital importance in the prosecution of the British bomber effort in the dark days of 1941 and 1942, and thereafter became just as important in a number of secondary roles.

had already accepted the fact that the combination of significant bomb load and useful range required the power and fuel capacity that could be offered only by four-engined aircraft.

By the autumn of 1941 no fewer than three four-engined heavy bombers had entered service with Bomber Command: the Short Stirling could carry 14,000lb (6,350kg) of bombs for 590 miles (949km), while the corresponding figures for the Handley Page Halifax were 5,800lb (2,631kg) carried over 1,860 miles (2,993km). Undoubtedly the finest of the trio, however, was the celebrated Avro Lancaster that could carry 14,000lb (6,350kg) of bombs over a range of 1,660 miles (2,671km), and also possessed a bomb bay large enough to carry considerably heavier special weapons over shorter ranges, for specific missions such as dam-busting, bridge destruction and the penetration of reinforced concrete U-boat pens. With the Halifax and Lancaster as its primary weapons, Bomber Command could begin to take the air war to Germany with increasing effect.

Throughout 1941, Bomber Command was learning the lessons of area bombing by night, and was building up its strength and skills for the heavy bombing campaign. Unlike the Americans, who were confident that their heavily armed daylight bombers could fight their way through the German defences, using their advanced Norden bombsights to succeed in pinpoint attacks on small targets of strategic importance, Bomber Command was convinced that night bombing was the only solution to anti-aircraft guns and fighter defences. The targets would have to be large industrial areas, in which bombing would damage industry and demoralise the civilian population, whilst keeping to a minimum the number of bombers lost to the German night-fighters.

The steadily improving capability of Bomber Command spurred a comparable development in the size and capability of the German night-fighter arm. Ground radar was developed to vector the Ju 88 and Bf 110 fighters into the correct area, and airborne interception sets installed in these night-fighters were used to locate the bombers at short range. British losses began to climb alarmingly during the early summer of 1941, but a counter to this trend was found in the form of 'Window'. This comprised specially-sized strips of metal foil, which were dropped in their millions to reflect the German radar beams and cause a totally confused picture of the situation on German radar screens.

The device was used with great success in 'Gomorrah', an operation that involved four Bomber Command raids in late July and early August 1943. 'Gomorrah' almost completely destroyed the great port of Hamburg. Thereafter, Bomber Command's growing fleet of heavy bombers turned its attention to the Battle of Berlin: a series of 16 great raids launched against the German capital in the winter of 1943 and spring of 1944.

During the summer of 1943, the heavy bombers of the US 8th Army Air Force began to complement the effort of Bomber Command in ever-increasing strength. Catapulted into World War II by the Japanese attack on Pearl Harbor on 7 December 1941, the United States had agreed with the United Kingdom that Germany was the prime enemy and should be destroyed first, and that only after this had been achieved would the full weight of the Allies be turned on the Japanese.

Most of 1942 was spent building up the US air forces in the United Kingdom, but from the summer onwards Boeing B-17 Flying Fortress and Consolidated B-24 Liberator heavy bombers started to undertake daylight

Undoubtedly the best and also the most widely remembered British heavy bomber of World War II, the Avro Lancaster was powered in most of its marks by four Rolls-Royce Merlin engines, was well defended, and could carry up to 18,000lb (8,165kg) of bombs or, in a special version, one 22,000lb (9,979kg) 'Grand Slam' bomb, the heaviest air-dropped weapon of World War II. This is a Lancaster B.Mk III, which was identical to the Lancaster B.Mk I except for its powerplant of four Merlin 22 or 24 engines, each rated at 1,640hp, made in the USA by Packard. The Lancaster B.Mk III accounted for 3,020 of the 7,378 Lancasters built, and its primary data included a crew of seven, a span of 102ft 0in (31.09m), length of 69ft 6in (21.18m), empty weight of 37,000lb (16,780kg), maximum take-off weight of 70,000lb (31,750kg), maximum level speed of 287mph (462km/h) at 11,500 ft (3,500m), climb to 20,000ft (6,095m) in 41 minutes 0 seconds, service ceiling of 24,500ft (7,465m), and range of 1,660 miles (2,675km) with a bomb load of 14,000lb (6,350kg). The type's defensive armament was eight 0.303in (7.7mm) Browning trainable machine guns located in three power-operated turrets: one in the nose with two guns, one in the dorsal position with two guns, and one in the tail with four guns.

probes into northern Europe. At first the US forces enjoyed some success. Then, in August 1943, the 8th Army Air Force launched its first raid deep into Germany. Warned by radar of the American build-up over the Channel, German fighters scrambled to attack the bomber formations, which were cruising at high altitude and producing highly visible 'vapour trails'. The German fighters picked up the American bombers while they were still a considerable distance from their target, and there followed a running battle to and from the target of Schweinfurt. The American bombers suffered crippling losses to the massed fighter attacks. A second attempt in October proved even more disastrous, and deep penetration raids were temporarily halted.

The problem lay in the fact that the bombers' defensive machine-guns lacked the weight and concentration to defeat the Germans' cannon-armed fighters. The bombers needed long-range escort fighters to protect them, but these were not available until the end of the year. At the time, the 8th Army Air Force's fighter squadrons were equipped only with the single-engined Republic P-47 Thunderbolt, a machine that was later to gain an enviable reputation as a heavy attack fighter, and with the twin-engined, twin-boom Lockheed P-38 Lightning that was too large and heavy to dogfight with the German single-engined machines. There was also an increasing number of North American P-51 Mustang fighters, but these were early American-engined variants that offered their best performance at low altitude, and were therefore unsuited to the high-altitude escort role. None of the American fighters had sufficient range to escort the heavy bombers deep into Europe, so they were confined to escort duty for the Martin B-26 Marauder and North American B-25 Mitchell medium bombers, creating havoc over the north of the continent.

One of the most important strategic uses of air power in World War II was the Japanese attack on the ships and base of the US Pacific Fleet at Pearl Harbor in the Hawaiian Islands in December 1941. The attack was a huge success in obvious tactical terms, for large numbers of American major warships were sunk or badly damaged, but in strategic terms it was a failure as it drew the USA into World War II and, by not finding the Americans' three carriers in the Pacific and failing to destroy Pearl Harbor's repair facilities and fuel supplies, could not deliver a knock-out blow.

Consolidated Liberator

BUILT in larger numbers than any other American warplane in history, a fact that is all the more remarkable as the type was a four-engined aeroplane planned for the long-range heavy bombing role, the Liberator was a truly excellent machine notable for its very long range (resulting from the use of well turbocharged engines to allow economical cruising flight at high altitude with the aid of its high-aspect-ratio wing) and the versatility that permitted its use in a number of basically related but operationally diverse roles.

In its baseline bomber version, the Liberator was the B-24 with a powerplant of four Pratt & Whitney R-1830 air-cooled radial engines each rated at 1,200hp. The first genuine production model of this series was the B-24D with a maximum bomb load of 8,800lb (3,992kg) and a defensive armament of 10 0.5in (12.7mm) Browning trainable machine guns installed as two hand-held weapon in the nose position, single hand-held weapon in the two beam positions, and two weapons in each of the power-operated dorsal, ventral and tail turrets. These 2,738 aircraft were followed by 791 examples of the B-24E with different propellers, 430 examples of the B-24G with a power-operated nose turret carrying two 0.5in (12.7mm) machine guns, 3,100 examples of the B-24H with an improved nose turret, 6,678 examples of the B-24J upgraded version of the B-24H with an improved autopilot, 1,250 examples of the B-24L version of the B-24J with two manually operated guns in the tail, and 2,593 examples of the B-24M revised version of the B-24J.

The maritime patrol version was the PB4Y-1 Liberator based on the B-24D and later bomber variants, and 977 if these aircraft were included in the totals listed above. An improved model was developed as the PB4Y-2 Privateer with the Liberator's twin endplate vertical surfaces replaced by a single, considerably taller vertical tail surface, and 736 of these aircraft were delivered for service after World War II.

The other main developments were the C-87 transport for the US Army Air Forces, the C-109 fuel transport for the USAAF in the Far East where fuel had to be lifted over the eastern Himalayas from India to China, the RY transport for the US Navy, the AT-22 flying classroom for the USAAF, and a number of Liberator variants for the RAF in the bomber, maritime reconnaissance and transport roles. Total production of the Liberator series was 18,482 aircraft excluding 782 examples of the PB4Y-2 Privateer and its few derivatives.

The Consolidated B-24 Liberator, seen here in the form of a B-24H, was used in virtually every American theatre of War, and is seen here in the form of a late-production aeroplane with a power-operated nose turret. Notable features were the high-aspect-ratio wing, tricycle landing gear with short nose unit to keep the fuselage as low to the ground as possible, good al-round defensive capability provided by the well-sited gun armament, and bomb carriage in two lower-fuselage weapon bay accessed not by conventional doors but by roller-blind doors that retracted out and then up round the lower fuselage.

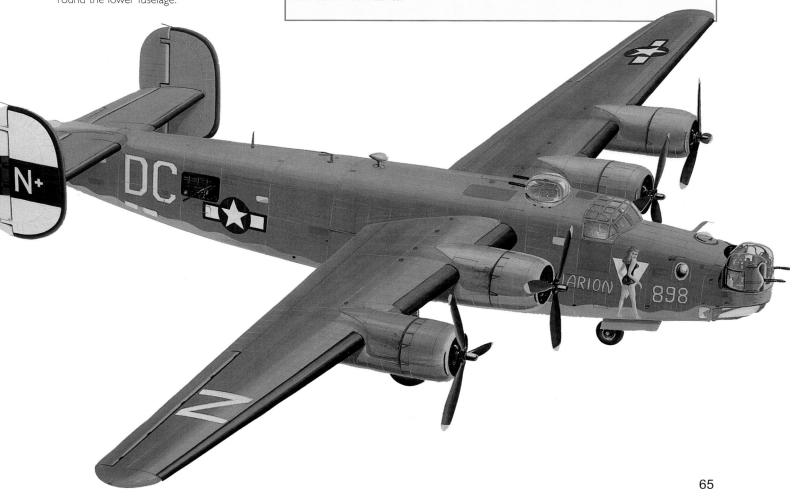

The British Spitfires and new Hawker Typhoons also undertook escort duties over Europe, but none of the Allied fighters had the range to penetrate the area where the main German fighter defences operated. Since the beginning of the combined bomber offensive, which had been launched on a highly organised co-operative basis by the 'Pointblank' directive issued by Prime Minister Winston Churchill and President Franklin D. Roosevelt in January 1943, the Germans had increased their fighter forces in Western Europe, and had taken a heavy toll of the Allied bombers.

The Mustang suffered an inauspicious entry into service, but was the fighter that ultimately provided the ideal answer to the Americans' escort problem. Designed to a British specification and produced in prototype form over a period of just 117 days, the Mustang was a departure from contemporary American practice in being powered by an inline, rather than a radial, piston engine. An Allison powerplant gave the new fighter excellent performance at low and medium altitudes, but the decision was taken to change to a British engine, the Rolls-Royce Merlin, and the Mustang became perhaps the best fighter of the war. Armed with six 0.5in (12.7mm) heavy machine-guns and able to use drop tanks (light external fuel tanks which could be dropped once their fuel had been exhausted, or on entering combat), the Mustang had excellent range and, once the drop tanks had been released, superb performance and the type of agility that allowed it to dogfight on equal terms with the best of the opposing German fighters. The Americans now had a fighter that could escort bombers as far as Berlin and back, and from December 1943 the 8th Army Air Force ranged deep into Europe with ever-increasing success. This success could be measured not only in the number of targets attacked and destroyed by the bombers, but also in the swelling total of German fighters despatched by the American escorts.

Joined from the beginning of 1944 by the 15th Army Air Force based in

The North American P-51 Mustang was the escort and multi-role fighter *par excellence* of World War II. Conceived to a British requirement and powered in its original versions by the Allison V-1710 liquid-cooled engine, the type was originally restricted by its indifferent altitude performance to the fighter-bomber and tactical reconnaissance fighter roles, but then the adoption of the Packard V-1650, which was the American-made version of the Rolls-Royce Merlin liquid-cooled engine, transformed the type's altitude performance while the addition of drop tanks allowed a considerable increase in range. The type reached its World War II mass-production apogee with the P-51D that introduced a cut-down rear fuselage to permit the adoption of a clear-view canopy providing improved fields of vision.

The North American P-51 Mustang offered a virtually ideal blend of performance, agility, firepower, viceless handling characteristics, and rugged strength to create a superb air combat fighter that could operate in the escort fighter and fighter-bomber roles. The definitive P-51D Mustang was powered by a Packard (Rolls-Royce) V-1650-7 Merlin engine rated at 1,510hp, and among its other data were a fixed forward-firing armament of six 0.5in (12.7mm) Browning machine guns, disposable armament of two 1,000lb (454kg) bombs or ten 5in (127mm) unguided air-to-surface rockets, span of 37ft 0in (11.28m), length of 32ft 3in (9.83m), empty weight of 7,125lb (3232kg), maximum take-off weight of 11,600lb (5,262kg), maximum speed of 437mph (703km/h) at 25,000ft (7,620m), service ceiling of 41,900ft (12,770m), and range of 2,080 miles (3,347km) with drop tanks.

Italy, the combined bomber offensive went from strength to strength, the Americans raiding by day and the British by night. German industrial potential was seriously affected, and the Luftwaffe's daylight losses were compounded by the increasing number of more expensive twin-engined and radar-equipped night-fighters destroyed by the British. The heavy losses suffered on the Eastern Front in the previous year, combined with the falling standard of pilot training, served to reduce the efficiency of the German fighter arm and ease the task of the Allied fighters.

In May and June 1944, the Allied heavy bombers turned their attention to isolating France from the rest of German-held territory, in preparation for the Allied invasion of Normandy. Canals were breached, spans were removed from bridges, railway lines and marshalling yards were turned into giant scrapyards, and all types of transport were harried unmercifully throughout north-western Europe. The German ground forces were virtually paralysed, and so heavy were the attacks on airfields that the remnants of the German air units in France were pulled back to Germany or southern France.

When the strategic bomber campaign resumed in July 1944, the British and Americans devoted their full attention to the German transport system and all types of power production, from electricity-generating stations to synthetic oil plants. Germany was virtually paralysed by the end of the year, with her armed forces desperately short of fuel. By the spring of 1945 the bombing campaign had brought Germany to the verge of collapse, and there were few worthwhile strategic targets remaining.

Meanwhile the Allies had evolved a tactical air power in most respects superior to anything the Germans had deployed between 1939 and 1941. The forcing ground for this Allied development had been North Africa, where a see-saw war had swayed across the continent from Egypt to Tunisia for some 30 months. The British had gradually evolved an effective and very flexible technique of close air support, based on the use of RAF controllers alongside the forward army troops to call in fighter-bombers and medium bombers as required from the 'cab-ranks' of such aircraft orbiting above the battlefield. By the end of 1942 the Allies had gained almost total air superiority over North Africa, and tactical air power played a decisive part in the final defeat of Axis forces on the ground by May 1943.

Although the tactical use of the fighter-bomber had been pioneered by the Germans over southern England, the real impetus for the development of tactically decisive fighter-bombers came from the British in the desert campaign. At first, obsolescent types such as early Hurricane fighters were fitted with makeshift bomb racks for use when the opportunity arose. There was soon a demand for

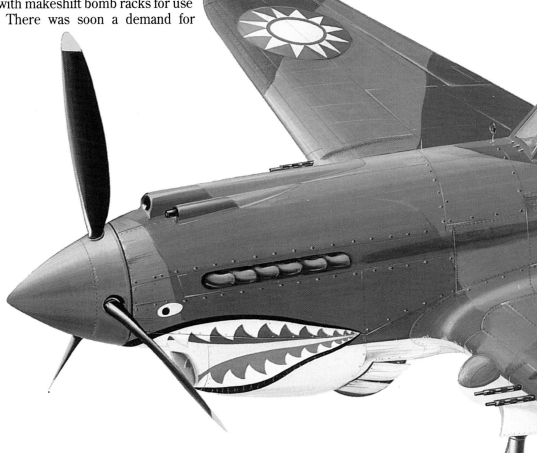

In its original and final forms, the Curtiss P-40 Warhawk series was powered by the Allison V-1710 liquid-cooled Vee piston engine, but in some of its most useful variants was engined with the Packard V-1650 version of the Rolls-Royce Merlin liquid-cooled Vee piston engine.

Known to the Americans and their allies by names such as Tomahawk, Kittyhawk and Warhawk, the Curtiss P-40 series of single-engined fighters resulted from a development programme in the later 1930s but was not a match in air combat for the best of European or Japanese-designed fighters. This meant the relegation of the P-40, seen here in the form of an aeroplane with Chinese markings, to the ground-attack role, and here the type's good low-level performance, steadiness as a weapons platform, load-carrying capability, and sturdiness were all assets that turned the P-40 from an indifferent fighter into a first-class ground-attack warplane.

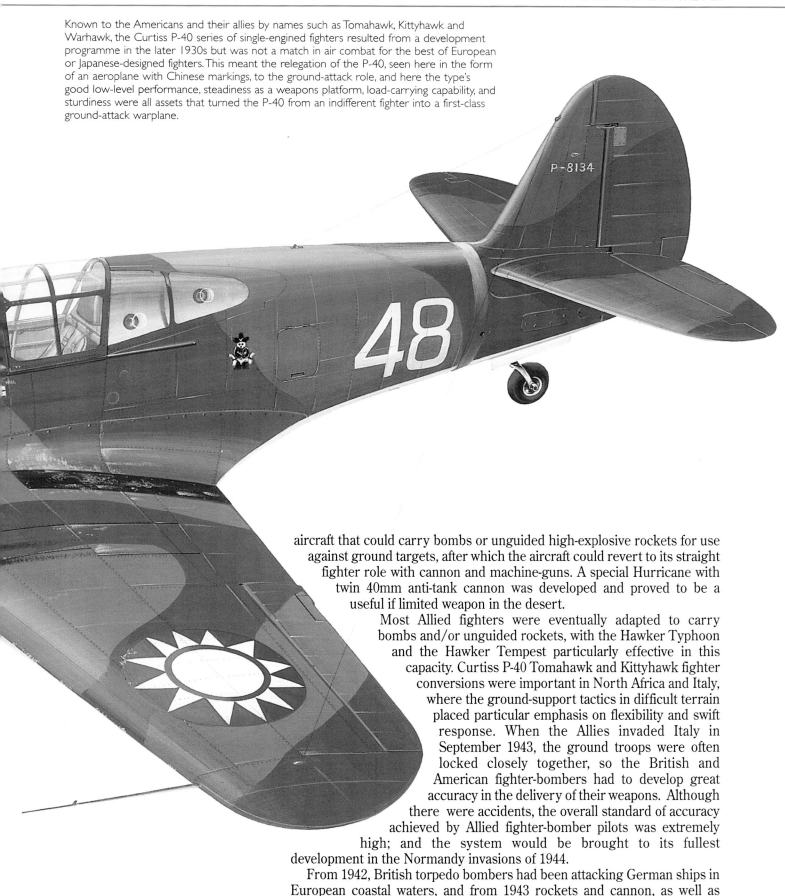

aircraft that could carry bombs or unguided high-explosive rockets for use against ground targets, after which the aircraft could revert to its straight fighter role with cannon and machine-guns. A special Hurricane with twin 40mm anti-tank cannon was developed and proved to be a useful if limited weapon in the desert.

Most Allied fighters were eventually adapted to carry bombs and/or unguided rockets, with the Hawker Typhoon and the Hawker Tempest particularly effective in this capacity. Curtiss P-40 Tomahawk and Kittyhawk fighter conversions were important in North Africa and Italy, where the ground-support tactics in difficult terrain placed particular emphasis on flexibility and swift response. When the Allies invaded Italy in September 1943, the ground troops were often locked closely together, so the British and American fighter-bombers had to develop great accuracy in the delivery of their weapons. Although there were accidents, the overall standard of accuracy achieved by Allied fighter-bomber pilots was extremely high; and the system would be brought to its fullest development in the Normandy invasions of 1944.

From 1942, British torpedo bombers had been attacking German ships in European coastal waters, and from 1943 rockets and cannon, as well as bombs, were used on an increasing scale by Beaufighters and Mosquitoes,

Above: The Focke-Wulf Fw 200 Condor was designed in the period leading up to World War II as a transatlantic passenger transport, but was then pressed into more martial service as a long-range maritime reconnaissance bomber. As such, the Condor ranged deep into the Atlantic in the search for Allied convoys plying between the USA and the UK, vectoring in the U-boat 'wolf packs' or alternatively attacking ships with its modest but nonetheless useful bomb load. The Condor was also used as a launch platform for primitive anti-ship missiles.

severely restricting the movement of German coastal shipping and of Axis supply convoys operating between Italy and North Africa.

The main threat to the Allies at sea was the German U-boat fleet, and aircraft eventually helped suppress this threat. During the early stages of the war, anti-submarine operations were mainly undertaken by two aircraft: one was an obsolescent British machine, the Avro Anson, and the other an excellent American type, the Lockheed Hudson. But Hudsons were in short supply, and they lacked the range for long ocean patrols. Operations were therefore confined initially to coastal and offshore waters.

The requirement for four-engined aircraft offering the range for oceanic anti-submarine operations was appreciated at an early date. Bomber Command refused to relinquish sufficient numbers of land-based aircraft for conversion to this role, so Coastal Command's mainstay remained the reliable Short Sunderland flying boat. Gradually, however, Coastal Command acquired small numbers of Consolidated B-24s and Handley Page

The Consolidated PBY series, named Catalina by the British and almost universally known by that name today, was built in larger numbers than any other seaplane before or since, and was invaluable in the prosecution of the Allied war effort in most theatres. The type was originally developed and built as a pure flying boat, but in its PBY-5A form became an amphibian with retractable tricycle landing gear to enhance its operational versatility.

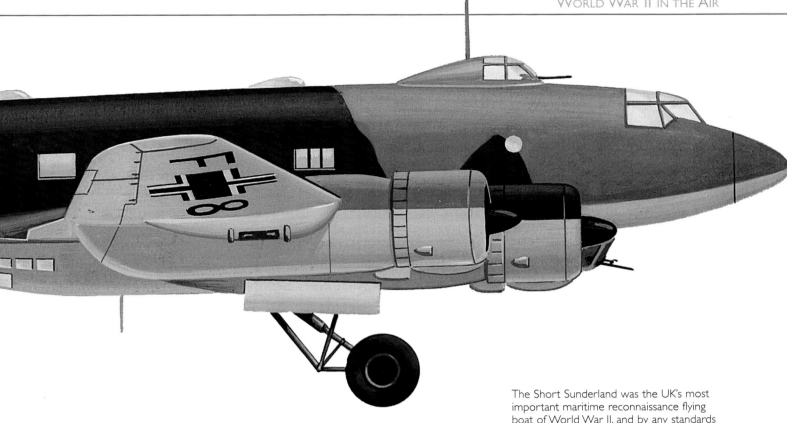

Halifaxes, which were soon operational over areas of the Atlantic Ocean where U-boats had previously been out of range of air attack.

With the new aircraft entering service, and with weapons effective against underwater targets, the 'Atlantic gap' between the limits of aircraft based in the United Kingdom and the United States was slowly narrowed. It was finally closed by naval aircraft operating from escort carriers, while the American Consolidated PBY Catalina flying boat was also used extensively. Gradually the Allied war against the U-boat became one of

The Short Sunderland was the UK's most important maritime reconnaissance flying boat of World War II, and by any standards was a classic 'boat of its type. It was extremely strong, possessed adequate speed and good range, and was well protected by multiple machine-gun turrets. When attacked by German fighters, whose pilots called the type the 'flying porcupine', the Sunderland generally descended to low altitude so that the German pilots could not attack its undefended lower portions, and then fought off the fighters with the guns in its power-operated turrets.

techniques with radar and weapons, and by 1944, aircraft and escort craft had combined to reduce the U-boat threat to manageable proportions.

Germany's main maritime aircraft was the Focke-Wulf Fw 200 Condor, a conversion of the pre-war airliner, which was used as a patrol bomber and a reconnaissance type. The Condor was adequate as a bomber, sinking large tonnages at times, but poor serviceability and structural weakness prevented it from becoming a major threat. The Condor made a first-class reconnaissance aeroplane, however, and had the Luftwaffe and German navy co-operated fully to exploit the type of information that could have been provided by the small Condor force, the U-boat successes would have been far greater, at least in 1941 and 1942. Other German aircraft that saw extensive use in the maritime role included two land based planes, the Heinkel He 111 and Junkers Ju 88 for torpedo and other attack modes, and flying boats of Blohm und Voss and Dornier manufacture.

By the end of World War II a revolutionary type of aeroplane had appeared. In the early years of the war, a considerable amount of work had been devoted to the jet engine, with the object of improving its power and reliability, and by 1943 both the British and Germans had experimental combat aircraft flying. Not only were they fast, but they allowed the designers to dispense with the large, vibrating piston engine in the nose of fighters, instead giving the pilot a much better field of vision and simplifying the task of installing a heavy battery of forward-firing cannon. Germany had advanced more rapidly than the United Kingdom, but official vacillation and Hitler's later insistence that jet aircraft be used as bombers had delayed the service debut of the world's first true jet-powered combat aircraft. Nevertheless, Germany had the Messerschmitt Me 262 twin-jet fighter and the Arado Ar 234 twin-jet bomber in service by 1944.

These were both greatly superior to Allied aircraft, but tactical misuse, shortages of fuel and of top-class pilots, and a variety of operational problems dictated that the few German jets produced could do little more

Right: The Mistel (mistletoe) was one of the expedients to which Germany was reduced during the closing stages of World War II in an effort to create a weapon decisive against point targets. The Mistel composite comprised two aircraft (in this instance a Focke-Wulf Fw 190 upper component and Junkers Ju 88 lower component) of which the lower carried a very large charge of explosive instead of the normal crew. The whole contraption was flown by the pilot in the smaller upper aeroplane, who controlled the flight and then, when within sight of a target such as a major bridge, locked the lower aeroplane on course and detached his fighter, leaving the explosive-laden bomber to crash onto the target.

Below: By the standards of carrierborne attack warplanes, the Douglas SBD Dauntless two-seat dive-bomber was relatively small and light, which made it quite nimble for a warplane of its class. Powered by a Wright R-1820-60 Cyclone air-cooled radial engine rated at 1,200hp, the definitive SBD-5 had a fixed forward-firing armament of two 0.5in (12.7mm) Browning machine guns, a defensive armament of two 0.3in (7.62mm) Browning machine guns in the rear of the 'glasshouse' cockpit, a disposable armament of one 500 or 1,000lb (227 or 454 kg) bomb carried on the centreline crutch and supplemented by two 100lb (45kg) bombs carried under the wing, or alternatively two 250lb (1,13kg) depth charges in its late-war role against submarines.

The Junkers Ju 88 was Germany's most versatile warplane of World War II, and rivals its British equivalent, the de Havilland Mosquito, for the honour of having been the most versatile warplane ever placed in production. The type was schemed as a high-speed medium bomber, but was then developed into other variants for roles as diverse as unmanned attack (see above), torpedo bombing, night-fighting, heavy attack and anti-tank work, and reconnaissance.

than show their manifest superiority, giving the Allies a disagreeable surprise before the end of the war. The only Allied jet fighter to see service was the Gloster Meteor, which was introduced in time to help defeat the V-1 flying bomb menace and take part in action over north-west Europe.

The Germans produced a fair number of experimental jet aircraft, along with the extraordinary Messerschmitt Me 163 Komet (comet) rocket-powered interceptor, and some of these types might have made a significant impact had the war continued. It was clear that German jet aircraft were aerodynamically superior to their Allied counterparts, and after the Allied victory there was a race between the Soviets, Americans and British to secure as much German research material as possible.

Before the jet engine reached a fully operational stage, however, several superb piston-engined fighters were developed as the last generation of such aircraft. These aircraft all possessed a maximum speed in the order of 475mph (765km/h): among the British offerings were the Supermarine Spiteful, Hawker Fury and de Havilland Hornet; American competitors included the Republic XP-47J Thunderbolt and North American P-82 Twin Mustang; and the primary German contender was the Focke-Wulf Ta 152.

Above: One of only three turbojet-powered aircraft to enter operational service in World War II, the Arado Ar 234 Blitz was a high-speed bomber, and was an excellent type that was virtually immune to Allied interception. As with a number of other advanced German weapons, however, it was a question of too little too late, andonly a few aircraft that were completed could be flown as Germany was desperately short of fuel.

Opposite top: Affectionately known as the 'Jug', abbreviated from Juggernaut, the Republic P-47 Thunderbolt was the largest and heaviest single-engined single-seat fighter to enter service in World War II, and found its *métier* as a devastating fighter-bomber with very good performance and a heavy disposable load.

Though none of these aircraft saw full-scale service in the war, some of them served as interim types pending the arrival of fully developed jet aircraft in the late 1940s.

The war against Japan also involved large-scale air warfare. Although the tactics used in the Pacific theatre were similar to those evolved in the European war, a number of differences were forced upon the combatants by the geographical circumstances of the campaign. The limitations of the aircraft, too, played an important part in both tactical and strategic developments. General Douglas MacArthur's reconquest of New Guinea, for example, took the particular form it did so that his land forces could enjoy all the benefits of superior air power, and the advances to the Marianas and Iwo Jima were largely dictated by the need for the former as a heavy bomber base, and for the latter as a base for escort fighters and as an emergency landing ground for bombers crippled over Japan.

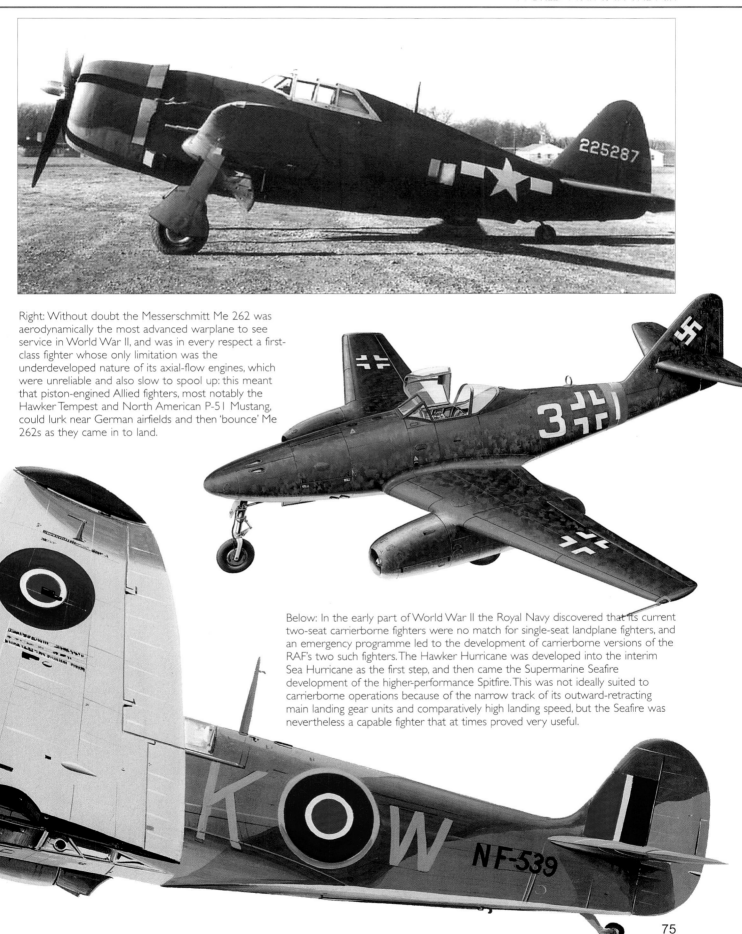

Right: Without doubt the Messerschmitt Me 262 was aerodynamically the most advanced warplane to see service in World War II, and was in every respect a first-class fighter whose only limitation was the underdeveloped nature of its axial-flow engines, which were unreliable and also slow to spool up: this meant that piston-engined Allied fighters, most notably the Hawker Tempest and North American P-51 Mustang, could lurk near German airfields and then 'bounce' Me 262s as they came in to land.

Below: In the early part of World War II the Royal Navy discovered that its current two-seat carrierborne fighters were no match for single-seat landplane fighters, and an emergency programme led to the development of carrierborne versions of the RAF's two such fighters. The Hawker Hurricane was developed into the interim Sea Hurricane as the first step, and then came the Supermarine Seafire development of the higher-performance Spitfire. This was not ideally suited to carrierborne operations because of the narrow track of its outward-retracting main landing gear units and comparatively high landing speed, but the Seafire was nevertheless a capable fighter that at times proved very useful.

At an individual level, Japanese aircraft proved much more manoeuvrable than their Allied counterparts, especially in the first year of the war. Although a number of Japanese fighters had only machine-guns for armament, the redoubtable Mitsubishi A6M Reisen (Zero Fighter, nicknamed 'Zeke' by the Allies) also had cannon, enabling it to decimate the clumsier Allied fighters such as the US Navy's Brewster F2A Buffalo and Grumman F4F Wildcat, as well as the US Army's Bell P-39 Airacobra and Curtiss P-40, whose only defence lay in breaking off combat by means of a high-speed dive.

Gradually, the Allies introduced better fighters, and tactics were evolved to exploit the higher performance, superior firepower and better protection of these fighters to counter the superior agility of the Japanese machines.

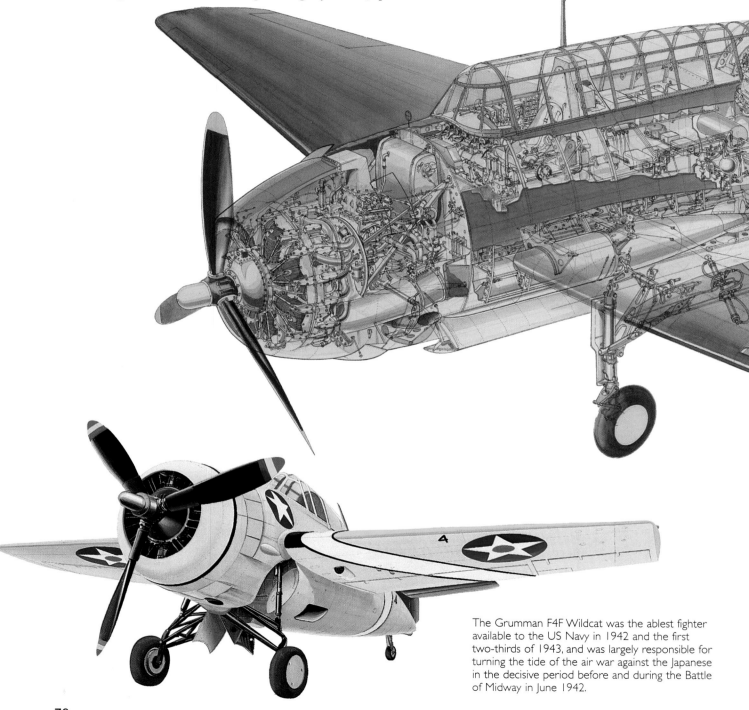

The Grumman F4F Wildcat was the ablest fighter available to the US Navy in 1942 and the first two-thirds of 1943, and was largely responsible for turning the tide of the air war against the Japanese in the decisive period before and during the Battle of Midway in June 1942.

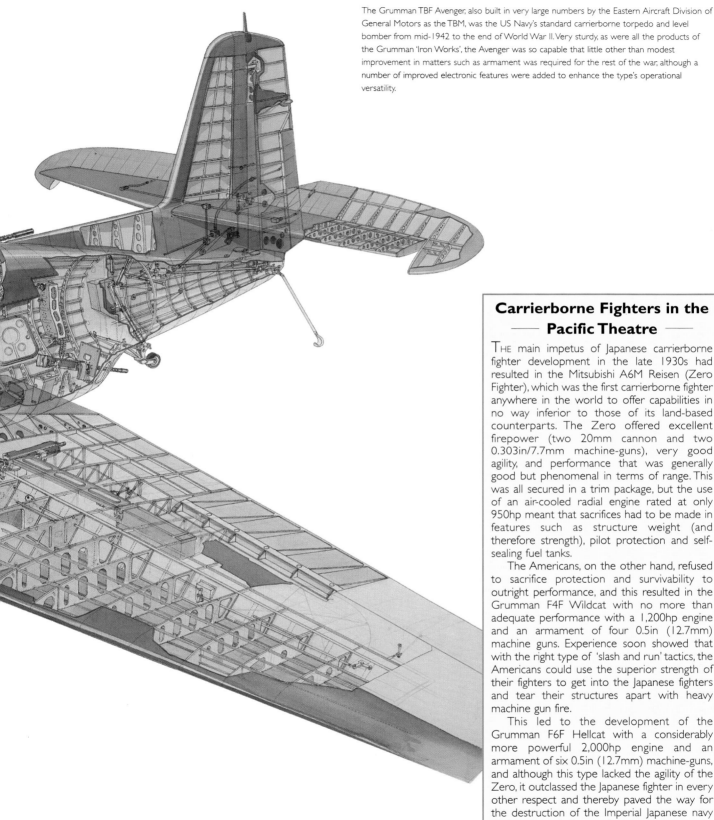

The Grumman TBF Avenger, also built in very large numbers by the Eastern Aircraft Division of General Motors as the TBM, was the US Navy's standard carrierborne torpedo and level bomber from mid-1942 to the end of World War II. Very sturdy, as were all the products of the Grumman 'Iron Works', the Avenger was so capable that little other than modest improvement in matters such as armament was required for the rest of the war, although a number of improved electronic features were added to enhance the type's operational versatility.

Carrierborne Fighters in the Pacific Theatre

THE main impetus of Japanese carrierborne fighter development in the late 1930s had resulted in the Mitsubishi A6M Reisen (Zero Fighter), which was the first carrierborne fighter anywhere in the world to offer capabilities in no way inferior to those of its land-based counterparts. The Zero offered excellent firepower (two 20mm cannon and two 0.303in/7.7mm machine-guns), very good agility, and performance that was generally good but phenomenal in terms of range. This was all secured in a trim package, but the use of an air-cooled radial engine rated at only 950hp meant that sacrifices had to be made in features such as structure weight (and therefore strength), pilot protection and self-sealing fuel tanks.

The Americans, on the other hand, refused to sacrifice protection and survivability to outright performance, and this resulted in the Grumman F4F Wildcat with no more than adequate performance with a 1,200hp engine and an armament of four 0.5in (12.7mm) machine guns. Experience soon showed that with the right type of 'slash and run' tactics, the Americans could use the superior strength of their fighters to get into the Japanese fighters and tear their structures apart with heavy machine gun fire.

This led to the development of the Grumman F6F Hellcat with a considerably more powerful 2,000hp engine and an armament of six 0.5in (12.7mm) machine-guns, and although this type lacked the agility of the Zero, it outclassed the Japanese fighter in every other respect and thereby paved the way for the destruction of the Imperial Japanese navy air force's carrierborne air arm.

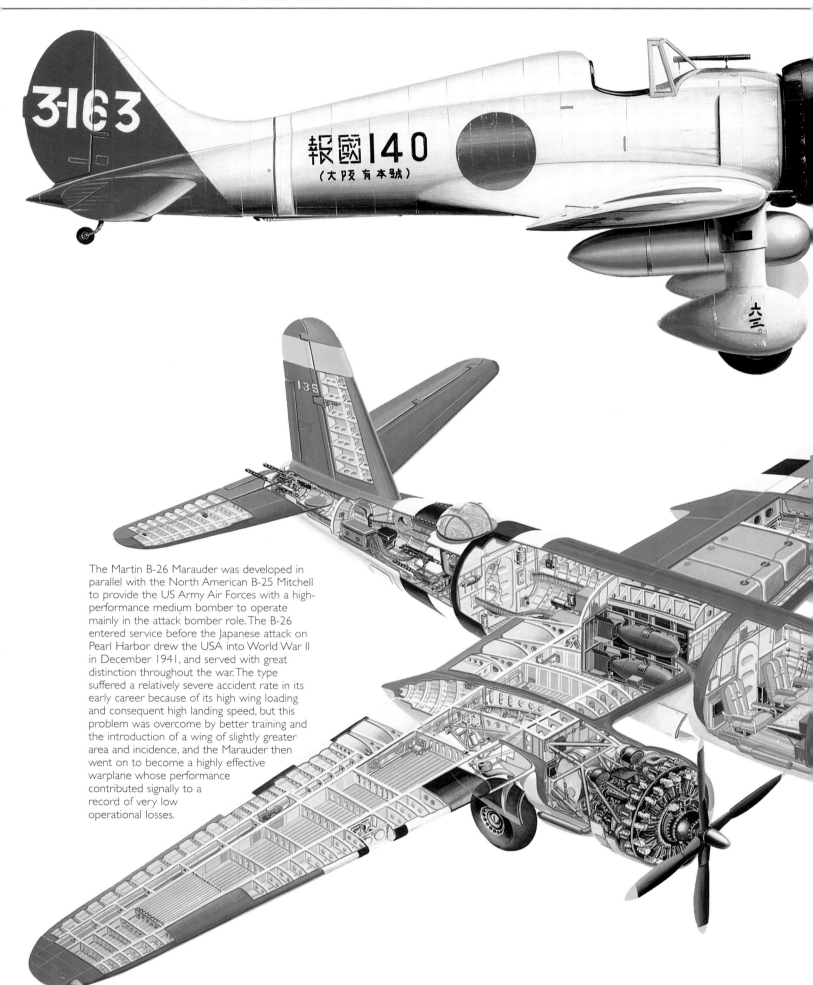

The Martin B-26 Marauder was developed in parallel with the North American B-25 Mitchell to provide the US Army Air Forces with a high-performance medium bomber to operate mainly in the attack bomber role. The B-26 entered service before the Japanese attack on Pearl Harbor drew the USA into World War II in December 1941, and served with great distinction throughout the war. The type suffered a relatively severe accident rate in its early career because of its high wing loading and consequent high landing speed, but this problem was overcome by better training and the introduction of a wing of slightly greater area and incidence, and the Marauder then went on to become a highly effective warplane whose performance contributed signally to a record of very low operational losses.

Left: In the mid-1930s the Imperial Japanese navy air force led the world in the development of monoplanes for carrierborne deployment. Still convinced that success in combat would accrue from a combination of great agility and good performance, the service adopted the Mitsubishi A5M, later allocated the Allied reporting name 'Claude', as its first monoplane fighter. This could be fitted with a centreline drop tank for additional range (a pioneering development for the time) and had fixed landing gear with nicely faired main units, for the service decided that the additional weight and complexity of retractable main units would more than offset the possible slight gain in speed. The armament of two 0.303in (7.7mm) fixed forward-firing machine-guns was decidedly light, and an anachronistic feature was the open cockpit, which was demanded by pilots after the company had first developed the fighter with an enclosed cockpit.

Above: The North American P-82 Twin Mustang appeared very slightly too late for service in World War II, and was a successful attempt to create an escort fighter with even longer range than the classic P-51 Mustang. The Twin Mustang was in essence the fuselages and outer wing panels connected by a constant-chord wing centre section and tailplane.

Martin B-26 Marauder

ALTHOUGH it saw service first in the Pacific theatre (initially with bombing attacks on Japanese-occupied New Britain from New Guinea, then as a torpedo bomber and level bomber in the Midway and Aleutian campaigns), the Marauder is best remembered for its part in the European campaign against the Germans. Here the B-26 was flown mainly by the 9th Army Air Force based in the UK and the 12th Army Air Force based in Italy, and was also operated by the British and, at a later date, French air forces.

Total production of the B-26 series was 4,708 aircraft including minor variants, and the first variant in this sequence was the B-26 of which 201 were built with the original wing spanning 65ft 0in (19.81m), a powerplant of two Pratt & Whitney R-2800-5 air-cooled radial engines each rated at 1,850hp, and a defensive armament of single 0.3in (7.62mm) Browning trainable machine guns in the manually operated nose and tail positions, and two 0.5in (12.7mm) Browning trainable machine guns in a power-operated dorsal turret. There followed 139 examples of the B-26A with increased weights, provision for a torpedo in place of the standard bomb load of 5,200lb (2,359kg), and a defensive armament of four 0.5in (12.7mm) machine guns. The B-26B, of which 1,883 were produced, introduced the uprated powerplant of two R-2800-41 engines each rated at 2,000 hp, revised armament including a package of four 0.5in (12.7mm) fixed forward-firing machine guns on the sides of the forward fuselage and, in the last 1,242 aircraft, a wing of increased span and area. The 1,235 examples of the B-26C were completed at a different factory to the basic B-26B standard, and the 300 examples of the B-26F were to an improved B-26C standard. The final major production model, of which 893 were delivered, was the B-26G development of the B-26F with equipment changes.

The B-26G may be taken as typical of late-production Marauder bombers, and its primary features included a crew of seven, a powerplant of two R-2800-43 engines each rated at 2,000hp, a disposable load of 4,000lb (1,814kg) carried in a lower-fuselage weapons bay, and a gun armament of eleven 0.5in (12.7m) Browning machine guns disposed as four fixed forward-firing weapons 'blistered' onto the sides of the forward fuselage, one trainable forward-firing weapon in the manually operated nose position, single manually operated laterally-firing weapons in the two beam positions, two trainable weapons in the power-operated dorsal turret, and two trainable rearward-firing weapons in the power-operated tail turret. Other details of this important warplane included a span of 71ft 0in (21.64m), length of 56ft 1in (17.09m), empty weight of 25,300lb (11,476kg), maximum take-off weight of 38,200lb (17328kg), maximum speed of 283mph (455km/h) at 5,000ft (1,525m), initial climb rate of 1,000ft (305m) per minute, service ceiling of 19,800ft (6,035m), and range of 1,100 miles (1,770 km).

The two most important fighters were the Grumman F6F Hellcat and Vought F4U Corsair, both high performance machines capable of carrying large offensive loads. The main strike aircraft were the Grumman TBF/TBM Avenger torpedo-bomber and Douglas SBD Dauntless dive-bomber later supplanted by the Curtiss SB2C Helldiver, all of which performed with great distinction.

The campaign against the Japanese in China was the responsibility of the Nationalist Chinese with support from the US Army, and Boeing B-29 Superfortress strategic heavy bombers began the strategic campaign against Japan from airfields in south-east China. From late 1944 they were joined by similar machines from bases on the islands of Saipan, Tinian and Guam in the recently captured Marianas group. The B-29s, carrying large bomb loads at high speed and over great distances, gradually eroded Japan's ability to fight, and caused severe civilian casualties with a series of devastating incendiary raids on the major Japanese cities.

It was the Pacific war, moreover, that finally proved the efficiency of strategic bombing. After the high-explosive and incendiary raids, two atomic bombs were dropped on Hiroshima and Nagasaki on 6 and 9 August 1945 respectively, and the terrible devastation caused by these weapons finally persuaded Japan that the war had to be ended without further delay.

A single aeroplane with just this devastating weapon could cripple a nation. For better or for worse, air power was supreme.

Conceived for the delivery of heavy bomb loads over considerable ranges by means of a high-altitude cruise, the Boeing B-29 Superfortress can be regarded as the first genuinely effective strategic bomber, for it was a warplane of this type that dropped the single atomic bombs on Hiroshima and Nagasaki during August 1945, finally to end World War II by forcefully persuading the Japanese that further resistance was pointless.

The symbol of the new era of warfare ushered in at the end of World War II was the mushroom cloud, which was the visible evidence of the ghastly destruction wrought at its base by the explosion of a nuclear weapon.

The Age of Turbine Propulsion

The de Havilland Vampire single-seat fighter was something of an oddity. Appearing just too late for service in World War II, it was an advanced type with propulsion by a single centrifugal-flow turbojet, but somewhat anachronistic in its early forms in retaining for its central nacelle the type of plywood/balsa/plywood sandwich construction typical of de Havilland aircraft from the late 1930s. Later models switched to an all-metal structure, and the light and nimble Vampire was at first a useful fighter, then a capable fighter-bomber, and finally an effective trainer in its variants with side-by-side accommodation in a wider nacelle.

URING the closing stages of World War II, the major powers gained sufficient experience of turbojet propulsion both to appreciate its manifest advantages for military aircraft and to discover some of its attendant problems. Even in its original primitive state, the turbojet was designed, developed and produced in two basic forms: as the axial-flow turbojet and the centrifugal-flow turbojet. In the former, the air drawn through the inlet at the front of the engine is compressed longitudinally as it moves through a series of axial compressors on its way to the combustion chamber; in the latter, the indrawn air is compressed radially by a centrifugal compressor before being turned through a second right angle on its way to the combustion chambers arranged round the back of the engine casing.

The axial-flow turbojet was pioneered by the Germans, and the centrifugal-flow turbojet was the particular enthusiasm of the British. At first, the simple engine pioneered by Air Commodore Frank Whittle and built in prototype form by Power Turbojets was more than adequate in its core conceptual layout, and development of this core concept was entrusted to companies such as de Havilland, Metropolitan-Vickers, Rolls-Royce and Rover. From this process emerged the first two operational turbojets to power British

fighters, namely the de Havilland Goblin installed in the de Havilland Vampire, and the Rolls-Royce Welland used in the Gloster Meteor. Such centrifugal-flow turbojets were more than adequate for the performance limits imposed by the aerodynamic knowledge of the time, but late in the war the British began to appreciate some of the inherent disadvantages possessed by this engine layout, namely its considerable bulk (especially in diameter), and its need to turn the air flow through at least two right angles. Combined with thoughts of pushing forward towards high subsonic performance from the levels currently imposed by straight-wing aerodynamic theory, the disadvantages were sufficient to persuade British industry into the process of designing and developing axial-flow turbojets.

Perhaps a more urgent problem was that of fuel consumption. One of the

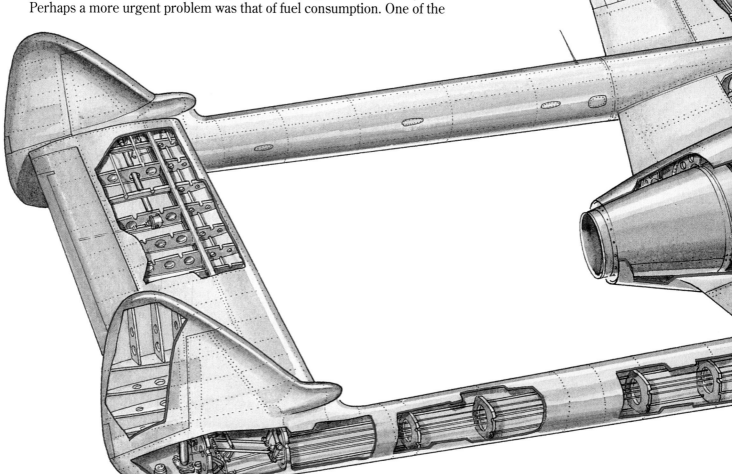

de Havilland Vampire

REMAINING in service into the 1980s in its trainer variants, the de Havilland Vampire was schemed as a pure fighter with single-seat accommodation and an inbuilt armament of four 20 mm Hispano fixed forward-firing cannon in the nose, was developed as a fighter-bomber with underwing racks for two 1,000lb (454kg) bombs or eight air-to-surface rockets each carrying a 60lb (27kg) warhead, and then revised with a wider central nacelle for the accommodation of two men in its trainer and then night-fighter models, the latter with airborne interception radar in the nose.

The Vampire FB.Mk 6 may be taken as typical of the fighter-bomber variants. It was powered by one de Havilland Goblin DGn.3 turbojet rated at 3,300lb st, spanned 38ft 0in (11.58m), was 39ft 9in (9.37m) long, possessed weights increasing from an empty figure of 7,200lb (3266kg) to a maximum take-off figure of 12,290lb (5,600kg), and was typified by performance including a maximum speed of 548mph (883km/h) at optimum altitude, initial climb rate of 4,800 ft (1,463m) per minute, service ceiling of 44,000ft (13,410m), and range of 1,400 miles (2,253km) with the two drop tanks that could be carried as an alternative to underwing weapons.

The rationale behind the de Havilland Vampire's configuration was the need to accommodate the bulky centrifugal-flow turbojet and to reduce thrust losses within the engine by using a jetpipe that was as short as possible. This suggested the incorporation of the engine in a short central nacelle, where it was aspirated via two wing-root inlets and exhausted immediately to the rear of the nacelle, and this in turn dictated that the tail unit should be carried on small-diameter booms extending rearward from the wing trailing edges and outboard of the exhaust plume.

turbojet's great advantages is its ability to operate on a fuel as simple as kerosene, but the early turbojet was so thirsty for fuel that the range of aircraft with such a powerplant was severely curtailed from that of piston-engined aircraft with the same fuel capacity. As a result, considerable effort was devoted to research designed to find a solution to the turbojet's high specific fuel consumption (the quantity of fuel burned to produce a given power for a given period).

Aerodynamicists were also discovering that, at high speeds, the air approaching and hitting the aeroplane's wings and fuselage was being compressed around the leading edges of the wings and other airflow entry areas. This compression resulted in considerable turbulence and drag, leading in turn to extreme buffeting that could cause structural failure. An early solution, applied in the North American P-51 Mustang and other piston-engined fighters, was the laminar-flow wing, which was much thinner in section than earlier types and was designed to smooth the flow of air round it, thus reducing both turbulence and drag. But even this solution could not alleviate the main problem, which was the high-pressure shock wave streaming back and out from the nose, the first part of the aeroplane to meet the airflow.

Despite their failure to co-ordinate research and apply its lessons effectively, the Germans had discovered the answer: sweeping the wings back out of the line of the shock wave. With a top speed of 870km/h (541mph), the Messerschmitt Me 262 twin-turbojet fighter that entered service in 1944 had modestly swept wings. This planform was adopted for structural and other aerodynamic reasons as much as for avoidance of the shock wave, but the success of this slight sweep, combined with the data revealed in captured German aerodynamic research, gave the Americans and Soviets an insight into the manner in which the effects of air compression could be overcome.

Even so, there was still much to be learned before aircraft would be capable of approaching the 'sound barrier'. Although there was an immediate reduction in the financial resources available for military hardware after the war, the lessons of the 1920s had been learned and a high

Designed in the closing stages of World War II for effective service from the second half of the 1940s, the Lockheed Neptune maritime patrol and anti-submarine warplane was a truly phenomenal machine that was originally designated as the P2V and from 1962 as the P-2. The type carried a substantial warload in the lower-fuselage weapons bay and under the wings, and in its original forms had powerful gun armament. The combination of two large piston engines and considerable fuel capacity provided moderately good performance together with great range and endurance, and in latter models two turbojets were added under the outer wing panels for boosted 'dash' performance. Finally, constant improvement and augmentation of the onboard electronics ensured that the Neptune was constantly a match for the warships and more particularly the submarines that were its main prey.

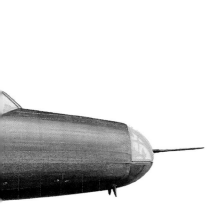

level of research was encouraged so that new military hardware could be developed quickly, should such a need materialise. The USSR and the United States took a quick lead in devoting a large proportion of their research effort to high-speed flight, and soon emerged with some formidable combat aircraft and impressive research types. Yet while they were absorbing German engine technology, most of the world's military powers used British turbojet engines, either imported or built under licence. The importance of the turbojet engine was well appreciated in the United Kingdom, and research and development continued as a high priority.

The Gloster Meteor had been the only Allied turbojet aircraft to serve operationally in World War II. After the war, the Meteor was quickly joined by the delightful Vampire, perhaps the last first-class fighting aeroplane of an unsophisticated type to enter service with any of the major powers. Although turbojet-powered, the Vampire in its initial form included a wooden central nacelle for the pilot, but had excellent handling characteristics despite the fact that its controls were unpowered. Good aircraft for their time, both the Meteor and the Vampire were considered more than adequate for their tasks by the government of a financially impoverished United Kingdom, and so no priority was afforded to research data that would be required for the creation of a more advanced type; the British government even opined that supersonic aircraft would be superfluous. This policy proved to be shortsighted.

The United States' main turbojet fighter of World War II had been the highly disappointing Bell P-59 Airacomet, which had not seen active service. Already on the drawing board, however, was the Lockheed P-80 (soon to be the F-80) Shooting Star, which would use a British-designed engine. Like the Meteor and Vampire, the Shooting Star did not feature a swept wing, but was clearly superior to the Meteor, which had established a world speed record of 975km/h (606mph) in 1946.

In 1947, North American, a firm that had been left behind in the race to build turbojet-powered fighters because of its commitment to the P-51 Mustang and P-82 Twin Mustang programmes, produced a classic fighter that succeeded largely because it incorporated the results of German research. This aeroplane was the F-86 Sabre, the West's first swept-wing fighter. The Sabre's lines were pleasing and, despite its lack of a suitably powerful engine, it was transonic (on or about the speed of sound) in a shallow dive. A year later the type was in service with the US Air Force (as the US Army Air Force was now known, having been made fully independent of the US Army). Export orders had been received, and several

First flown in the early 1960s and operational into the late 1980s, the Yakovlev Yak-28 was slightly supersonic and provided the USSR with a multi-role warplane type that was produced and operated in variants, identified by NATO as the 'Brewer' attack bomber with a glazed nose and capable of carrying a small nuclear weapon in its lower-fuselage weapons bay (most aircraft later being rebuilt for the electronic warfare and reconnaissance roles), the 'Firebar' interceptor with two medium-range and sometimes two short-range air-to-air missiles supported by airborne interception radar in a 'solid' nose, and the 'Maestro' two-seat advanced trainer.

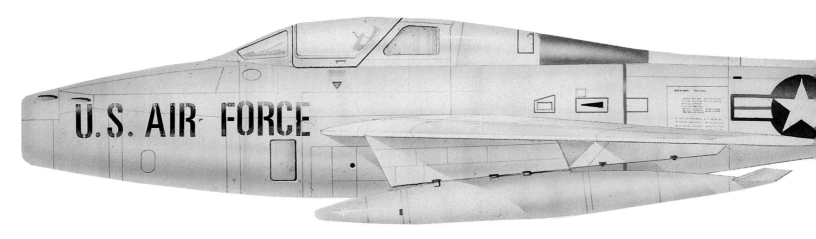

countries were interested in the possibilities of licensed production and development with different engines (the Orenda in Canada and the Rolls-Royce Avon in Australia), and different gun armament (two 30mm cannon in Australian aircraft replacing the standard American battery of six 0.5 in/12.7mm machine-guns). Far more advanced than other Western type, when introduced, 10,000 Sabre aircraft were eventually built.

Yet the Sabre had been preceded into the air by a Soviet type that would prove its greatest foe, the Mikoyan-Gurevich MiG-15, which first flew in July 1947, just three months before the Sabre. Although not as neat as the Sabre, the MiG-15 fully incorporated the results of German and Soviet research, and featured swept flying surfaces. Power was provided by a British-designed engine, for which the Labour government had granted export licences. Like most Soviet aircraft of the 1930s and 1940s, the MiG-15 was crude in finish and equipment, but was rugged, reliable and an excellent performer in the air.

Although the MiG-15 had entered widespread production and service use as early as 1948, later receiving the NATO reporting name 'Fagot', the Soviets had been more than normally secretive about their new fighter's performance. Thus, when American pilots first encountered the MiG-15 after the outbreak of the Korean War in 1950, they were completely startled. Indeed, it was the success of the MiG-15 against straight-winged American fighters that persuaded the US Air Force that the Sabre had to be deployed to this theatre. Even then, pilots soon discovered that the Sabre was marginally inferior to the MiG-15 in overall combat terms, but the combination of the American pilots' superior training and the Sabre's incorporation of a radar-aided gunsight enabled the American pilots to 'turn the tables' on their Soviet opponents.

By the early 1950s, the development costs of new aircraft had risen so sharply that governments and manufacturers alike were determined to wring every last particle of development potential out of basic designs. To the Western powers this usually meant the minimum of alteration to the

Designed and developed as successor to the classic Republic P-47 Thunderbolt heavy fighter from the later 1940s, the Republic F-84 fighter matured, like its predecessor, in the attack fighter rather than interceptor role, and many thousands of the type were delivered in the 1950s, not just as the mainstay of the US Air Force's tactical air arm but also as the core of the modern air forces being created by the European NATO countries against the threat of an aggressively minded Warsaw Pact alliance under the control of the USSR. The series was developed in three basic forms: as the Thunderjet fighter with a nose-aspirated engine and straight flying surfaces, as the Thunderstreak with a nose-aspirated engine and swept flying surfaces for higher subsonic performance, and as the Thunderstreak with inlets in the wing roots (leaving the nose free for reconnaissance equipment) and swept flying surfaces. The aeroplane illustrated here is an F-84F Thunderstreak, able to carry a small nuclear weapon.

basic airframe and engine, but constant updating of the avionics (aviation electronics), which are largely responsible for combat efficiency.

The first Western aeroplane of this type was the F-86D Sabre, which featured an advanced avionics package that provided an all-weather capability, and also enabled the fighter to engage targets automatically after the pilot had selected his objective. Once locked on to the target, the F-86D's radar and computer instructed the pilot as to course and speed until the target was in range: the computer/radar complex then extended the retractable rocket pack under the nose, fired the requisite weapons at the target, and retracted the pack.

Although some later American fighters (especially those of the US Navy) were fitted with a multiple cannon battery, from the Korean War until the late 1960s the Americans in general and the US Air Force in particular, preferred a primary armament of missiles. Initially these were unguided rockets rather than true guided missiles, and were fired at the target in salvoes in the case of the 2.75in (70mm) calibre Folding-Fin Air Rocket series, or individually in the case of the MB-1 Genie with its command-detonated nuclear warhead. Developed from the early 1950s, however, guided missiles with heat-seeking infra-red (IR) or radar guidance were in common service by the end of the decade. The radar-guided missiles fell into two basic categories depending on the specific nature of their guidance package: the active radar guidance system sends out its own search pulses and then homes on them, while the semi-active guidance system homes on the target, radar-illuminated by the attacking fighter, the guidance system steering the missile towards the source of the electromagnetic echoes it receives from the illuminated target.

Another improvement introduced on the F-86D was the use of afterburning, or 'reheat' as it is often called. In this system, extra fuel is injected into the exhaust gases of the engine, to mix and burn with the oxygen surviving in the exhaust gases, and so producing more thrust for little extra weight and complexity – but considerably increased fuel consumption. Such a system was commonplace on all high-performance military aircraft by the early 1960s.

The Republic F-84 Thunderjet was made superfluous as a fighter by the availability to the USA, and later to its allies, of the superlative North American F-86 Sabre fighters, exemplified here in action against a Mikoyan-Gurevich MiG-15 fighter, its primary foe in the Korean War. With a General Electric J47 axial-flow turbojet and swept flying surfaces, the Sabre was capable of high subsonic performance and was also a good dogfighter, especially in its later variants with a number of aerodynamic improvements. The type was also built in Canada with the Orenda turbojet for slightly improved performance, and in Australia with the Rolls-Royce Avon turbojet and the standard sextet of 0.5in (12.7mm) Browning machine-guns replaced by a pair of 30mm Aden cannon for better all-round performance and a much heavier air-to-air punch.

Even with afterburning and a fully developed engine, the Sabre was limited by its aerodynamic layout to transonic speeds. North American had recognised this factor, however, and had designed a Sabre-derived fighter that would be fully supersonic in level flight. Wings of markedly increased sweep and reduced thickness/chord ratio were added to a beautifully streamlined fuselage to create the Sabre 45 (the figure of the wing sweep angle), which was accepted for service as the F-100 Super Sabre. This was the first of the US Air Force's 'century' series of supersonic fighters, and introduced in 1954, at the start of a service career that lasted to the mid-1980s with some of the United States' allies.

Lockheed was also well aware of the limitations suffered by the current generation of fighters – for its F-80 Shooting Star and F-94 Starfire had received a rough handling from the MiG-15s in the Korean War, and the company now produced a thoroughly supersonic fighter. This was based on a design concept entirely different from that of the Super Sabre, however. Rather than use a high angle of sweep to reduce the problems of air compression, the Lockheed design team opted for an extraordinary layout that made its fighter resemble a missile, in that it was based on a large and basically cylindrical fuselage accommodating the pilot, electronics, a very powerful afterburning turbojet and most of the fuel. To this were added a large T-tail and a tiny but unswept wing that was tapered on its leading and trailing edges; thus the aeroplane relied on high engine thrust and its extremely thin wing to cut through the compression barrier. This F-104 Starfighter first flew in 1954 and was ordered into production for the US Air

A turbojet-powered warplane of the first-generation type, the Lockheed P-80 (later F-80) Shooting Star fighter was just too late for service in World War II, but was built in moderately large numbers in the late 1940s. The F-80 proved obsolete as a fighter in the Korean War, but was used with some success as a fighter-bomber and paved the way for the F-94 Starfire radar-equipped interceptor, and also for the T-33 trainer development that was built in considerably larger numbers and is still in widespread service during the mid-1990s for trainer and counter-insurgency roles.

Fighter Electronics

THE fighter emerged from World War II with the reflector or, gyro gunsight as its most advanced item of operational equipment. Developments in the later 1940s added the ranging radar to the gyro sight, and this helped to maintain the fighter as an excellent air combat platform. During this period, however, the bomber carrying nuclear weapons became an increasingly major threat, and although fighters could be vectored into an intercept position by ground radar, the control of collision-course interceptions gradually came to demand the adoption of lightweight interception and fire-control radar, the latter capability being required for accurate delivery of heavier gunfire or, more significantly, salvoes of air-to-air unguided rockets and the first generation of air-to-air missiles.

Throughout the 1950s the range, target-tracking and general capabilities of such equipment continued to improve to the point at which it became feasible for the Western nations to move away from the rigid implementation of ground-controlled interception techniques, in favour of a system that allowed the fighters to complete the interception on their own after being guided into the right general area.

A major breakthrough came with the development in the 1960s of miniaturised electronics in which thermionic valves were replaced by transistors to permit the creation of radar equipments that were considerably smaller and lighter, yet offered significantly improved reliability and overall capability. This permitted the development of radars that did not just search for targets, but also prioritising the tracked targets in order of probable threat, looking for targets below the fighter's flightpath in the ground 'clutter' that had previously made this impossible, and scanning the ground itself for navigation features and surface targets.

This process continued through the 1970s and 1980s, making the radar at once more capable and also less 'visible' to enemies so that the radar of today is a major element of the fighter's comprehensive sensor suite, which can also include infra-red and optronic systems for combination in the computer before presentation to the pilot on his head-up and head-down displays.

Force, which ultimately ordered only a small number of Starfighters, due to a change in its equipment policies.

The type was saved by a large order from the new West German air force for the F-104G, a much developed multi-role fighter, also ordered by several other European nations as well as by Canada, Japan, and a number of other American allies. The F-104G remained one of the most valuable combat aircraft used by the European countries of NATO until the mid-1980s, and is still in limited service with some American allies. It is also worth noting that Italy, in addition to participating on the European licensed production programme for the F-104G, developed its own variant as the Aeritalia (now Alenia) F-104S for service with the Italian and Turkish air forces.

The USSR had an avionics capability considerably inferior to that of the United States or even the European nations during the 1950s, and therefore concentrated its efforts on the full exploitation of current types. Thus there was a marked similarity between the MiG-15 and the MiG-17 'Fresco', which first flew in 1952. The structural problems and aerodynamic limitations which had caused the loss of many MiG-15s were overcome, and power was provided by a greatly uprated engine so that handling and performance were both improved considerably. Roughly contemporary with later models of the F-86, the MiG-17 had a higher performance than its rivals, but was not met in combat by its Western contemporaries. However, the MiG-17 was later passed to a number of Soviet allies and clients including North Vietnam and many Arab states. The North Vietnamese used the MiG-17 to good effect against the American 'century' series fighters in the early part of the Vietnam War during the mid- to late-1960s, capitalising on the Soviet fighters' agility and heavy firepower to close with their American opponents and engage in the type of turning fight that best suited the MiG-17's capabilities. The Arabs also used the MiG-17 in combat against French- and American-built fighters, although in this instance flown by the Israeli air force. In the Middle Eastern theatre the MiG-17 did not fare as well as in the Far Eastern theatre, for the Arab pilots were poorly trained and suffered heavily at the hands of the very able Israeli pilots. Thereupon, the Arab air force relegated the MiG-17 largely to the ground-attack role.

Just one year after the appearance of the MiG-17, however, the same design bureau produced its MiG-19 'Farmer'. This was the first Soviet fighter capable of supersonic performance in level flight, and in most respects it was a match for, if not actually superior to, the F-100. The MiG-19 had clear conceptual links with the MiG-17 and MiG-15, but was altogether a more refined design based on considerably improved aerodynamics, and a greatly improved powerplant comprising two Soviet-designed axial-flow turbojets in place of the earlier fighters' single British-type centrifugal-flow turbojet. The greater power and compact dimensions of the side-by-side engine installation allowed the design team to refine the somewhat tubby lines of the earlier types in preparation for supersonic flight. The USSR had also begun to catch up with advanced avionics, and the MiG-19 appeared in a number of models with different avionics packages for a variety of roles, including limited all-weather interception with radar and up to four primitive beam-riding air-to-air missiles.

Like the F-100, the MiG-19 enjoyed a long operational career, so it is right to say that both these Mach 1.3 fighters stood the test of prolonged service very well. The greatness of the MiG-19 can be measured in the fact that while the F-100 was soon switched from the pure fighter to the tactical fighter role, the Soviet fighter generally retained its pure fighter role. Even after it had been superseded in the USSR by more advanced fighters, the type remained a mainstay of the air forces of most Soviet allies, clients and satellites. By the mid-1960s, the West generally regarded the MiG-19 as obsolescent if not obsolete by comparison with the latest Western fighters offering Mach 2+ performance. Events in the Vietnam War and the Arab Israeli Wars of 1967 and 1973 then revealed the error of this judgement: its heavy cannon armament and light wing loading made the MiG-19 an excellent air-combat fighter at high subsonic speeds. This factor is still important in the mid-1990s, and the MiG-19 (including its Chinese-built Shenyang J-6 variants) remains in comparatively widespread service.

The pace of turbojet development was quite dramatic during the 1950s,

The Mikoyan-Gurevich was one of the most under-rated fighters of its day. The type was the USSR's first supersonic fighter, and as such the Soviet counterpart of the USA's North American F-100 Super Sabre. The Super Sabre later matured as a highly capable fighter-bomber and nuclear strike fighter, but the MiG-19 was generally retained in the air combat role. The type was a phenomenal achievement in aerodynamic and structural terms, for genuine supersonic performance was achieved with a powerplant of two small afterburning turbojets, and the long and very thin wing was remarkably stiff, allowing the incorporation of outboard ailerons (rather than the F-100's type of inboard ailerons) for rapid response in the rolling plane. Full appreciation of the MiG-19 and its Chinese-built J-6 variants came only in the late 1960s and early 1970s, when American pilots in Vietnam found that their highly supersonic fighters soon lost energy and thus manoeuvring capability in any sort of turning engagement, and thus became moderately easy prey for fighters such as the MiG-19 which could maintain high energy levels at high subsonic speeds.

Mikoyan-Gurevich MiG-19 series

ALTHOUGH it was a comparatively simple type, the Mikoyan-Gurevich can be used as an example of how the fighter was developed during the 1950s and 1960s. Vying with the North American F-100 Super Sabre for the historical niche as the world's first operational warplane capable of sustained supersonic performance in level flight, the MiG-19 resulted from a Soviet appreciation that the MiG-17, good as it was, was little more than a considerably improved MiG-15 and that truly supersonic flight performance could be provided only by a new design. Yet even when the MiG-19 had entered service, the Soviets pressed ahead with the development of Mach 2 fighters and thus undervalued the MiG-19. It was only later, with the advent of the Chinese version of this fighter, that the world came to realise the very real virtues of this high-performance fighter as a superb air-combat dogfighter, owing to its aerodynamic design and light wing loading.

The requirement for a supersonic fighter was issued in the autumn of 1949, and the Mikoyan-Gurevich design team soon decided that while the basic configuration of its earlier turbojet-powered fighters could be retained, albeit in much refined form, a new powerplant and a number of more advanced features were required. The Soviet centrifugal-flow turbojets derived from a British engine, the Rolls-Royce Nene, had too large a cross-section for sensible installation in a fuselage of the right fineness for supersonic flight, and had also reached the end of their useful development lives. The design team therefore decided to adopt an axial-flow turbojet of the afterburning type, together with flying surfaces with a leading-edge sweep of 58 degrees. As it previous MiG fighters, the wing was located in the mid-set position and was a truly remarkable structure of considerable area, high aspect ratio and low thickness/chord ratio, yet was immensely strong and also stiff enough in aero-elastic terms to allow the incorporation of outboard ailerons without any fear of aileron-reversal problems.

Work proceeded rapidly in the early 1950s, and as there were several engine options open to it, the design bureau designed its Aircraft SM in several prototype forms. The first of these to fly, in October 1952 was the I-350 with a powerplant of one Lyul'ka AL-5 or AL-5F turbojet. The I-360 second prototype flew toward the end of the year with a radically different powerplant of two small Mikulin AM-5 (later called Tumanskii RD-5) turbojets arranged side-by-side in the rear fuselage. The I-370 third prototype, which also flew in 1952, was powered by two Klimov VK-7F turbojets. It is thought that the first and second prototypes had the same pattern of tail unit as the MiG-15 and MiG-17, with the horizontal surface located part-way up the vertical tail surface, but that the third prototype may have introduced the type of tail unit adopted for the production model, with the tailplane lowered from the vertical surface to the upper part of the rear fuselage.

Trials revealed the superiority of the I-360's powerplant, and this was adopted for the pre-production model, which was authorised in 1953 with the designation MiG-19F and subsequent NATO reporting designation of 'Farmer-A'. The first of these aircraft flew during September 1953, and the type was delivered for service evaluation from December with a powerplant of two AM-5F turbojets each rated at 6,702lb st (29.81kN) with afterburning.

Later redesignated MiG-19SF, the MiG-19S 'Farmer-C' was the first major production version, and was developed under great pressure to overcome the longitudinal control problem encountered at transonic speed by the first two variants, which used a fixed tailplane and separate elevators. The MiG-19S introduced an all-moving slab tailplane with anti-flutter masses ahead of the leading edge. This effectively cured the longitudinal control problem, and other changes introduced with the MiG-19S were a powerplant of two redesignated RD-9B (later improved RD-9BF) turbojets, spoilers for improved roll control, an additional air brake in the ventral position, a revised control system, and a gun armament of three long-barrel 30mm cannon in place of the mixed battery of 23 and 37mm weapons carried by the earlier aircraft.

The MiG-19PM 'Farmer-D' was the limited all-weather development of the MiG-19SF with the cannon armament deleted and four underwing hardpoints added for a quartet of RS-2 or K-5 (AA-1 'Alkali') air-to-air missiles (AAMs) employed in conjunction with the 'Scan Odd' radar used for target acquisition and guidance of the beam-riding AAMs. The type was also produced in China as the Shenyang J-6, and the variants of this series included the J-6 'Farmer' version of the MiG-19SF 'Farmer-C', produced after the signature of a licence agreement in January 1958. Deliveries began in December 1961 of the J-6 in its initial form with an armament of three 30mm cannon. Since that time the type has been built in large numbers and also exported with the designation F-6, impressing customers with the excellence of the finish and the great attention paid to detail during the design and manufacturing processes.

The J-6A 'Farmer' is the Chinese equivalent of the MiG-19PF with a fixed armament of two 30mm cannon (in the wing roots) and radar to provide limited all-weather interception capability. The type was exported as the F-6A. The J-6B 'Farmer' is the Chinese equivalent of the MiG-19PM 'Farmer-D' with the two 30 mm cannon supplemented by two PL-1 semi-active radar-homing AAMs derived from the Soviet RS-2 or K-5 (AA-1 'Alkali') and used in association with interception radar. The J-6C 'Farmer' is a development for the day-fighter role with the brake chute relocated to a bullet fairing at the base of the rudder. The J-6Xin 'Farmer' is a development of the J-6A with Chinese radar in a sharp-tipped radome on the splitter plate rather than Soviet radar in the inlet centrebody.

Built by Tianjin rather than Shenyang, the JJ-6 'Farmer' is a trainer, development equivalent to (but not identical with) the MiG-19UTI that was developed in prototype form in the USSR but not placed in production. The JJ-6 has its forward fuselage lengthened forward of the wing to provide volume for the insertion of a tandem-seat cockpit.

however, and the F-104, which appeared only a year after the MiG-19, was far superior in terms of legend performance, with a maximum level speed in excess of Mach 2 and a far superior climb rate and service ceiling.

In the early 1950s, Republic also produced a supersonic fighter, developing the F-84F Thunderstreak from the F-84 Thunderjet, the substitution of swept wings for straight flying surfaces on a fuselage that was otherwise little modified affording a useful increase in overall performance. This produced an improved fighter at minimal cost, but the Thunderstreak was only an interim type, despite a long and distinguished career as a fighter-bomber and reconnaissance aeroplane with the US Air Force and several allied nations.

To create a truly supersonic type, the Republic design team echoed the North American team in the adoption of highly swept flying surfaces, a sleek fuselage and a powerful turbojet with full afterburning. First flown in 1955, this Republic aeroplane was the F-105 Thunderchief, one of the classic US Air Force aircraft of the period after World War II. Although it was classified as a fighter, the Thunderchief was in reality a massive and hard-hitting strike and attack aeroplane, characterised not only by its high supersonic performance but also by its incorporation of an internal weapon bay to supplement the hardpoints that had become standard for the carriage of external drop loads. Nicknamed 'Thud', the Thunderchief also featured an advanced avionics suite that created a number of maintenance problems but found a new lease of life in the 1960s during the Vietnam War. Even though many analysts had decided that the nuclear-capable F-105 was obsolescent, the type was revealed by operations to be versatile and capable of absorbing the levels of battle damage that would have downed most other types. Even

The Republic F-105 Thunderchief was conceived as a highly capable supersonic strike warplane able to deliver nuclear weapons in the operational and tactical roles. After a number of difficult teething problems caused by its very advanced nature, the type was used in the conventional attack role during the Vietnam War and proved highly successful. The Thunderchief could also be refuelled in the air by the US Air Force's standard system of the type, namely the flying boom carried by the Boeing KC-135 Stratotanker: this boom was 'flown' into a receptacle on the receiver warplane by an operator in the tanker, and fuel was passed down the boom after a positive lock had been achieved between the boom and the receiver warplane.

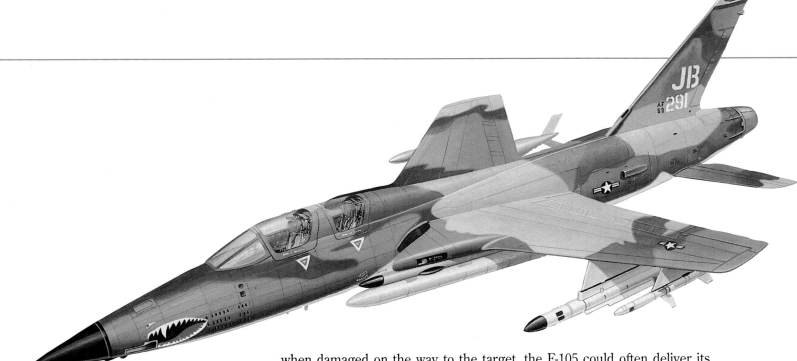

The two-seat trainer model of the Thunderchief was also pressed into active service after conversion to the 'Wild Weasel' configuration with additional electronics for the detection and localisation of enemy air-defence radars that could then be destroyed by the high-explosive/fragmentation bombs or specialist anti-radar missiles (typically the AGM-45 Shrike or AGM-78 Standard ARM) carried by the Thunderchief, or alternatively by the weapons carried by accompanying warplanes supplied with the required targeting information by radio or data-link.

when damaged on the way to the target, the F-105 could often deliver its weapons load (now generally carried on one under-fuselage and four under-wing hardpoints) with pinpoint accuracy and only then turn for home.

With their powerful engines and advanced aerodynamic features, multi-role fighters could, by the late 1950s, carry an offensive load far greater than could be stowed inside the airframe, even if it had been possible to locate a weapons bay among the masses of avionics equipment accommodated throughout the fuselage. Pioneered during World War II, streamlined pylons under the wings and fuselage could accept a dazzling variety of under-wing stores. Not only bombs, but unguided rockets either singly if they were of large calibre or in multiple launcher pods if they were of small calibre, guided missiles of the air-to-air and/or air-to-surface varieties, napalm tanks, chemical tanks, drop tanks for extra fuel, and other offensive stores could be carried. The mass of wiring and plumbing needed to connect the stores and tanks to onboard computers and the aeroplane's main fuel system greatly increased the complexity of the problems faced by the large design teams.

Meanwhile, the Europeans were advancing more slowly than the Americans and the Soviets. World War II, had devastated Europe, and of the major aeronautical powers before World War II, only the United Kingdom and France were in any position to design and construct advanced combat aircraft. Yet the British government could foresee no war before the late 1950s and, with finance in short supply, the development of new fighting aircraft received a low priority. In France the work of reconstruction after World War II was more urgent and, despite a number of interesting experiments, the combat aircraft brought into service were chosen for their serviceability rather than for inspirational design or high performance.

The limitations of the United Kingdom's Meteor and Vampire as front-line fighters were highlighted by the Korean War, but the lack of research and development in the previous years had left the British aircraft industry in no position to advance the production of a new fighter. In 1952, the United Kingdom was placed in the humiliating position of having to accept 430 Sabres built by Canadair and paid for by the American and Canadian governments. Two years later, however, as several supersonic types were being introduced in the USSR and the United States, two swept-wing but only transonic British fighters entered service after prolonged development.

The first of these was the Supermarine Swift, whose production programme was curtailed as a result of the type's intransigent aerodynamic

problems; the second was the classic Hawker Hunter, perhaps the best transonic fighter and ground-support aircraft of its kind. With clean lines, excellent handling characteristics and a good load-carrying capacity, the Hunter was built in greater numbers than any other post-war British aeroplane, and is still in first-line service with several smaller air forces during the mid-1990s.

French fighter aircraft have been supplied almost exclusively by the firm set up in 1945 by Marcel Bloch, whose aircraft manufacturing company had been nationalised in 1937 as part of the SNCASO group. Returning from Germany, where he had been incarcerated during the war, he changed his surname to Dassault (his codename in the wartime resistance), and built up the company bearing his new name into the biggest military aircraft manufacturer in France. The machines supplied by Dassault have been based on sound engineering and inspired design, with costs carefully kept down by repeating as many components and ideas as possible from design to design.

Below left: The most successful European-built fighter in numerical as well as operational terms, the Dassault Mirage III resulted from a requirement for a lightweight interceptor but matured as a medium-weight interceptor that was soon rendered superfluous in its designed fast-climbing role by the disappearance of the high-altitude bomber after the introduction of effective surface-to-air missile systems. The type's development then centred on the creation of the Mirage IIIE multi-role fighter and Mirage IIIR reconnaissance variants.

Opposite: The English Electric Lightning was initially conceived as a supersonic research type but later developed as an interceptor and finally as a fighter-bomber. The most notable features of the Lightning were its angular flying surfaces and the use of a twin-engined powerplant in which the engines were superimposed to avoid the possibility of asymmetric control problems in the event of one engine failing. Both engines were aspirated via a circular nose inlet whose centrebody contained the antenna for the airborne interception radar. The Lightning was very fast and possessed a superb rate of climb but, in common with most other British-designed fighters, was notably short of range on internal fuel and was only lightly armed with a mere two short-range air-to-air missiles on the sides of the forward fuselage. Both these limitations were addressed in later models, which introduced a large ventral installation in which the forward part carried two 30mm Aden fixed forward-firing cannon and the rear part extra fuel. The last models for export, to Kuwait and Saudi Arabia, had underwing and overwing hardpoints for the carriage of missiles and/or bombs.

The first turbojet-powered Dassault fighter was the Ouragan (hurricane), which was built in moderate numbers for the French and Indian air forces before being replaced by the more advanced swept-wing Mystère. The Mystère was built in some numbers, both for the home market and for export, and was the first French aircraft to exceed the speed of sound, although only in a shallow dive. Just as the F-100 had been evolved in concept terms from the F-86, the Super Mystère, of which Dassault flew in prototype form in 1955, was the truly supersonic development of the Mystère. With its more streamlined fuselage, a Rolls-Royce Avon axial-flow afterburning turbojet and very thin wings, it proved a first-class fighter, and served the Israeli air force well in combat.

The first Mach 2 European fighter was the English Electric (later British Aircraft Corporation and finally British Aerospace) Lightning. This had entered service in 1960, after a 13-year design and development period that had turned a supersonic research aeroplane into a phenomenal fast-climbing interceptor whose two main limitations were indifferent armament and poor range.

The Dassault Mirage III, adopted in 1961, appeared six years after the first flight of the Mirage I lightweight prototype. The prolonged gestation periods of these fighters, comparing poorly with the speed at which the Soviets and Americans were able to put new types into service, was a clear indication of weakness in the European aeronautical industry and the strength of the superpowers.

The Mirage III has been the most successful European combat aeroplane designed since World War II, and has formed the basis of a large number of advanced and high-performance combat aircraft. Essentially a scaled-up Mirage III, the Mirage IV is a Mach 2 bomber for the delivery of France's atomic bombs.

The Mirage 5 was designed to an Israeli requirement as a simplified clear-weather version of the all-weather Mirage III for use as a ground-attack fighter, but since upgraded in most cases to Mirage III standards or higher as miniaturised electronics were developed.

The most successful exponent of the Dassault Mirage III series in operational terms has been the Israeli Defence Force/Air Force, which used its aircraft to devastating effect in the first hours of the 1967 'Six-Day War'. Knowing that Egypt, Jordan and Syria were planning to launch a combined offensive to crush it, Israel planned and executed a militarily decisive pre-emptive campaign that resulted in the capture of the Sinai from Egypt, eastern Jerusalem and the 'East Bank' of the Jordan river from Jordan, and much of the Golan Heights from Syria. The key to this extraordinary success was Israel's incredible series of preliminary air raids, which caught most of the Arab air power on the ground and destroyed at least three-quarters of it for virtually no Israeli losses. The most advanced type used in these raids was the Mirage III, which provided air cover as well as delivering crushing attacks on surface targets.

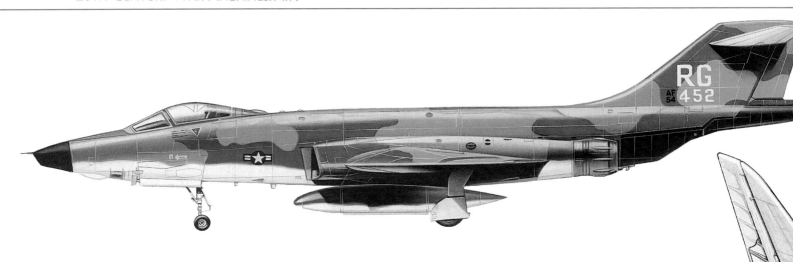

The Mirage F1 was designed as a multi-mission fighter and attack aeroplane, based on the Mirage III's fuselage but with new swept wings and tailplane.

Israel was concerned that deliveries of its Mirage 5 force might be delayed by Arab political and economic pressure on France, and embarked upon a programme of indigenous but wholly unlicensed production and further development of the Mirage III. This foresight paid handsome dividends when delivery of the Mirage 5 force was later embargoed completely, and Israel Aircraft Industries was able to respond with its Nesher (eagle) version of the Mirage III as work continued on the much upgraded Kfir (lion cub) derivative with an American turbojet and an advanced suite of Israeli electronics. Israel used its Mirage IIIs to stunning effect in the 1967 'Six-Day War' and had introduced the Nesher in time for the 'Yom Kippur' War of 1973.

Surplus Neshers were later exported to Argentina with the name Dagger, and were used against the British during the Falklands campaign. In Israel, further development of the Kfir produced the Kfir-C2, with canard foreplanes to improve field performance and to enhance manoeuvrability in air combat, and Israel has continued to develop this useful type in variants with more refined aerodynamics, greater power from a 'tweaked' engine and, most importantly of all, increasingly sophisticated electronics in single- and two-seat variants.

Many exported Mirage IIIs and Mirage 5s have been upgraded to a comparable standard, and South Africa undertook a comparable upgrade effort to produce the Atlas Cheetah, by rebuilding French aircraft delivered before the imposition of a United Nations' embargo of arms supplies as a supposed counter to South Africa's policy of separate racial development. This embargo was lifted in 1994 after the swearing-in of a new multi-racial South African government, and this has opened the possibility of South African exports or involvement in further Mirage III/5 upgrades.

The basic design of the remarkable Mirage III has proved enormously adaptable and, with different engines, flying surfaces, avionics and armament can undertake a variety of combat tasks ranging from short-range interception to medium-range operational-level nuclear strike bombing, all-weather fighting, training, daylight ground attack and reconnaissance. The Mirage III and Mirage 5 are still operational in some numbers with European air forces although they are now rapidly declining in importance as more advanced types have assumed primary roles, but they are likely to remain among the most valuable combat types of several South American and African countries for many years. Indeed,

Opposite: The McDonnell F-101 Voodoo was planned as a fighter that could escort American strategic bombers as they penetrated Soviet air space, but range of the required order was impossible with the turbojet engines of the period, and the F-101 was therefore developed initially as a day interceptor, then as an all-weather interceptor, and finally as a reconnaissance aeroplane. In this last capacity the RF-101 was extensively used in the dangerous days of the Cuban Missile Crisis of 1962, and was one of the key elements that allowed the USA to determine the extent and nature of the Soviet involvement in Cuba.

McDonnell Douglas A-4 Skyhawk

ONE of the most remarkable warplanes of all time, the Skyhawk was designed by Douglas, before its merger with McDonnell, as the A4D carrierborne light-attack bomber which first flew in June 1954 but then matured during the 1960s as the A-4 multi-role land-based as well as carrierborne warplane. The design team's objective was to produce the smallest, lightest and therefore cheapest type that could fulfil the complete mission expected of it, and so successful was the result that the prototype turned the scales at a maximum weight only half that fixed by the US Navy as its upper limit, yet it was capable of high subsonic speed and, in unladen form, fighter-like agility.

As might be expected of so important a type, the Skyhawk went through a number of forms with steadily increasing capabilities (in terms of weapons load and electronics, the latter accommodated in an enlarged 'hump' fairing to the rear of the cockpit enclosure), a switch from the anti-ship to the land-attack role with a larger load of different weapon types, and two different turbojet engine types: the early models were powered by the Wright J65 (an Americanised and not altogether successful version of a British engine, the Armstrong Siddeley Sapphire), but in new-build models from the A-4E the standard engine became the Pratt & Whitney J52.

The definitive late-production model was the A-4M Skyhawk II with the powerplant of one J52-P-408A turbojet rated at 11.200lb (5,080kg) st, span of 27ft 6in (8.38m), length of 40 ft 3.25 in (12.27 m), empty weight of 10,465 lb (4747 kg), maximum take-off weight of 27,420lb (12,437kg), maximum speed of 670mph; 1,078km/h) at optimum altitude, initial climb rate of 8,440ft (2,572m) per minute, service ceiling of 49,000ft (14,935m), and range of about 920 miles (1,480km) with the maximum external weapons load. This last comprises 9,155lb (4,153kg) of stores as diverse as 'dumb' bombs of the free-fall or retarded types, cluster bombs, dispenser weapons, rocket-launcher pods, cannon pods, and air-to-surface missiles. The Skyhawk also carries a fixed forward-firing armament of two 20mm Mk 12 cannon or, in a number of export aircraft, two 30mm DEFA cannon.

Pakistan bought a large number of ex-Australian Mirage IIIs during the early 1990s, with a view to supplementing its current fleet of Mirages with an upgraded variant.

A notable factor in fighter design since the early 1950s has been the wide range of tasks which operators expect of their smaller combat aircraft. Up to the middle of World War II, it was possible to build a combat aeroplane for one specific role, but development costs have since been prohibitively high for such development to be considered by any country other than one of the two superpowers. The tendency has been towards the creation of multi-role aircraft, and this tendency was discernible even during World War II in the evolution of supremely versatile types such as the de Havilland Mosquito and Junkers Ju 88.

Each role demands its own electronics package and specialised weapons, but this fact has actually eased the designers' task. Providing the electronics packages for all-weather interception, reconnaissance and ground-attack roles can be accommodated in the same fuselage, the basic aeroplane can be used in a number of roles. Reduced to its simplest terms, the designer's task from the mid-1950s until recently has been to produce an aeroplane capable of high performance at all altitudes and in all conditions, but with the ability to carry a heavy offensive load on the exterior hardpoints and sufficient internal volume for accommodation of the relevant avionics. Although simple in concept, such design is vastly complex in practice, and has been complicated further by the realisation that missiles have some disadvantages in combat. Internally mounted guns, with all their bulky ammunition and fire-control radars, must now be designed into the airframe.

Advanced combat aircraft are so prohibitively expensive that the economies of the United Kingdom and France were severely strained by the development and production of machines such as the Lightning and Mirage.

Other European countries, apart from Sweden, could not match this expenditure, and so bought aircraft from one of the main producers, or concentrated on less advanced types with limited capabilities.

Italy produced the lightweight G91 close-support aircraft, and developed its two most important turbojet-powered trainers into useful but limited light-attack types: the single-seat attack version of the MB-326 sold moderately well, but the comparable version of the MB-339 (an evolutionary development of the MB-326 with a revised forward fuselage offering vertically stepped accommodation) failed to attract any purchasers. This has been a growing trend since the mid-1960s, followed by countries such as the

Designed and developed with considerable speed in the period immediately after World War II but still in modest service with a number of countries, the Ilyushin Il-28 'Beagle' was planned as a tactical light bomber with a powerplant of two simple turbojet engines, and was therefore in the same basic class as the English Electric Canberra. There was little complexity in the design, which has a three-man crew, a straight wing but swept tail surfaces, tricycle landing gear, two Klimov VK-1 turbojets each rated at 5,792lb (2,700kg) st which are installed in underwing nacelles, and a primary armament of 4,409lb (2000kg) of bombs carried in a lower-fuselage weapons bay. The gun armament comprises four 23mm NR-23 cannon, two of them fixed forward-firing weapons in the nose whilst two are trainable weapons in the manned tail turret.

United Kingdom, France, Spain, Romania and the former Yugoslavia. Such machines are still sold to Third World nations as primary combat aircraft, and provide a secondary attack capability for the home air forces. Virtually no trainer designed since 1970, even in the United States and the USSR, has lacked this secondary attack capability.

The US Air Force's inventory of modern combat aircraft designed between the late 1940s and late 1950s, ranging from the F-86 Sabre to the Convair F-102 Delta Dagger and F-106 Delta Dart interceptors, was impressive. It was then matched by just one truly superlative type, the McDonnell (later McDonnell Douglas) F-4 Phantom II multi-role fighter, developed for the US Navy but then adopted for the US Air Force. Design began in 1954, and by 1960 the type was recognised as the best all-round combat aeroplane developed in the United States since the end of World War II. With a lowering, aggressive appearance, the Phantom II was first conceived as a carrierborne attack aeroplane but was built in prototype form as a two-seat carrierborne fleet defence fighter (the first aircraft capable of undertaking the whole interception mission without support from surface ships). It then evolved into strike, attack, close support, electronic pathfinder, defence suppression and reconnaissance forms, and is still used by a number of Western air forces apart from those of the United States, where the type is due for retirement from US Air Force service in the second half of the 1990s.

The lessons of combat in Vietnam during the late 1960s and early 1970s led to the development of a new model with fixed gun armament, in the form of the redoubtable 20mm Vulcan six-barrelled rotary cannon capable of a rate of fire in the order of 6,000 rounds per minute This convinced the governments of most countries of the need for fighters with a fixed gun

In the early 1950s NATO became very concerned about the vulnerability to missile and bomb attack of the large air bases required for its increasingly capable, complex and expensive warplanes. The organisation therefore sponsored a number of design competitions to produce lighter, less complex and less expensive warplanes that could operate from fields or strips of undamaged road in times of crisis. The only one of these types to enter full production in its planned form was the Fiat G91 light-attack fighter adopted in Italy (its parent country) and West Germany but later passed on to Portugal. In its original forms as the G91R reconnaissance and light attack fighter and G91T combat-capable advanced trainer, the type had a powerplant of one Bristol Orpheus turbojet, but later development resulted in the G91Y with a powerplant of two General Electric J85 turbojets for improved performance and greater flight safety.

armament, and further evidence was provided by Israeli aircraft in the 'Six-Day War', when cannon proved as useful as guided missiles, especially at the low speeds and short ranges at which air combat was joined.

Immediately after the end of World War II, the main strength of the US Navy's air arm lay with piston-engined types such as the Grumman F8F Bearcat fighter, the Vought F4U Corsair fighter and fighter-bomber, and the Douglas AD Skyraider attack bomber, which was still flying over Vietnam in the early 1970s. Interim turbojet-powered types were under development, however, and by the early 1950s the US Navy and US Marine Corps had accepted a number of new aircraft such as the Grumman F9F fighter (in its straight-winged Panther and swept-wing Cougar forms), the McDonnell F2H Banshee and F3H Demon fighters, and the Douglas F3D Skyknight all-weather fighter.

Seen in company with a pair of intercepting McDonnell Douglas F-4 Phantom II fighters, the Tupolev Tu-95 'Bear' was a remarkable technical and operational triumph. First flown in prototype form during 1954, the type was planned as a less advanced back-up to the Myasishchyev M-4 'Bison' turbojet-powered strategic bomber. Range was always a problem with the thirsty turbojets of the day, so the Tu-95 was planned with the odd combination of fully swept flying surfaces and a powerplant of four extremely potent turboprop engines each driving an eight-blade contra-rotating propeller unit. As a result the Tu-95 offered near-jet speed together with considerably greater range, and the type was therefore placed in large-scale production, eventually exceeding that of the disappointing M-4 by a considerable degree. The Tu-95 also proved to be very versatile, the original bomber version soon being supplemented by missile-carrying models with large stand-off missiles, multi-sensor reconnaissance models optimised for the maritime role, and maritime patrol models optimised for the anti-submarine role. Later production aircraft were to the somewhat improved Tu-142 standard that was phased out of production only in the early 1990s after delivery in anti-submarine and cruise missile launch platform versions.

Later in the 1950s, the Douglas A3D Skywarrior attack bomber and A4D Skyhawk light-attack aeroplane appeared, and the US Navy moved into the supersonic age with the Vought F8U Crusader fighter whose configuration was later scaled-down to create the LTV A-7 Corsair II strike and attack aeroplane. The largest and heaviest carrierborne aeroplane, the Mach 2 North American A3J Vigilante attack bomber, entered service in 1960.

All these aircraft operated in Vietnam, and constant updating of their engines and avionics kept them in the forefront of military technology well into the 1970s. The US Navy types were resilient and versatile machines, disproving the theory that turbojet-powered aircraft and their avionics would be susceptible to battle damage. The only US Air Force aeroplane to match the Navy machines was the F-105, and this had serviceability problems that would never have been permitted in a carrierborne combat aeroplane.

By the 1970s, the only other countries to develop carrierborne aircraft were France and the United Kingdom. Re-formed towards the end of World War II, the French naval air arm initially operated American naval aircraft, and in the mid-1990s still operates the Crusader, which was redesignated as the F-8 in 1962 as part of the rationalisation of the US forces' previously separate tri-service designation systems into a single system. From the early

147

McDonnell Douglas F-4 Phantom II

THE F-4 Phantom II must be considered as one of the greatest warplanes of all time. The type has been used with great success in a number of wars and has revealed great 'developability' in its primary and increasing number of secondary roles. Angular, brutish and pugnacious in appearance, the Phantom II is notable for its very good performance, reliable twin-engined powerplant, good agility despite its large size and considerable weight, and overall amenability to improvement.

The original F-4A version was a pilot-production model that entered service only in small numbers, so the first major models were the F-4B and RF-4B carrierborne fighter and reconnaissance models. There followed the F-4C and RF-4C versions of the F-4B and RF-4C for the US Air Force, the F-4D more fully optimized USAF model, the F-4E and RF-4E definitive land-based fighter and reconnaissance models with the inbuilt cannon armament lacking from the previous models, the F-4F air-superiority fighter for the West German air force, the F-4G 'Advanced Wild Weasel' defence-suppression rebuild of the F-4E, the F-4J improved carrierborne model with all-round improvements, the F-4K and F-4M anglicised versions for the Fleet Air Arm and RAF with a powerplant of two Rolls-Royce Spey turbofans in place of the otherwise standard General Electric J79 turbojets, and the F-4S equivalent to the F-4J produced as F-4B conversions.

The F-4E may be regarded as the definitive model. This has a crew of two (pilot and systems operator), an armament of one 20mm M61A1 Vulcan six-barrel cannon and up to 16,000lb (7257kg) of highly diverse unguided and guided weapons carried on one under-fuselage and four underwing hardpoints, a powerplant of two J79-GE-17A turbojets each rated at 17,900lb (8,120kg) st with afterburning, maximum speed of 1,500mph (2,414km/h) of Mach 2.2 at high altitude, initial climb rate of 28,000ft (8,534m) per second, service ceiling of more than 60,000ft (19,685m), and range of 1,750 miles (2,817km) without external weapons.

1960s, however, the Dassault Etendard IVM proved itself a more than adequate carrierborne attack aircraft, and the Breguet 1050 Alizé (tradewind) has also served well in the anti-submarine role.

The Fleet Air Arm (FAA) of the Royal Navy possessed few high-performance aircraft during World War II, apart from converted landplanes such as the Supermarine Seafire adaptation of the Spitfire. In the years after 1945, it soldiered on with piston-engined types such as the Hawker Sea Fury fighter, Fairey Firefly reconnaissance fighter and Fairey Barracuda torpedo bomber, as well as a number of more advanced American aircraft such as the Grumman Avenger that was operated in the airborne early warning (AEW) role. The FAA acquired its first turbine-powered types in the early 1950s: the Supermarine Attacker and Hawker Sea Hawk fighters, and the Fairey Gannet anti-submarine aeroplane which was powered by a turboprop engine, like its French contemporary, the Alizé.

By the late 1950s, three swept-wing aircraft designs were under development for the FAA, and entered service late in the 1950s and early in the 1960s. These were the Supermarine Scimitar interceptor and strike fighter, the de Havilland (later Hawker Siddeley) Sea Vixen interceptor and the Blackburn (later Hawker Siddeley) Buccaneer strike aeroplane. The Buccaneer was a particularly good machine, with excellent performance 'on the deck' through careful aerodynamic design, and first-class landing characteristics as a result of a 'super-circulation' boundary-layer control system.

Despite its many virtues, the Buccaneer was long resisted by the RAF, which wanted the considerably more advanced British Aircraft Corporation (BAC) TSR-2 tactical strike and reconnaissance aeroplane. In the mid-1960s, however, the RAF reluctantly agreed to accept surviving ex-FAA aircraft when the Royal Navy's force of large aircraft-carriers was retired later in the decade. The TSR-2 project had been cancelled, and much to its surprise the RAF found the Buccaneer to be a truly great aeroplane. It was then ordered in large numbers, the last examples being retired only in 1994.

The USSR's air force moved into the Mach 2 era with the Mikoyan-Gurevich MiG-21 'Fishbed' fighter, designed to supersede the highly successful MiG-19. Small and compact for a Mach 2 aircraft, the MiG-21 had a delta wing but conventional, highly-swept tail surfaces, and proved both popular and successful. Lacking the size, weight and versatility of the Phantom II, the MiG-21 was designed for the short-range interception mission in clear weather conditions, using ground-controlled interception (GCI) techniques. Total production in the USSR, several Warsaw Pact countries and India numbered more than 6,500 aircraft, and an additional large but unspecified quantity has been built in China as the Chengdu J-7 series, which has in turn spawned the export-oriented F-7M Airguard derivative with its large proportion of Western avionics.

Although conceived for the clear-weather interception role and first flown in 1955 with comparatively light armament, the MiG-21 was successfully evolved into a limited all-weather type capable of interception and ground-attack roles as a result of upgraded avionics and additional armament capability. The MiG-21 family also included several reconnaissance models and three tandem-seat operational conversion trainers, and during its long production career the MiG-21 was built in many variants with three basic engine types, increasingly large dorsal spines allowing a major increase in internal fuel capacity and, in the last model, a completely re-engineered airframe.

The MiG-21 series was built in larger numbers than any other Soviet warplane since World War II, and was used by virtually every Soviet ally,

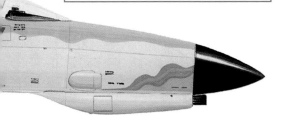

client and satellite. Although the type had disappeared from Soviet first-line service by the early 1990s, the type survives in large numbers with the air forces of most other Soviet-bloc countries, and the mid-1990s are witnessing a scrambled contest as the Russian parent organisation competes with several Western countries for the lucrative upgrade of these obsolescent aircraft. The update requested by most operators is concerned mainly with the MiG-21's avionics and weapons capabilities, and although India has opted for a Russian upgrade with Russian radar, it has also specified Western items for a large proportion of other features. It is likely that many of the other upgrade customers will follow a similar course.

In its heyday the Soviet fighter, because of its small size and low wing loading, could usually outfly contemporary American aircraft, and the MiG-19 helped to demonstrate that the art of dogfighting, a useful element of the fighter pilot's inventory of skills, had not disappeared. Part of the MiG-21's undoubted export popularity lay in its relative cheapness; in general, this trim fighter cost between one-quarter and one-third of the price for a Phantom II.

The nearest Soviet equivalent to the mighty F-105 Thunderchief as an attack aeroplane was a series of sturdy swept-wing designs originating in the design bureau of Pavel Sukhoi. The Su-7 'Fitter' series equipped most of the air forces in the Soviet sphere of influence, but although it has much the same performance as the F-105, the Su-7 cannot carry the same offensive load and is also notably deficient in range even when carrying two drop tanks in place of disposable armament. The Su-7 series may be regarded as a short-range close-support fighter whereas the F-105 was a long-range strike and attack fighter. In its milieu, however, the Su-7 was unrivalled until the late 1980s, for it was very fast at low level, monumentally strong, and a superb weapon platform because of its low gust response.

Even though the Su-7 was a superb operational aeroplane, especially in its

The Breguet (now Dassault) Alizé is typical of the type of small anti-submarine aeroplane forced on lesser naval air arms by the modest size of their aircraft-carriers. Powered by a single Rolls-Royce Dart turboprop, whose considerable fuel economy offers useful endurance, the Alizé has a crew of three, carries moderately advanced electronics, and can lift a useful weapons load in its lower-fuselage weapons bay and on underwing hardpoints. The type is operated only by the French and Indian navies.

An altogether more sophisticated approach to the problems of carrierborne anti-submarine operations was possible for the US Navy, which operates a greater number of aircraft-carriers all with considerably larger flight-decks. The solution for the US Navy is represented by the Lockheed S-3 Viking, which it achieves extraordinary success in the difficult feat of packing maximum electronics, weapons and fuel in an airframe capable of undertaking long-endurance missions yet small enough (with its wings folded) to be carried in useful numbers on aircraft-carriers packed with a host of other warplane types. The Viking is powered by two fuel-economical General Electric TF34 turbofan engines pod-mounted below wings that contain large integral fuel tanks, and the basically rectangular-section fuselage carries the crew of four, a mass of very advanced electronic equipment (radar, magnetic anomaly detector, acoustic data-processing equipment and associated droppable sonobuoys, electronic support measures equipment and the systems to combine their data into a complete tactical picture) and a lower-fuselage weapons bay for a decisive quantity of anti-submarine weaponry that can be complemented by missiles such as the McDonnell Douglas AGM-84 Harpoon anti-ship missile on two underwing hardpoints.

later variants with short take-off and landing (STOL) capability which enabled operation from semi-prepared airstrips immediately behind the front line, the Soviet air forces were unhappy with the type's very poor payload/range performance, and from 1960 the design bureau started work on a variable-geometry derivative offering improved payload/range performance. For a combination of technical and production reasons it was decided to pivot only the outer half of each wing, but this proved adequate to transform the basic close-support fighter's payload/range performance. The resulting aeroplane entered service in 1971 as the Su-17 'Fitter-C', which was also produced in differently engined Su-20 and Su-22 forms. With the outer wing sections in their minimum-sweep position, the Su-17 series aircraft had much improved field performance and greater tactical radius; and with the wings in the maximum-sweep position, speed was comparable with that of the Su-7. The net result was that the Su-17 series could carry 250 per cent more payload over 30 per cent greater tactical radius.

Unlike the other half of the Mikoyan-Gurevich prototype series, which did not lead to a production swept-wing aeroplane, the other half of the Sukhoi prototype series resulted in a production aeroplane with a tailed-delta layout. The first of this series was the Su-9 'Fishpot' interceptor that was reserved for Soviet use from the time of its introduction in mid-1959. From 1966, it was complemented by the improved Su-11 'Fishpot', and production of the two models totalled some 2,000 aircraft. These were gradually supplanted from the early 1970s by the Su-15 'Flagon', which was probably designed to replace the Yakovlev Yak-28P 'Firebar' Mach 1.9 interceptor. The Su-15 was altogether a more advanced interceptor, offering Mach 2+ performance both as a result of its more refined airframe incorporating a large measure of area-ruling, and its considerably more potent twin-engined powerplant aspirated via wing-root inlets rather than the earlier types' nose inlet. This latter fact allowed the incorporation of a much superior interception radar with its antenna in the large nose radome. The last Su-15 interceptors were retired only in the late 1980s.

Also in service with the USSR's forces until this time was the Tupolev Tu-28P 'Fiddler', the largest interceptor fighter in service anywhere in the world, and intended primarily for poor-weather operations in the USSR's northern regions. These areas were poorly equipped with air bases, but lay on the optimum trans-polar route that would probably have been used by American strategic bombers attacking the USSR. The only way to provide effective patrol and interception capabilities in these regions was therefore through the development of a moderately supersonic interceptor with an airframe large enough to carry considerable fuel, a two-man crew, an extremely powerful radar system, and four large long-range air-to-air missiles.

Not all the energy of the world's military aircraft designers went into the evolution of fighters, however. With the destruction of Hiroshima and Nagasaki, the strategic bomber had proved its value beyond all doubt. The invention of an immensely destructive device such as the A-bomb (fission or nuclear bomb) opened the possibility of true strategic air power in the form of just a few aircraft, each crewed by less than a dozen men. The theories of men such as Douhet, Mitchell and Trenchard in the 1920s were finally proved by the destruction of Hiroshima and Nagasaki, and their concept of strategic bombing as the arbiter of war was made still more terrible by the development of the even more powerful H-bomb (fusion or thermonuclear bomb) shortly after the end of World War II.

It was inevitable that these weapons should come to dominate military thinking in the late 1940s. It was assumed that long-range guided missiles, based on the German V-2 of World War II, would eventually be developed as a delivery system for such weapons, but in the short term the only practical solution seemed to lie with the long-range manned bomber, and then the long-range unmanned bomber, which was essentially a surface-to-surface missile of the type that would now be classified as a cruise missile, albeit of considerably larger size than anything in service today. The manned

Designed at much the same time as the Mikoyan-Gurevich MiG-21 'Fishbed' lightweight tactical fighter, the Sukhoi Su-7 'Fitter' was also designed as a tactical fighter but emerged as a somewhat larger and heavier type optimized for the attack-fighter role. The type saw extensive service with the USSR and its allies and clients between the 1960s and 1980s, and acquired something of a mixed reputation. On the credit side, the Su-7 was recognised as rugged, fast at low level, and an extremely good weapons platform, while on the debit side were the type's extremely thirsty Lyul'ka AL-7 afterburning turbojet engine and limited external weapons carriage capability. The former meant that even with two drop tanks the tactical radius was exceptionally short while the latter meant that, even before two hardpoints were lost to the inevitable drop tanks, only a very modest weapons load could be lifted. The situation was improved somewhat in the later Su-17 'Fitter' series, which adopted hinged outer wing panels to improve field and cruise performance, resulting in lowered fuel consumption.

bomber, therefore, became the single most important type of weapon in the arsenals of the United States, the USSR and the United Kingdom, the only three countries with nuclear weapons in the 1950s. Heavy bombers were always designed with the capacity to carry such weapons, even if the specific type of bomb had not been fully developed at the time.

The only turbojet-powered bomber in operational service when the war ended was a German type, the Arado Ar 234 Blitz (lightning). The Germans had been experimenting with several other types of turbojet-powered bomber, most notably the Junkers Ju 287. This extraordinary aeroplane had a forward-swept wing, and the powerplant comprised four turbojets which were installed as two under the wing and two on the sides of the forward fuselage. Fascinating experimental data on the use of forward-swept wings as a means of combating the worst effects of high-speed compression were obtained by the Americans and the Soviets, but as yet no military aircraft with forward-swept wings has entered production.

By 1946, both the superpowers had instituted top-priority programmes to develop a strategic bomber capable of carrying nuclear bombs over very long ranges. At the same time, the USSR was abandoning its virtually exclusive concentration on tactical air power for a more mixed approach. This reflected the fact that while the Soviet air force had shown itself to be the most powerful support arm in the world, aiding the Red Army in its massive pushes into Germany, the Soviet leaders had been greatly impressed by the devastation wrought on Germany and Japan by the combined Western bomber offensive. The Soviets began by building the Tupolev Tu-4 'Bull', a reverse-engineered derivative of the Superfortress, as their first strategic bomber type.

The United States had become convinced during World War II that it needed a completely new generation of bombers, and had therefore begun a large-scale research and development programme. Yet just after the war, before the new bombers could be placed in service, the most important aircraft in the Strategic Air Command (SAC) was the Boeing B-50 development of the B-29, with more advanced systems, better armament and uprated engines. Even so, the very fact of the SAC's formation indicated the importance attached to the United States' concept of nuclear strategic bombing.

The B-50 was essentially an interim type, pending the arrival of one of the oddest and most controversial aeroplanes of all time, the Convair B-36. This had its origins in the American decision of 1943 to build a fleet of advanced bombers, but design and prototype construction were delayed initially by the more immediate demands of World War II. When this important programme was later undertaken as a matter of high priority, it was soon discovered that the pace of technical development in this forcing period of history had been so fast, that the planned type was already on the verge of obsolescence in all features but its payload/range performance, which ensured that a heavy bomb load could be delivered over intercontinental ranges. Development and procurement of the B-36 continued, however, and the type entered service in the late 1940s. With a wing spanning no less than 230ft (70.1m), the monstrous B-36 was powered by six 3,500hp radial piston engines buried in the wings, driving pusher propellers located behind the wing trailing edges.

At a time when advanced turbojet-powered fighters were opening the possibility of combat operations at high subsonic speeds, the B-36 was judged too slow for survivability in its basic piston-engined form. Thus the B-36D featured a boosted powerplant, with the original piston engines supplemented by four turbojet engines in pods, each accommodating two

Soviet Parallel Design Concepts

IN December 1949, Pavel Sukhoi and about half of the team of his designers were subordinated to the over-pressed Tupolev bureau, Sukhoi himself was allowed to continue a measure of basic research and collaborated with the Central Aerodynamics and Hydrodynamics Institute (TsAGI), in the development of two basic design concepts.

These were both tailed types, one based on a conventional wing swept (the S type) and the other on a delta wing (the T type). The first of at least five S-1 research aircraft flew in mid-1955, and in the following two years the series was used for a major programme of research and development.

In the early 1950s the Soviet air forces issued a requirement for an advanced fighter to counter the first two of the US Air Force's 'century' series fighters, namely the North American F-100 Super Sabre and McDonnell F-101 Voodoo. The result was a series of warplanes that were larger and heavier than their Western counterparts, with the required performance provided by a higher-rated powerplant drawing its fuel from a relatively smaller internal capacity.

Designs to meet the Soviet air forces' requirement were drawn up by the Mikoyan-Gurevich and Sukhoi bureaux, the former offering the I-380 that was broadly similar to the Sukhoi design in configuration and powerplant. Sukhoi's response to the requirement was based on his team's experience with the experimental configurations mentioned above, and the basic S-1 was accordingly evolved into a more advanced form with an area-ruled airframe incorporating flying surfaces characterised by a leading-edge sweep angle of 62 degrees, slab tailplane halves, artificial feel in the powered control surfaces, four air brakes on the rear fuselage, an improved wing with kinked trailing edges for greater area, a less tapered nose providing a larger inlet for greater airflow in combination with suck-in auxiliary doors, a translating inlet centrebody containing the antenna for the SRD-5 intercept radar, a clamshell cockpit canopy, and a ribbon-type brake chute in a box under the rear fuselage.

The Convair B-58 Hustler was the world's first supersonic bomber. The main conceptual problem facing the designers of this aircraft was that the internal carriage of the nuclear weapon payload and all the fuel for both outward and inward legs of the mission would result in an aeroplane so large that supersonic performance would not really be possible even with the new and potentially superb General Electric J79 afterburning turbojet that was the best available engine for the bomber. The solution that offered itself to the design team was elegant yet daring: create a small bomber without internal weapons accommodation or fuel for more than one leg of the mission, and add both these in the form of a large and nicely streamlined pod carried under the fuselage and carrying both the nuclear payload and the fuel for the outward leg of the mission. The whole assembly was supersonic, but over the target the pod containing the bomb and now-surplus fuel tankage was dropped, reducing the weight and drag of the bomber for higher exit speed and a return to base on the internal fuel tankage. The B-58 entered service in the early 1960s, and provided a very high degree of capability although only at the expense of complex maintenance. The type was withdrawn from service in 1970.

side-by-side engines, attached under the outer wing panels. This boosted the maximum speed to 435mph (700km/h), considerably below the figure attainable by current fighters, but which, in conjunction with the bomber's prodigious defensive armament of paired 20mm cannon, was deemed to offer at least a measure of survivability.

Although the B-36 had the neccessary range of 7,500 miles (12,070km) for global missions, the US Air Force soon appreciated that the very size of the aeroplane was a hindrance to its survivability and therefore its likely success in combat. The B-36's radar signature was enormous, for example, and this made the type highly detectable even by the comparatively primitive ground-based radars then available to the Soviets.

The Americans reasoned that they should replace the B-36 with a smaller, faster and less detectable bomber. But a smaller airframe also entailed reduced fuel capacity and thus restricted range at a time when the SAC was being developed as the United States' primary method of strategic power projection. The answer lay in aerial refuelling, which had been attempted as early as the 1920s, but was now being brought to an acceptable operational capability by the British and the Americans. Britain opted for the hose-and-drogue type of refuelling, in which the receiver aeroplane noses its refuelling probe into a basket trailed at the end of a hose by the tanker, whilst the Americans developed the flying boom, which an operator in the tanker 'flies' into a receptacle of the receiver aeroplane.

The B-36 was an interim type, and was replaced from the early 1950s by the remarkable Boeing B-47 Stratojet and Boeing B-52 Stratofortress turbojet-powered bombers operating in the medium and heavy strategic

Changing Concepts of Bomber Design

THE imminent debut of turbojet-powered fighters in the middle stages of World War II rightly persuaded the US Army Air Force in 1943 that, in the future, bombers would only survive against turbojet-powered fighters if they adopted a similar powerplant for much higher speed and service ceiling. By 1944, five companies were involved in the design of jet-powered bombers, their initial thoughts being centred on conventional (and thus straight-winged) aircraft with turbojets in place of piston engines. Boeing proposed its Model 424 that was in essence a scaled-down Model 345 (B-29 Superfortress) with four turbojets in podded pairs under the wings. The proposal failed to interest the USAAF, and the company revised the concept into the Model 432 with all four engines buried in the fuselage. The new proposal aroused limited interest, and Boeing was contracted for design definition and a mock-up of this XB-47.

As the company was proceeding with these initial steps, a team of its designers and engineers was allowed in the summer of 1945 to visit captured German factories and research centres, in the process discovering the advantages of swept flying surfaces for aircraft of high subsonic performance. Boeing therefore recast the Model 432 as the Model 448 with a thin wing characterised by a quarter-chord sweep angle of 35 degrees. At this stage the USAAF raised objections to the grouping of the engines in the fuselage, where they would be highly vulnerable to disablement by a single hit, and Boeing thus recast the design as the Model 450 with six engines located under the wings as two podded pairs inboard and two podded singletons outboard, each pod unit being placed below and ahead of the wing leading edge in a position that interfered minimally with the flow of air over the wing and also offered structural advantages in reducing the long, thin wing's tendency to bow under load.

This was the definitive design, and was optimised for the carriage of current nuclear weapons, which were both large and heavy, in a large weapon bay on high-altitude missions to attack area targets deep in enemy territory. The Model 450 thus began to mature as a high-altitude type with a crew of three including two pilots in a fighter-type cockpit, all-swept flying surfaces including a cantilever high-set wing of laminar-flow section, and bicycle-type landing gear with tandem twin-wheel units under the fuselage (fore and aft of the weapon bay) and small single-wheel stabiliser units extending from the underside of the twin-engine pods. The first of two XB-47 (Model 450-3-3) prototypes flew in December 1947 with a powerplant of six General Electric J35-GE-2 turbojets each rated at 3,750lb (1,701kg) st, while the second prototype had a powerplant of six General Electric J47-GE-3 turbojets each rated at 5,000lb (2,268kg) st. The indifferent power of these engines advocated the use of booster rockets for take-off, and the XB-47s had provision for 16 solid-propellant RATO units in the fuselage sides aft of the wing. The new bomber clearly possessed exceptional potential and the US Air Force, as the USAAF had now become, ordered the type as the B-47 Stratojet, which entered service in the early 1950s as the USA's first turbojet-powered strategic bomber.

roles respectively. The B-47 was a version developed from one of five turbine-powered experimental bomber designs ordered by the US Army Air Force in 1943. A superbly clean and sleek type whose swept-wing design was finalised only after the Americans had digested the implications of German research data captured at the end of World War II, the Stratojet revealed how the aerodynamics hitherto applied only to small fighters could be successfully used on a large aeroplane with its wings swept at 35 degrees. Although it was classified as a medium bomber, its range of 4,000 miles (6,437km/h) and maximum speed of 600mph (966km/h) made the B-47, with a bomb load of 22,000lb (9,979kg), a far more formidable combat aeroplane than the larger and theoretically more devastating B-36.

The United Kingdom at last entered the field of strategic nuclear bombing with turbojet-engined aircraft. The first of these, essentially an interim type, was the Vickers Valiant, a four-engined machine with pleasing lines, and the first of the United Kingdom's 'V-bombers' to enter service. The Valiant's performance was limited by its intermediate design, which resulted in a wing of only modest sweep, but the type was used for developing the tactics of British nuclear bombing, and also for testing the British fission and fusion weapons.

The Americans followed the Stratojet with the B-52 Stratofortress, which entered service with the SAC in 1955. The family likeness to the B-47 was immediately apparent, but the B-52 is an altogether larger and more powerful aeroplane with a maximum speed of 660mph (1,062km/h), a range of 10,000 miles (16,093km), and a normal bomb load of up to 27,000lb (12,247kg) of nuclear weapons carried internally, that can be increased in some models to a maximum of 75,000lb (34,020kg) of conventional weapons carried internally, and externally. Powered by eight engines in four twin-engined under-wing pods, and fitted with the same type of landing gear arrangement as the B-47, the B-52 has proved to be an enormously versatile strategic bomber, used to such devastating effect for tactical bombing in the Vietnam War. In 1961, the B-52G variant entered service with the capability

The demands of night and all-weather interception of heavy bombers during the late 1940s and early 1950s presented designers with acute problems: high speed was necessary to ensure rapid interception, so turbojet propulsion was required; long endurance was essential for sustained patrols, so a substantial, fuel-filled airframe was inevitable; and the airborne interception radar of the period was bulky and needed a dedicated operator, so still further demands were made on airframe size and weight. This meant that almost all of the night- and all-weather fighters of the period were large machines with a twin-engined powerplant to ensure that performance was not adversely affected by the drag and weight of the airframe. A typical example of this trend was the Gloster Javelin, a British fighter carrying its radar in the large nose, and with a delta wing of great area and considerable thickness to accommodate the engines and large quantity of fuel. Knowledge of the aerodynamic factors associated with delta wings was still poor at this time, so the Javelin was also given a large horizontal tail surface mounted at the head of the vertical surface to provide full longitudinal control.

to carry and launch two North American AGM-28 Hound Dog nuclear-tipped air-to-surface missiles, and from 1981 the last two variants (the B-52G and turbofan-powered B-52H) were revised for carriage of the Boeing AGM-86 air-launched cruise missile. Although the B-52 was supplanted as the SAC's most important strategic bomber from 1986 by the Rockwell B-1 Lancer, the type is still in comparatively widespread service as a conventional bomber and sea-control aeroplane.

The United Kingdom's small fleet of Valiant bombers had to be grounded and scrapped in 1964 because of fatigue problems, but by this time the RAF's two primary V-bombers were in service. These were the Avro Vulcan, the first large delta-wing aeroplane to enter service anywhere in the world, and the more conventional Handley Page Victor whose 'crescent' flying surfaces featured a sweep angle that gradually reduced from root to tip. Both of these long-range heavy bombers (medium range by US standards) resulted from a requirement drafted as early as 1946, but official vacillation resulted in both types going into production, with a consequent increase in aircraft unit costs and a complete doubling of training, spares and procedures. The only redeeming feature of this duplication was that the Victor emerged as an excellent tanker, and the Vulcan as a low-level attack bomber. The last few Vulcans were rescued from retirement in 1982 to participate in the Falklands campaign, when very long flight-refuelled missions were flown from a forward base on Ascension Island in the South Atlantic. The last Victor tankers were retired only in the mid-1990s when their airframe hours were exhausted after intensive operations in the 1991 UN-led campaign to expel the Iraqi occupiers from Kuwait.

Convair B-36 'Peacemaker'

AFTER World War II, the US Air Force invited both Boeing and Consolidated to prepare design studies for a bomber able to reach 450mph (724km/h) at 25,000ft (7,620m), cover a range of 12,000 miles (19,312km) with a bomb load of 4,000lb (1,814kg), deliver a bomb load of 10,000lb (4,536kg) to a radius of 3,400 miles (5,472km), and reach an altitude of 35,000ft (10,670m).

Consolidated had already considered such a type with a tail unit carrying endplate vertical surfaces and with a powerplant of six pusher engines to improve airflow over the wings, and submitted this Model 35 design in May 1941. The company refined this design during the summer of 1941 as Boeing (together with Douglas and Northrop) pressed ahead with rival concepts. In November 1941 the USAAF contracted with Consolidated for two XB-36 prototypes that were to be delivered in 1944. The definition of the design resulted in considerable growth of size and weight, requiring the use of six huge R-4360 radials buried in the wings where they could be reached for inflight maintenance and were supplied with fuel from an internal capacity of 17,583 Imp gal (79,932.5litres) in six wing-mounted tanks. The envisaged bomb load was 42,000lb (19,051kg) carried in four bomb bays below a tunnel 85ft (25.91m) long for the wheeled cart that moved on twin rails to provide a means of transfer between the two pressurised compartments (forward crew and rear gunners' sections).

Up to the summer of 1944 the whole programme was seriously delayed by its low priority, but the high cost to the US forces of capturing the Mariana Islands to provide the bases needed for the strategic bombing of Japan by Boeing B-29 Superfortresses then persuaded the USAAF to afford the B-36 a higher priority. The first XB-36 flew in August 1946 with a flush flight-deck canopy and main landing gear units each carrying a single wheel 9ft 2in (2.79m) in diameter. These units exerted so great a ground pressure that there were only three airfields in the continental USA with runways offering concrete of the required 22in (0.56m) thickness; the XB-36 was therefore revised with a four-wheel bogie on each main landing gear unit, reducing the required concrete thickness to 13.5in (0.34m). The machine was also fitted with the raised flightdeck glazing that was adopted as standard, and took to the air in this revised form during June 1948.

The Convair B-58 Hustler supersonic bomber entered service in 1960. Powered by four podded turbojets, the delta-winged Hustler was capable of 1,385mph (2,229km/h) and had a service ceiling of 60,000ft (18,290m). To maintain a clean fuselage for minimum drag and maximum speed, the designers placed both the weapon load and the fuel for the outward leg of the mission in a streamlined pod under the fuselage. This pod was designed to be jettisoned over the target, enabling the unencumbered bomber to fly home at maximum speed.

The Hustler was not entirely successful, however, and in the late 1960s its task assumed by the General Dynamics F-111 series. The first major combat aeroplane to enter service with a variable-geometry wing planform, the F-111 was planned for the US Air Force, but a subsequent political decision dictated its development as a carrierborne fleet air-defence fighter for the

US Navy, as the use of a single airframe/powerplant combination being thought likely to reduce development, procurement and operating costs. Powered by a pair of advanced turbofan engines, the F-111 has a speed well in excess of Mach 2, and proved itself capable of undertaking the strike, attack and reconnaissance roles previously performed by a number of different types.

In many respects the F-111 lived up to expectations from the beginning of the programme, but rising costs, engine limitations and airframe weight all caused problems. Nonetheless the TFX, as the type was known before it first flew in 1964, has proved a versatile and hard-hitting aircraft, eventually meeting or exceeding most of its performance requirements in a highly successful service career intended to continue into the next century. It should be noted, however, that the F-111B naval version was cancelled at an early stage of its development due to intractable weight problems. The real virtues of the machine were initially obscured by political controversy over its cost, and worries about a basic design flaw after several early aircraft were lost for no apparent reason in the Vietnam War. A simple technical problem was then diagnosed and cured, and the F-111 matured as an exceptional combat aeroplane.

The Tupolev Tu-4, the Soviet copy of the B-29, was in service in 1947, less than two years after work on the project began. And if two years seems a long time merely to copy another aeroplane and put it into mass production, it must be remembered that the Soviet designers had to dismantle the American aircraft, produce working drawings of every component, and supervise all the modifications that had to be effected to suit the type to

The Vickers Valiant was the first of the three British 'V-bombers', and was planned as a comparatively simple type to provide Bomber Command with an interim nuclear bombing capability in the period it took to develop the two more advanced types, the Avro Vulcan with its large delta wing and the Handley Page Victor with its crescent-shaped wing. The Valiant proved successful in service and could have been developed into a successful low-level bomber of the type that began to become essential from the late 1950s as the availability of surface-to-air missile systems made high-altitude penetration of Soviet airspace increasingly problematic. The availability of the Vulcan and Valiant scotched this concept for a Valiant B.Mk 2, and the original Valiant B.Mk 1 bombers were retired in 1965 as a result of wing spar fatigue problems.

The Boeing B-52 Stratofortress was the manned bomber mainstay of the US Air Force's Strategic Air Command between the time it entered service in its initial B-52B production form during 1955 until it was complemented by the Rockwell B-1B Lancer in the later 1980s.

Developed in the late 1940s by English Electric, the Canberra was intended as a light tactical bomber with the ability to deliver a small nuclear weapon as an alternative to conventional free-fall weapons. The aeroplane proved immensely versatile, and was thus evolved into a number of other forms for tasks as diverse as night intruding, reconnaissance, electronic warfare and training. The type illustrated here is a Canberra T.Mk 17, which was produced in small numbers as a conversion of the Canberra B.Mk 2 bomber for the electronic warfare training role. The Canberra is still in limited first-line service with a number of smaller air forces, and also with the Royal Air Force as a trainer.

Soviet production techniques and methods. Metallurgists had to discover what alloys the Americans had used and instruct Soviet producers to achieve the same results; and the engineers and planners had to produce entirely new factories and techniques to build a type markedly different from any of their own. Yet the advantages were colossal: in the B-29 the Soviets found good examples of all the latest American systems, and these they could copy and modify without a long preliminary research phase.

This treasure trove was quickly exploited in the Tu-16 'Badger', the USSR's first turbojet-powered strategic bomber, which appeared in 1954 and inherited much from Tupolev's continued effort to evolve bombers, transports and even airliners from the basic Tu-4. The wings of the Tu-16 are well swept, and the two Soviet-designed engines are neatly buried in the wing roots. The Tu-16 was a match for its Western contemporaries in every

The British started to develop their own nuclear weapons in the period after World War II, and in 1946 the Royal Air Force issued an ambitious requirement for a bomber to carry such a 10,000lb (4,536kg) 'special weapon' or a heavy load of conventional bombs over a great range at high subsonic speed at an altitude of over 50,000ft (15,240m). Among the several companies who responded to this requirement were the two companies which had supplied the RAF's two most important heavy bomber types in World War II, the Avro Lancaster and the Handley Page Halifax. That from Avro was the Type 698, which was based on a circular-section fuselage that accommodated, from front to rear, the large bombing radar, pressurised flightdeck, twin-wheel nose unit of the retractable tricycle landing gear, fuel tankage, weapon bay, and bays for avionics and electronic countermeasures. The fuselage supported the large vertical tail surface and the wing centre section, which was a deep structure that carried two Bristol BE.10 (later Bristol Siddeley Olympus) turbojets on each side. Outboard of the centre section were the main panels of the delta wing, each swept at 50 degrees, accommodating one of the main landing gear units (each carrying four small twin-tired wheels) and five large fuel tanks, and carrying on their trailing edges two-section inboard elevators and two-section outboard ailerons. Two Type 698 prototypes were ordered. The first of these made its first flight in August 1952 with an interim powerplant of four Rolls-Royce Avon RA.3 turbojets each rated at 6,500lb (2,948kg) st, but these were soon replaced by Armstrong Siddeley Sapphire ASSa.6 turbojets each rated at 7,500lb (3,402kg) st and later by Olympus BOl.1/28 turbojets. The second prototype was closer to the planned production standard with its forward fuselage lengthened by 1 ft 4 in (0.406 m) to accommodate the longer nose unit leg that had been installed to provide the wing with a greater angle of incidence at take-off. The name Vulcan had by now been selected for the bomber, and the first Vulcan B.Mk 1 to emerge from the production line flew in February 1955 with the Olympus Mk 100 turbojet that was soon replaced by quartets of steadily more powerful Olympus variants. Production totalled 45 aircraft that entered service from February 1957.

respect, and more than a match in defensive armament.

Tupolev sprang a further surprise on the aviation world in 1955, with the very large Tu-95 'Bear' bomber. Powered by four 14,795hp (10,030kW) Kuznetsov turboprop engines driving very large contra-rotating propeller units, the Tu-95 was sleek and the wings were moderately swept. The type had an excellent range of 7,457 miles (12,000km) and a maximum speed in the order of 559mph (900km/h).

Both the Tu-16 and Tu-95 remain in service with the Russian air force, the former usually employed in roles such as maritime reconnaissance, missile launching and air-to-air tanking, and the latter in longer-range

Generally known in the West as the 'Badger', the Tupolev Tu-16 strategic medium bomber was a remarkable type for the time of its design and development in the late 1940s and early 1950s, achieving considerable payload/range performance with two notably powerful turbojet engines. Built in substantial numbers, the Tu-16 was initially used in the level bombing role, but was then adapted in considerable numbers for other tasks such as inflight refuelling, launch of large nuclear-tipped missiles, multi-sensor reconnaissance, and electronic warfare. The type is still in useful service, but is finally being phased out of first-line service.

The Mikoyan-Gurevich MiG-23 'Flogger' was designed as an air-combat fighter to succeed the MiG-21 'Fishbed', and was most notably different from its predecessor not only in its greater size, weight, power and electronic sophistication, but also in its adoption of a variable-geometry wing planform in which the minimum-sweep position provided good take-off and landing performance. The medium-sweep position provided a good blend of speed and range, and the maximum-sweep position provided the highest possible performance. This variant is a MiG-23MF 'Flogger-B', which was the first large-scale production model.

maritime reconnaissance, missile launching and strategic bombing. A modernised variant of the TU-95 was evolved as the Tu-142, which is used for the long-range anti-submarine role.

The other important heavy bomber developed by the Soviets in the 1950s was the Myasishchyev M-4 'Bison', which entered service in 1958. Like the Boeing bombers, it perched on a tandem main landing gear arrangement with outrigger units for ground stability. Finally removed from service in the late 1980s, the M-4 was powered by four turbojets buried in the wing roots, but while it was nearly as large as the B-52, the M-4 could carry only a 22,046lb (10,000kg) weapon load, and both its speed and range were inferior to that of its American counterpart. The Soviets judged early in the type's career that the M-4 was operationally inferior to the Tu-95, despite the latter's reliance on a turboprop powerplant, and the M-4 was switched to the shorter-range strategic role before being converted as an air-to-air tanker.

To match the B-58 supersonic bomber, the Soviets revealed the existence of the Tu-22 'Blinder' in 1961. This is another sleek aeroplane of aggressive but somewhat unusual appearance as its two engines are located above the tailplane, one on each side of the vertical tail surfaces. The Tu-22, which also came as a shock to the West, is capable of Mach 1.5 but was considered deficient in range by the Soviets.

These aircraft were kept in the forefront of Soviet bomber capability for as long as possible by updating their electronics and improving their engines. The aircraft were adapted for carrying more advanced weapons, including stand-off missiles, but they grew in obsolescence during the mid-1960s, and many were converted for the maritime reconnaissance role, as their economical cruising range was more important than outright speed or weapon-carrying capability.

The USSR's next strategic bomber was a formidable aircraft, the variable-geometry Tu-22M 'Backfire'. Capable of Mach 2.3 at high altitude, the 'Backfire' can carry the largest free-fall nuclear weapons or a pair of stand-off missiles.

The Americans did not continue with the concept of supersonic medium bombers after the B-58, but decided instead designed a supersonic   heavy

The Tupolev Tu-95 was one of two swept-wing strategic bombers developed in the USSR from the late 1940s, initially as a back-up in the event of problems with the conceptually more advanced Myasishchyev M-4 'Bison' with turbojet propulsion. The Tu-95 resulted from a 1950 initial decision to design and develop a technically less risky bomber that could fill the operational gap that would be left should the M-4 prove unsuccessful, and was based on the extraordinarily powerful NK-12 turboprop. The engine and its contra-rotating propeller unit were a great technical risk, but in structural terms the Tu-95 was not, for it was derived ultimately from the Tu-4. The Tu-95/1 first of two proto-types flew in September 1955 and revealed generally satisfactory performance and handling even though there were severe engine/propeller problems that were probably responsible for the loss of this aeroplane. The Tu-95/2 second prototype followed the Tu-95/1 into the air in February 1955. With the engine/propeller problems reduced – though not eliminated – the new bomber entered service early in 1956 as the Tu-95M that soon received the NATO reporting name 'Bear-A'.

bomber for the penetration role. This aeroplane was the Rockwell B-1, which offered excellent capabilities in a role that became obsolete in the face of a steadily improved Soviet surface-to-air missile capability. The B-1 project was therefore cancelled in its high-supersonic B-1A form, only to be reinstated later as the more modestly supersonic B-1B Lancer, optimised for the low-level role. As an alternative to the B-1A, the Americans decided to procure more ballistic missiles (both submarine- and land-launched) and large numbers of the new generation of cruise missiles. These small turbofan-powered 'aircraft' carry a potent warhead, and are guided by an inertial navigation system (INS) that is updated over major landmarks by

Light bombers have been in decline since the end of World War II, principally because attack fighters can pack almost as great a punch and are considerably cheaper to build and operate. There have been two classic examples: the British-built English Electric Canberra, and the Soviet Ilyushin Il-28 'Beagle'. The Canberra was conceived in 1945, and the first prototype flew in 1949. Since then the aircraft has served with great distinction in many air forces, including that of the United States, and still has a limited future in smaller air forces. Extremely versatile and manoeuvrable, the Canberra could outfly most of the fighters of its heyday, and established a number of records. The Il-28 flew two years before the British bomber, and despite its obsolescence is still a popular aeroplane in the countries within the former Soviet sphere of influence.

The Americans have not relied on conversions of bombers for their maritime reconnaissance aircraft, but have produced such excellent machines as the Lockheed P2V Neptune, and the Lockheed (now Lockheed Martin) P-3 Orion, derived from the Electra airliner. After years of service from the Avro Shackleton derivative of the Lincoln, the RAF currently deploys the four-engined Hawker Siddeley Nimrod, based very loosely on the Comet airliner. This is possibly the best maritime reconnaissance aeroplane in the world, and combines long endurance on two engines with a high-speed dash capability when using all four. The Nimrod is the only such aeroplane in the world powered by turbojets rather than turboprops. Several other countries have also produced useful maritime reconnaissance

The Saab 35 Draken was the first genuinely supersonic warplane of Western European design to enter production, and was a remarkable achievement for the small Swedish aircraft industry as the Draken offered basically the same performance as the English Electric Lightning with only half the power (one rather than two Rolls-Royce Avon turbojets fitted in this instance with a Swedish-designed afterburner). The key to this remarkable performance was the creation of a long aeroplane with most of the major masses piled one behind the other, resulting in an aeroplane of very small frontal area supported in the air by a 'double-delta' wing whose highly swept inboard sections were little more than the inlet ducts for the turbojet engine installed in the rear fuselage.

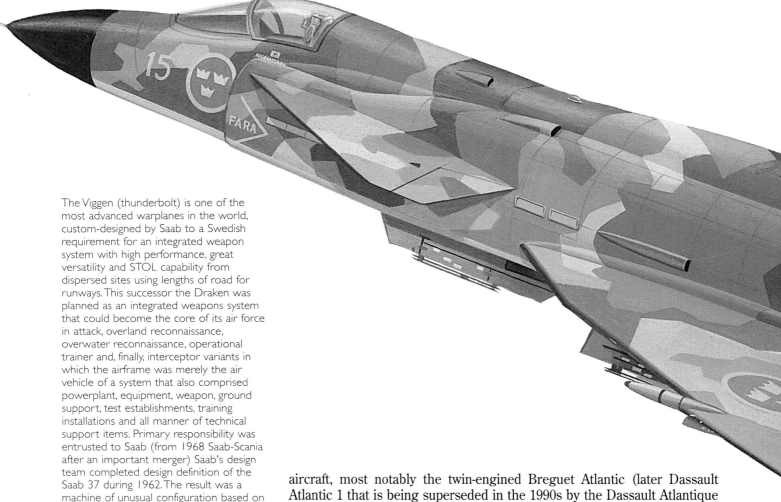

The Viggen (thunderbolt) is one of the most advanced warplanes in the world, custom-designed by Saab to a Swedish requirement for an integrated weapon system with high performance, great versatility and STOL capability from dispersed sites using lengths of road for runways. This successor the Draken was planned as an integrated weapons system that could become the core of its air force in attack, overland reconnaissance, overwater reconnaissance, operational trainer and, finally, interceptor variants in which the airframe was merely the air vehicle of a system that also comprised powerplant, equipment, weapon, ground support, test establishments, training installations and all manner of technical support items. Primary responsibility was entrusted to Saab (from 1968 Saab-Scania after an important merger) Saab's design team completed design definition of the Saab 37 during 1962. The result was a machine of unusual configuration based on a large double-delta wing, though this reversed the planform of the Draken's wing in having greater sweep outboard than inboard. This was only the start of the story, however, as the need for real STOL capability drove the rest of the basic design in a direction that was for its time most radical. Thus the double-delta wing was located at the rear of the fuselage in the low-set position, and complemented by canard foreplanes set in the shoulder position on the inlet trunks just to the rear of the cockpit. Whereas the conventional delta-winged warplane must use up-elevon to raise the nose for take-off, thereby imposing an overall download, the canard delta-winged warplane employs the lift of the canard foreplane halves to raise the nose, thereby creating an overall upload for highly beneficial effects on take-off run.

aircraft, most notably the twin-engined Breguet Atlantic (later Dassault Atlantic 1 that is being superseded in the 1990s by the Dassault Atlantique 2) landplane from France, the four-engined ShinMaywa (originally Shin Meiwa) PS-1 flying boat from Japan, and the four-engined Ilyushin Il-38 'May' landplane from the USSR.

The only other country to have produced advanced combat aircraft is Sweden, whose policy of strongly armed neutrality led to the development of the highly original and very interesting Saab 35 Draken (dragon) double-delta and Saab 37 Viggen (thunderbolt) canard multi-role aircraft, both capable of performance in the region of Mach 2. The success of these two Swedish aircraft should have been an object lesson for the West: the authorities decided what they needed, and then every effort was made to develop the right machine for the specification. Although costly, such a programme never approached the vastly expensive competitive programmes initiated in other countries.

The vast cost of advanced aircraft determined that aircraft produced by other nations have been of limited performance. In the 1960's, even the rich European countries reached the stage where collaborative projects became both financially and politically attractive: only in this way could the costs be spread to a sufficient number of taxpayers, and large, relatively economical production runs assured. Excellent examples of the trend were the SEPECAT strike, attack and reconnaissance fighter built by the United Kingdom and France, the Panavia Tornado variable-geometry multi-role combat aeroplane built by the United Kingdom, West Germany and Italy,

Developed by McDonnell Douglas in association with British Aerospace, which includes the Hawker company that developed the original Harrier, the AV-8B Harrier II is a considerably more advanced warplane that the Harrier with an uprated engine, a revised cockpit offering better fields of vision and more advanced instrumentation, a larger and more sophisticated wing of all-composite construction, superior lift-improvement devices, and provision for a somewhat larger load of more diverse and capable weapon types. These basic changes are complemented by a more advanced nav/attack system that has been complemented in later subvariants by a forward-looking infra-red sensor for passive night-attack capability, and radar for full all-weather capability.

About to enter a mid-life upgrade programme in the later 1990s, the Panavia Tornado is a collaborative British, German and Italian type optimised for the long-range interdiction role but also developed in air-superiority and electronic warfare/reconnaissance variants for the British and the Germans and Italian respectively. The Tornado IDS baseline variant illustrated here can carry a heavy external weapons load, possesses STOL capability as a result of its high-lift devices and thrust-reversing engines, can cruise over long ranges with its variable-geometry wing in the minimum- or intermediate-sweep positions, can fly very fast at very low level with its wings in the maximum-sweep position, and can undertake blind first-pass attacks with very considerable accuracy with its advanced avionics, which include terrain-following radar and an inertial navigation system.

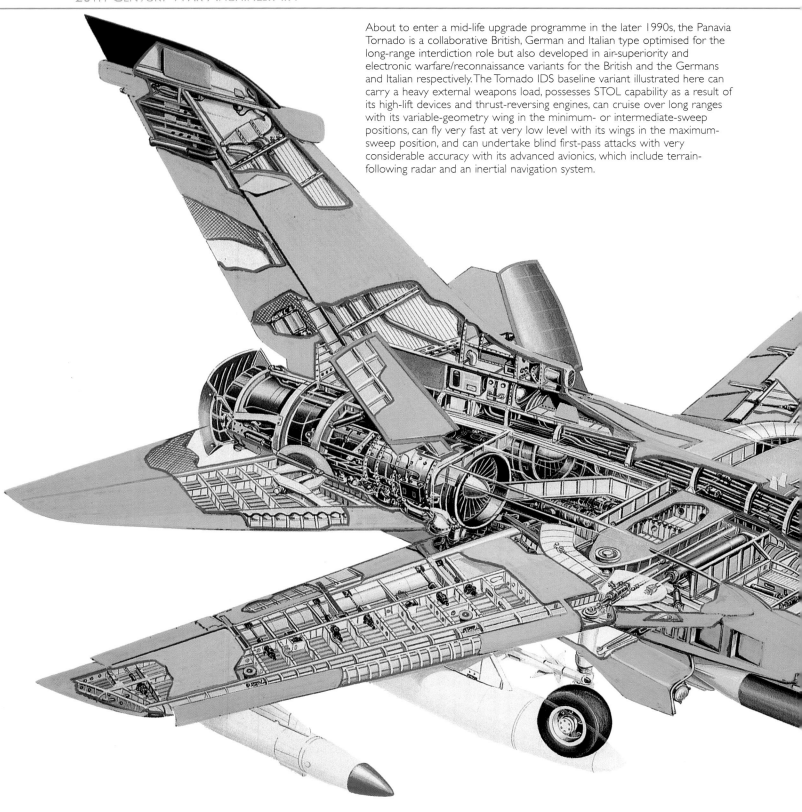

and the Dassault/Dornier Alpha Jet light attack/trainer aeroplane built by France and West Germany. Such co-operation was financially reasonable for the countries concerned and gave opportunities for the creation of exciting new aircraft.

The Hawker Siddeley (now British Aerospace) Harrier vertical take-off and landing (VTOL) aeroplane, with its radical arrangement of vectoring jetpipes to deflect the engine's thrust, was one of the last major combat aircraft to be built by a single nation, along with examples from the United States, Russia, France, China and Sweden.

During the first half of the 1980s, the United Kingdom was actively seeking partners for the collaborative development of the Agile Combat Aircraft technology demonstrator, to be built as a vital step towards the evolution of a new European combat aircraft based on the British Aerospace P.110 design, with contributions from West German and French companies: this effort finally matured as the Eurofighter 2000. The Harrier concept crossed the Atlantic to the United States, where McDonnell Douglas was largely responsible for the much enhanced AV-8B Harrier II for the US Marine Corps and, in British-assembled form, the Harrier GR.Mk 5 for the RAF.

In the field of combat aircraft capability, the features being developed in the 1980s were not performance factors as such, but were consentrated on improved combat capability through aspects such as increased agility, weapons flexibility, accuracy of navigation and weapons delivery, and operational reliability. Advances were thus being made in the sphere of avionics and the control of aircraft in all flight regimes by the use of electronically signalled control movements ('fly-by-wire' control system), advanced aerodynamics and engines with considerably improved power-to-weight ratios.

This led to a new generation of combat aircraft, epitomised by production machines such as the General Dynamics F-16 Fighting Falcon and McDonnell Douglas F/A-18 Hornet, and planned developments such as the ACA, a re-winged version of the F-16 evaluated as the F-16XL, and the Saab JAS 39 Gripen (griffon) fighter. Much was also being achieved in the enhancement of existing capabilities, exemplified by the provision of canard foreplanes on the Dassault Mirage 4000 prototype and the Israel Aircraft Industries Kfir-C2 production fighter, and by the increasing use of improved targeting aids carried as external pods.

Through the Present Into the Future

THE manned aeroplane is here to stay for the foreseeable future. During the period from the late 1950's to the early 1970s, there were hints that the manned warplane would soon be replaced by guided missiles, but this evolution has not taken place for a number of pressing technical reasons and because of the importance of an onboard crew to the operational versatility and flexibility of the warplane.

The importance of human intervention is nowhere better attested than in the control of the strategic nuclear deterrents of the two superpowers up to the time of the USSR's collapse in 1989. The USA and USSR each had large numbers of surface- and underwater-launched ballistic missiles, but they retained comparatively small but significant manned bomber forces that could be re-targeted after 'launch', could be recalled, could undertake a variety of approaches to the target, and could fly other missions with the aid of additional or different equipment.

The Soviets' most important such assets, which are still operated by some of the USSR's successor states in the Commonwealth of Independent States (CIS), such as Russia and the Ukraine, are the Tupolev Tu-22M 'Backfire' and the Tu-160 'Blackjack' variable-geometry bombers. The Tu-22M is a radical development of the disappointing Tu-22 'Blinder' fixed-wing bomber, while the TU-160 bears a striking likeness to the Rockwell B-1 Lancer, the American type designed as successor to the Boeing B-52 Stratofortress. The B-52 was designed for long-range subsonic missions, carrying free-fall nuclear weapons, but in its last B-52G and B-52H variants it was revised for ow-level penetration of Soviet airspace, armed with two North American AGM-28 Hound Dog air-to-surface supersonic cruise missiles later replaced by 12 or more Boeing AGM-86 air-to-surface subsonic cruise missiles. As a result of its extreme targeting accuracy and relative immunity to interception due to its very low-level

---

Lockheed Martin F-16 Fighting Falcon

THIS illustration shows the original F-16A with a number of its weapon options. The current F-16C differs externally only in a number of minor features such as a larger tailplane, but has the option of two considerably more powerful engines as well as a much improved suite of flight and mission avionics for a considerably improved as well as expanded capability. The primary details of the F-16C, whose pilot sits on a semi-reclining McDonnell Douglas ACES II zero/zero ejector seat and controls the fighter with his right-hand sidestick controller and left-hand throttle, include a powerplant of one General Electric F110-GE-129 or Pratt & Whitney F100-P-229 turbofan rated respectively at 29,588 or 29,100lb (13,421 or 13,200kg) st with afterburning, span of 32ft 9.75in (32.00m) including wing-tip missiles, length of 49ft 4in (15.03m), maximum take-off weight of 42,300lb (19,187kg), maximum speed of more than 1,320mph (2,124km/h) or Mach 2.0 at high altitude, service ceiling of more than 50,000ft (15,240m), tactical radius of 852 miles (1,371km) with two 2,000lb (907kg) bombs and two AIM-9 Sidewinder air-to-air missiles, and an armament of one 20 mm M61A1 Vulcan six-barrel cannon and up to 12,000lb (5,443kg) of stores carried on nine hardpoints.

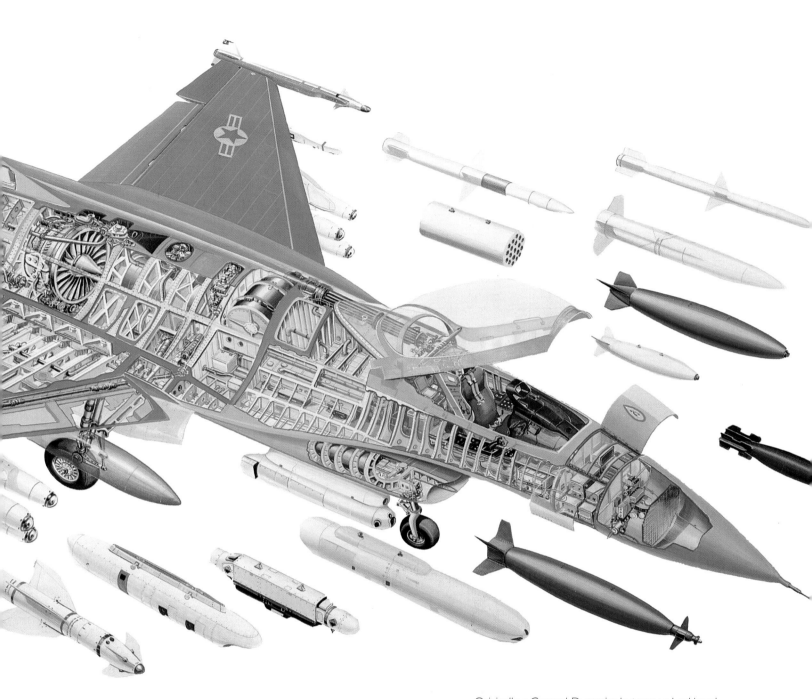

Originally a General Dynamics but now a Lockheed Martin product, the F-16 Fighting Falcon was developed initially as a light-weight fighter technology demonstrator with a fly-by-wire control system and an airframe of relaxed static stability, the combination of the two offering a level of agility considerably higher than that of machines such as the McDonnell Douglas F-4 Phantom II. So successful were the YF-16 prototypes, however, that the type was ordered into production and has since been developed into a superb multi-role fighter.

121

This trio of Lockheed (now Lockheed Martin) S-3 carrierborne anti-submarine aircraft reveals a number of interesting features. The aeroplane nearest the camera shows the magnetic anomaly detector 'sting' in the extended position for the detection of a submerged submarine by the localised effect of its large ferrous mass on the Earth's magnetic field, and the aeroplane farthest from the camera is a KS-3A inflight-refuelling tanker conversion with its drogue-tipped hose in the trailed position so that a receiver aeroplane can manoeuvre its refuelling probe into the drogue and take on fuel.

cruise altitude and 'stealthy' design, the AGM-86 offered far higher penetration capability than the AGM-28.

The B-1A was designed for high supersonic performance at high altitude, but the growing sophistication of the Soviet air-defence capability led to the type's cancellation, although it was later reinstated as the B-1B with lower overall performance, but with superior capabilities in the penetration role achieved through a large complement of cruise missiles and/or free-fall nuclear weapons. In simple financial terms, it is hard to appreciate how the B-1B programme could be justified as truly cost-effective, but in strategic and political terms there can be no doubt that the type provides the United States with important capabilities in the power-projection role, which demands extreme operational flexibility up to the moment of weapon release.

The B-1B is an exceptional illustration, inasmuch as the cost and complexity of a single-role aeroplane makes such types rare in modern air forces, where single-role aircraft are generally dedicated either to specialised reconnaissance – as exemplified by the Lockheed (now Lockheed Martin) SR-71 and the TR-1 updated version of the classic U-2 in

Concerned that a planned Super Mirage (Mirage IIIG8A with a powerplant of two SNECMA M53-3 turbofans) for the Avion de Combat Futur requirement would prove too costly for the French air force, Dassault offered the service a smaller multi-role fighter with a delta wing and single engine, this design having been prepared in 1972 as the Delta 1000. During 1975 the French air force belatedly reached the same conclusion as Dassault about the cost of the Super Mirage program, and in December of that year cancelled the ACF requirement in favour of four prototypes (complemented by a company-funded fifth machine) of the delta-winged type in a revised form dubbed Mirage 2000. Dassault was wrongly convinced that the Mirage 2000 would be much cheaper to develop and build than the Super Mirage, but was correct in anticipating that the use of the latest CCV (Control-Configured Vehicle) concepts in concert with advanced technology would make the Mirage 2000 into a warplane offering capabilities enormously superior to those of the Mirage III with basically the same layout. The core of this superior capability was the combination of relaxed static stability, an area-ruled fuselage, a cambered wing carrying automatically scheduled full-span slats on its leading edges and full-span elevons on its trailing edges, and a fly-by-wire control system. The first prototype flew in March 1978, and the type entered service in July 1984 as the Mirage 2000C fighter. The type has since been developed in a number of single- and two-seat variants for a host of roles.

American service, or the Myasishchyev M-17/55 'Mystic' entering Russian service in the mid-1990s – or to control as exemplified by the Boeing E-3A Sentry, developed from the Model 707 transport, and the Ilyushin A-50 'Mainstay' developed from the Il-76 'Candid' transport. These extremely costly aircraft have good survival chances as they are not intended for operations in the combat zone.

The SR-71 'Blackbird' was retired from first-line service in the early 1990s, but is still in limited use for experimental tasks, and a few aircraft were restored to operational capability in 1995. The SR-71 is a truly remarkable aeroplane, and remains the current holder of the world's absolute speed and altitude records. Its origins are still veiled, but it is clear that the type was planned as the launch platform for supersonic reconnaissance drones, developed initially into the YF-12A experimental interceptor and later into the SR-71 strategic reconnaissance platform. The 'Blackbird' is a massive delta-wing machine with the fuselage contours faired laterally into a lifting shape, and is powered by two afterburning bleed-turbojets running on special low-volatility fuel. Prodigiously expensive to build and to maintain, the SR-71 fleet provided the US forces with a mass of reconnaissance information after Mach 3+ flights at exceptionally high altitudes.

For the control of its armed forces, the United States deploys two types modified from civil airliners. As noted above, the Boeing E-3 Sentry is an adaptation of the Boeing 707, with a large rotodome above the fuselage containing the antenna for the very capable Westinghouse APY-1 radar. Operating at high altitude on long patrols, the E-3 can monitor all air activity within a radius of 250 miles (402km) at any altitude, while an onboard tactical team uses computers to assess data from this radar and other sources, and then directs friendly forces to deal with the threats revealed. The United States planned a fleet of 40 Sentries but in fact ordered just 34 aircraft, while later purchasers were NATO with 18, Saudi Arabia with five, France with four and the United Kingdom with seven. The USSR's first such aeroplane was the considerably less sophisticated Tupolev Tu-126 'Moss', replaced early in the 1990's by the A-50 'Mainstay' derivative of the Il-76 'Candid' transport.

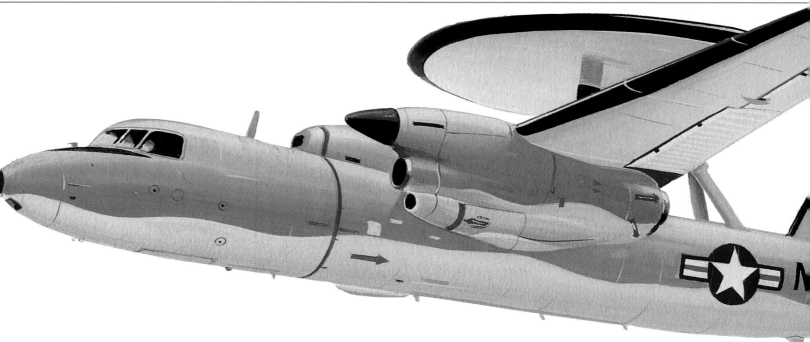

These airborne warning and control system aircraft (AWACS) are exceedingly complex yet efficient adjuncts to the tactical control of air power: essentially, they are airborne command posts, generating data for themselves and receiving inputs from other aircraft, satellites and surface forces. Each aeroplane is capable of controlling the entire range of air activities in a complete theatre of war.

The control of tactical air operations has also become increasingly important, and the world's most successful exponent of this art is the Grumman (now Northrop Grumman) E-2 Hawkeye, which was developed for carrierborne use by the US Navy and has proved itself particularly effective, notably during the Israeli invasion of Lebanon in early 1982. The E-2 was still in production during the mid-1990s for the US Navy, which had ordered almost 200 such aircraft by that time, and other purchasers include Egypt, France, Israel, Japan, Singapore and Taiwan.

Although expensive, this type of aeroplane can increase the efficiency of combat aircraft, hence the description of such aircraft as 'force multipliers'. It is probable, therefore, that AWACS aircraft are likely to figure prominently in the future plans of the major air forces. However, just as it is desirable to make full use of one's own AWACS aircraft, it is equally important to prevent the enemy from making full use of his. It seems likely, therefore, that the role of electronic counter-measures (ECM) aircraft will be extended from

Below: Better known in the West as the 'Flogger', the Mikoyan-Gurevich MiG-23 was developed as successor to the MiG-21 'Fishbed', and was better optimised for the tactical situation that developed from the later 1960s in being a larger and more comprehensively equipped (and also armed) type with a considerably more powerful engine and, perhaps most importantly of all, a variable-geometry wing planform in which the minimum-sweep position offered good field performance, the intermediate-sweep position provided good cruise performance, and the maximum-sweep position helped to generate high overall performance at the upper end of the speed range. The type was extensively developed up to the late 1980s as the MiG-23 for the fighter and to a limited extent fighter-bomber roles, and as the somewhat modified MiG-27 for the dedicated attack role with an armoured forward fuselage, and greater weapon capability.

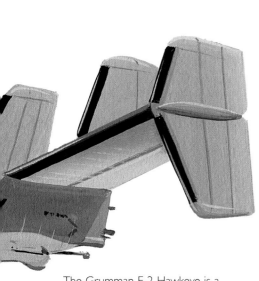

The Grumman E-2 Hawkeye is a remarkable carrierborne aeroplane offering an AWACS (Airborne Warning And Control System) capability in no way inferior in qualitative terms to that of the larger, land-based Boeing E-3 Sentry. The features that have been sacrificed to secure the capability for operations from the flightdecks of the US Navy's aircraft carriers are airframe size and engine power, and this means that the E-2 has a lower speed and shorter endurance than the E-3, although both of these elements are adequate for naval operations.

its already prominent position. The US Air Force pioneered the use of such aircraft over Vietnam in the 1960s and early 1970s, and they have proved themselves valuable aids to combat aircraft, jamming the radar of enemy ground and air missiles and hampering the use of early warning systems.

The deployment of electronic warfare aircraft increased considerably during the 1980s, primarily in the USA. Few countries can afford to purchase single-role aircraft such as the US Navy's Grumman (now Northrop Grumman) EA-6 Prowler all-weather type, which has capabilities at strategic, operational and tactical levels, and therefore rely on the extensive use of podded ECM equipment located on underwing hardpoints otherwise dedicated to the carriage of weapon and/or drop tanks. There is little doubt, however, that the increased survivability of combat aircraft carrying ECM pods more than offsets their reduced disposable warload. ECM pods are standard on the combat aircraft of all air forces with any claim to modern equipment.

Two other AEW aircraft worthy of mention are the Grumman (now Northrop Grumman) EF-111 Raven (or 'Electric Fox'), of which 42 were produced for the US Air Force as conversions of obsolescent General Dynamics F-111A long-range interdictors but with a highly automated version of the same Raytheon ALQ-99 Tactical Jamming System as carried by the EA-6 Prowler; and the Panavia Tornado ECR development of the Tornado multi-role warplane for electronic combat and reconnaissance roles, which include the detection and elimination of radars associated with enemy air-defence systems.

The United States, the former USSr, and Western European nations have introduced new combat aircraft in recent years. The most important of these are: the Mikoyan-Gurevich MiG-23 'Flogger' variable-geometry tactical fighter, the MiG-27 'Flogger' attack fighter derivative of the MiG-23, the Sukhoi Su-24 'Fencer' variable-geometry strike and attack aeroplane, and the Su-25 'Frogfoot' close-support and anti-tank aeroplane for the Warsaw Pact forces; the Fairchild Republic A-10 Thunderbolt II anti-tank aeroplane, the General Dynamics F-16 Fighting Falcon air-combat and multi-role fighter, the Grumman (now Northrop Grumman) F-14 Tomcat carrierborne multi-role fighter with a variable-geometry wing platform, the McDonnell Douglas F-15 Eagle air-superiority fighter, and the McDonnell Douglas/Northrop F/A-18 Hornet carrierborne dual-role fighter/attack aeroplane for the United States; the Dassault-Breguet Mirage F1 and Mirage 2000 for France; and the variable-geometry Panavia Tornado multi-role combat aeroplane for Italy, the United Kingdom and Germany.

Although most of these are large, expensive combat aircraft, the American F-16 and F/A-18 are lighter aircraft designed to cope with the

The McDonnell Douglas F-15 Eagle is the air-superiority counterpart of the Lockheed Martin F-16 Fighting Falcon air-combat fighter, and like its smaller colleague has been developed into a true multi-role type able to carry a heavy load of diverse 'smart' and 'dumb' air-to-surface weapons as an alternative to its primary load of short- and medium-range air-to-air missiles. The F-15 was planned as successor to the McDonnell Douglas F-4 Phantom II in its Sidewinder and Sparrow missile-armed form, and possesses a core similarity to the earlier type in its substantial twin-engined airframe with a large wing for considerable internal fuel capacity and a high rate of climb to a considerable service ceiling.

Above: Originally known as the U-2 and then as the TR-1 before returning to U-1 once more, this Lockheed Martin type is essentially a jet-powered 'glider' able to operate at very high altitudes in the reconnaissance role.

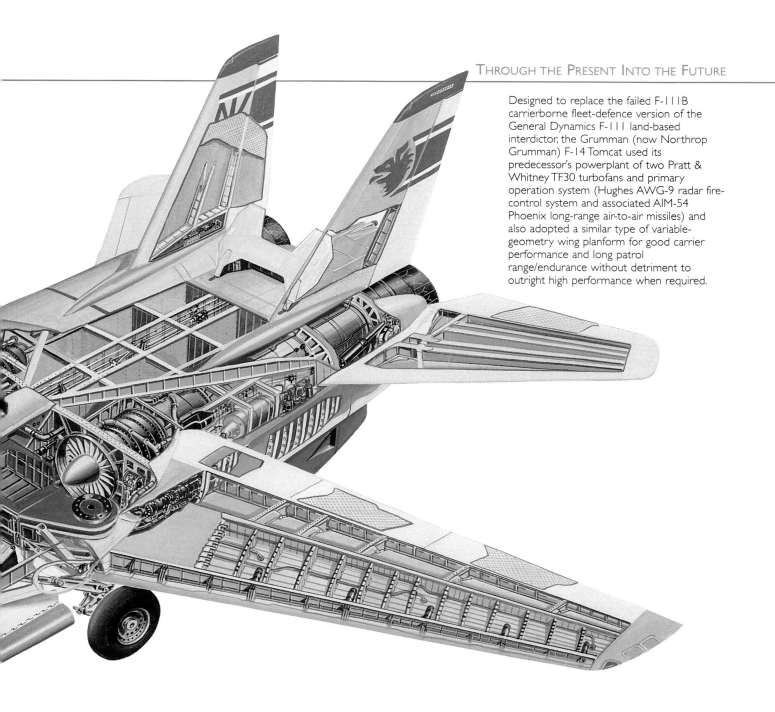

Designed to replace the failed F-111B carrierborne fleet-defence version of the General Dynamics F-111 land-based interdictor, the Grumman (now Northrop Grumman) F-14 Tomcat used its predecessor's powerplant of two Pratt & Whitney TF30 turbofans and primary operation system (Hughes AWG-9 radar fire-control system and associated AIM-54 Phoenix long-range air-to-air missiles) and also adopted a similar type of variable-geometry wing planform for good carrier performance and long patrol range/endurance without detriment to outright high performance when required.

Northrop Grumman F-14 Tomcat

CERTAINLY the most powerfully armed carrierborne fighter in the world and, despite its age, still one of the most capable air-superiority fighters of any type anywhere in the world, the F-14 Tomcat (seen here in its original F-14A version before development of the F-14D version with a different powerplant) is a high-performance platform for carriage of the AWG-9 radar system and AIM-54 Phoenix long-range AAM, of which a maximum of six can be carried, reduced to four if the underwing hardpoints are used for four AIM-9 Sidewinder short-range AAMs or alternatively for two AIM-9s and two AIM-7 Sparrow medium-range AAMs, which can also replace the AIM-54s on the underfuselage stations; there is also a 20 mm M61A1 Vulcan six-barrel cannon for dogfighting engagements. The F-14A has a crew of two (pilot and systems operator) in tandem on Martin-Baker GRU7A zero/zero ejector seats, a powerplant of two Pratt & Whitney TF-30-P-414A turbofans each rated at 20,900lb (9,480kg) st with afterburning, span of 64ft 1.5in (19.55m) spread reducing to 38 ft 2.5in (11.65m) swept, length of 62ft 8in (19.10m), empty weight of 40,104 lb (18,191kg), maximum take-off weight of 74,349 lb (33724 kg), maximum speed of 1,564mph (2,517km/h) or Mach 2.27 at 36,000ft (10,975m), initial climb rate of more than 30,000 ft (9145 m) per minute, service ceiling of more than 56,000ft (17,070m), and range of 2,000 miles (3,220km) in interceptor configuration with drop tanks.

attentions of heavier and more sophisticated combat aircraft through their extraordinary agility and the sophisticated electronics. In Europe, this tendency is illustrated in the later Dassault fighters and the SEPECAT Jaguar strike fighter. The move towards variable-geometry layouts combines economy and low landing speed with high combat speed, while new alloys and materials such as carbon-fibre and high-strength plastics are also being introduced.

At a purely tactical level, the tendency away from Mach 2+ performance towards much reduced performance is best exemplified by the A-10 Thunderbolt II, which is a twin-engined type intended for the battlefield anti-tank and close-support roles. Almost ugly in appearance, the A-10 has a combination of exceptional strength and complete redundancy of principal systems, providing a high level of battlefield survivability. Comparatively cheap to buy, operate and maintain, the A-10 performs well in terms of endurance and agility at low altitudes with a large payload, and is capable of delivering heavy offensive loads of free-fall or precision-guided weapons very accurately in the face of intense anti-aircraft fire. Other nations have already experimented with this type of machine, but usually in the form of a counter-insurgency aircraft based on light aircraft or primary trainers. The Soviet (now Russian) equivalent to the A-10 is the Sukhoi Su-25 'Frogfoot', which was revealed to be in limited service over Afghanistan in 1982, and has since been developed both into a carrierborne and a land-based attack fighter, offering offensive capabilities

The McDonnell Douglas F-15 Eagle is a thoroughbred fighter with much in common with the same company's F-4 Phantom II at the conceptual level in features such as the large and only modestly swept wing, and the boomed carriage of the tail unit: on this F-4 this is a single unit above the twin-engined powerplant, but on the F-15 it comprises paired units outside the twin-engined powerplant.

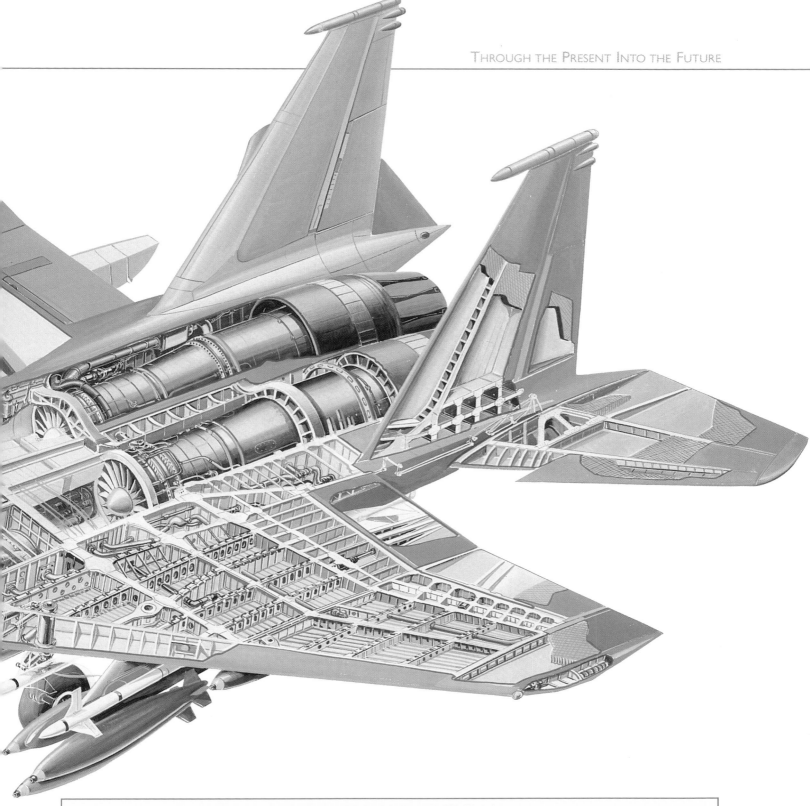

McDonnell Douglas F-15 Eagle

THE McDonnell Douglas F-15 Eagle air-superiority fighter is a large and highly capable type offering multi-role as well as interception capabilities, and is notable for its ability to carry CFTs (Conformal Fuel Tanks) on the outsides of its inlet trunks for considerably more fuel and tangential weapon-carriage capability. The single-seat variants are the baseline F-15A with APG-63 radar and a powerplant of two Pratt & Whitney F100-P-100 turbofans each rated at 23,380lb (10,809kg) with afterburning, and the F-15C with significantly enhanced APG-70 radar and an uprated powerplant. The two-seat models are the combat-capable F-15B and F-15D equivalent to the F-15A and F-15C respectively, and the F-15E long-range interdictor with CFTs and much enhanced weapons capability. The F-15C is powered by two Pratt & Whitney F100-P-220 turbofans each rated at 23,450lb (10,637kg) st with afterburning. The fighter's other data include a span of 42ft 9.75in (13.05m), length of 63ft 9in (19.43m), maximum take-off weight of 68,000lb (30,844kg), maximum speed of more than 1,650mph (2,655km/h) or Mach 2.5 at 36,000ft (10,975m), initial climb rate of more than 50,000ft (15,240m) per minute, service ceiling of 60,000ft (18,290m), and tactical range of 1,222 miles (1,967km) in the interception role. The F-15C is armed with one 20 mm M61A1 Vulcan six-barrel cannon and can carry 23,600lb (10,705kg) of external stores on nine hardpoints.

comparable with those of the A-10 in addition to slightly higher performance. By the end of the 1980s the US Air Force had decided that the A-10 was obsolescent, and planned to adopt a derivative of the F-16 as its close air support/battlefield air interdiction (CAS/BAI) type. This plan was proceeding in the mid-1990s despite the fact that the A-10 proved itself a truly formidable aeroplane in intended role during the 1991 UN-led campaign to liberate Kuwait. Indeed, the success of the A-10, attracted considerable interest from countries looking to purchase second-hand aircraft.

Another type that had proved its military attractions, but yet failed to secure the success it really deserves is the VTOL aeroplane exemplified by the British Aerospace Harrier. Modern airfields, with their large expanses of runway and taxiway, are very vulnerable to the type of air and/or missile attack that can render them unusable even if they are not actually destroyed, and this poses enormous practical problems for the continued viability of conventional air power. The VTOL aeroplane is immune to this limitation, as it can operat from just behind the front line of even a highly mobile campaign.

The original Harrier was supplanted during the late 1980s and early 1990s by the Harrier II, developed jointly by McDonnell Douglas and British Aerospace for service with the US Marine Corps and RAF as the AV-8B and Harrier GR.Mk 5 respectively. The Harrier II is altogether superior to the original model in most operational aspects, as a result of its larger yet lighter wing, improved cockpit, greater load-carrying capability, more powerful engine and enhanced lift-improvement devices. Continued development has produced the Night-Attack Harrier with provision for the sensors that make possible an electronically silent night attack, and the radar-equipped Harrier II Plus which is under final development in the mid-1990s.

The only derivative of the original Harrier to remain in service in the mid-1990s is the British Aerospace Sea Harrier, which was evolved towards the end of the 1970s to provide the FAA with a radar-carrying multi-role fighter, reconnaissance and strike (attack) aeroplane able to operate from the three small Royal Navy aircraft-carriers. The type was rushed into service in time to play a highly distinguished role in the 1982 recapture of the Falklands Islands from Argentine occupation. The original Sea Harrier FRS.Mk 1 is being supplemented by the Sea Harrier F/A.Mk 2 (previously FRS.Mk 2), with superior radar and the ability to carry a larger load of more advanced weapons.

An Anglo-French collaborative programme, the SEPECAT Jaguar was planned as a supersonic advanced trainer, but proved so successful that most production aircraft were completed in single-seat attack form. The type has STOL field performance, the stalky landing gear provides good ground clearance for the loading of bulky external stores, and the availability of a high-grade nav/attack system (without radar) provides for blind first-pass attack capability.

With a larger wing and more powerful engine than the BAe (originally Hawker Siddeley) Harrier, the McDonnell Douglas/BAe AV-8 Harrier II STOVL (Short Take-Off and Vertical Landing) warplane offers a significantly improved weapon-carriage capability, and had been adopted by Italy and Spain in addition to the USA and UK.

Seen here in the form of the first of two YA-10A prototypes, the Fairchild Republic A-10A Thunderbolt II is a dedicated tank-killing and close support warplane with great strength, large quantities of armour, redundant structures and systems, and a twin-engined powerplant provided with enhanced survivability by the wide separation of the two engines and the shielding against ground fire offered by the wing and tail. The primary armament is one 30 mm GAU-8/A Avenger seven-barrel cannon firing depleted uranium projectiles, and up to 16,000 lb (7528 kg) of disposable stores (including up to six Hughes AGM-65 Maverick air-to-surface missiles) carried on 11 hardpoints.

The United States and the United Kingdom are collaborating in a project for a supersonic short take-off, vertical landing (STVOL) combat aeroplane; the only other contender in this major but wholly underestimated field has been the former USSR, where the VTOL/STOVL development is the work of the Yakovlev design bureau, whose first operational aeroplane of this type was the Yak-38 'Forger' carrierborne attack aircraft. The bureau designed the Yak-141 'Freehand' as a supersonic successor, but a number of crashes and an acute shortage of funding led to the cancellation of this programme.

The performance plateau reached with current military aircraft results from reliance on aluminium alloys as the primary structural medium, and this precludes sustained speeds in excess of Mach 2.25. Titanium is used in cases where heat is likely to be extreme, but the cost of this metal prohibits its use on a large scale. Composite materials of various kinds became more common during the 1980s, but their costs were also high and their applications somewhat specialised. Later in the decade, however, continued development of aeronautical materials made feasible the greater use of composite materials for load-carrying structures and increased use of advanced alloys of lithium and aluminium. The gradual acceptance of these high-technology materials

131

The McDonnell Douglas F/A-18 Hornet is the single most important warplane in the US Navy's carrierborne inventory, for it is a single type that can undertake both the fighter and the attack roles by a simple change of software in the mission computer. The type emerged from the same light-weight fighter technology demonstration programme as the General Dynamics (now Lockheed Martin) F-16 Fighting Falcon, and was originally a Northrop design.

did not indicate any desire for higher performance, but rather the desire to reduce weight without sufficient strength, and to simplify the production and maintenance of complex structures.

In the context of the performance plateau, it is worth noting that experience in combat has provided ample evidence that Mach 2 performance is more than adequate under most operational and tactical conditions; in the Vietnam conflict, the Arab Israeli wars and the Falklands campaign, supersonic combat proved exceptionally rare. Even when combat was initiated at supersonic speed, the combatants were soon slowed to subsonic speed as they lost energy in supersonic manoeuvres. The lesson learnt from these wars therefore, is that while supersonic performance may be useful for the approach to combat and for interception when targets may be engaged beyond visual range, most military aircraft gain little real advantage from supersonic performance. More important are the factors of

good manoeuvrability at high subsonic speed and an armament that includes a gun capable of high rates of fire for short-range engagements where missiles cannot be used.

Manoeuvrability cannot easily be improved on an existing aircraft except in small measure, by palliatives such as special flap settings. However, there are exceptions such as delta-wing aircraft whose agility can be enhanced very considerably by the addition of canard foreplanes. These smooth the airflow over the wing at high angles of attack and, if movable, supplement the trailing edge elevons to produce considerable increases in longitudinal control response. Such foreplanes were added to the IAI Kfir (lion cub), the unlicensed Israeli-built derivative of the Dassault Mirage, to produce the markedly superior Kfir-C2 and its Kfir-C7 upgraded version, and in 1982 the French manufacturer decided to follow IAI's lead and offer a similarly upgraded Mirage III/5 as either new-build aircraft or, as has proved more popular, retrofit of existing aircraft. South Africa later moved along the same path to produce its Atlas Cheetah upgrade of the Mirage III with canard foreplanes, a much revised wing, and more advanced electronics of the same basic type fitted in the Kfir.

During the Vietnam War, the Americans found that their primary Mach 2+ fighters were not proving to be as successful as anticipated against the

When France refused to deliver the Dassault Mirage 5 clear-weather fighters for which it had paid in advance, Israel responded by developing its own derivative of the Mirage III as the IAI Kfir with more advanced Israeli electronics, the more powerful General Electric J79 turbojet and, in its definitive form, canard foreplanes for considerably improved field performance and combat agility.

Now disappearing from service, the Lockheed F-104 Starfighter was developed after the Korean War to provide the US Air Force with a 'manned missile' for the fast-climbing interception role. Only modest numbers were built for the USAF in the interceptor and adapted tactical fighter roles, but then came very large orders for the F-104G multi-role fighter version.

The Dassault Mirage 2000 is an extremely capable multi-role warplane that uses modern aerodynamics, a design of relaxed static stability, and a fly-by-wire control system to overcome the energy-sapping tendencies of the delta wing planform in lower-altitude manoeuvring flight.

less advanced Mikoyan-Gurevich fighters operated by the North Vietnamese air force. It was this air campaign that revealed the value of agility at high subsonic speeds, when the MiG-17 'Fresco', MiG-19 'Farmer' and MiG-21 'Fishbed' fighters managed to outfly machines such as the F-100 Super Sabre, Lockheed F-104 Starfighter, F-105 Thunderchief, F-4 Phantom II and F-8 Crusader. The US forces, and especially the US Air Force, instituted a massive research programme that resulted in the creation of two of history's most important military aircraft. The General Dynamics YF-16 prototype proved so superb that it was placed in production as the F-16 Fighting Falcon, while the Northrop YF-17 provided the starting point for the McDonnell Douglas/Northrop F/A-18 Hornet. These aircraft were designed to complement he heavier and less agile McDonnell Douglas F-15 Eagle and Grumman (now Northrop Grumman) F-14 Tomcat respectively, whose origins pre-dated the experiences of Vietnam. While the heavier fighters had a power-to-weight ratio close to or exceeding unity, which gave them excellent speed and rate of climb for the interceptor role, the lighter fighters were machines with less outright performance but far greater agility in the air combat role.

The F-16 was among the first service aircraft (with the Panavia Tornado) to use 'fly-by-wire' control, in which the pilot is linked to his control surfaces not by mechanical or hydraulic systems, but by means of computer-

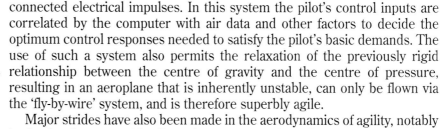

connected electrical impulses. In this system the pilot's control inputs are correlated by the computer with air data and other factors to decide the optimum control responses needed to satisfy the pilot's basic demands. The use of such a system also permits the relaxation of the previously rigid relationship between the centre of gravity and the centre of pressure, resulting in an aeroplane that is inherently unstable, can only be flown via the 'fly-by-wire' system, and is therefore superbly agile.

Major strides have also been made in the aerodynamics of agility, notably in the development of leading-edge root extensions (LERXes) by Northrop for its YF-17 experimental fighter. These LERXes are highly important in the F/A-18 Hornet, and have been incorporated in the Northrop F-5 Tiger II light fighter; they were also featured in the superb Northrop F-20A Tigershark multi-role fighter that could have entered service in the late 1980s or early 1990s but failed to secure a production order for a variety of reasons, many of them politically inspired. Other aerodynamic advances have been made possible by the development of new materials that permit the use of forward-swept wings, which offer the same advantages as the swept-back wing while affording distinct improvement in flight at high angles of attack.

Although it was weel known that the Soviets' huge numerical advantage over the Western alliance was more than counterbalanced by the technical superiority of weapons fielded by the West, it became clear through the 1970s and 1980s that the Soviets were rapidly closing the technological gap. Indeed, this fact was stunningly revealed when the West was first allowed to gain a glimpse of two new-generation Soviet combat aircraft, the Mikoyan-Gurevich MiG-29 'Fulcrum' and Sukhoi Su-27 'Flanker', which appeared in the late 1980s as the Soviet counterparts of the F-16 and F-15. Exhibition flights demonstrated that both Soviet aircraft possessed incredible agility,

The Northrop (now Northrop Grumman) F-5 series was developed in the later 1950s to provide the less technically sophisticated of the USA's allies with a slightly supersonic warplane that could use small and poorly equipped air bases, would be cheap to buy and affordable to operate, and yet would still provide useful capabilities for defensive warfare. The series started with the F-5A single-seat fighter and F-5B two-seat trainer variants of the radarless Freedom Fighter model, and then progressed to the F-5E single-seat fighter and F-5F combat-capable two-seat trainer of the radar-fitted Tiger II series with a number of aerodynamic improvements as well as an uprated powerplant.

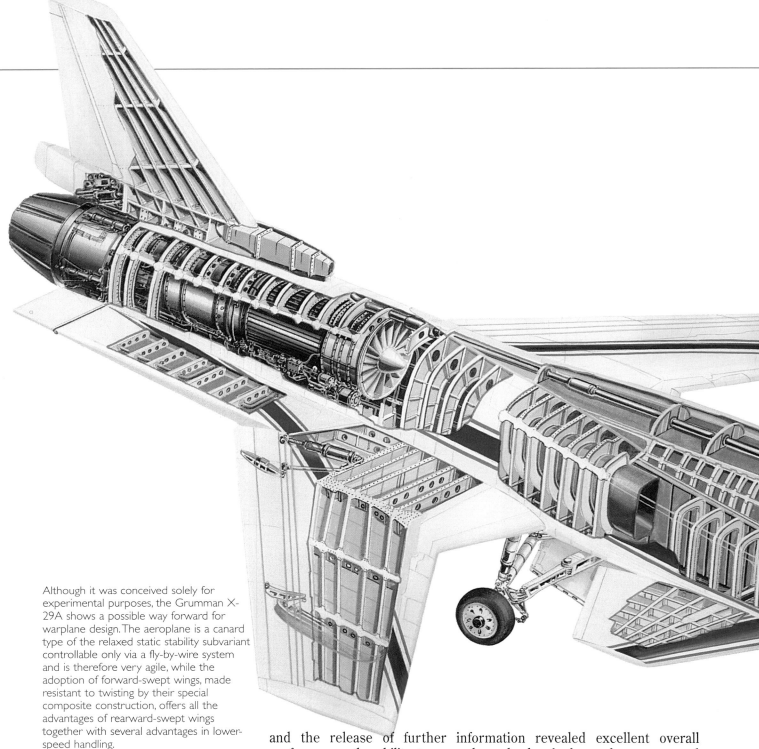

Although it was conceived solely for experimental purposes, the Grumman X-29A shows a possible way forward for warplane design. The aeroplane is a canard type of the relaxed static stability subvariant controllable only via a fly-by-wire system and is therefore very agile, while the adoption of forward-swept wings, made resistant to twisting by their special composite construction, offers all the advantages of rearward-swept wings together with several advantages in lower-speed handling.

and the release of further information revealed excellent overall performance, the ability to carry large loads of advanced weapons, and electronic capabilities generally equal to those of their Western counterparts, and in some areas (notably the IR search and track sensors) superior to anything available in the West.

The technologically and industrially advanced nations of the Western alliance are gradually overhauling this marginal Russian lead, however, with a new generation of combat aircraft. The US Air Force, for example, began to operate very small numbers of the Lockheed (now Lockheed Martin) F-117 Sky Knight 'stealthy' attack fighter and Northrop Grumman B-2 Spirit strategic bomber from 1983 and 1994 respectively, and another advanced type scheduled for delivery early in the next century is the Lockheed Martin/Boeing F-22 Rapier advanced tactical fighter. These aircraft mark a quantum advance over their predecessors in terms of low-observability, which is the 'stealthiness' that allows them to operate with minimal chance

The CF-18A is the Canadian land-based counterpart of the McDonnell Douglas F/A-18A Hornet single-seat fighter and attack warplane operated by the US Navy and US Marine Corps, but differs on no significant detail from the F/A-18 baseline version.

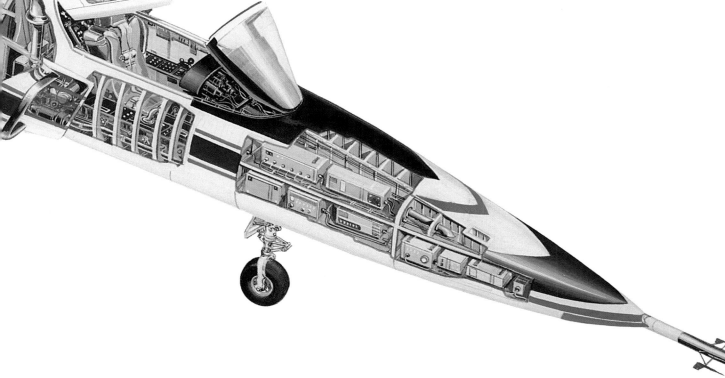

137

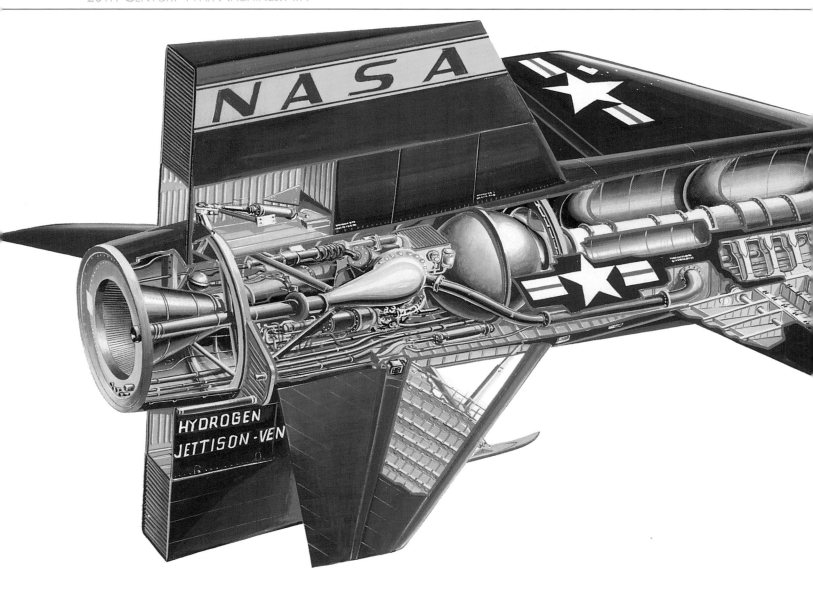

HYDROGEN
JETTISON-VEN

Another type that was conceived and operated exclusively in the experimental arena, the North American X-15 was a rocket-powered type launched at high altitude from a motherplane for the exploration of highly supersonic flight conditions in the upper atmosphere, or rather in the interface between the atmosphere and space, and for the testing of ablative coatings for re-entry vehicles. Even so, many of the lessons learned with the X-15 were applied to later generations of military aircraft.

of detection by any enemy air-defence systems. This 'stealthiness' is derived from very careful internal and external design to minimise angles or flat sections that can reflect radar signals, equally careful design of the exterior surfaces and engine exhausts to minimise visual, acoustic and thermal signatures, and reliance on passive sensors in place of earlier aircraft's active sensors such as radar. (A radar beam is as 'visible' in its sector of the electromagnetic spectrum as the light beam of a lighthouse on a dark night in the visual light sector of the spectrum.) The emphasis on such aircraft, in terms of development urgency and procurement totals, has been scaled down following the collapse of the former USSR, but the fact that US forces may still face high-technology threats in other parts of the world is constantly borne in mind.

Russia is still actively involved in the development of advanced combat aircraft, but is beset by political and financial problems, and is therefore unlikely to emerge as a realistic successor to the USSR in terms of military power. The country inherited the bulk of the USSR's military machine, with lesser portions going to the Ukraine and the other ex-Soviet republics that now constitute the CIS.

It was the threat from the USSR that spurred the development of other

modern weapons for the Western bloc. So far as aircraft are concerned, these range from light multi-role tactical fighters such as the Italo-Brazilian AMX to advanced tactical combat aircraft such as the Dassault Rafale (squall) for the French air force and naval air arm, and the Eurofighter 2000 for the British, German, Italian and Spanish air forces. The AMX is operational, and the Rafale and Eurofighter 2000 are due to enter service at the beginning of the next century, although some of the programmes' most advanced elements have been curtailled and planned procurement has been scaled down. It is worth noting that the Rafale and Eurofighter 2000, together with the JAS 39 Gripen (griffon) that is further advanced towards production for the Swedish air force, are of the 'modern' configuration with canard foreplanes and an aft-mounted delta wing controlled via a 'fly-by-wire' system for extreme agility and the capability to fly at very high angles of attack.

All three Western types are inherently 'stealthy', have advanced powerplants offering a very high power-to-weight ratio in afterburner, and have electronics based on a digital databus system for the maximum exploitation of active and passive sensors, advanced computers, and the very latest in disposable weapons. These are all features of the combat aircraft ofthe next century.

The Lockheed Martin F-117 Night Hawk is a 'stealthy' attack warplane designed for subsonic flight but possessing the ability to tackle and destroy high-value point targets with precision-guided munitions by using its special structure and design to avoid detection and therefore interception and destruction.

Above: A YF-22 refuels while a F-16 flies in support. The F-22 was created by a consortium of Lockheed, General Dynamics, and Boeing to make the first American fighter of the 21st century.

Below: A F-117 ready for takeoff. The F-117 Stealth fighter was announced in November 1988 by the U.S. Government. Lockheed was commissioned to build a radar-evading fighter. It took only 31 months to produce this unconventional plane and achieve its first flight. The shape of the aircraft is arranged to absorb or reflect enemy radar beams away from it.

Right: A B-2 Stealth Bomber flying on a test flight over the desert in the American West. Details of this aircraft are closely guarded by the U.S. Government. The B-2 is a strategic long-range, heavy bomber, meant to be invisible to enemy radar and sensors.

Helicopters

The Early Helicopter

T HE earliest type of flying machine of which there is still definite evidence was a model helicopter. It resembled a small horizontal four-bladed windmill that lifted into the air when its spindle was rotated by a drawstring. The image of this model dates from about 1325, so it seems likely that the concept of what we now call the helicopter has fascinated aviation pioneers since the early fourteenth century.

In about 1500 the great Italian polymath, artist and inventor, Leonardo da Vinci, turned his fertile mind to the helicopter, although he had no concept of true aerodynamic lift. His drawing for a helicopter demonstrates its designer's natural genius and could possibly have risen into the air if built in model form, but the design was very eccentric – it was basically an airscrew in the literal sense of the word: a helical wing which, if rotated, would have 'screwed' itself up into the air.

This and later designs might have worked in model form but would have been completely impractical in full-size form because they ignored the problems of control, most especially over the effects of the rotor's torque. Like the aeroplane, the helicopter in its definitive form is based on the concept of aerodynamic lift. While a conventional aeroplane is propelled forward so that the circulation of air past the wings generates lift, the helicopter relies on the rotation of the rotor to create the flow of air past the rotor blades for the generation of lift.

The concept of helicopter flight, incorporating as its major elements the possibility of vertical take-off and of hovering, continued to fascinate men in the centuries after Leonardo's death. Extraordinary and sometimes technically interesting models were developed, but all these pioneers lacked two essentials: a true understanding of the nature of lift and an engine of adequate power-to-weight ratio. Sir George Cayley drew up plans for a helicopter in 1796 and 1853, and in 1842 W.H. Phillips produced a fascinating model driven by a steam engine: the most interesting feature of the Phillips model were the steam jets issuing from the tips of the rotor blades to drive the lifting elements, in a torqueless fashion that still attracts the designers of helicopters.

Only with the invention of the light petrol engine towards the end of the nineteenth century, however, was it possible for the pioneers to move forward from models towards full-sized machines. Here they came face to face with the first basic problem of helicopter development, how to control the reaction to the torque of the spinning rotor: in practical terms, this means that as the blades of the rotor turn around their vertical shaft, the fuselage

Arguably the first successful helicopter, the Focke-Achgelis Fa 61 (originally the Focke-Wulf Fw 61) of 1937 was a workable although clumsy machine with two counter-rotating rotors, each possessing a diameter of 22ft 11.625in (7.00m), carried at the tips of two long outrigger arms. The helicopter was powered by a Siemens-Halske Sh.14A radial piston engine rated at 160hp (119kW), had a maximum take-off weight of 2,100lb (953kg), and was characterised by performance that included a cruising speed of 62mph (100km/h) at sea level, service ceiling of 8,600ft (2,620m) and range of 143 miles (230km).

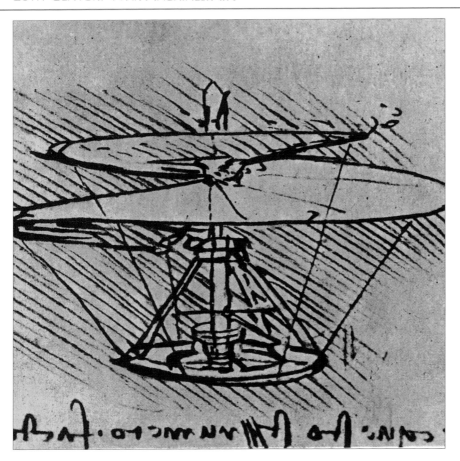

A remarkable achievement for its time (the end of the fifteenth and beginning of the sixteenth centuries, the 'helicopter' designed by Leonardo da Vinci was really a type of helical airscrew but lacked adequate motive power and also any means of control.

tends, by reaction, to rotate in the opposite direction. The pioneers saw several ways of overcoming this problem, such as the use of contra-rotating rotors on co-axial shafts, counter-rotating rotors on different shafts, or a small propeller mounted vertically at the rear end of the fuselage to hold the tail steady against the torque reaction. They could even suggest a practical means of moving the helicopter forward, backward and sideways: the axis of the rotor would be tilted to provide lift in the direction the pilot wished to take.

The problem that caused most difficulty in the development of fully practical helicopters, however, was cyclic pitch control of the type first expounded by

The Breguet-Richet Gyroplane II of 1908 was powered by a 55hp (41kW) Renault engine and was basically of aeroplane configuration with a fuselage and tail unit as well as small wings that provided an additional 538sq ft (50sq m) of lifting area to supplement the two forward-tilting rotors, each with a diameter of 25ft 9in (7.85m) for a total rotary lifting area of 1,041.9sq ft (96.8sq m). The machine made a number of successful flights in the summer of 1908 before being damaged in a heavy landing, and was then rebuilt as the Gyroplane II bis that made only one test flight before a storm wrecked the machine in its hangar during May 1909.

The Breguet-Richet Gyroplane II bis is pictured during its brief life in 1909. The loss of this machine helped to persuade Louis Breguet, also discouraged by the current lack of piston engines offering a high power-to-weight ratio, to cease work on rotary-wing aircraft until the 1930s, when he returned to the fray with the Breguet-Dorand Gyroplane Laboratoire that was probably completed in November 1933.

G.A. Crocco in 1906: when a helicopter lifts vertically in still air, the speed of the airflow over all the rotor's blades is equal and so too is the lift generated by each blade right through a complete rotation; but when the helicopter moves forward, the movement of air over any advancing blade is greater than that over any retreating blade, resulting in greater lift on the side of the advancing blades and thus a tendency to roll in the direction of the retreating blades. The solution was as readily appreciated as the problem, but the means of turning this solution into a practical method of cyclic pitch control (the adjustment of rotor blade pitch so that the lift is equal on each side of the central shaft) was altogether more taxing.

This concept of altering the rotor blades' angle of incidence as they turned, with the objective of balancing the lift by decreasing the angle of incidence of the advancing blades and increasing that of the retreating blades, was fraught with technical problems and few engineers seemed to realise exactly what was needed. The isolated figure of the Danish pioneer J.C. Ellehammer, who made interesting advances in the design of fixed-wing aircraft, was perhaps the first man to build a helicopter with adequate provision for incidence control, in 1912. The machine was unsuccessful, however, and like his fixed-wing designs it failed to become well known because of Ellehammer's solitary way of life. This was a hindrance to the evolution of flight, for Ellehammer conceived a number of technical advances that had to await reinvention by later designers.

By 1912, two French helicopters had left the ground, although neither could be said to have flown in the proper sense of the word since neither had cyclic pitch control nor any other means of adopting a given course in the air. The first was built by the Breguet brothers. Powered by a 50hp (37.3kW) Antoinette engine, this Breguet-Richet Gyroplane I first rose into the air at Douai in September 1907: four men, one at each corner of the machine, had to steady

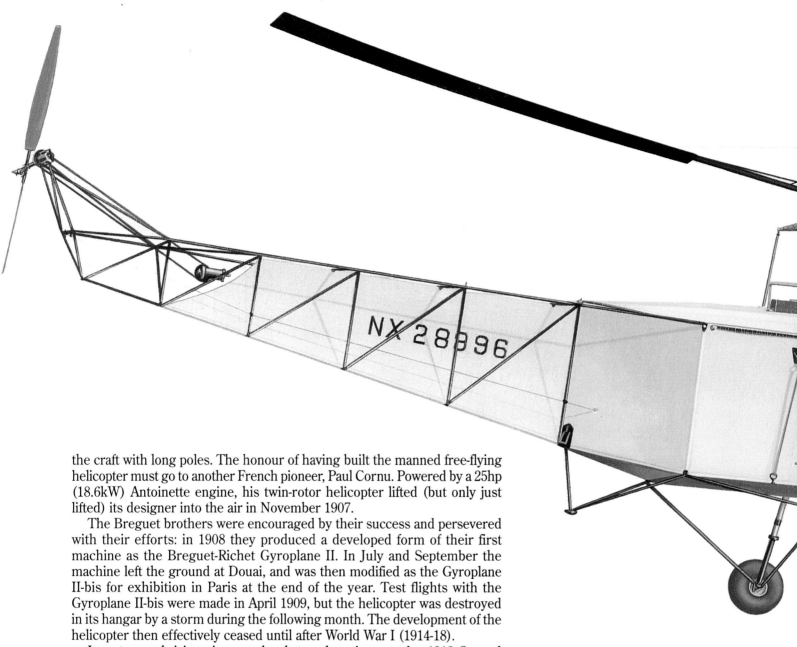

the craft with long poles. The honour of having built the manned free-flying helicopter must go to another French pioneer, Paul Cornu. Powered by a 25hp (18.6kW) Antoinette engine, his twin-rotor helicopter lifted (but only just lifted) its designer into the air in November 1907.

The Breguet brothers were encouraged by their success and persevered with their efforts: in 1908 they produced a developed form of their first machine as the Breguet-Richet Gyroplane II. In July and September the machine left the ground at Douai, and was then modified as the Gyroplane II-bis for exhibition in Paris at the end of the year. Test flights with the Gyroplane II-bis were made in April 1909, but the helicopter was destroyed in its hangar by a storm during the following month. The development of the helicopter then effectively ceased until after World War I (1914-18).

Inventors and visionaries were hard at work again soon after 1918. Several experimental types managed to rise into the air, but none of them achieved anything more than that. It was May 1924 before another French pioneer, Etienne Oehmichen, made the world's first closed-circuit helicopter flight of 0.62 miles (1km) in his four-rotor Oehmichen No.2 machine, at Arlonans. This was an advance, but only a marginal advance, for the problems of control were still formidable.

Incidence and pitch control were at last brought to a practical level by the experiments of an Argentine pioneer, the Marquis Raoul Pateras de Pescara, who produced a series of helicopters in Spain and France between 1919 and 1925. Yet this far-sighted man, whose machines had clearly overcome the main problem of unequal lift, was denied fame by his failure in the matter of torque control. In other respects the Pescara helicopters were good machines, and showed what could be anticipated once full control had been achieved.

Other pioneers active in the early 1920s were the American Henry Berliner, who made a successful hovering flight in 1922 after having considered the

Opposite: The photograph shows Igor Sikorsky himself at the controls of the VS-300 prototype during 1940. This reveals the prototype in its original form with a small enclosed tailboom carrying the anti-torque rotor.

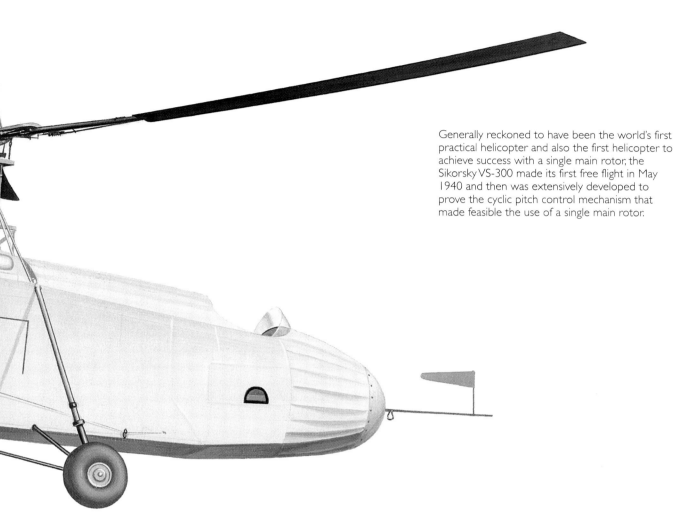

Generally reckoned to have been the world's first practical helicopter and also the first helicopter to achieve success with a single main rotor, the Sikorsky VS-300 made its first free flight in May 1940 and then was extensively developed to prove the cyclic pitch control mechanism that made feasible the use of a single main rotor.

problem since 1905, de Bothezat also in the United States, and Louis Brennan, superintendent of the United Kingdom's torpedo factory during World War I and later head of the rotorcraft department at the Royal Aircraft Establishment at Farnborough. Like Oehmichen, all these men saw their hopes founder on the problems of cyclic pitch control.

The key figure in the development of rotary-wing flight was a Spaniard, Juan de la Cierva. The machine he invented (and patented as the Autogiro) was not a helicopter, however, but rather the gyroplane or, as it later became, the autogyro. In this type of machine, the lifting rotor is unpowered: lift is generated by the freely windmilling overhead rotor as an engine and conventional propeller drive the machine through the air. Most early autogyros had a tractor engine/propeller combination at the front of the aeroplane-type fuselage, while most later autogyros have used a pusher engine/propeller combination at the rear of a fuselage nacelle that also supports the conventional tail unit by means of a boom extending rearward under the propeller. The autogyro depends on forward motion in the air, without which the rotor will stop revolving and the machine will fall, albeit safely with some lift still generated by the freely windmilling rotor.

Cierva's driving passion was the creation of heavier-than-air craft that could not be stalled, as had happened in the fatal crash of his first fixed-wing aeroplane. Cierva's first three Autogiros, the C.1 to C.3 built and tested between 1920 and 1922, failed because of their use of inflexible rotor blades. In 1922, however, Cierva built a model with articulated hinges that permitted the blades to flap: as they rotated the blades were thus free to fall as they retreated at a lower relative speed and rise as they advanced at a higher relative speed, thereby modifying the apparent angle of attack and equalising the amount of lift generated on each side of the rotor. This system was applied to the C.4 Autogiro that made its first successful flight during January 1923. Cierva had understood the full nature of the problem and had found a practical solution to it. The real beauty of the system lay in its simplicity: the blades moved automatically until the whole rotating system was in equilibrium.

Opposite: Another photograph reveals Igor Sikorsky at the controls of the VS-300 prototype during April 1941, after the machine had been revised with a more fully enclosed fuselage and twin-float alighting gear for trials into the helicopter's suitability for waterborne operation.

The Flettner Fl 185 that first flew in 1936 was an overly complex prototype with a single 160hp (119kW) Siemens-Halske Sh.14A radial engine mounted in the nose to drive the overhead rotor, the two anti-torque rotors located on outriggers extending from the sides of the fuselage, and a small fan that helped to cool the engine.

In 1925, Cierva decided to move to the United Kingdom, where he hoped there would be a better market for his Autogiro. The flapping mechanism became very sophisticated in later models, but remained essentially the same as in the C.4, operating entirely automatically and under the influence of purely aerodynamic forces. Although its success gave helicopter designers a clear indication of what they should be looking for, the autogyro system could not be used as it stood: the application of power to the rotor prevented the system from operating automatically.

Cierva enjoyed moderate success as his fully developed Autogiros became popular with both the public and the military. For this he was indebted to the exhibitions and test flights undertaken by his two most important assistants, Harold F. Pitcairn in the United States, and Captain Frank Courtney in the UK. The Autogiro's primary limitation, it should be noted, was its related inability to take-off vertically or to hover motionless in the air.

The second aspect did not worry Cierva unduly, but he was determined to find some practical method for allowing vertical take-off, for this would increase the military utility of the Autogiro. Cierva had already introduced a system for spinning the rotor before take-off, thus shortening the ground run, and a pitch-changing mechanism was fitted to Autogiros in the late 1920s to supplement the flapping motion in equalising lift. The final link, a clutch device, was demonstrated in July 1933. Power from the engine at the nose of the fuselage was now taken along a series of shafts through the fuselage and up to the rotor. This was engaged to the drive and was spun to flying speed before lift was allowed to develop, the clutch was

released, and all the power was applied to the propeller that pulled the machine through the air as soon as the spun-up rotor had lifted it into the air.

In this way the Autogiro could make a jump start into the air, where the propeller provided the forward speed which made the rotor turn on its own. The key to rotor spin-up on the ground was the pitch-control mechanism, which kept the rotor blades at zero incidence, preventing them from generating asymmetric lift until the moment when the clutch was disengaged and the rotor resumed its natural performance. The whole machine 'jumped' some 20ft (6.1m) into the air before the propeller took over.

These Autogiros were a startling sight in operation and proved very successful, continuing in service well into World War II (1939-45). After this time they faded into obscurity until rescued in the 1960s by a wave of enthusiasm for miniature types intended only for sporting use. The main users of Autogiros in World War II were the British, who used the type's ability to stay almost in one spot to help calibrate radar equipment, a function that could not have been undertaken readily by conventional aircraft.

The Germans developed an experimental unpowered autogyro, the Focke-Achgelis Fa 330 Bachstelze, for possible use as an observation platform for U-boats. This simple yet effective little machine could be dismantled into small units for stowage; in operation, the U-boat would tow the Fa 330 at the end of a wire, thus giving it the necessary forward speed for its rotor to windmill and thereby generate lift. From some distance behind and above the parent U-boat the observer in the autogyro enjoyed an excellent field of vision and could search for prey reported to the U-boat via a telephone wire attached to the towing cable. This ingenious and workable system was not used operationally, however, since it meant that the U-boats would stay on the surface for dangerously prolonged periods, and a crash dive would sacrifice the pilot and autogyro as the towing cable was severed.

The success of the Autogiro built by Cierva and his licensees and of the autogyro built by other designers had the fortunate effect of spurring on the development of the helicopter, for here at last was clear proof that rotor-lifted aircraft were practical flying machines. The most important figures in this final stage were Professor Heinrich Focke, one of the parent figures of the

Focke-Wulf company, and the Russian-born Igor Sikorsky, well known before World War I for his giant four-engined aircraft and as the designer and manufacturer of many flying boats and amphibians since emigrating to the USA after the Russian Revolution of 1917.

Focke was the first to achieve any success when his Fw 61 was developed into a production machine. Its maiden flight was in 1936, a year after Breguet had flown the Breguet-Dorand Gyroplane Laboratoire as a successful helicopter using co-axial twin rotors to overcome torque reaction effects. The Breguet helicopter progressed no further, however, leaving the field to Focke and his partner Gerd Achgelis, with whom he had worked in 1932 after leaving Focke-Wulf. Achgelis had been a Focke-Wulf employee and was a superb aerobatic pilot, which was a useful background for learning to handle a new type of aeroplane.

The prototype of the world's first successful helicopter flew in June 1936 and soon proved its worth. Powered by a 160hp (119kW) Bramo (Siemens-Halske) Sh.14A radial piston engine, the Fw 61 was lifted and propelled by a pair of counter-rotating rotors mounted on the ends of two steel-tube outriggers set out from the fuselage based on that of the Focke-Wulf Fw 44 Stieglitz basic training aeroplane. As in the Breguet type but rather more clumsily, the torque reaction of each rotor cancelled that of the other rotor and made the machine directionally stable. The Fw 61 set up some impressive world records for helicopters, including a distance of 143 miles (230km), speed of 76mph (122km/h), endurance of 1 hour 20 minutes 49 seconds, and altitude of 11,243ft (3,427m).

The Flettner Fl 282 Kolibri (humming bird) was one of the most advanced helicopters designed in World War II, and its use of closely spaced intermeshing twin-rotors produced a compact design that appealed most strongly to the German navy for shipboard applications. The Fl 282 was powered by a 160hp (119kW) Bramo (Siemens-Halske) Sh.14A radial piston engine, and its primary data included rotor diameters of 39ft 2.875in (11.96m), fuselage length of 21ft 6.25in (6.56m), height of 7ft 2.625in (2.20m), maximum take-off weight of 2,205lb (1,000kg), maximum speed of 93mph (150km/h) at sea level, service ceiling of 10,825ft (3,300m), and range of 106 miles (170km).

The Fw 61 was fully controllable and thereby proved that helicopters were practical flying machines, but it was only a prototype and therefore lacked the power-to-weight ratio that permitted the carriage of a payload. So the designers decided to refine and lighten their basic concept before producing a production model. Four years passed before the Focke-Achgelis Fa 223 Drache was ready for production in 1940, and even after the type was ordered for German military service, production was hampered by Allied air attacks and only nine production-standard Fa 223s were completed during the war; another three were built after the war from salvaged parts.

Igor Sikorsky became interested in rotary-wing flight during his pioneer period in Russia, and built his first helicopter in 1909: this machine was powered by a 25hp (18.6kW) Anzani engine and would not leave the ground. In 1910, Sikorsky built a second prototype, but although this could rise into the air it was incapable of lifting both itself and a pilot. Realising that rotary-wing aircraft were beyond the capabilities of current technologies, Sikorsky turned his attention to a series of large fixed-wing aircraft, culminating in the Ilya Muromets bomber of 1914 that was the world's first successful four-engined aeroplane. After the Bolshevik Revolution of 1917 that turned Russia into the USSR, Sikorsky left the country and settled in the USA during 1919, turning his attention to the design of flying boats and amphibians. Sikorsky rose to the position of engineering manager of the Vought-Sikorsky Division of the United Aircraft Corporation, and in 1938 he decided to capitalise on years of reflection by addressing the problems of rotary-wing flight.

Receiving authorisation to proceed with the design and construction of a helicopter prototype, Sikorsky produced the VS-300 that first flew in tethered mode during September 1939 with a 75hp (55.9kW) Lycoming air-cooled radial piston engine. The VS-300 underwent a major development programme, and made its first free flight in May 1940 with a Franklin engine rated at 90hp (67.1kW). The VS-300 became the world's first truly practical helicopter of

the single main rotor type in December 1941, when it was flown successfully as the VS-300A with the definitive cyclic pitch control system (developed to practical status by Landgraf) and a single anti-torque tail rotor. Testing and development continued through 1942 with power increased to 150hp (112kW) to create the final VS-300B form, and this epoch-making helicopter was retired to the Henry Ford Museum in 1943. Whereas the Breguet-Dorand and Fw 61 must be reckoned to have been the world's first successful helicopters, in that they could take-off and land vertically, and undertake forward, backward and sideways manoeuvres in the air, the VS-300 must similarly be reckoned as the world's first practical helicopter as it combined these features with the factor that allowed its development into a production type also capable of carrying a payload.

Although the type was planned for large-scale production, the Flettner Fl 282 Kolibri was in fact produced only in prototype and pre-production models for the evaluation of its technical and operational capabilities. This model is typical of the type as trialled for the observation role, with a Plexiglas-covered forward fuselage providing good fields of vision.

Impressed with the potential of the VS-300, the US Army Air Corps (known as the US Army Air Forces (USAAF) later that year) had contracted in the spring of 1941 for an improved experimental type with two-seat accommodation. This VS-316A was evolved as a development of the VS-300A/B, retaining the earlier type's heavy-gauge steel-tube fuselage structure with all except the extreme tail covered in fabric, but featuring a powerplant of one 165hp (123kW) Warner R-500-3 radial piston engine driving a fabric-covered three-blade main rotor via a gearbox that turned the drive angle through 90 degrees, enclosed side-by-side accommodation with side doors and optional dual controls, and fixed tailwheel landing gear whose main wheels could be replaced by two inflated rubber pontoons for amphibious capability. This prototype first flew in May 1942 as the XR-4, and was followed by another 30 helicopters for service trials. These were three YR-4A and 27 improved YR-4B machines (including three diverted to the US Navy with the designation HNS-1), with a main rotor whose diameter was increased from the XR-4's figure of 36ft 0in (10.97m) to 38ft 0in (11.58m) and driven by the more powerful 180hp (134kW) Warner R-550-1 engine.

These machines proved the practical nature of the helicopter in trials as diverse as arctic operations and maritime capability from a platform on an oil tanker. There followed an initial production batch of 100 R-4B helicopters delivered in 1944: 20 of these were diverted to the US Navy for use by the US Coast Guard with the designation HNS-1, and 45 were transferred to the Royal Air Force (RAF) and Fleet Air Arm (FAA) with the designation Hoverfly Mk I that was also applied to seven YR-4Bs transferred to the UK. In 1948, the helicopters still operational with the new US Air Force (USAF), as the USAAF had become in 1947, were allocated the revised designation H-4B, signalling the change from the R-for-Rotary wing to H-for-Helicopter category.

The USAAF never considered the R-4 as anything other than a trials type that could explore both the practicality and utility of the helicopter in military service, and this limited expectation of the type was justified by the type's service life, which revealed only marginal capabilities with two men on board. What was needed was a more powerful version of the same basic type, and this was ordered in 1942 as the R-5 that was designed as the VS-327. While this new type was being developed and prepared for production, the USAAF decided that it needed a refined version of the R-4 for continued examination of the helicopter's capabilities. Ordered in 1943 as the R-6, this was designed as the VS-316B to reflect the fact that the type was essentially an improved VS-316A with the same rotor and transmission systems but powered by the 225hp (168kW) Lycoming O-435-7 flat-six piston engine. The fuselage was completely revised into the tadpole type that became typical of Sikorsky helicopters of the next generation: this had a formed Plexiglas cockpit section and a metal semi-monocoque boom to support the anti-torque tail rotor.

The XR-6 prototype first flew in October 1943, and in March 1944 established impressive world helicopter altitude, distance and endurance records during the course of non-stop flight between Washington, DC and Dayton, Ohio, in which the machine covered 387 miles (623km) in 4 hours 55 minutes, with an altitude of 5,000ft (1,525m) recorded during the crossing of the Allegheny mountains. There followed 31 service test and development helicopters each powered by the 240hp (179kW) Franklin O-405-9 flat-six piston engine: these were five XR-6A and 26 YR-6A helicopters built respectively by Sikorsky and Nash-Kelvinator. The latter won the contract for 193 R-6A production machines. Production started in 1945, and it is uncertain whether or not the full total was completed. Some 36 of the helicopters were diverted with the designation HOS-1 to the US Navy, which used the type for the search-and-rescue (SAR) role and also received three XH-6As with the revised designation XHOS-1, and another 26 were delivered to the UK for use by the RAF and FAA with the designation Hoverfly Mk II.

The R-6A was beset by engine problems, but the helicopters that survived to 1948 received the revised designation H-6A.

In 1942 the USAAF decided that the helicopter had considerable potential as an air observation post machine, but only if it provided better payload and performance than the R-4. To meet the resulting requirement, Sikorsky designed the VS-327 as a conceptual offspring of the R-4, although it was a completely new design and introduced a number of features that were soon to become standard on early Sikorsky helicopters. The core of the new design was the powerplant, which comprised a 450hp (336kW) Pratt & Whitney R-985 radial piston engine located with its crankshaft vertical to drive a much larger main rotor via a clutch and cooling fan arrangement. The central fuselage carried the engine and was of welded steel-tube construction covered with resin-bonded shaped plywood panels rather than fabric as in the R-4, the slim forward fuselage carried the crew of two (observer in front of the

The Focke-Achgelis Fa 223 Drache (kite) was a large helicopter that adhered to the design concept pioneered in the Fa 61 with two large counter-rotating propellers at the tips of the fuselage-mounted outriggers. The Fa 223 was powered by a 1,000hp (746kW) Bramo 323Q03 radial piston engine, and its other details included rotor diameters of 39ft 4.5in (12.00m), overall span of 80ft 4.625in (24.50m), fuselage length of 40ft 2.25in (12.25m), height of 15ft 9in (4.80m), maximum take-off weight of 9,500lb (4,315kg), maximum speed of 75mph (120.5km/h) at sea level, service ceiling of 23,295ft (7,100m), and range of 199 miles (320km).

Built in the UK under licence from Cierva, the Avro Rota Mk I was an Autogiro used in modest numbers by the Royal Air Force before and during World War II. The key features of the design were an aeroplane-type fuselage with a 140hp (104kW) Armstrong Siddeley Genet Major radial piston engine located in the nose and driving a tractor propeller, wide-track main landing gear units, a substantial tail unit, and an unpowered three-blade rotor carried above the fuselage on a substantial quadruped pylon. The details of this useful type included a rotor diameter of 37ft 0in (11.28m), fuselage length of 19ft 8.5in (6.01m), height of 11ft 1in (3.38m), maximum take-off weight of 1,900lb (862kg), maximum speed of 110mph (177km/h) at sea level, service ceiling of 8,000ft (2,440m), and range of 250 miles (402km).

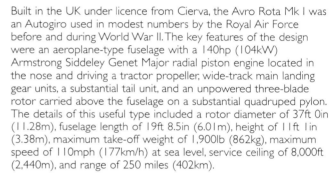

Rotor Control

THE main problem encountered in early helicopters was the tendency of the machine to roll laterally in the direction of the retreating rotor blades as the advancing blades passed through more air and generated greater lift than the retreating blades that passed through less air. This problem was eventually solved by the introduction of a flapping hinge in the rotor head, which allowed the advancing blade to climb slightly, thereby reducing its angle of attack and the amount of lift generated, while the retreating blade fell slightly, thereby increasing its angle of attack and the amount of lift generated, so that the turning rotor blades generated an equal amount of lift on each side of the shaft. The other two main features of the helicopter's control system, which are operated by the pilot, are the collective and cyclic pitch controls. The collective pitch control is the method by which the pilot controls the helicopter's ascent and descent by the increase or decrease simultaneously (i.e. collectively) of the pitch angle of all the main rotor blades, thereby increasing or decreasing the amount of lift generated by the whole of the rotor disc. The cyclic pitch control is the method by which the pilot controls the helicopter's direction in level flight by altering the pitch angle of each main rotor blade consecutively (i.e. cyclically) at a given geometric position in each revolution, thereby tilting the main rotor disc's theoretical axis of rotation in the desired direction; to tilt the rotor disc forward to create forward motion from the hover, for example, the pitch angle of each advancing blade is reduced and that of each retreating blade increased.

pilot) in an extensively glazed metal monocoque structure, and the boom was a wooden monocoque structure. The landing gear was of the fixed type in a reversed tricycle arrangement with the main units well forward and the stalky rear unit located at the junction of the central fuselage and boom sections.

The USAAF ordered an eventual five prototypes in 1943, and the first of these XR-5 helicopters flew in August 1943 with the R-985-AN-5 engine; two of the prototypes were later retrofitted to British specification and received the revised designation XR-5A. There followed 26 examples of the YR-5A service test type of which two were diverted to the US Navy with the designation HO2S-1, and in 1948 the surviving helicopters were allocated the revised designation YH-5A; five of the YR-5As were modified with dual controls with the designation YR-5E that was changed to YH-5E during 1948. The USAAF also ordered 100 examples of the R-5A (from 1948 H-5A) production model, but in the event only 34 were built with provision for a litter carrier on each side of the fuselage.

Some 21 of these helicopters were later modified to R-5D (from 1948 H-5D) standard with internal accommodation for a second passenger, a rescue hoist, conventional tricycle landing gear, a powerplant of one 600hp (447kW) Pratt & Whitney R-1340 radial piston engine, and provision for auxiliary fuel in an external tank. Intended primarily for the civil market, the S-51 model was a development of the R-5D with the R-985 Twin Wasp engine and accommodation for a pilot and up to four passengers. The type first flew in February 1946 and received civil certification during March of the same year, paving the way for deliveries to start in August. In 1947 the new USAF received 11 S-51 helicopters with the service designation R-5F (from 1948 H-5F), and followed in 1948-49 with 39 examples of the H-5G variant equipped with power-boosted controls, untapered rotor blades and a rescue hoist for the SAR role, together with 16 examples of the H-5H variant with updated equipment and provision for pontoon alighting gear in place of the standard wheeled landing gear.

The USAF allocated most of its helicopters to the Air Rescue Service, which flew the type extensively during the Korean War (1950-53) with an enclosed litter carrier on each side of the fuselage. The same basic type was used by the US Navy for the planeguard and general observation roles, and deliveries amounted to some 97 machines. The more important of these models was the HO3S-1 of which 88 were built for delivery from November 1947 and for full service from May 1948. Nine similar aircraft were procured on behalf of the US Coast Guard, which allocated the designation HO3S-1G to the type in the SAR role. A number of other S-51s were delivered to the air arms of other countries.

The most important aspect of the fully developed VS-300 and its Sikorsky successors was the cyclic pitch control, perfected by Landgraf and first fitted in definitive form during December 1941. This now became the heart of the helicopter in every form, and many forms of helicopter were tried successfully during the 1940s. In the USA, Kellett, who had previously produced autogyros, developed a helicopter with counter-rotating twin rotors, set on angled shafts so that the blades intermeshed, helping to reduce the overall 'span'.

Friedrich von Doblhoff, an Austrian, made his mark with the first jet-propelled helicopter, the Doblhoff WNF 342. This introduced the unusual concept of feeding compressed air and fuel into combustion chambers at the tips of the rotor blades, where the vapour mixture was burned to provide thrust. The generation of power at the rotor tips rather than in the fuselage avoided torque problems and made the tail rotor unnecessary. Experimental models with this sort of propulsion have been tested ever since, but despite its clear advantages the type has never found favour. Another major contender within the German Reich was Anton Flettner, with the Flettner Fl 282 Kolibri. Flettner remains one of the lesser known pioneers of rotary-wing flight, which is remarkable given the fact that his first fully practical helicopter, the Fl 265, was superior to the Fw 61 and made its first successful free flight several months before the VS-300 began its initial tethered flights. Flettner had been a devotee of rotary-wing flight since the early 1930s, and was particularly anxious to overcome the torque-reaction problem associated with a lifting rotor driven by a fuselage-mounted engine. This preoccupation was evident in Flettner's first helicopter design, completed in 1930, which was based on a large two-blade rotor powered directly by two Anzani piston engines, each rated at 30hp (22.4kW) and installed on one of the rotor blades to drive a small tractor propeller.

The prototype of this helicopter was overturned by a gust of wind and destroyed during 1933 in the course of tethered trials. Flettner then designed a two-seat autogyro as the Fl 184 with enclosed two-seat accommodation, fixed tailwheel landing gear with cantilever main units, a three-blade rotor fitted with a cyclic pitch control system, and a powerplant of one 140hp (104kW) Sh.14 radial piston engine located in the nose to drive a two-blade tractor propeller. This machine was also built in prototype form, but was lost in 1936 after suffering an inflight engine fire. The talented Flettner now turned to the Fl 185 design that was intended to operate as a helicopter when the rotor was powered for vertical flight and as an autogyro when the rotor was unpowered in horizontal flight: the Fl 185 had fixed tricycle landing gear, a three-blade rotor, and a powerplant of one Sh.14A engine. The powerplant was nose-mounted inside a long-chord cowling and drove a frontal cooling fan as well as a gearbox that drove the rotor and/or

Seen here on the production line, the Sikorsky R-4 was developed as the VS-316A (first flight in January 1942) and was the primary definitive evolution of the concepts first embodied in the VS-300, and as such was the first helicopter in the world to enter full-scale production, as the German Fa 223 Drache and Fl 282 Kolibri helicopters had failed to reach this stage. The R-4 introduced fully enclosed accommodation and dual controls for the two-man crew.

two variable-pitch propellers mounted at the tips of outriggers extending from each side of the fuselage: when the rotor was powered, the propellers provided thrust in the opposite direction to counteract the torque reaction, but when the rotor was unpowered, the propellers absorbed the full power of the engine to provide forward thrust. The Fl 185 made only a few test flights before being scrapped.

By this time, however, Flettner had come to his definitive concept of how to obviate torque reaction, namely a side-by-side pair of intermeshing two-blade rotors that were mounted at the heads of two outward-inclined drive shafts and turned in opposite directions so that the torque reaction of one cancelled that of the other. Flettner appreciated that this system would produce a seriously turbulent airflow pattern, but felt that the problems associated with this airflow would be more than offset by the advantages of the torqueless rotor system and the reduced drag that would result from a

design that ob-viated the need for any external rotor-carrying structure. The new rotor system was first used on the Fl 265, of which the German navy ordered six prototypes in 1938. The fuselage of the Fl 265 was based on that of the Fl 185 but revised with the intermeshing rotor system and without the two propeller outriggers. The same type of powerplant arrangement was used and, to improve the helicopter's controllability, a conventional tail unit was provided with a trimmable tailplane, and a large vertical tail surface incorporating a rudder was used to supplement the directional control provided by differential collective-pitch change in the two rotors. The Fl 265 V1 first prototype made its maiden flight in May 1939 and, despite its loss a mere three months later when the rotor blades struck each other, soon proved the general success of Flettner's design concept. The five other prototypes were used for a number of successful trials in several military applications, and in 1940 the German navy ordered Flettner to initiate full production of the type. By that time, Flettner had moved forward to a more advanced design and the production order was switched to this more capable type, namely the Fl 282 Kolibri. This was designed as a two-seater so that, at the expense of range, an observer could be carried in a rearward-facing seat that was installed behind the rotor assembly. The design was created with sufficient range in the permissible centre of gravity position so that the helicopter could be flown as a single- or two-seater without trim changes, and its most obvious role was observation in land and naval applications.

The design was completed in July 1940 and work started immediately on no fewer than 30 prototype and 15 pre-production helicopters. Flight trials were scheduled to begin in 1941, and while the first three machines were completed as single-seaters with accommodation for the pilot in an enclosed cockpit, the others were finished as two-seaters with open accommodation. The Fl 282 marked a departure from previous Flettner practice in the location of the Sh.14A engine, which was installed in the centre of the fuselage with a wooden cooling fan that drew air through slots in the underside of the fuselage, and drove a forward-mounted transmission unit that turned the drive through 155 degrees to a 65-degree upward and backward angle to power, via a transmission shaft, the upper transmission unit that drove the two rotor shafts. The latter were inclined outward at 12 degrees and forward at 6 degrees, and carried the two rotors. These were each of the two-blade type, each blade having a steel spar, wooden ribs, and a skinning of plywood covered in fabric: each blade was attached to its rotor hub by flap and drag hinges. The fuselage was of welded steel-tube construction covered over its central portion by light alloy panels and over its rear section by fabric, and carried at its rear the conventional tail unit, which comprised a trimmable horizontal surface and a large vertical surface with a rudder to supplement differential collective-pitch change of the two rotors for directional control. The pilot was accommodated in an open steel-tube structure at the extreme nose, and the airframe was completed by the fixed tricycle landing gear with a single wheel on each unit. The Fl 282 V1 first prototype flew in 1941, and as additional machines became available and the pace of the development programme was accelerated, the Fl 282 soon proved itself to be an admirable helicopter that combined great reliability with viceless handling characteristics.

Operational trials were undertaken from 1942, and so useful was the Fl 282 that, from 1943, about 20 of the 24 completed development helicopters were used for the convoy escort role in the Mediterranean and Black Seas. In 1944 the German air ministry ordered 1,000 production examples of the Fl 282 from BMW, but no production helicopters were completed as a result of the programme's dislocation by Allied bombing. Only three of the Fl 282 helicopters survived to VE-Day in May 1945, many of the others having been destroyed to prevent their capture by the Allies.

The other major American pioneer of the single-rotor helicopter was Bell. During World War II, Bell cut its rotary-wing teeth on the Model 30 design, of which five were built as research helicopters. From the third of these machines the company developed the Model 47 as a practical helicopter paving the way for a production model. The first of 11 prototype and service test helicopters flew in December 1945 with an open fuselage structure, quadricycle landing gear, and a powerplant of one 175hp (130.5kW) Franklin horizontally opposed piston engine, and in March 1946 the Model 47 became the first helicopter in the world to receive civil certification.

This was the first of 27 Sikorsky YR-4B helicopters built to a contract issued by the US Army Air Forces for evaluation machines that were operated by the USAAF, US Navy and Royal Air Force to the extent of 17, three and seven machines respectively. The YR-4B was powered by a 180hp (134kW) Warner R-550-1 radial piston engine driving a main rotor with a diameter of 38ft 0in (11.58m), and also had a larger cockpit than that of the initial XR-4 and YR-4A machines, of which one and three respectively were built. The XR-4 was powered by a 165hp (134kW) Warner R-500-1 radial engine driving a main rotor with a diameter of 36ft 0in (10.97m), but a larger engine and rotor were introduced on the YR-4As. The YR-4Bs were used for trials under arctic and tropical conditions, and it was a YR-4B that undertook the first helicopter evacuation of a wounded soldier, an event that took place in Burma during 1944.

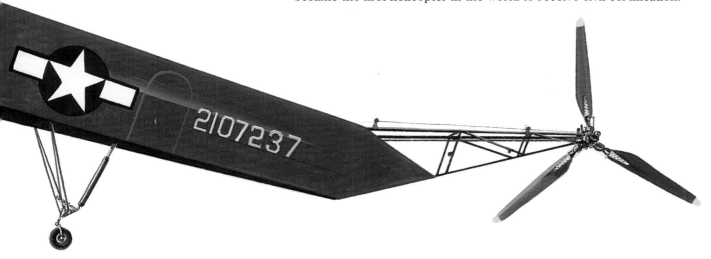

The first production version was the two-seat Model 47B, of which 78 were completed with the 175hp (130.5kW) Franklin 6ALV-335 engine. There followed a number of mainly civil Model 47 variants that also secured orders with an increasing number of the world's air arms. The most important of these were the Model 47D with the Franklin 6V4-178-B32 engine rated at 178hp (133kW) and a blown Plexiglas canopy in place of the Model 47B's car-type windscreen; the definitive three-seat Model 47G with the 200hp (149kW) Franklin 6V4-200-C32AB engine and a small horizontal tailplane at the tail; and the four-seat Model 47J Ranger with the 220hp (164kW) Lycoming VO-435 flat-six piston engine. The Model 47G and Model 47J were built respectively in 10 and six subvariants, distinguishable by their different engines.

The Model 47 soon attracted the attention of the USAAF, which saw the type as a useful utility helicopter, and in 1947 the service received 28 Model 47A helicopters with the 175hp (130.5kW) Franklin O-335-1 engine for evaluation under the designation YR-13. Ten of the helicopters were diverted to the US Navy, and three of them were modified to YR-13A standard suitable for operation in cold climates.

The first full production order was placed by the US Army, which in 1948 contracted for 65 examples of a Model 47D variant for service under the H-13B designation with the 200hp (149kW) Franklin O-335-3 engine and a bubble canopy with a removable top. The 15 H-13C helicopters were H-13Bs stripped of their rear fuselage covering and revised with twin-skid landing gear for use in the casevac role, with a litter pannier carried externally on each side of the fuselage. The H-13D military version of the model 47D-1, of which 87 were delivered, had single rather than dual controls, skid landing gear, and the 200hp (149kW) O-335-5 engine, and in 1962 the surviving helicopters were redesignated OH-13D in the rationalisation of the US tri-service designation system. Some 490 of the H-13E derivative of the H-13D

A type that saw limited operational use as a means of increasing the spotting horizon for U-boats, the Focke-Achgelis Fa 330 Bachstelze (water wagtail) was a kite autogyro towed to spotting height by a moving submarine. The type's primary details included a rotor diameter of 24ft 0in (7.315m), fuselage length of 14ft 6in (4.42m), empty weight of 180lb (82kg), and a minimum air speed of 17mph (27km/h) to maintain flight.

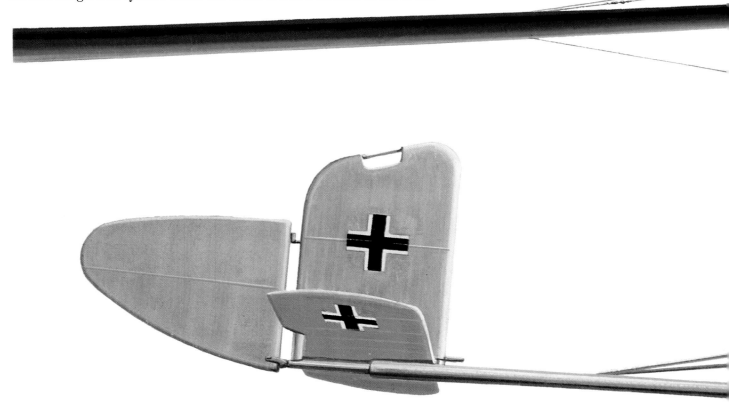

were delivered with dual controls, three seats, a new main transmission and tail, and the 200hp (149kW) O-335-5B engine, and in 1962 the surviving helicopters were redesignated OH-13E Sioux. More than 260 of the H-13G military derivative of the Model 47G were delivered with a controllable stabilizer, relocated and larger fuel tankage, a number of stability-enhancing features, provision for two external litter panniers, and the 200hp (149kW) Lycoming VO-435 engine, and in 1962 the surviving helicopters were redesignated H-13G. Some 470 of the H-47H military derivative of the Model 47G-2 were delivered with dual controls, provision for two external litter panniers, revised skid landing gear, bonded all-metal rotor blades, and the 250hp (186kW) VO-435-23 engine, and in 1962 the surviving helicopters were redesignated OH-13H. The H-13J, of which just two were delivered, was a three-seat presidential transport derivative of the Model 47J with more comfortable accommodation and the 240hp (179kW) VO-435-21 engine, and in 1962 the helicopters were redesignated UH-13J. The OH-13S, of which 265 were delivered to succeed the H-13H, was the military derivative of the Model 47G-3B with the tail boom lengthened by 1ft 2in (0.356m), main rotor blades extended by 1ft 0in (0.305m), and power provided by the 260hp (194kW) TVO-435-25 engine. The TH-13T military derivative of the Model

47G-3B-1, of which 411 were delivered for the instrument training role, featured considerably more advanced avionics than earlier models, the cabin was widened by 8in (0.203m) by comparison with that of the OH-13S, and power was provided by the 270hp (201kW) TVO-435-25 engine.

The US Navy also appreciated the potential of the Model 47 as a helicopter trainer, and evaluated the basic type's capabilities in the form of 10 YR-13 helicopters transferred with the naval designation HTL-1. The service followed with an order for 12 of the HTL-2 version of the Model 47D, and later orders added variants up to the HTL-7. The US Navy also perceived the Model 47's application in the utility and icebreaker patrol roles, and 28 of the HUL-1 naval derivative of the Model 47J variant were delivered, the surviving helicopters being redesignated UH-13P in 1962. Two HUL-1s diverted to the US Coast Guard for the SAR role in arctic conditions were designated HUL-1G, and in 1962 the helicopters were redesignated HH-13Q.

The Model 47 was built extensively under licence in Italy by Agusta, in Japan by Kawasaki and in the UK, under sub-licence from Agusta, by Westland. Large-scale production of the Model 47 in all its military and civil variants lasted from 1945 to the 1980s and resulted in several thousands of civil and military helicopters in a bewildering number of variants with open and enclosed cockpits and steadily increasing engine power. The Model 47 proved especially useful in urban areas and for various types of short-range flying. It was not long before the implications of the helicopter's independence from specially constructed landing sites became clear. New buildings began to feature landing pads on their roofs, and police departments realised that the helicopter, with its slow flying speed and ever-increasing endurance, was ideally suited for traffic surveillance and similar activities.

The helicopter's only major drawback in an urban environment has been its noisiness. At first this was not an acute problem, for the smaller engines used in the early 1950s were relatively quiet and the public was less concerned about the environment. But the growing size and increasing weight of helicopters required the use of more powerful and consequently noisier engines.

At the same time, improvements to both control and rotors allowed the helicopter to undertake a wider variety of roles with an increasingly heavy payload. This tendency was further increased by the development of a turbine engine suitable for helicopter installations. This is the turboshaft, which has a considerably higher power-to-weight ratio than the radial piston engine. In itself this has improved the helicopter's payload capability, but other important advantages of a turboshaft powerplant are greater fuel economy, relatively vibration-free running, increased reliability, reduced volume, and lighter weight. These last two factors have been particularly important, for they opened the way for the powerplant to be relocated from the fuselage to a position above the cabin and close to the rotor shaft: this made greater fuselage volume available for payload, and also resulted in a further lightening of the dynamic system by removing the need for long transmission shafts connecting any fuselage-mounted engine with the gearbox located at the base of the rotor shaft.

The USA had pioneered the practical helicopter, and this allowed American companies other than Sikorsky and Bell (most notably Hiller, Hughes, Kaman, Piasecki and Vertol) to develop a thriving international business as well as excellent sales within the USA. Vertol (later Boeing-Vertol and now Boeing Helicopters), Piasecki and Kaman concentrated on particular designs of twin-rotor helicopters, the first two on long-bodied machines with counter-rotating rotors at each end of the fuselage, and the last on short stumpy designs with an intermeshing arrangement of counter-rotating rotors.

By the 1950s, several European companies had entered the arena of helicopter design and manufacture. Westland, Saunders-Roe and Bristol were early leaders in the UK, but by the 1960s, Westland, licence-holders for Sikorsky designs, had achieved dominance. Sud-Est (later part of Aérospatiale) took most of the market in France, Bölkow (later MBB, now part of Eurocopter) led the field in Germany, and Agusta was dominant in Italy. Perversely, as the number of aircraft manufacturers declined in the 1960s and 1970s, that of helicopter manufacturers increased, especially in Latin America and Japan, although many of these produced only a few machines or just a single type before fading into obscurity.

The Mil design bureau achieved a virtual monopoly in the USSR, now the Commonwealth of Independent States (CIS), with some outstanding designs in several categories of medium single-rotor and heavy twin-rotor machines. The most important designer of naval helicopters, however, has been the Kamov bureau, which concentrates on helicopters of compact design through the use of a co-axial arrangement of two contra-rotating rotors.

The Boeing CH-47 Chinook is typical of the modern tandem-rotor transport helicopter: the long fuselage has a rectangular-section cabin accessed by a ventral ramp/door arrangement for the carriage of anything from troops to light vehicles, provision under the fuselage for the lifting of external loads on a three-point lift system, fuel carried in the external pannier tanks to leave the fuselage free for payload, landing gear of the quadricycle type for great stability on the ground, and the twin-rotor dynamic system that provides great lifting capability and also gives great flexibility in the centre of gravity position. The rotor system is based on two three-blade rotors indexed at 30 degrees to each other so that their blades can intermesh in the longitudinal plane without touching, and these rotors are powered by two turboshafts installed in nacelles on the sides of the pylon carrying the rear rotor and driving a transmission system that allows either engine to drive both rotors.

Helicopter Types

In the course of a life now amounting to some 60 years, the helicopter has been developed in a number of forms offering particular advantages and disadvantages. The first helicopters used a pair of contra-rotating rotors arranged on outriggers extended from the fuselage and generally used to support the main landing gear units. The primary advantage of this system, as first displayed in the Focke-Achgelis Fa 61, is the fact that it removes the need for an anti-torque rotor at the tail and permits the use of two simple rotors without complex hinges and controls; the primary disadvantage is the overall width. The width factor was tackled and overcome in helicopters such as the Flettner Fl 282 with the counter-rotating rotors installed on masts located close to each other but inclined slightly outward, so that the two rotor discs could intermesh without the blades touching. The definitive expression of two closely spaced main rotors is found in the helicopters of Nikolai Kamov, who adopted contra-rotating rotors with one installed above the other in a co-axial fashion so that the torque reaction of each rotor is cancelled by that of the other, and this allowed the creation of notably compact helicopters well suited to shipboard applications. The other main employment of two main rotors is in the tandem-rotor system in which the two counter-rotating rotors are located at the forward and rear ends of a longer fuselage with the rear rotor located above the front unit. Helicopters of this type were designed by Bristol, Yakovlev and Piasecki, the last's types being the most successful, as the company became known as Vertol that eventually became part of Boeing and is still responsible for the Model 107 and Model 114 series that are in service as the H-46 Sea Knight and H-47 Chinook series respectively. The primary advantage of the tandem-rotor layout is the ability to lift heavy loads whose position relative to the helicopter's centre of gravity is less critical than in single-rotor designs. This leaves the 'standard' helicopter pioneered by Sikorsky with a single main rotor whose torque reaction is controlled by a small rotor (or now the lateral expulsion of engine exhaust gases) at the tail.

From Piston to Turbine Power

THE most striking attribute of the helicopter is its versatility, a capability appreciable from the mid-1950s after the adoption of the turboshaft in place of the air-cooled piston engine as the standard type of powerplant in all but the lightest helicopters. Some helicopters were built for specific roles, but most of them proved able to undertake other tasks, especially as the power-to-weight ratio of the helicopter had been improved with the introduction of turboshaft engines. Moreover, in contrast to aircraft built since the end of World War II, many civilian and military helicopters have been evolved on the basis of a common airframe and rotor system. This factor resulted mainly from the fact that, up to the late 1960s, the helicopter was intended mainly as a transport vehicle.

While the basic helicopter could carry passengers on a commercial basis for civilian operators, it could also be adapted for use as an anti-submarine weapon, an SAR or air-sea rescue type, or a heavy-lift machine by adding the relevant equipment. This adaptation made economic sense, and was entirely feasible before helicopters were streamlined for operations in a hostile environment. This development occurred in the late 1960s when the helicopter's success in the Vietnam War combined with new technology and design ideas to foster a division between civil and military machines.

After the United States, the USSR was the next major power to produce a helicopter of its own design. The Mil Mi-1 'Hare' entered production in 1948 as a light transport type, but was soon supplanted by the Mi-2 'Hoplite' that was also built in large numbers. A year later the American, Stanley Hiller, introduced his Hiller 12 series of light utility helicopters, of which eventually more than 2,000 were built. Helicopters as small as these represented the only early designs which could not readily be adapted for other uses, as their payloads were so small. Training, observation and light communications were the only tasks that could be undertaken with any real efficiency.

The helicopter thus began to come into its own only during the early 1950s, partly as a result of the celebrated successes of American 'choppers' in Korea. New production facilities were built in other countries and numerous helicopter designs appeared in the first half of the decade. Sud-Est, a French nationalised group, produced its first model in 1951. A utility helicopter, the Alouette (lark) then proved outstandingly successful and the most versatile helicopter of French design. Production variants were the Alouette II and enlarged Alouette III which were each developed in variants with the Turbomeca Artouste and later the Turbomeca Astazou turboshafts.

The Sikorsky S-55 entered service with the US Air Force as the H-19, the US Army as the H-19 Chickasaw, the US Navy as the HO4S and the US Marine Corps as the HRS, and introduced the definitive form of the Sikorsky concept of piston-engined single-rotor helicopters for utility employment. The features that contribute to this 'definitive' nature included quadricycle landing gear, a 'pod-and-boom' fuselage with the high-set boom supported by a triangular fillet and the pod optimised for the transport role with considerable internal capacity and sliding lateral doors, the high-set cockpit, and the radial piston engine located low in the extreme nose to drive the rotor system via a long transmission shaft extending obliquely backward and upward to the main gearbox.

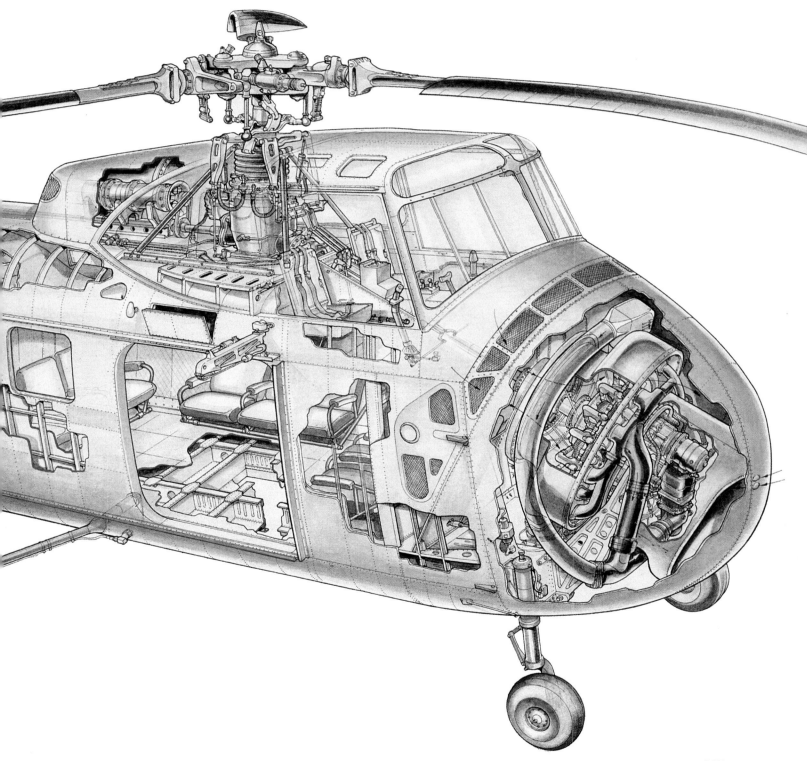

The Yakovlev Yak-24 'Horse' appeared in the same year, and was the world's largest helicopter at the time. Intended as a military transport, the Yak-24 set a number of world rotorcraft records but was built only in small numbers because of intractable handling problems.

In 1952, Mikhail Mil designed a large helicopter that was clearly inspired by the Sikorsky S-55 of 1949. Built over a period of more than 10 years by the parent company to the extent of 1,281 helicopters for the civil and military markets, the S-55 was the first Sikorsky helicopter to be built in very large numbers, and the production total was swelled beyond the American figure by licensed construction in France (five helicopters built by Sud-Est), Japan (71 machines built by Mitsubishi) and the UK (485 examples of the somewhat different Westland Whirlwind as an improved version of the baseline model).

The origins of the S-55 can be traced back to the technical success of the VS-327 built for the US forces as the R-5 (later H-5), and the S-51 series produced for the USAF and US Navy as the H-5 (later models) and HO3S respectively. This basic model had proved that the helicopter was a practical machine for military use, but also revealed that genuine utility required greater payload through the adoption of a larger airframe that would need a larger main rotor driven by a considerably more powerful engine. Sikorsky evolved such a type as the S-55, and rightly reasoned that the only place to locate the hold was under the main rotor, where changes in payload would not adversely affect the helicopter's centre of gravity position. The hold was accessed by a large starboard-side sliding door, and was planned with a length of 10ft 0in (3.05m), width of 5ft 3in (1.60m) and height of 6ft 0in (1.83m): this meant that unless the fuselage was to be lengthened to a significant degree, the cockpit had to be located above rather than ahead of

Opposite: Piston-engined light helicopters such as the Bell Model 447, seen here in military form as the H-13G, came into their own during the early 1950s for tasks such as observation, liaison and, as is apparent here, casualty evacuation with one or two wounded men loaded onto panniers attached to the sides of the helicopter for rapid evacuation to medical facilities more comprehensive than those on the front line.

Below: The Sikorsky S-51 series was widely used by American allies, this being a helicopter of the series in service with the Royal Canadian navy.

the hold. Because the hold was located on the centre of gravity, it was impossible to install the voluminous and weighty radial piston engine in the same place and, given the choice of positions fore or aft of the hold, the Sikorsky design team opted for a nose installation.

This allowed the engine to be fitted inside large clamshell doors that provided good access for maintenance, but demanded that the rotor system be driven via a long and heavy transmission shaft running obliquely to the gearbox immediately under the main rotor. The fuel tankage was placed below the hold, and the design of the S-55's fuselage was completed by a circular-section boom (installed at right angles to the rear face of the hold) for the anti-torque tail rotor, and by fixed quadricycle landing gear with a single wheel on each unit; twin metal or inflated rubber pontoons could be fitted in place of the wheels for amphibious capability, and there was also provision for the wheeled landing gear units to be fitted with inflatable pontoons for flotation in the event of a ditching. The rotor system comprised a three-blade main rotor and a two-blade tail rotor.

Impressed with the payload-carrying potential of the S-55, the USAF ordered five YH-19 prototypes for evaluation, and the first of these flew in November 1949 with a powerplant of one 550hp (410kW) Pratt & Whitney R-1340 radial piston engine. The second prototype introduced a large triangular fillet in the angle between the rear of the hold section and the underside of the boom, and this became standard on all subsequent helicopters of the family. The type entered production as the S-55A, with a powerplant of one 600hp (447kW) R-1340-57 radial piston engine.

The primary variants of the S-55A initial production model for the US forces were 50 examples of the H-19A for the USAF in the utility role; 72 examples of the H-19C Chickasaw for the US Army in the transport role; 10

examples of the HO4S-1 for the US Navy in the general-purpose role; and 161 examples of the HRS for the US Marine Corps in the assault transport role, with self-sealing fuel tanks and accommodation for eight troops: the HRS was delivered from April 1951 in two variants as the baseline HRS-1 (60 helicopters) and the HRS-2 (101 helicopters) with improved equipment; a number of HRS-2s were transferred to the UK for use by the FAA under the designation Whirlwind HAR.Mk 21. In the 1962 tri-service rationalisation of the US services' designation systems, surviving examples of the USAF and US Army models became the UH-19A and UH-19C Chickasaw respectively, while the small number of SH-19A and SH-19B helicopters (H-19As and H-19Bs converted to the rescue role) received the revised designations HH-19A and HH-19B respectively.

These S-55A variants had a main rotor with a diameter of 49ft 0in (14.94m). Delivered from 1952, the improved S-55B/C introduced the 700hp (522kW) Wright R-1300-3 radial piston engine, a main rotor with a diameter of 53ft 0in (16.15m), a boom that was angled down by 3.5 degrees to provide better clearance between its upper surface and the rotor blades under extreme circumstances (specifically the S-55C model), a horizontal stabilizer in place of the inverted-Vee finlets, a proper fin in place of the original pylon to carry the tail rotor, and improved equipment. This improved type was built for the USAF as the H-19B (264 helicopters redesignated UH-19B in 1962); for the US Army as the H-19D Chickasaw (301 helicopters redesignated UH-19D Chickasaw in 1962); for the US Navy as the HO4S-3 (79 helicopters redesignated UH-19F in 1962); for the US Coast Guard as the HO4S-3G (30 hoist-equipped helicopters redesignated HH-19G in 1962); and for the US Marine Corps as the HRS-3 (105 helicopters redesignated CH-19E in 1962). A number of HO4S-3s were transferred to the UK for use by the FAA with the designation Whirlwind HAS.Mk 22.

The designation S-55T is now applied to any piston-engined helicopter of the S-55 series revised by Aviation Specialties or Helitec with the 650hp (485kW) Garrett TSE331-3U-303 turboshaft powerplant, whose higher

Opposite: The Mil Mi-4 helicopter, known in the West by the reporting designation 'Hound', was clearly inspired by the Sikorsky S-55 design but was somewhat larger and more powerfully engined than its American counterpart. The type's primary details include a powerplant of one 1,700hp (1,267.5kW) Shvetsov ASh-82V radial piston engine, main rotor diameter of 68ft 11in (21.00m), fuselage length of 53ft 11in (16.435m), height of 13ft 8.25in (4.17m), maximum take-off weight of 17,196lb (7,800kg), maximum speed of 130mph (210km/h) at 4,920ft (1,500m), service ceiling of 18,045ft (5,500m) and range of 155 miles (250km).

An early example of a successful tandem-rotor transport helicopter was the Vertol (originally Piasecki) PV-18 that was ordered by the US Navy as the HUP Retriever and, as seen here, by the US Army as the H-25 that was universally known as the Army Mule. The type was powered by a single 575hp (429kW) Continental R-975-42 radial piston engine driving a transmission system that turned both rotors, and the location of this engine in the rear part of the fuselage is indicated by the use of tailwheel landing gear with the divided main units located well aft on the lower part of the fuselage, as the weight of the air-cooled engine prevented the machine toppling onto its nose.

power-to-weight ratio improves payload capability through a major reduction of empty weight, generally enhances performance, and offers the advantages of lower vibration levels.

This American helicopter was one of the world's most successful types ever brought into production, and small numbers are still operational in a variety of civilian and military capacities. Its Soviet counterpart, the Mi-4 that received the NATO reporting designation 'Hound', was a general-purpose machine, and by adapting the main features of the S-55, Mil's design team was able to reduce the time otherwise needed for development.

One year later, Sikorsky responded with the S-56, the world's first twin-engined helicopter, built to a 1950 US Marine Corps requirement for an assault transport helicopter able to carry 26 fully equipped troops or an equivalent weight of freight including light vehicles (three Jeeps) or a 4.13in

Seen here in the form of a machine operated by the French navy for the assault transport of marine forces, the Sikorsky S-58 was a larger and considerably more powerful evolution from the concept of the S-55, offering greater payload and performance.

Compared with the S-55, the Sikorsky S-58 had a four- rather than three-blade main rotor, a more conventionally configured fuselage with considerable payload volume still accessed by sliding lateral doors, and fixed tailwheel landing gear. The type was operated by the US forces as the H-34 Choctaw (US Army), HSS Seabat (US Navy) and HUS Seahorse (US Marine Corps) and by several other armed services around the world, and was also built under licence in France and the UK, in the latter as the Westland Wessex that reached its definitive form with a turboshaft powerplant.

(105mm) howitzer and its crew. Sikorsky designed the S-56 round a hold 30ft 1in (9.17m) long, 7ft 3in (2.21m) wide and 6ft 7in (2.01m) high, accessed by hydraulically powered clamshell doors in the lower nose (as well as by a rear cargo door) and fitted with a winch on an overhead rail for movement of freight items. Of necessity, the hold had to be arranged under the centre of gravity, and this determined the overall layout of the helicopter. The rest of the fuselage comprised a flightdeck above the clamshell nose doors and a comparatively short rear fuselage that supported the upward-angled pylon carrying the four-blade tail rotor. In the absence of turboshaft engines,

The Italian company Agusta has produced helicopters of its own design but is best known as the licensee of Bell, Boeing and Sikorsky. This is an Agusta (Bell) AB.47J of the Italian army.

In 1962 all the S-58 series helicopters in US service were redesignated in the H-34 series as part of the rationalisation of the three separate systems used up to that time. This is a UH-34D (originally HUS-1 Seahorse) used for the recovery of an astronaut from a Mercury orbiter capsule in the 1960s.

which appeared just a few years later and would have transformed the S-56's capabilities as a result of their smaller size and higher power-to-weight ratio, the required power could only be provided by a pair of large fan-cooled radial piston engines. There was inadequate room in the fuselage for these units, which were thus installed in large nacelles at the tips of stub wings, with their transmission shafts extending inward to the gearbox below the five-blade main rotor. The nacelles also carried the retractable main units of the tailwheel landing gear.

The capabilities promised by the S-56 were good, and the US Marine Corps ordered four XHR2S-1 prototypes with a powerplant of two 1,900hp (1,417kW) R-2800-50 Double Wasp radial piston engines, and the first of these machines flew in December 1953. Successful trials paved the way for the delivery of 55 (out of an initially ordered 91) examples of the HR2S-1 production model with modified engine nacelles, twin-wheel main landing gear units, and a triangular dorsal fillet bracing the tail-rotor pylon to the rear fuselage.

The first HR2S-1 flew in October 1955, and deliveries were completed between July 1956 and February 1959. The designation was changed to CH-37C in the 1962 rationalisation of US designation systems. Impressed by the HR2S's payload capability, the US Navy thought that the type could be developed into a useful radar-equipped airborne early warning (AEW) type, and this resulted in an order for two HR2S-1W helicopters delivered in 1957 with the nose extensively revised with a bulbous radome for the APS-20E surveillance radar, whose consoles and operators were accommodated in the modified hold. Endurance and service ceiling were both poor, however, and no further orders for this AEW version were placed.

The US Army was also interested in the S-56 and, after successful evaluation of one HR2S-1 with the revised designation YH-37, in 1954 ordered the first of an eventual 94 helicopters for service from 1956 with the designation H-37A Mojave that was altered in 1962 to CH-37A Mojave. The initial helicopters were delivered with R-2800-50 engines but later machines had improved R-2800-54 engines, and production was completed in May 1960. In June 1961 the service began to receive 90 helicopters rebuilt to the improved H-37B Mojave (from 1962 CH-37B Mojave) standard with a Lear-developed autostabilization system, a redesigned cargo door and cabin

Generally known in the West by the reporting designation 'Horse', the Yakovlev Yak-24 was designed as a medium transport but was never effective because of continued resonance problems with its tandem-rotor configuration. The details of this type, in its Yak-24U form with a dynamic system that comprised two Mil Mi-4 rotors and associated engines, included a powerplant of two 1,700hp (1,267.5kW) Shvetsov ASh-82V radial piston engines each driving a rotor with a diameter of 68ft 10.75in (21.00m), fuselage length of 69ft 10.5in (21.30m), height of 21ft 4in (6.50m), maximum take-off weight of 32,276lb (14,640kg), maximum speed of 158mph (254km/h) at sea level, service ceiling of 18,045ft (5,500m) and range of 298 miles (480km). The helicopter could carry 40 troops, or 18 litters, or two anti-tank guns with crews and limited ammunition, or two command cars, or three staff cars.

hatch, crash-resistant fuel tanks, the ability to load and unload while hovering, and other operational improvements.

One year after the appearance of the S-56, Sikorsky introduced the S-58 as a general-purpose type that was quickly followed by a specialised anti-submarine version. The S-58 was an outstanding design, and earned very substantial orders from the US armed forces and from other users. The model was also built under licence in the United Kingdom as the Westland Wessex with a turboshaft powerplant of the type later adopted for a number of S-58 conversions. Westland had previously built the S-55 under licence as the Whirlwind, again with a turboshaft powerplant.

The designation S-58A was used for the civil and military general-purpose helicopter that first flew in prototype form during March 1954 as a far more capable machine than the preceding S-55 series, due to the use of a considerably more powerful engine and a replanned fuselage incorporating a larger cabin. The basic S-58 design resulted from a US Navy requirement for an anti-submarine helicopter offering much better capabilities than the HO4S naval version of the S-55, which had been used to a limited extent in the anti-submarine warfare (ASW) role with dunking sonar and an armament or one or two lightweight homing torpedoes, but had revealed wholly inadequate payload/range performance for effective use in this exacting role. The US Navy's hopes for a highly capable shipborne ASW helicopter were based primarily on the Bell Model 61 tandem-rotor type powered by a single 2,400hp (1,789kW) Pratt & Whitney R-2800 Double Wasp radial piston engine, but development was slow and the eventual helicopter was disappointing in performance, and only 50 of these very large HSL-1 helicopters were built.

In the circumstances, therefore, it was fortunate that Sikorsky had begun work during 1951 on the S-58. This was based on an engine offering nearly double the power of that used in the S-55, although this engine was still located in the nose behind clamshell access doors and drove the transmission system by means of a long shaft running obliquely through the forward fuselage to the gearbox under the main rotor. Other changes were four- rather than three-blade main and tail rotors, replacement of the S-55's combination of a pod-and-boom fuselage and quadricycle landing gear by a more conventional fuselage with tailwheel landing gear, and provision for

The first successful helicopter for the design bureau headed by Mikhail Mil, the Mi-1 was dubbed 'Hare' in the Western system of reporting names for Soviet equipment, and was built in substantial numbers in the USSR before production was transferred to WSK-PZL Swidnik in Poland, where the type was further developed into a family of SM-1 variants. The SM-1WS was typified by a powerplant of one LiT-3 (Polish-built Ivchyenko AI-26V) radial piston engine rated at 575hp (429kW), main rotor diameter of 47ft 1in (14.35m), fuselage length of 39ft 8.5in (12.10m), height of 10ft 10in (3.30m), maximum take-off weight of 5,204lb (2,360kg), maximum speed of 96mph (155km/h) at sea level, service ceiling of 9,845ft (3,000m) and range of 373 miles (600km).

the main rotor blades and the complete rear fuselage (with tail pylon and anti-torque rotor) to be folded for easier shipborne stowage.

In June 1952 the US Navy ordered three XHSS-1 prototypes, and the first of these flew in March 1954 with a powerplant of one R-1820-84 radial, a crew of two, and provision for 16 passengers or eight litters. The type was ordered into production as the HSS-1 Seabat (from 1962 SH-34G or, stripped of mission equipment for the utility transport role, UH-34G). Despite its greater power, the HSS-1 still lacked the payload/range performance for effective use in the combined submarine hunter and killer roles, however, so the type was generally operated in pairs with one helicopter flying as a submarine hunter with dunking sonar and the other as a submarine killer with one or two lightweight homing torpedoes carried on the fuselage sides. Production totalled 215 helicopters, and this initial model was followed by 167 examples of the HSS-1N (from 1962 SH-34J or, stripped of mission equipment for the utility transport role, UH-34J) night/adverse-weather variant with improved avionics, an autostabilization system, an automatic hover coupling system, and Doppler navigation.

The US Marine Corps adopted the same basic type as the HUS-1 Seahorse (from 1963 UH-34D) of which 516 were delivered with accommodation for 12 fully armed troops and provision for 0.3in (7.62mm) pintle-mounted machine guns in the cabin doors. Other major variants for the USMC were the HUS-1A Seahorse (from 1962 UH-34E) amphibious version of which 40 were delivered with pontoon floats on the three units of the landing gear, and the HUS-1Z Seahorse (from 1962 VH-34D) of which seven were delivered as VIP transports.

The US Army adopted a derivative of the HSS-1 as the H-34A Choctaw (from 1962 CH-34A), and ordered 359 of the type in a utility configuration that was converted in a few cases to VH-34A VIP/staff transport and the upgraded CH-34B and CH-34C standards, the last with airborne search equipment. The CH-34A's hold is 13ft 7in (4.14m) long, 5ft 0in (1.52m)

Developed from the PV-3, the PV-17 first flew in 1949 and was built to the extent of just five Vertol (Piasecki) HRP-2 Rescuer helicopters, used by the US Marine Corps for 10-seat assault transport training with a powerplant of one 600hp (447kW) Pratt & Whitney R-1340-AN-1 Wasp radial piston engine.

The PD-22 design was based on that of the PV-17 with a larger-capacity fuselage and a considerably uprated powerplant, and the type was ordered as the H-21 series for service with the US Air Force and US Army with the names Work Horse and Shawnee respectively. The type reached its definitive form as the Vertol Model 43 (H-21C Shawnee), of which 334 were delivered to the US Army with accommodation for 20 troops or capability for the carriage of freight including a slung load on a ventral lifting hook, powerplant of one 1,425hp (1,062.5kW) Wright R-1820-103 radial piston engine driving two rotors each with a diameter of 44ft 0in (13.41m), fuselage length of 52ft 6in (16.00m), height of 15ft 5in (4.70m), maximum take-off weight of 14,704lb (6,669kg), maximum speed of 125mph (202km/h) at sea level, service ceiling of 7,750ft (2,360m) and range of 403 miles (649km).

wide and 5ft 10in (1.78m) high, and is accessed by a large starboard-side sliding door.

The USAF operated only 10 HH-34D rescue helicopters converted from ex-naval CH-34Ds for the USAF Reserve. Other S-58s were built for civil use and for export to the air arms of allied nations, raising Sikorsky production to 1,821 helicopters. Another 166 helicopters were built under licence in France by Sud-Aviation with no major divergence from the US basic pattern, and a somewhat different version was built in the UK as the Westland Wessex. The type is still in limited service, and most survivors conform in general terms to the standard described above. The designation S-58T is used for S-58s revised with a turbine powerplant, namely one 1,875hp (1,398kW) Pratt & Whitney Canada PT6B-6 Turbo Twin Pac coupled turboshaft. The revised powerplant results in improved reliability and payload, the latter deriving from the turboshaft's considerably better power-to-weight ratio. Sikorsky flew the first such conversion in August 1970, and a similar package is available in the early 1990s from California Helicopter International.

Enter the Turboshaft

The Sikorsky HH-53 Super Jolly was developed from the CH-53 Sea Stallion for the combat search-and-rescue role with a rescue hoist, armour protection, armament, all-weather flight and navigation instrumentation, and additional fuel capacity that could be supplemented in flight via a retractable refuelling probe on the lower starboard side of the forward fuselage.

MOST of the helicopters built up to the mid-1950s, in any part of the world, had a cruising speed of just under 100mph (160km/h) and a range in the order of 250 miles (400km). The main differentiating factor in their performance, therefore, had been the load they could carry. This increased rapidly in later types, and in the next generation of helicopters the performance also improved.

The reason for this improvement was a combination of two factors, one of them relatively simple and the other considerably more important. The simple factor was the general improvement in the helicopter concept during this period, witnessed by the adoption of improved structures and the introduction of more sophisticated aerodynamic and control features. The more important factor, however, was the replacement of the air-cooled radial or opposed piston engine by the turboshaft. The major advantages offered by the turboshaft over the piston engine were its comparatively vibration-free running (as the core of the engine consisted of rotating rather than reciprocating parts), its much improved reliability, its greater economy of fuel, and its radically reduced size and weight. This last advantage allowed the engine or engines to be installed above the cabin close to the rotor mast rather than in the lower fuselage, at a stroke removing the need for long and weighty transmission shafts and removing a bulky item whose volume could now be used for payload. The overall effect of the change from a reciprocating to a turbine engine was therefore a powerplant offering not only higher power in absolute terms but also a significantly higher power-to-weight ratio.

An indication of general improvement came in 1955 with the performance of the turboshaft-powered Alouette II: cruising speed rose to nearly 115mph (185km/h) and range to 400 miles (645km), and the model sold widely to civil and military operators in many parts of the world. The Alouette was the world's first turboshaft-powered helicopter to enter full production, and its origins can be traced back to the Sud-Est SE.3120 Alouette three-seat helicopter designed largely for agricultural use. This first flew in July 1952 with a powerplant of one 200hp (149kW) Salmson 9NH radial piston engine. The airframe was then completely revised to accept a turboshaft powerplant, the 360hp (269kW) Turbomeca Artouste I, and this SE.3130 prototype first took to the air in March 1955, being followed in 1956 by three pre-production helicopters.

The type entered production in 1956 as a utility helicopter for the civil as

well as military markets, but when Sud-Est merged with Sud-Aviation in 1957, the designation was altered to SE.313B. The Sud-Aviation and Nord-Aviation organisations merged in January 1970 to create Aérospatiale, and it is as a product of this manufacturer that the Alouette series is generally known despite the fact that surviving helicopters really come under the aegis of Eurocopter France, as Aérospatiale became upon its merger with the German company MBB (that became Eurocopter Deutschland).

The Alouette II soon proved itself a very capable general-purpose helicopter, being distinguished particularly for its excellent capabilities at higher altitudes, and at its peak served with some 22 air arms. Production amounted to 923 helicopters for civil and military operators. Apart from what was for the time good performance, the Alouette II was notable for its ability to carry a slung load of 1,323lb (600kg). The type is now obsolete except in the communications role but is still in fairly widespread service with a powerplant of one Turbomeca Artouste IIC6 turboshaft derated from 530 to 360shp (395 to 269kW).

The SE.3140 Alouette II, a development of the SE.3130 powered by one 400hp (298kW) Turbomeca Turmo II turboshaft, did not enter production, so the next model was the SA.318C Alouette II Astazou. First flown in January 1961, this is a much-improved version of the SE.313B, with the more fuel-efficient Astazou IIA turboshaft derated for greater reliability in this application. Production lasted into 1975, some 350 helicopters being built, and of the Alouette II series some 963 went to military operators, many of these machines remaining in service as utility helicopters.

The year in which the Alouette II first flew also saw the introduction of the first variants of the world's only truly successful co-axial twin-rotor helicopter series, namely the Kamov Ka-15 'Hen' and Ka-18 'Hog'. These entered service with the Soviet army and navy, and were also used by Aeroflot, the Soviet airline organisation. The performance of these two

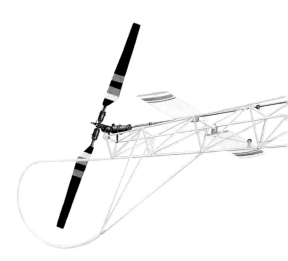

Kamov helicopters was inferior to that of the Alouette II, but their importance lies in the fact that they paved the way for the Ka-25 'Hormone'.

Further development of the Alouette II concept resulted in the more capable, better known, more widely produced and still useful SA.316A Alouette III. Designed as the SE.3160 in the period after the 1957 merger between Sud-Est and Sud-Aviation, the Alouette III was a basic upgrading and updating of the Alouette II, and featured greater power, a fully covered pod-and-boom fuselage, a larger cabin, improved equipment and other enhancements to offer greater payload and better performance together with the reliability and altitude performance of the Alouette II. The prototype first flew in February 1959, and production followed in 1961 with a powerplant of one 870hp (649kW) Turbomeca Artouste IIB turboshaft derated to 570hp (425kW) and matched to an upgraded transmission system. The type soon revealed exceptional high-altitude performance even with a substantial load, and this was a great spur to military as well as civil sales.

The SA.316B Alouette III improved model was introduced in 1968 with the uprated powerplant of one Artouste IIIB turboshaft, a strengthened transmission and improved landing gear for a further increase in payload. The type was also built under licence in Switzerland by FFA. The SA.316C Alouette III was a limited-production version powered by the Artouste IIID turboshaft, but the definitive model was the SA.319B Alouette III Astazou. Just as the SA.318C was developed as an Astazou-powered SE.313B, the SA.319B was produced and first flown in 1967 as a more economical and reliable machine than the SA.316B. Production of the Alouette III series

Left and below: The Aérospatiale (now Eurocopter France) SA. 318 Alouette II series was the first turboshaft-powered helicopter in the world to enter large-scale production, and its overall superiority to piston-engined light helicopters was rewarded by large orders. In its definitive SA. 318C Alouette II Astazou form, this helicopter can carry its pilot and up to four passengers, and its other details include a powerplant of one 530hp (395kW) Turbomeca Astazou IIA turboshaft derated to 360hp (268kW), a main rotor diameter of 33ft 5.6in (10.20m), fuselage length of 31ft 11.75in (9.75m), height of 9ft 0.25in (2.75m), maximum take-off weight of 3,630lb (1,650kg), maximum speed of 127mph (205km/h) at sea level, service ceiling of 10,825ft (3,300m) and range of 62 miles (100km) with a 1,323lb (600kg) payload.

began only in 1973 and amounted to 1,453 helicopters, the greater portion of them for military service in a number of roles. The HAL Chetak is the Indian licence-built version of the SA.316B, which HAL has developed into role-optimised land and naval subvariants. The land version is designed for the anti-tank role with four air-to-surface missiles (ASMs) and a stabilized roof sight, while the naval version is intended for the shipborne anti-submarine role and is armed with two Mk 44 or Mk 46 anti-submarine torpedoes (only one torpedo is carried if the optional podded magnetic-anomoly detection (MAD) kit is fitted), a harpoon-type downhaul system for ship capability under adverse weather and sea conditions, and folding rotor blades for economical shipboard stowage. The last basic development of the Alouette series was the SA.315B Lama, which was evolved from a time late in 1968 by Sud-Aviation to meet an Indian requirement for a general-purpose helicopter with good hot-and-high performance for Himalayan operations. The SA.315B first flew in March 1969, and is the airframe of the Alouette II combined with the dynamic system of the Alouette III. The type entered service in 1970, and the versions built under licence in India and Brazil are the HAL Cheetah (built from 1972 and still in low-volume production in the mid-1990s) and the Helibras HB 315B Gaviao.

The most important helicopter adopted by the US forces up to that time appeared in 1956. This was the Bell Model 204, which was the US forces' first turbine-powered helicopter and was designed as a nine-seat utility type that entered service as the HU-1 (later UH-1) Iroquois but is best remembered as the 'Huey' of the Vietnam War. In the basic model, the continued improvement in helicopter performance was indicated by a cruising speed of 126mph (205km/h) combined with a range of 320 miles (515km). The Model 204 variants were powered by variants of the Lycoming T53 turboshaft rated at between 770 and 1,100hp (574 and 820kW), and these were followed by larger numbers of the Model 205 variants with accommodation for 15 men including the pilot, and an uprated T53 powerplant rated at between 1,100 and 1,400hp (820 and 1,044kW). Variants of these two basic types were converted and developed into a host of special combat roles, the most significant of which was the Model 209 HueyCobra

The piston-engined helicopter was not immediately replaced by the turboshaft-powered type once the turboshaft had emerged as an effective powerplant in the mid-1950s, and helicopters such as this Kaman H-43A Huskie, with a powerplant of one 600hp (447kW) Pratt & Whitney R-1340-43 radial piston engine, lingered in its primary task of base rescue with the US Air Force. The type was then transformedby the adoption of a turboshaft powerplant, the 860hp (641kW) Lycoming T53-L-1B, to create the H-43B.

The Aérospatiale (now Eurocopter France) Alouette III was developed as an enlarged and more powerful version of the Alouette II, with an uprated engine, a higher-rated transmission and an enclosed tailboom. The original model was the SA. 316C Alouette III with accommodation for the pilot and up to six passengers, or two litters and two attendants, or 1,653lb (750kg) of freight, a powerplant of one 870hp (649kW) Turbomeca Artouste III turboshaft derated to 570hp (425kW), main rotor diameter of 36ft 1.75in (11.02m), fuselage length of 33ft 4.375in (10.17m), height of 9ft 10.125in (3.00m), maximum take-off weight of 4,960lb (2,250kg), maximum speed of 136mph (220km/h) at sea level, service ceiling of 13,125ft (4,000m) and range of 298 miles (400km). Like the Alouette II series, the Alouette III was produced in Artouste and higher-rated Astazou-powered forms that sold well on both the civil and military markets, and was also developed in specialised forms with armament and the appropriate sensors.

armed combat helicopter. This was evolved for the close support of the troops landed from 'Huey' helicopters, and was in essence a narrow-fuselage derivative of the Model 204 with the dynamic system of the Model 205. Setting a pattern that has remained essentially unaltered in the intervening years, the fuselage accommodated the pilot above and behind the co-pilot/gunner: the pilot could fire the disposable armament carried on the four hardpoints under the HueyCobra's stub wings, but the primary weapon operator was the co-pilot/gunner who also handled the chin-mounted traversing turret with its elevating armament of one multi-barrel machine gun and one grenade launcher. Quickly evolved and simply equipped, the HueyCobra was then evolved into more powerful variants with heavier and more versatile armament aimed with the aid of increasingly sophisticated avionics.

The HueyCobra is still in widespread service in its latest AH-1S form (four subvariants). A two-engined version was developed for use by the US Marine Corps, and the original AH-1J SeaCobra has since been replaced by the upgraded AH-1T Improved SeaCobra and the AH-1W SuperCobra. All these Model 204, Model 205 and Model 209 variants retain the two-blade type of main rotor introduced on the original HU-1, but Bell is continuing development of the narrow-fuselage marque and offers a much enhanced model with a four-blade main rotor.

The origins of the 'Huey' series can be traced back to the Korean War, which revealed the importance of the helicopter for a number of utility roles including, most importantly of all, casualty evacuation. A study undertaken after the war by Bell indicated that much improved operational capability could only be achieved in a helicopter that was both larger and more powerful than those currently in service, and in 1954 the US Army issued a

requirement for a utility helicopter able to carry a payload of 800lb (363kg) over a radius of 115 miles (1,85km), fly at a speed of 115mph (185km/h), hover at 6,000ft (1,830m) out of ground effect, and be air-portable in transports such as the Douglas C-124 Globemaster and Lockheed C-130 Hercules.

The requirement elicited 20 design proposals, and in June 1955 the US Army announced that the winner of the design competition was Bell with its Model 204 concept that was initially ordered in the form of three XH-40 prototypes. The core of the new helicopter was the new Lycoming T53 turboshaft, a basically simple and conservative engine that offered early maturity and considerable growth potential from its initial rating of 700hp (522kW). In overall terms, the advantages that the US Army found in the turboshaft by comparison with the piston engine were less vibration, reduced mechanical complexity, smaller volume, lower weight, much improved power-to-weight ratio, reduced fire risk, and the ability to run on a wide range of fuels.

With this turboshaft as the heart of its design, Bell based the all-metal Model 204 on a tadpole-shaped fuselage with a broad forward section accommodating the flightdeck area (accessed by two hinged doors) forward of the payload area (accessed by two large sliding doors), twin-skid landing gear, and the turboshaft located above the fuselage at the junction of the tail boom with the main pod section. The gearbox was installed in front of the engine and drove a two-blade main rotor (of the standard Bell type with broad blades and a stabilizing bar located at right angles to the blades) and a two-blade anti-torque rotor located on the port side of the pylon that was placed well behind the tailplane on the tail boom.

The Sikorsky CH-3C was developed as a purely land-based derivative of the SH-3 Sea King with its boat hull and stabilizing floats, and proved very useful in the utility transport role.

The Westland Wessex was a British-developed version of the Sikorsky S-58 with a turboshaft powerplant that initially comprised a 1,450hp (1,081kW) Napier Gazelle Mk 161 but later two 1,250hp (932kW) Rolls-Royce Gnome Mk 112 (licence-built General Electric T58) turboshafts. This is a Wessex HU.Mk 5 assault transport with details that included a rotor diameter of 56ft 0in (17.07m), fuselage length of 48ft 4.5in (14.74m), height of 14ft 5in (4.39m), maximum take-off weight of 13,500lb (6,124kg), maximum speed of 132mph (212km/h) at sea level, service ceiling of 14,100ft (4,295m) and range of 478 miles (770km).

The first XH-40 flew in October 1956 with a powerplant of one 700hp (522kW) XT53-L-1 turboshaft, and by this time the US Army had also ordered six YH-40 service test helicopters with a powerplant of one 700hp (522kW) T53-L-1A turboshaft, the cabin lengthened by 1ft 0in (0.305m) to allow the carriage of four litters, greater ground clearance, and improved controls. The two types were later redesignated XHU-1 and YHU-1, as the pre-production model was to be the first type in the US Army's new HU (Helicopter Utility) category. The pre-production model, of which just nine were delivered from June 1959 with the 860hp (641kW) T53-L-1A turboshaft flat-rated at 770hp (574kW), was the HU-1 Iroquois (redesignated UH-1 in the 1962 rationalisation).

After the HU-1 had entered production for the US Army, Bell evolved a civil version as the Model 204B with a powerplant of one 1,100hp (820kW) Lycoming T53-L-1A turboshaft for the carriage of 10 passengers, and some of these helicopters entered limited military service with export customers. After the delivery of the nine HU-1 (UH-1) pre-production helicopters, full-production helicopters entered service from June 1959 with the designation HU-1A (later UH-1A). With a powerplant of one T53-L-1A turboshaft driving a main rotor on a shorter mast, the type accommodated a crew of one or two plus up to five passengers or two litters, or alternatively 3,000lb (1,361kg) of freight in a cabin that was 8ft 6in (2.59m) long, 7ft 10in (2.39m) wide and 4ft 10in (1.47m) high. Later helicopters of the same basic variant switched to the 960hp (716kW) T53-L-5 turboshaft for improved performance with the same load, and the type could be armed with two 0.3in (7.62mm) pintle-mounted machine guns and thirty-two 2.75in (70mm) unguided rockets in two packs on the fuselage sides. Production up to March 1961 amounted to 173 helicopters, of which 14 were converted into TH-1A Iroquois dual-control trainers.

Introduced to service in March 1961, the HU-1B (soon UH-1B) was an

185

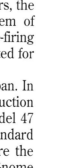

updated version with a powerplant of one 960hp (716kW) T53-L-5 turboshaft or, in later examples of the same basic variant, one 1,100hp (820kW) T53-L-9/9A or T53-L-11 turboshaft driving a main rotor with wider-chord blades and located on top of a taller rotor mast. The type can carry seven troops, or three litters and two seated casualties plus one attendant, or 3,000lb (1,361kg) of freight, and can be fitted with the same armament installations as the UH-1A. Production between 1961 and 1965 totalled 1,014 helicopters including the four service test helicopters.

The UH-1C model, introduced to service in September 1965, is based closely on the UH-1B but with a longer fuselage, increased fuel capacity, a main rotor with blades of even wider chord for a modest improvement in speed, and much greater manoeuvrability as a result of a reduced main rotor blade stall tendency. Production amounted to 749 helicopters.

Entering service from February 1964, the UH-1E was the UH-1B/C variant designed to fulfil the US Marine Corps' assault support helicopter (ASH) requirement, with an all-aluminium structure to mitigate the effects of salt-water corrosion, a rotor brake, increased fuel capacity, a rescue winch, and a payload of eight troops or 4,000lb (1,814kg) of freight. Production between 1964 and 1966 amounted to 192 helicopters, and there were also 20 examples of the TH-1E crew trainer variant.

The UH-1F that entered service from September 1964 was the UH-1B utility version for the USAF, with a completely different powerplant in the form of one 1,290hp (962kW) General Electric T58-GE-3 turboshaft flat-rated at 1,100hp (820kW) for the carriage of a payload comprising 10 passengers or 4,000lb (1,814kg) of freight in the missile site-support role. Production between September 1964 and 1967 amounted to 119 helicopters excluding 26 examples of the TH-1F dual-control trainer variant.

The HH-1K was the SAR variant of the UH-1E for the US Navy, but powered by the 1,400hp (1,044kW) T53-L-13 turboshaft. Production amounted to 27 helicopters delivered from May 1970. The UH-1L was the utility variant of the UH-1E for the US Navy, but powered by the T53-L-13 turboshaft derated to 1,100hp (820kW). Production amounted to eight helicopters delivered from November 1968, and there were also 90 examples of the TH-1L dual-control trainer delivered from 1969. The UH-1M designation was applied to a small number of UH-1Cs upgraded with the T53-L-13 turboshaft, provision for six AGM-22A (French AS.11) wire-guided anti-tank missiles and, in some helicopters, the Hughes Iroquois night fighter and night tracker (INFANT) system of searchlights and a low-light-level TV to illuminate targets for the side-firing armament. The UH-1P designation was applied to 20 UH-1Fs converted for psychological warfare.

The Model 204 series was also built under licence in Italy and Japan. In Italy the type was known as the Agusta (Bell) AB 204B, and its construction was a logical development from Agusta's production of the Bell Model 47 light helicopter as the Agusta (Bell) AB 47. This was powered as standard by the Lycoming T53-L-11A turboshaft, but alternative engines were the General Electric T58-GE-3 and Bristol Siddeley (later Rolls-Royce) Gnome

Designed as the Model 204, the Bell UH-1 Iroquois, universally nicknamed 'Huey' after its initial pre-1962 HU-1 designation, was the first turboshaft-powered helicopter to enter large-scale production in the USA and was one of the weapons that may be said to have defined the nature of the Vietnam War, in which American forces were involved between 1961 and 1973. The UH-1B may be taken as typical of the early 'Huey' helicopters, and could carry the pilot and up to eight soldiers, or two litters and one attendant, or 3,000lb (1,361kg) of freight. Other details included a powerplant of one 96hp (716kW) Lycoming T53-L-5 turboshaft, main rotor diameter of 44ft 0in (13.41m), fuselage length of 42ft 7in (12.98m), height of 12ft 8.5in (3.87m), maximum take-off weight of 8,500lb (3,856kg), maximum speed of 138mph (222km/h) at sea level, service ceiling of 14,000ft (4,265m) and range of 230 miles (371km).

H.1000 or H.1200 turboshafts. The first AB 204B flew in May 1961, and the four main subvariants of the baseline utility helicopter were the AB 204B-11 with the H.1000 engine and a main rotor diameter of 44ft 0in (13.41m), the AB 204B-12 with the H.1000 engine and a main rotor diameter of 48ft 0in (14.63m), the AB 204B-21 with the H.1200 engine and the smaller-diameter main rotor, and the AB 204B-22 with the H.1200 engine and the larger-diameter main rotor.

The most important development, however, was the AB 204AS dedicated anti-submarine helicopter: this was powered by the T58-GE-3 turboshaft, its armament comprised two Mk 44 or Mk 46 lightweight homing torpedoes, and its mission equipment included dunking sonar, all-weather instrumentation, automatic stabilisation and approach to the hover, and optional search radar. Production of the AB 204 series continued to 1974 and totalled 238 helicopters.

In January 1962, Bell granted a licence for the Model 204 to Mitsui, which in turn sub-licensed the type to Fuji for manufacture as the Fuji (Bell) UH-1B with the tail rotor relocated from the port to the starboard side of the tail pylon and with power provided by the T53 turboshaft assembled in Japan as the Kawasaki KT53. Deliveries totalled 124 helicopters, all but 34 of these going to the Japanese Ground Self-Defense Force.

Service experience revealed that the Model 204, in its UH-1 military form, was limited in tactical utility by its comparatively small payload volume and indifferent performance under hot-and-high conditions, both of these being factors that were to come to the fore in operations over South Vietnam during the Vietnam War (American involvement between 1961 and 1973). Bell therefore decided to exploit the greater power available from the T53-L-11 engine in the development of a Model 204 derivative with a larger main rotor and a bigger cabin for the carriage of a considerably greater payload: not counting its one pilot, this could include 12 troops, or six litters plus one attendant, or 4,000lb (1,814kg) of freight.

The new type was designed as the Model 205, and in July 1960 the US Army ordered seven examples with the service test designation YUH-1D. The first of these helicopters flew in August 1961 with a powerplant of one 1,100hp (820kW) Lycoming T53-L-11 turboshaft, a main rotor with a diameter of 48ft 0in (14.63m) rather than 44ft 0in (13.41m), and a fuselage stretched by 3ft 5in

The Agusta (Bell) AB 204B was the version of the civil Bell Model 204B made in Italy for military as well as civil applications. A notable feature is the typical Bell main rotor design, with two wide-chord blades and, at right angles to them, the stabilizing bar with small weights at its tips.

Operational experience revealed that the UH-1 'Huey' was too small, in its original Model 204 variants, for genuinely effective practical use, so Bell developed the Model 205 with a revised fuselage allowing the incorporation of a cabin large enough to carry up to 14 troops, or six litters and an attendant, or 3,880lb (1,759kg) of freight. The type entered service as the UH-1D, and this is the AB 205 variant built in Italy by Agusta, one of Bell's European licensees. The details for the definitive UH-1H variant include a powerplant of one 1,400hp (1,044kW) Lycoming T53-L-13 turboshaft, main rotor diameter of 48ft 0in (14.63m), fuselage length of 41ft 10.75in (12.77m), height of 14ft 6in (4.42m), maximum take-off weight of 9,500lb (4,309kg), maximum speed of 127mph (204km/h) at 5,700ft (1,735m), service ceiling of 12,600ft (3,840m) and range of 320 miles (515km).

(1.04m). In concert with a relocation of the enlarged fuel cells, the fuselage stretch increased cabin volume by slightly more than 50 per cent and made possible the carriage of the planned maximum payload in any of its forms.

The Model 205 was intended mainly for the US military, but Bell appreciated that the type also had civil attractions and therefore introduced the Model 205A-1 upgraded version that also secured a number of export military sales. First flown in 1963, the type is powered by a 1,400hp (1,044kW) Lycoming T53-13-B turboshaft derated to 1,250hp (932kW) and can carry a slung load of 5,000lb (2,268kg) as an alternative to an internal payload of 14 passengers.

The initial production version of the Model 205 for the US Army entered service from August 1963 as the UH-1D with a powerplant of one 1,100hp (820kW) T53-L-11 turboshaft, and production amounted to 2,008 helicopters excluding the seven YUH-1D service test helicopters. Profiting from its experience with the Model 205A-1 and its T53-13-B turboshaft, Bell developed an improved version of the UH-1D as the UH-1H with a more powerful engine for better hot-and-high performance, especially in the hover in regions such as South Vietnam. The type was delivered from September 1967, and American production amounted to 4,890 helicopters including 3,573 for the US Army, which plans to maintain some 2,700 helicopters of this type in service into the next century with updated features such as composite main rotor blades (glassfibre and Nomex with polyurethane leading edges protected over their outer sections by a stainless steel capping), an infra-red (IR)suppressor, a crash-resistant auxiliary fuel system, and more modern electronics including a radar-warning receiver and IR jammer, improved radio gear, and possibly a more modern powerplant offering marginally greater power but, more importantly, reduced fuel consumption and better 'maintainability'.

Among the American fleet are several special-purpose models, the most important being the EH-1H. During the early 1980s a few UH-1Hs were converted to the battlefield electronic countermeasures (ECM) standard with the 'Quick Fix I' communications interception, direction-finding and jamming equipment together with the Racal RACJAM airborne communications jamming system. The increasing threat to battlefield helicopters during this period was reflected by other changes such as the addition of a radar-warning receiver, radar jammer, chaff/flare dispenser, IR jammer, and missile detection and countermeasures implementation system. Another battlefield development of the UH-1H was the UH-1H stand-off target acquisition system (SOTAS) targeting helicopter fitted with a General Dynamics radar (with moving target indication facility) using a ventral antenna.

Some 220 UH-1Hs were also converted into UH-1V casevac/medevac helicopters during the 1980s. The designation HH-1H is applied to 30 USAF on-base rescue helicopters based on the UH-1H but carrying special equipment for rescue of aircrew from crashed aircraft.

The Agusta (Bell) AB 205 is the Italian licence-built version of the UH-1D/H differing only in small details from the US pattern, and from 1969 the company produced the slightly improved AB 205A-1. Production ended in 1988 after the delivery of 490 helicopters, mostly to air arms. The AIDC (Bell) UH-1H is the Taiwanese-built version of the UH-1H, of which 118 were delivered by the Aero Industry Development Center between 1969 and 1976. The Dornier (Bell) UH-1D is the German-built version of the UH-1D: after assembling an initial four helicopters from Bell-supplied kits, Dornier produced 140 UH-1Ds for the West German air force (which also received two such helicopters directly from Bell), and another 204 for the West German army. The Fuji (Bell) HU-1H is a version of the UH-1H built under licence by Fuji under sub-licence from Mitsui with the 1,400hp (1,044kW) Kawasaki (Lycoming) T53-K-13B turboshaft with a tractor rather than pusher tail rotor. The first HU-1H flew in July 1973, and military production totalled 107 including 52 with the ability to carry mine dispensers.

The Bell Model 206 was designed in an effort to win a US Army order for a light observation helicopter, but initially lost to the Hughes Model 369 that was ordered as the OH-6 Cayuse, was then developed into the Model 206A for civil sales and finally ordered into large-scale production for the US Army as the OH-58 Kiowa after the Kiowa's delivery rate decreased and its price rose. This is an AB 206 built by Agusta for the Italian army's air corps. The details of the Model 206A include accommodation for the pilot and three passengers or light freight, powerplant of one 317hp (236kW) Allison 250-C18 turboshaft, main rotor diameter of 33ft 4in (10.16m), fuselage length of 31ft 2in (9.50m), height of 9ft 6.5in (2.91m), maximum take-off weight of 3,000lb (1,361kg), maximum speed of 150mph (241km/h) at sea level, service ceiling of 17,000ft (5,180m) and range of 391 miles (629km).

During the early 1960s Bell decided that the only practical way in which its in-service Model 205 (UH-1 Iroquois) utility helicopter could be improved in overall capabilities was through the adoption of an uprated powerplant. There were no single-turboshaft powerplants offering adequate output, however, so the company's thoughts turned to a twin-engined layout. In 1964, Bell converted a UH-1D helicopter to Model 208 Twin Delta configuration with a Continental XT67-T-1 coupled turboshaft: offering 1,240hp (925kW), this powerplant comprised two T72-T-2 Model 217 power units driving a single shaft via a combining gearbox. The Model 208 first flew in April 1965 and offered some performance and payload enhancements over the basic UH-1C, but also the far greater safety factor of a powerplant either of whose power sections could support the helicopter in level flight. It was this latter factor that appealed to the Canadian forces, which needed a twin-engined UH-1 version for the extra reliability and safety required for operations in remote areas. In May 1968, therefore, Canada contracted for the development of the Model 212 Twin Two-Twelve as a derivative of the UH-1H with a Canadian coupled-turboshaft powerplant.

The first Model 212 flew in April 1969 with the 1,290hp (1,150kW) Pratt & Whitney Canada PT6T-3 Turbo Twin Pac driving a semi-rigid rotor of two-blade configuration. Later production models feature the PT6T-3B version of the Turbo Twin Pac with improved single-engine performance. The Model 212 received civil certification in June 1971, and since that time significant numbers of the basic commercial version have been built for the civil market and for the export military market. In October 1983, Textron agreed with the Canadian government to switch production of its current generation of unarmed helicopters to Canada, and the transfer of Model 212 production was completed in August 1988. The Canadian company handles sales to the Canadian government and civil operators, but also supplies helicopters to the parent company for resale to American and other customers. The Model 212 is also built under license in Italy as the Agusta (Bell) AB 212 by Agusta, which has also developed the specialised AB 212ASV/ASW version for the maritime role.

The Bell OH-58 Kiowa was developed during the 1980s into the altogether more capable OH-58D Kiowa Warrior (company designation Model 406) to serve as an advanced scout and target-designation helicopter with an uprated powerplant, refined nose contours, a four-blade main rotor offering greater lift and reduced noise, provision for light armament and, most importantly of all, a mast-mounted sight located above the main rotor. The availability of this multi-sensor item allows the OH-58D to lurk behind cover such as trees or hilltops, where it is relatively immune to the enemy's weapons, but still see the target area with the sensors in the spherical head, which is all that protrudes above the skyline.

Seen here with the wings that can be fitted to offload the six-blade main rotor in forward flight, the Mil Mi-6 'Hook' is an elderly type that still offers considerable heavy-lift capabilities as, with a crew of five, it can carry 90 troops, or 41 litters and two attendants, or 26,455lb (12,000kg) of freight in the hold, or alternatively a slung load of 17,637lb (8,000kg). The type has a powerplant of two 5,499hp (4,100kW) Soloviev D-25V (TV-2BM) turboshafts, rotor diameter of 114ft 10in (35.00m), fuselage length of 108ft 10.5in (33.18m), height of 32ft 4in (9.86m), maximum take-off weight of 93,700lb (42,500kg), maximum speed of 186mph (300km/h) at optimum altitude, service ceiling of 14,765ft (4,500m) and range of 621 miles (1,000km) with a 17,637lb (8,000kg) payload.

Transport Helicopters

HELICOPTERS optimised for the heavy transport role can take one of two primary forms, especially in the USSR (now CIS) that was and remains the primary exponent of such helicopters for civil as well as military purposes. The more obvious of these configurations, as epitomised by the Mil Mi-6 'Hook' and considerably larger and more modern Mi-26 'Halo', is the large fuselage. The floor and lower sides of such a fuselage are generally completed with specialised attachments that allow the insertion of a large number of seats for the passenger-carrying role or, in the more common military role, provide for the firm lashing of freight items. The cabin is generally of rectangular section to maximise the amount of freight that can be loaded onto the strengthened floor, and the capability for straight-in loading and unloading of such freight is provided by the incorporation of rear doors of either the clamshell type with a detachable ramp or, more usually, the rear ramp/door type built into the lower part of the rear fuselage. Such ramp/doors are also a feature of the larger types of American medium transport helicopter such as the Boeing H-46 Sea Knight and H-47 Chinook and also the Sikorsky H-53 Sea Stallion and Super Stallion. The other type of heavy-lift helicopter is the flying crane, which is optimised for the lifting role with a vestigial fuselage reinforced for the attachment of a substantial slung load. Helicopters of this type include the Soviet Mil Mi-10 'Harke' and American Sikorsky H-54 Tarhe. These helicopters generally have tall, wide-straddling quadricycle landing gear of the type that allows the helicopter to taxi over a large load for the attachment of the lifting strop, but the nature of this landing gear also makes it possible to attach a payload pod to the underside of the fuselage or alternatively a payload platform to the inner sides of the landing gear legs.

The Model 212 was adopted by the US military with the designation UH-1N, and deliveries were made from 1970 to the USAF (79 helicopters), and more importantly from 1971 to the US Navy and Marine Corps (221 helicopters of which the last was handed over in 1978). The variant's cabin is 7ft 8in (2.34m) long excluding the cockpit, 8ft 0in (2.44m) wide and 4ft 1in (1.24m) high, and is accessed on each side by a large rearward-sliding door. The sole derivative of this baseline model is the VN-1N presidential and VIP transport helicopter. Production amounted to just two new-build helicopters, although six more were produced as UH-1N conversions.

The Model 412 is a useful helicopter developed as an upgraded version of the Model 212 with a four- rather than two-blade main rotor and greater fuel capacity to increase speed and range. The type first flew in August 1979, and immediately revealed not only better performance but also reduced noise and vibration levels with its powerplant of one 1,800hp (1,342kW) Pratt & Whitney Canada PT6T-3B-1 Turbo Twin Pac coupled turboshaft flat-rated at 1,308hp (975kW) for take-off and 1,130hp (843kW) for continuous running. The type was designed primarily for the civil market, but a number of military orders were also won. The type is also built under licence in Italy as the Agusta (Bell) AB 412.

The Military 412 is the attack transport derivative of the Model 412, and was originally designated Model 412AH. The type has a Lucas undernose

turret (fitted with one 0.5in/12.7mm Browning M3 heavy machine gun and 875 rounds) aimed via a Honeywell Head Tracker helmet sight, provision for 0.3in (7.62mm) machine guns pintle-mounted in the cabin doors, and capability for externally carried weapons such as two pods carrying either two 0.3in machine guns or one 0.5in heavy machine gun, or two pods each carrying one 20mm cannon, or two multiple launchers each carrying seven or nineteen 2.75in (70mm) unguided rockets, or two multiple launchers each carrying four 2.75in unguided rockets. Other variants of the Model 412 include the Model 412SP upgraded version of the Model 412 with an increased maximum take-off weight and some 55 per cent more internal fuel capacity, the Model 412HP 1991 model with improved transmission for a higher hovering ceiling despite the type's greater weight, and the IPTN Bell-412 Indonesian license-built version of the Model 412SP without any significant differences from the baseline version.

As the Western world was concentrating its design and production efforts on the creation of light and medium helicopters for the battlefield role, the USSR was concentrating more on the development of medium and heavy helicopters for tactical and battlefield use. The first of these was the Soviet Mil Mi-6 'Hook', which brought a new dimension to heavy-lift helicopter capabilities, setting world records with payloads of more than 44,092lb (20,000kg). First flown in September 1957, the Mi-6 'Hook-A' was for its time the world's largest helicopter and is still a prodigious machine powered by two 5,499hp (4,100kW) PNPP 'Aviadvigatel' (Soloviev) D-25V (TV-2BM) turboshafts and capable of lifting a substantial slung load as an alternative to the internal payload of troops, freight and light vehicles in the hold, which is accessed by clamshell rear doors and ramps, and is 38ft 6in (11.72m) long, 8ft 8.25in (2.65m) wide and a minimum of 6ft 6in (2.00m) high, with a winch available for cargo handling. An unusual feature of the design is the removable wing, which offloads the main rotor by some 20 per cent in forward flight. Production totalled more than 800 such helicopters, about half of them for dedicated military service and the remainder mainly for the resources-exploitation industry with reversion to military service in times of crisis.

Produced only in small numbers, the Mi-6VKP 'Hook-B' is the airborne command post variant with the cabin fitted out for its role with specialised communication and plotting equipment. The type is distinguishable by its different antennae, which include four blade antennae arranged around the rear of the boom and a large rectangular frame antenna farther forward under the boom. Other changes include the omission of the starboard-side external fuel tank and the installation farther forward on the port side of the fuselage of a heat exchanger associated with the helicopter's additional electronics. The Mi-6AYa 'Hook-C', otherwise known as the Mi-22, is a modernised airborne command post variant with a different electronic suite to that of the 'Hook-B'. The variant is readily identifiable by the large swept blade antenna above the boom, and by the cluster of antennae under the forward fuselage.

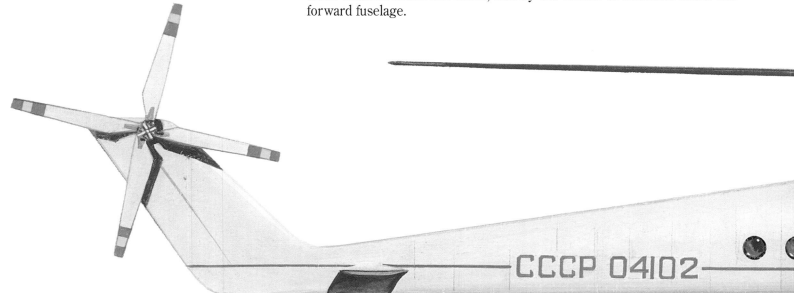

The Mi-10 'Harke' is the flying crane half-brother of the Mi-6 'Hook' with a cut-down fuselage and revised landing gear. The type is seen here with the platform that can be installed inside the landing gear units for the carriage of items such as this wheeled armoured personnel carrier. This and other heavy-lift helicopters have been produced in modest numbers for dual civil and military use: in civil service, the helicopters operate in tasks such as the supply of resources-exploitation industries in Siberia and similarly inhospitable regions lacking railways and major roads, but in times of crisis the helicopters are available to the military for the whole gamut of heavy-lift tasks.

The Mi-6 design led to the Mi-l0 'Harke' flying crane helicopter of 1960. This later model was intended to carry heavy, bulky loads, and has a widespread landing gear arrangement under the slim fuselage so that a load can be brought up under the helicopter and attached to the lifting points. First flown in V-10 prototype form during 1960, the type entered service in 1962 as the Mi-10 'Harke-A'. Above the line of the cabin windows, the Mi-10 is virtually identical to the Mi-6, although without provision for the detachable wings, and in its original form used the same powerplant of two PNPP 'Aviadvigatel' (Soloviev) D-25V (TV28-M) turboshafts each rated at 5,499hp (4,100kW) that were later replaced by two 6,504hp (4,850kW) PNPP 'Aviadvigatel' (Soloviev) D-25VF turboshafts. Below this level, the depth of the fuselage is reduced considerably and the boom is deepened so that the Mi-10 offered an unbroken lower fuselage line from nose to tail. The most unusual feature of the design is the quadricycle landing gear with twin wheels on each unit: the landing gear's track is 19ft 8.75in (6.01m), and its height allows the fully fuelled helicopter to taxi forward over loads up to 12ft 3.5in (3.75m) high for attachment to the underfuselage hook. The maximum external load is 33,069lb (15,000kg) including a platform that can be attached to the inside faces of the landing gear units, and which measures 28ft 0in by 11ft 7.25in (8.53m by 3.54m) for the carriage of suitable loads. As an alternative, the Mi-10 can carry 17,637lb (8,000kg) of freight as a slung load. Freight can also be carried in the cabin, which is 46ft 0.75in (14.04m) long, 8ft 2.5in (2.50m) wide and 5ft 6in (1.68m) high.

Introduced in 1966, the Mi-10K 'Harke-B' is an improved version with shorter landing gear units, a slimmer tail pylon and, perhaps most

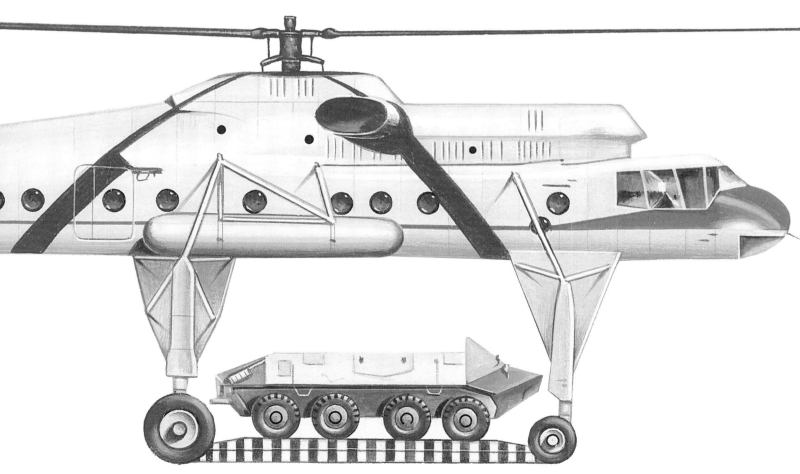

importantly of all, an undernose gondola with a rear-facing seat from which one of the two pilots can fly the helicopter in hovering flight for the loading and unloading of slung items. This improved model originally had the same powerplant as the Mi-10 and could carry a slung load of 24,250lb (11,000kg), but the retrofit of more powerful engines later improved payload to a marked degree. Production of the two types totalled some 55 helicopters up to 1977, when a small number of attrition replacement helicopters was built after a six-year break in production. Most of the Mi-10s and Mi-10Ks are operated in the resources-exploitation industry, but can be called into military service as required.

Further down the size and weight spectrum, but considerably more versatile in its tactical applications on the battlefield, is the Mi-8 that received the NATO reporting name 'Hip' and proved so successful that it has been maintained in production right up to the present in Mi-8 and improved Mi-17 variants. Basically a turbine-engined development of the piston-engined Mi-4 for civil and military applications, and flown in the first half of 1961 as the V-8 'Hip-A' prototype with a four-blade main rotor and a powerplant of one Soloviev (Ivchyenko) AI-24V turboshaft transmission-limited to 2,682hp (2,000kW), the Mi-8 was a capable machine but would clearly offer greater reliability as well as a better power-to-weight ratio with a twin-engined powerplant. The 'Hip-B' second prototype flew in September 1962 and pioneered an altogether more effective twin-turboshaft powerplant, though in this prototype form driving the same four-blade main rotor that was soon replaced by the definitive five-blade unit. Two more

Built by Aérospatiale (now Eurocopter France) as the SA. 366G Dauphin 2, this trim but somewhat underpowered search-and-rescue helicopter serves with the US Coast Guard as the HH-65A Dolphin. Other versions of the Dauphin 2 have a more directly martial application in the battlefield role with a moderately heavy weapons load.

The UH-1H is the definitive utility transport version of Bell's 'Huey' series in its single-engined form. The type still provides the ability to carry a useful number of men or light freight, but is noisy and increasingly expensive to maintain.

Despite the age of its basic design, which originated in the late 1950s for a first flight in September 1962, the Mil Mi-8 'Hip' is still the most important tactical transport helicopter operated by the Russian (originally Soviet) forces and a number of other air arms. The helicopter bears exactly the same relation to the Mi-4 'Hound' as does the Mi-2 'Hoplite' to the Mi-1 'Hare': the Mi-8 is therefore the turboshaft-powered development of the Mi-4, the prototype featuring a four-blade main rotor driven by a single 1,700hp (1,267.5kW) Soloviev turboshaft whereas the production model has a five-blade main rotor powered by two 1,700hp (1,267.5kW) Isotov TV2-117A turboshafts. The Mi-8 has a crew of three and can carry 24 troops or a freight load in the form of 8,818lb (4,000kg) carried internally or 6,616lb (3,000kg) lifted as a slung load. The type's other details include a main rotor diameter of 69ft 10.5in (21.29m), fuselage length of 59ft 7.5in (18.17m), height of 18ft 6.5in (5.65m), maximum take-off weight of 26,455lb (12,000kg), maximum speed of 161mph (260km/h) at 3,280ft (1,000m), service ceiling of 14,760ft (4,500m) and range of 276 miles (455km) with maximum payload. The two examples illustrated here are in service with the Finnish air force, and are a standard Mi-8 of the initial production civil/military series with circular cabin windows (above), and a dedicated military transport with rectangular cabin windows (below). The type is also operational with very heavy armament (unguided rockets and guided anti-tank missiles), and had also been upgraded to Mi-17 standard with an uprated dynamic system.

prototypes paved the way for the initial production model, the 'Hip-C' without the streamlined main landing gear fairings of the two prototype models. The first two models were the Mi-8P and Mi-8S with rectangular cabin windows, and were intended primarily for civil use although both saw some military service: the former was basically a convertible 28-passenger/freight transport and the latter an 11-passenger airliner. The Mi-8T 'Hip-C' was developed with a powerplant of two 1,500hp (1,118kW) TV-117 turboshafts as a utility transport with round windows and rail-mounted seats, and although developed initially for civil use was in fact built in much larger numbers for the military and with more powerful TV2-117A engines. The cabin is 7ft 8.25in (2.34m) wide and 5ft 10.75in (1.80m) high, with a length of 20ft 10.25in (6.36m) in the passenger model and 17ft 6.25in (5.34m) in the freight model, and this cabin is accessed by a large port-side forward sliding door and clamshell rear doors.

The military version has attachment points for two outrigger structures on the fuselage sides, each such structure being fitted with two hardpoints for multiple rocket launchers: these hardpoints were originally stressed for 16-tube launchers, but were later restressed for 32-tube launchers as a means of doubling the ability of the 'Hip-C' to saturate the landing zone with fire before touching down to disgorge its embarked troops. During the Mi-8's long production and service career, the Mi-8T and its successors have proved the basic concept to be excellent and highly reliable. Some of the helicopters have been upgraded to Mi-17 standard as the Mi-8MT 'Hip-C' and Mi-8MTV 'Hip-C', the latter optimised for operations under hot-and-high

Opposite top: The Aérospatiale (now Eurocopter France) SA319B Alouette III has been produced in original SA. 341 version with the 590hp (440kW) Turbomeca Astazou III turboshaft and the uprated SA. 342 version with the more powerful 870hp (649kW) Astazou XIV turboshaft. This is an example of the latter type in its SA. 342M form with an armament of four HOT tube-launched anti-tank missiles.

The Aérospatiale (now Eurocopter France) SA. 319B Alouette III Astazou was the final production model of the classic Alouette (lark) series, and is seen here in its armed form with provision under the outrigger arms for four wire-guided anti-tank missiles.

conditions with a powerplant of two 1,923hp (1,434kW) TV3-117MT turboshafts, and these are distinguishable by the relocation of the tail rotor from the starboard to the port side of the tail pylon. These two subvariants have the same weapons capability as the standard Mi-8T, but the rocket launchers are often of the B-8V20A type each carrying twenty 3.15in (80mm) S-8 unguided rockets packing a considerably heavier punch than the older 2.17in (55mm) S-5 type. There is also an Mi-8PS 'Hip-C' military VIP transport version based on the civil Mi-8 Salon executive transport.

The versatility of the Mi-8/Mi-17 series is attested by its development and production and/or conversion in a number of alternative forms. The Mi-8VZPU 'Hip-D', for example, is the airborne reserve command post version for the battlefield command and communications relay roles, and is distinguishable by its additional antenna arrays (above and below the boom) and supplementary electronic equipment carried in external box fairings attached to the hardpoints used for weapons in the 'Hip-C'.

The Mi-8TV 'Hip-F' is the export version of the 'Hip-E', with six AT-3 'Sagger' anti-tank missiles in place of the later and generally superior 'Swatters' of the Soviet type. Some of the helicopters have been further improved in capability to Mi-17 standard, and are also distinguishable by the tail rotor on the port side of the tail pylon.

The Mi-9 'Hip-G' is the airborne command post and battlefield communication relay helicopter based on the Mi-8T but distinguishable from the 'Hip-D' by detail differences such as its three 'hockey stick' antennae (two on the rear of the fuselage pod and one under the boom) and underfuselage strakes. Appearing in the early 1980s, the Mi-8SMV 'Hip-J' is an electronic warfare derivative of the basic series with a number of unspecified systems and external fittings (two box-type fairings and two 'handle' type antennae on each side of the fuselage) for the jamming of battlefield air-defence radars. Only a few such helicopters were produced, and later in the variant's career a small number were adapted for the electronic intelligence (Elint) role.

Another variant of the early 1980s, the Mi-8PPA 'Hip-K' is an advanced

ECM and communication-jamming variant with six cross-dipole antennae on each side of the rear fuselage, a large box fairing on each side of the cabin, six heat exchangers side-by-side under the fuselage for cooling of the electronic systems, but with no Doppler navigation.

The Mi-17 'Hip-H' is a much uprated and updated version of the Mi-8 that first flew in 1976 and entered service in 1981 with the dynamic system of the Mi-14, including a powerplant of two 1,925hp (1,435kW) Klimov (Isotov) TV3-117MT turboshafts and the tail rotor relocated to the port side of the fin for improved hot-and-high performance, especially in the hovering regime. The helicopter has a slightly larger cabin to facilitate carriage of the greater payload made possible by the improved powerplant, and can also carry additional weapons such as the UPK-23 gun pod containing the 23mm GSh-23L two-barrel cannon. In domestic military service this variant is generally not known as the Mi-17 but rather as the Mi-8MT or, with optimisation for operation in hot-and-high conditions, as the Mi-8MTV. Other improvements over the Mi-8TB standard include scabbed-on cockpit armour, a number of active countermeasures against IR- and radar-guided missiles, and exhaust diffusers.

The Mi-17-1 'Hip-H' version was introduced in 1989 with updated avionics and greater power in the form of two 2,072hp (1,545kW) TV3-117VM turboshafts allowing the carriage of a payload of 8,818lb (4,000kg) at altitudes up to 16,405ft (5,000m).

The Mi-17M/17V 'Hip-H' is the current production model built by the Kazan Helicopter Production Association with the same TV3-117VM powerplant as the Mi-17-1 and provision for nose radar and flotation equipment.

The Mi-17P 'Hip-K' is the Mi-17 counterpart of the Mi-8PPA and

The original Mil Mi-8 'Hip' versions are distinguishable from their later Mi-17 'Hip' offspring by a number of small features, and also by the location of the anti-torque rotor on the starboard rather than port side of the pylon extending upward and rearward from the end of the tailboom.

possesses the same NATO reporting name, but is based on the up-engined Mi-17 airframe with the Mi-8PPA's antenna array replaced by primary and secondary arrays on the rear fuselage and boom respectively. The primary array comprises a slightly concave rectangular fairing, with 32 circular antennae, on each side. The secondary array is considerably smaller and, located in line with the Doppler navigation, comprises two square fairings each containing four circular antennae.

Resulting from a programme launched in 1968 for a first prototype flight in 1973, the Mi-14PL (that received the NATO reporting name 'Haze-A') is a derivative of the Mil Mi-8 'Hip' for the considerably different land-based ASW role, with retractable landing gear (two forward-retracting single-wheel nose units and two rearward-retracting twin-wheel main units) and amphibious operating capability through the use of a boat hull and stabilizing sponsons. The planing bottom of the boat hull accommodates, from front to rear, the radome of the surveillance radar, the two nosewheel units (flanking the radome), the weapons bay, the dunking sonar (offset to starboard) and the two sonobuoy launcher tubes, while the two lateral sponsons also accommodate the main landing gear units.

The Westland (originally Saunders-Roe) Wasp HAS.Mk I seen above and below is the naval half-brother of the Scout AH.Mk I land-based model. The naval model has a slightly higher-rated powerplant, quadricycle rather than twin-skid alighting gear, a folding tail and folding main rotor blades, and naval avionics and armament for use from the quarterdeck platforms of frigates in the anti-submarine and anti-light surface vessel roles. The type has a flightcrew of two and can carry four passengers or a light freight load, and its other details include a powerplant of one 710hp (530kW) Rolls-Royce Nimbus Mk 503 turboshaft, main rotor diameter of 32ft 3in (9.83m), fuselage length of 30ft 4in (9.24m), height of 8ft 11in (2.72m), maximum take-off weight of 5,500lb (2,495kg), maximum speed of 120mph (193km/h) at sea level, service ceiling of 12,200ft (3,720m) and range of 270 miles (435km) with four passengers.

The greater demands of this exacting role dictated the introduction of an uprated powerplant, and this initially comprised two 1,700hp (1,268kW) Klimov (Isotov) TV3-117A turboshafts that were replaced in later helicopters by two 1,950hp (2,245kW) TV3-117MT turboshafts. The later helicopters also adopted a number of features of the Mi-17's dynamic system including the tail rotor switched from the starboard to the port side of the tail pylon, introduction of an externally mounted winch above the port-side sliding cabin door, and omission of the doors of the landing gear bays. The type can also be used in the SAR role with armament replaced by a rescue winch and other mission equipment.

In 1989 an improved variant was introduced as the Mi-14PLM with a number of detail improvements including a MAD installation.

The Mi-14BT 'Haze-B' is the mine countermeasures version of the 'Haze-A', identifiable by the strake and blister fairing (the former containing hydraulic tubing and the latter accommodating the relocated cabin heating and ventilation system) on the starboard side of the fuselage. The type can tow three different types of sled for the detonation of magnetic, acoustic and impact mines, and is visually differentiated from the Mi-14PL by its lack of the towed MAD 'bird' and by the windows installed in the

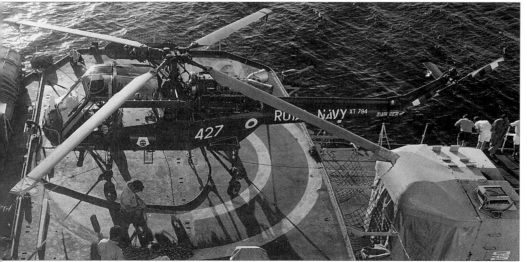

extreme rear of the fuselage pod to allow the mine counter measures (MCM) operator to keep watch on his towed equipment.

The Mi-14PS 'Haze-C' is the dedicated three-crew SAR variant of the 'Haze-B', retaining the starboard-side strake and pod but introducing a double-size door on the port side together with a retractable rescue winch with a three-person basket. The variant carries ten 20-person life-rafts, and the cabin is outfitted for the carriage of two litters and eight seated survivors. Other notable features of the Mi-14PS are its three searchlights and its ability to tow life-rafts containing survivors.

One of the best British designs appeared in 1958 in the form of the Westland Wasp/Scout evolutionary development of the Saunders-Roe P.531 prototype. A light general-purpose type, the helicopter was adopted by the Royal Navy as an anti-submarine helicopter and liaison machine with tricycle landing gear and the name Wasp, and by the army as an observation, liaison and light anti-tank type with twin-skid landing gear and the name Scout.

The same year also saw the appearance of the Kaman K-600, the first American helicopter powered by twin turboshafts. A general-purpose type, the K-600 was built in some numbers as the H-43 Huskie for the USAF, whose primary use for the type was to rescue the crews of aircraft involved in take-off and landing accidents.

Although developed for the Royal Navy, the Westland Wasp HAS.Mk I is now operated only by navies with have received ex-British 'Leander' class frigates or their Dutch-built counterparts of the 'Van Speijk' class.

The Kaman SH-2 Seasprite that first flew in 1959 was the world's first truly all-round helicopter, with the excellent speed of 155mph (250km/h) and a range of 450 miles (724km). The importance of the SH-2 lies in design features such as its retractable landing gear and watertight fuselage bottom, allowing the machine to sit in the sea, deceiving enemy submarines into thinking it had left the area, and making rescue operations easier. With advanced avionics and flying systems, the SH-2 has all-weather capability and can serve as an anti-missile defence when fitted with the appropriate electronics. The SH-2 was steadily upgraded in capabilities, and is still widely employed by the US Navy in its SH-2F Seasprite and SH-2G Super Seasprite twin-engined models.

The origins of the type can be traced back to 1956, when the US Navy issued a requirement for a high-performance utility helicopter capable of all-weather operations from smaller surface warships for the fulfilment of the whole range of utility missions. The most important of these roles was shipborne SAR, but other significant missions were planeguard, gunfire observation, reconnaissance, liaison, communications, vertical replenishment ('vertrep'), of ships at sea, casevac, and wirelaying for tactical air controller operations.

Kaman won the resulting design competition with its K-20 concept, which was a rarity among Kaman's designs in being a helicopter of conventional layout with a single main rotor and thus a longer rear fuselage supporting a small anti-torque rotor. Other features were tailwheel landing gear with retractable main units to facilitate the use of the rescue hoist that was one of the type's most important items of equipment, and a watertight hull so that the type could alight on the sea. The US Navy ordered four YHU2K-1 (from 1962 YUH-2A) prototypes, and the first of these flew in July 1959 with a crew of two, a payload that could include 12 passengers or two litters and four seated casualties, and a powerplant of one 1,025hp (764kW) General Electric T58-GE-6 turboshaft derated to 875hp (652kW). Flight trials confirmed that the K-20 could be a very capable helicopter, and the type was ordered into production with an uprated powerplant in the form of the 1,250hp (932kW) T58-GE-8 turboshaft.

The Kaman H-2 Seasprite has been developed through several versions initially with a single engine and then with two in variants of steadily more impressive multi-role capability. The type is still in service in two light airborne multi-purpose system (LAMPS) Mk I variants that provide the frigates and older destroyers of the US Navy with a helicopter that can undertake the anti-missile warning, anti-submarine, anti-light surface vessel, rescue and utility transport roles. Seen here is an SH-2D upgraded to SH-2F standard with a crew of three, powerplant of two 1,350hp (1,007kW) General Electric T58-GE-8F turboshafts, main rotor diameter of 44ft 0in (13.41m), overall length of 52ft 7in (16.03m), height of 15ft 6in (4.72m), maximum take-off weight of 13,500lb (6,123kg), maximum speed of 150mph (241km/h) at sea level, service ceiling of 22,500ft (6,860m) and range of 431 miles (695km).

Orders for this HU2K-1 initial production model totalled 84 helicopters that entered service from December 1962, by which time the designation had been altered to UH-2A. Ordered with the designation HU2K-1U (that had been altered before the type entered service), the UH-2B was a simplified version of the UH-2A and lacked all-weather flight capability. Production totalled 104 helicopters, most of which were later upgraded to UH-2A all-weather standard without any change in their designation.

In March 1965, Kaman completed a Seasprite conversion with a twin-engined powerplant. The use of two T58-GE-8B turboshafts, each rated at 1,250hp (932kW) and driving a transmission limited to a combined rating of 1,685hp (1,256kW), improved flight performance and, perhaps more importantly, enhanced safety in over-water operations as each engine was individually able to support the helicopter in level flight. The conversion caught the attention of the US Navy, which in 1966 ordered the similar alteration of two UH-2Bs to the UH-2C twin-engined standard for prototype trials. These confirmed the success of the revised powerplant, and many UH-2As and UH-2Bs were then converted to UH-2C standard for redelivery from August 1967 with a pair of T58-GE-8B turboshafts, slightly more tail area, and minor alterations of the cockpit and main rotor pylon. Many of the converted helicopters were later re-engined with two 1,350hp (1,007kW) T58-GE-8F turboshafts.

Another six UH-2As were converted to HH-2C Seasprite standard for the combat SAR role in the Vietnam War. These machines had a powerplant of two T58-GE-8F turboshafts, a more advanced main rotor, a four- rather than three-blade tail rotor, and twin- rather than single-wheel main landing gear units for operation at a higher maximum take-off weight. Other features were self-sealing fuel tankage, armour protection for the crew, a more advanced rescue hoist, and armament in the form of an undernose turret mounting one 0.3in (7.62mm) General Electric GAU-2B/A Minigun rotary six-barrel machine gun, and two 0.3in M60 machine guns pintle-mounted in the cabin doors. From February 1970, another 70 UH-2As were redelivered after conversion to the HH-2D standard that approximated that of the HH-2C except for its lack of armour and armament.

In the late 1960s the US Navy became increasingly concerned about the inadequacy of its anti-submarine and anti-ship missile defence capabilities at a time when the USSR was introducing several improved nuclear-powered attack submarine classes and specialised anti-ship missiles. Kaman proposed a development of its Seasprite to meet the resulting light airborne multi-purpose system (LAMPS) Mk I requirement, and the US Navy agreed that the type would make a useful interim type to operate from the helicopter facilities of its destroyers and frigates. In 1971, therefore, two HH-2Ds were modified to SH-2D standard with search radar using

Opposite top: The Sikorsky SH-3 Sea King was the first helicopter in the world to offer a full submarine hunter-killer capability in a single machine, and is here seen in the form of an SH-3H with its dunking sonar lowered so that the sensor is deep in the water as the helicopter hovers in search of a target.

Opposite bottom: The Agusta (Bell) AB 212 ASV/ASW is a medium-weight helicopter developed in Italy on the basis of the Bell Model 212 that entered service as the UH-1N twin-engined development of the earlier single-engined 'Huey' helicopters. The AB 212 ASV/ASW is well equipped and armed for the anti-submarine and anti-surface vessel roles.

Below: The Aérospatiale AS 365F Dauphin 2 (now Eurocopter France AS 565SA Panther) is optimised for the anti-ship or anti-submarine missions. The former is typical of the helicopter illustrated with chin-mounted radar and up to four AS.15TT lightweight anti-ship missiles.

an antenna in an undernose radome, an electronic support measures (ESM) system for the detection of possible threats through their electro-magnetic emissions, removable MAD system (with its sensor in a towed 'bird') on the starboard side of the fuselage and balanced by a port-side launcher for 15 sonobuoys, the associated displays and controls, and provision for armament in the form of two Mk 46 lightweight torpedoes.

The first of the two prototype conversions flew in March 1971. These conversions proved highly successful, and the US Navy therefore ordered the conversion of another 18 machines to a similar interim standard as Kaman completed work on the definitive LAMPS Mk I type that was now clearly available on the basis of the Seasprite. The SH-2Ds had all been delivered by March 1972.

Two HH-2Ds were later converted as YSH-2E prototypes to meet the full LAMPS Mk I requirement with improved radar and updated systems, and the first of these machines flew in March 1972. The planned SH-2E production model did not come to fruition, however, for the US Navy opted instead for the SH-2F improved version of the SH-2D with greater power, strengthened landing gear with the tailwheel moved farther forward, and a titanium rotor hub. The SH-2F entered service in May 1973 as the definitive LAMPS Mk I helicopter for the anti-submarine, anti-ship missile defence, SAR, and utility transport roles, tasks in which the SH-2F still offers capabilities unmatched in any helicopter of comparable size. The initial SH-2F fleet comprised 88 UH-2A, UH-2B and UH-2C conversions effected between 1973 and 1982, and this force was supplemented by 16 SH-2D conversions with a higher maximum take-off weight.

So successful did the SH-2F prove, moreover, that there was demand for greater numbers and the SH-2F fleet was therefore expanded by 54 new

helicopters built between 1985 and 1989. The new-build SH-2F differs from the SH-2G principally in its maximum ordnance load of 1,200lb (544kg) and powerplant of two 1,350hp (1,007kW) T58-GE-8F turboshafts driving an improved main rotor. The SH-2Fs still in US Navy service are being upgraded to virtual SH-2G standard with improved avionics and General Electric T700-GE-401 turboshafts for better performance (in terms of range and reliability) and greater commonality with the Sikorsky SH-60B Seahawk.

For service in the Persian Gulf since 1987, some 16 SH-2Fs were upgraded in defensive capability by the installation of an ESM system with rear-warning radar (RWR), ECM and passive targeting capabilities, two chaff/flare/decoy dispensers, one IR jammer, one missile warning system, one missile warning and jamming system and, under the nose, one forward-looking IR (FLIR) sensor.

The SH-2G Super Seasprite is a significantly improved SH-2F with a powerplant of two 1,723hp (1,285kW) T700-GE-401 turboshafts driving a new and slightly larger main rotor with composite-structure rotor blades. The variant also introduced a digital databus for full integration of the modern sensor and data processing systems, which include a much-enhanced acoustic data processor, an updated tactical navigation system, a global positioning system (GPS) receiver, an acoustic system data link, an FLIR sensor, improved ESM and dunking sonar. The prototype was a converted SH-2F that flew as an engine test bed in April 1985 and with full electronics in December 1989. The new type entered service in 1991 in the form of six new-build helicopters and a planned 97 examples converted from SH-2F standard but, in the event, the end of the 'Cold War' reduced the US Navy's requirement and only 17 'production' conversions were effected to complement the prototype conversion. The US Navy is to upgrade its in-service SH-2Gs with the improved defensive features of the SH-2Fs operated

Above: Westland developed its Sea King from the Sikorsky SH-3 with more sophisticated mission electronics, and the initial model was the Sea King HAS.Mk I illustrated here.

Above right: The Sea King HAS.Mk 5 is a considerably more capable anti-submarine helicopter than the Sea King HAS.Mk I, with more advanced sensors and processing equipment carried in a larger tactical compartment.

Left: The most important assault transport helicopter available to the US Marine Corps is the Sikorsky CH-53 Sea Stallion and Super Stallion series, which had been developed through a number of variants with two or three engines. This is an example of the definitive twin-engined model, the CH-53D.

in the Persian Gulf, together with the Magic Lantern-30 laser system for the detection of underwater mines. Kaman also offers the type in the anti-shipping role with stub wings for the carriage of AGM-65D Maverick ASMs, and is actively marketing rebuilds of up to 72 SH-2F helicopters now surplus to US Navy requirements.

Evermore advanced ideas reached the hardware stage during the late 1950s, and in 1960 the important Sikorsky S-61 emerged from the experimental shops. The type soon entered service with the US Navy as the SH-3 Sea King with a powerplant of two General Electric T58 turboshafts. The Sea King was of great operational importance at the time of its introduction as the world's first all-weather helicopter effectively combining the submarine hunter-killer roles that had previously required the efforts of two helicopters, one to hunt with sonar and the other to kill with depth charges and/or homing torpedoes; the US Coast Guard deploys a variant of the same basic type as a patrol and rescue helicopter. The USAF used the same basic airframe for transport missions and for rescuing aircraft and their crews, although these CH-3 and HH-3 Jolly Green Giant helicopters had a revised fuselage with retractable tricycle landing gear, a ventral ramp/door arrangement, and features such as improved armament and self-sealing fuel tanks. There were also two S-61 civil variants that secured modest but useful orders for the airliner and resources-exploitation support industries.

The S-61 was designed in the later 1950s to meet a US Navy requirement for an ASW helicopter to replace the Sikorsky HSS-1 Seabat, and combined, for the first time in such a machine, the hunter and the killer capabilities that previously required the teaming of two less capable helicopters. The transition to this more effective dual capability was made possible by the availability of the General Electric T58 turboshaft, which was a compact engine offering a considerably lower vibration level and also a very much higher power-to-weight ratio than any comparable piston engine. The incorporation of such an engine into the S-61 therefore resulted in a design that was somewhat different in conceptual terms from that of the S-58. This difference was reflected not so much in the basic configuration, which was little altered except for its full amphibious capability, but rather in the feasibility of a more reliable twin-turboshaft powerplant. This opened the way for the S-58's nose-mounted single piston engine to be replaced by two turboshafts located above the fuselage in positions flanking the gearbox and transmission for the five-blade main and tail rotors. This installation above the hold obviated the need for the S-58's long, heavy and obstructive transmission shaft and thus opened the way for a fuselage with greater useful capacity. Other notable features of the new design were a boat hull for emergency waterborne capability with stability enhanced by the outrigger sponsons that provided accommodation for the main units of the retractable tricycle landing gear, far greater payload, and provision for a more sophisticated mission suite in the hold, which was occupied by two sonar operators.

The specific variant for the US Navy was evolved as the S-61B, and the US Navy's go-ahead was signed in December 1957. The initial 10 machines were YHSS-2 prototype and service test helicopters, and the first of these flew in March 1959 with a powerplant of two 1,050hp (783kW) T58-GE-6 turboshafts. Evaluation of these helicopters confirmed the radical superiority of the S-61B over the S-58. This type was ordered into production as the HSS-2 Sea King (from 1962 SH-3A), with provision for an external payload of 6,000lb (2,722kg) carried on a sling with automatic touch-down release capability, mission equipment that included dunking sonar and an

Seen here in the form of a Sea King HAS.Mk 1, the Westland Sea King offers capabilities superior to those of its American SH-3 Sea King original by possessing the onboard tactical processing equipment that allows autonomous rather than ship-controlled anti-submarine operations. The radome to the rear of the powerplant/main rotor assembly covers the antenna for the Ekco AW391 surveillance radar that was replaced in the Sea King HAS.Mk 5 and later versions by the Marconi Sea Search radar.

autostabilization system providing for automatic transition to and from the hover as well as automatic altitude hold for effective sonar operation, and a powerplant of two T58-GE-6 turboshafts that were soon changed for two 1,250hp (932kW) T58-GE-8 or -8B turboshafts.

Production totalled 245 helicopters that entered service from September 1961. Numbers of SH-3A helicopters were later converted for different tasks, and these included three examples of the CH-3A for the USAF's role of supplying 'Texas Tower' radar outposts in the Atlantic; 12 examples of the HH-3A for the combat SAR role with T58-GE-8F engines, a 0.3in (7.62mm) General Electric GAU-2B/A Minigun rotary six-barrel machine gun in a barbette in the rear of each sponson, armour protection and provision for long-range fuel tanks; nine examples of the RH-3A for the exacting mine countermeasures role with the ASW equipment replaced by towed MCM equipment; and eight examples of the VH-3A for the presidential and VIP transport role. There were also three CH-3B conversions generally similar to the CH-3As and used for the same role. A total of 41 helicopters to SH-3A standard was produced for Canada (four built in the USA and the other 37 assembled in Canada) with the designation CHSS-2 that was later altered to CH-124.

The USAF was highly impressed with the capabilities of the ex-US Navy helicopters converted to S-61A amphibious transport standard with the designations CH-3A and CH-3B, and decided to procure a variant fully optimised for its particular requirements. Sikorsky developed this as the S-61R with a powerplant of two 1,300hp (969kW) turboshafts, an auxiliary power unit for independence from ground facilities, pressurised rotor blades for simple and quick inspection, a simplified lower hull, lateral fuselage sponsons into which the main units of the revised tricycle landing gear units

The original SH-3A Sea King version of the Sikorsky S-61 anti-submarine helicopter for the US Navy was austerely equipped for its primary task with just dunking sonar and an armament of depth charges or two homing torpedoes.

retracted, and the type of pod-and-boom fuselage that allowed the incorporation of a hydraulically-powered ventral ramp/door giving direct access to the hold, which was 25ft 10.5in (7.89m) long, 6ft 6in (1.98m) wide and 6ft 3in (1.91m) high, fitted with a winch for cargo handling, and additionally accessed by a jettisonable sliding door on the forward port side of the hold. The type was delivered from December 1963, and a total of 133 helicopters was ordered although only the first 41 were actually delivered to this initial standard, and the eventual production total, including the CH-3E, reached only 83.

Delivered from June 1966, the SH-3D was an improved ASW version with more powerful 1,400hp (1,044kW) T58-GE-10 turboshafts and improved dunking sonar. The US Navy ordered 73 such helicopters, and others were built for export. The type had a maximum official warload capability of 840lb (626kg) in the form of depth charges or two Mk 46 homing torpedoes, but the type had the ability to carry a slung load of 8,000lb (3,629kg), so the warload could be considerably higher than the quoted figure. The only current variant of this model in US Navy service is the VH-3D VIP transport, of which 11 were produced as SH-3D conversions.

The CH-3E was the improved standard introduced from the forty-second machine of the USAF's order for the CH-3. This was characterised by the introduction of a significantly more capable powerplant comprising two 1,500hp (1,132kW) T58-GE-5 turboshafts that was later retrofitted in the CH-3C. This uprated type was delivered from February 1966, and could lift 25 troops, or 15 litters, or a freight load of 5,000lb (2,268kg) internally or 8,000lb (3,629kg) externally, although a more important role was combat SAR in the Vietnam War with a powerful rescue hoist. For this difficult task, each helicopter was fitted with armament for the self-defence and fire-suppression roles: this armament comprised one Emerson TAT-102 turret

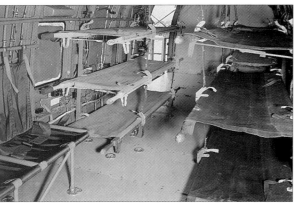

Above: The large cabin of the Westland Sea King is generally outfitted as a tactical compartment for the implementation of the whole anti-submarine task, but can be stripped out to turn the helicopter into a casualty evacuation machine of considerable capability.

on the outer end of each sponson and remotely controlled from sighting stations in the port and starboard personnel doors; each TAT-102 turret carried one 0.3in (7.62mm) General Electric GAU-2B/A Minigun rotary six-barrel machine gun with 8,000 rounds, and the combination of the turrets' positions and ability to traverse through an arc of more than 180 degrees meant that 360-degree fire capability was possible, with overlapping fields of fire toward the nose.

Service in Vietnam indicated the need for greater operational capabilities, and this led to the development of the HH-3E Jolly Green Giant, based on the armed CH-3E but fitted with protective armour, self-sealing fuel tanks, a retractable inflight-refuelling probe, jettisonable external tanks, a high-speed hoist, and other specialised equipment. Some 14 of the type were ordered, but only eight were completed as such and the total was boosted by the conversion of all the CH-3Es to this standard.

The designation HH-3F Pelican is applied to 40 of the US Coast Guard SAR version of the CH-3E, delivered from 1968 with search radar (using an antenna in a nose radome offset to port), a waterproofed fuselage, and provision for 15 litters and six seated survivors.

Under the SH-3G designation, 105 SH-3As and SH-3Ds were converted to utility helicopter standard with ASW equipment that can be removed to allow the installation of additional fuel tankage and seating for up to 15 passengers.

The SH-3H is the multi-role version of the SH-3G for the dual anti-submarine warfare and anti-ship missile defence roles, with upgraded ASW equipment including dunking sonar, active/passive sonobuoys and MAD gear with a towed 'bird' carried under the starboard stabilizing float, as well as specialist equipment including high-performance radar and a radar warning receiver for the fleet missile defence role, whose primary task is the detection and localisation of incoming anti-ship missiles. Some 112 SH-3As, SH-3Ds and SH-3Gs were upgraded to this standard.

Opposite Top; The Westland Sea King HC.Mk 4 is the primary assault transport helicopter for the delivery of Royal Marines in amphibious operations, and is a hybrid type that combines the folding tail and main rotor blades of the Sea King with the modified fuselage and landing gear of the Commando developed by Westland as a land-based tactical transport version of the Sea King.

The Westland Sea King Mk 45 is the version of the Sea King series for the Pakistani navy, with provision for the carriage and firing of the powerful AM.39 Exocet anti-ship missile.

The S-61A is the amphibious transport version of the Sea King for the export market, and is able to carry 26 troops, or 15 litters, or 12 VIPs, or a comparatively substantial freight load. The S-61D is the export variant of the SH-3D Sea King.

The Sea King has also been produced under licence in other countries, notably Italy, Japan and the UK. The Agusta (Sikorsky) ASH-3D is the Italian licence-built version of the SH-3D anti-submarine helicopter, differing only slightly from the original in items such as airframe strengthening, a revised tailplane and an uprated powerplant. The ASH-3D also has modified armament and avionics, the former including up to four Mk 46 torpedoes, each weighing 515lb (234kg), or two large anti-ship missiles, and the latter including SMA APS-705 surveillance radar or SMA APS-706 radar when the helicopter is fitted with the Marte Mk II system for Sea Killer Mk 2 anti-ship missiles. The ASH-3H is the Italian licence-built version of the SH-3H Sea King with role optimisation for anti-submarine and anti-ship warfare. The type can also lift a freight load of 6,000lb (2,722kg) carried internally or 8,000lb (3,629kg) carried externally as a slung load. Other tasks undertaken by the ASH-3H, which is fitted with dunking sonar as well as SMA APS-707 surveillance radar with its antenna in a chin radome, are anti-ship missile defence, early warning (EW) and tactical trooping. There is also an AS-61R SAR version of this helicopter, basically equivalent to the American HH-3F Pelican.

The Mitsubishi (Sikorsky) HSS-2 is the Japanese licence-built version of the SH-3A, and the Japanese company produced a total of 185 such helicopters including the HSS-2A and HSS-2B upgraded versions equivalent to the SH-3D and SH-3H respectively.

The Westland Sea King is the British licence-built version of the H-3 series. In 1959, Westland secured a licence not only to build but also to undertake further development of the S-61, but it was not until well into the following decade that Westland began to take advantage of this licence in the creation of a helicopter optimised for the Royal Navy's requirement for an advanced type to succeed the Westland Wessex as a shipborne anti-submarine helicopter with fully autonomous search-and-destroy capability over long ranges/endurances.

Although developed for the German navy as a search-and-rescue type, the Westland Sea King Mk 41 has since been upgraded to full combat capability with Ferranti Seaspray search radar and an armament of two or four Kormoran heavyweight anti-ship missiles.

A development of the piston-engined S-52, the turboshaft-powered S-59 did not enter service, but was useful in the development of features such as turboshaft propulsion and retractable landing gear to give helicopters higher speeds.

The first of four helicopters assembled from Sikorsky-supplied components flew in September 1967, and the success of these machines paved the way for the first British-built Sea King HAS.Mk 1 that flew in May 1969, leading the way for a service debut in February 1970 with a powerplant of two licence-built General Electric T58 turboshafts in the form of a pair of Rolls-Royce (Bristol Siddeley) Gnome H.1400 turboshafts each rated at 1,500hp (1,118kW) for take-off and 1,250hp (932kW) for continuous running. This variant was considerably better-equipped for the operational role than the baseline American model, and its avionics included surveillance radar with its antenna in a dorsal radome, dunking sonar and Doppler navigation, while its primary weapon options were up to four Mk 44 lightweight torpedoes or four Mk 11 depth charges. Production of the Sea King HAS.Mk 1 totalled 56 helicopters. There followed the Sea King HAS.Mk 2, which was a simple derivative of the Sea King HAS.Mk 1 but with a powerplant of two 1,660hp (1,238kW) Gnome H.1400-1 turboshafts and a number of features developed for Australia's Sea King Mk 50. Production totalled 21 helicopters, and all surviving Sea King HAS.Mk 1s were upgraded to the same standard with the designation Sea King HAS.Mk 2A. The model's cabin is 19ft 3in (5.87m) long in the ASW version, increasing to 24ft 11in (7.59m) in the SAR version, and its width and height are 5ft 6in (1.98m) and 6ft 3.5in (1.92m) respectively.

The designation Sea King AEW.Mk 2A is used for 10 Sea King HAS.Mk 2s converted to the AEW role with the Thorn EMI Searchwater low-altitude surveillance task (LAST) radar. This uses a 360-degree scan antenna in a pressurised radome on a swivelling arm attached to the starboard side of the fuselage: the arm and radome are turned to the rear for carrier operations and cruising flight, then swivelled down to the vertical position below the fuselage for patrol operations. In 1992 it was revealed that the helicopters

The Sikorsky HH-3E was developed from the US Air Force's CH-3 land-based transport version of the US Navy's SH-3 Sea King maritime anti-submarine helicopter, as a combat search-and-rescue helicopter for use in the recovery of aircrew whose warplanes had been forced down in hostile territory during the Vietnam War. The type soon became known as the 'Jolly Green Giant', and features that suited the type to its more intensive operational role were uprated engines, armour protection, an armament of two 0.3in (7.62mm) Minigun six-barrel rotary machine guns, additional fuel capacity, an extending inflight-refuelling probe, and a high-capacity rescue hoist with a weighted penetrator to reach the ground through a jungle canopy.

are to be upgraded electronically with the Searchwater radar modified to incorporate pulse-Doppler capability.

The Sea King HAR.Mk 3 is the dedicated SAR derivative of the Sea King HAS.Mk 2 for the RAF, which received 19 of the type for service from 1977 with no anti-submarine equipment but with additional avionics. The cabin is outfitted for the carriage of two dedicated mission crew (electronics/winch operator and loadmaster/winchman) and 19 seated survivors, or two litters and 11 seated survivors, or six litters. A subsequent order for six Sea King HAR.Mk 3A helicopters with improved avionics raised the Sea King HAR.Mk 3 variant's total to 25 machines.

The Sea King HC.Mk 4 is the assault transport version of the Commando Mk 2 (see below) for the Royal Marines, with the folding rotors of the Sea King series and able to carry 28 troops or 6,000lb (2,272kg) of freight internally, or alternatively a slung load of 8,000lb (3,629kg). The type is equipped for the troops to make parachute or

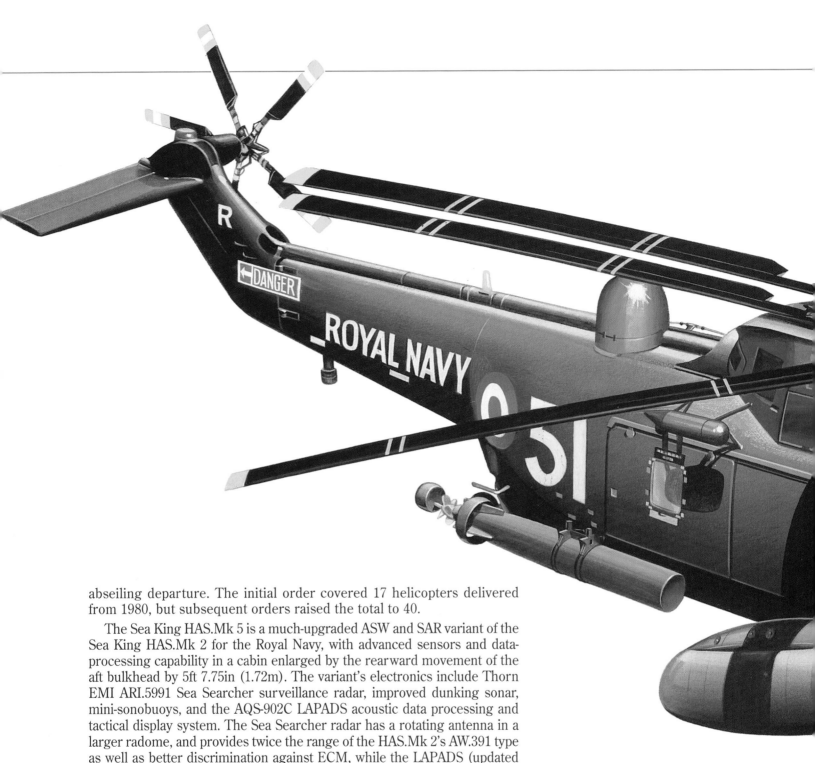

abseiling departure. The initial order covered 17 helicopters delivered from 1980, but subsequent orders raised the total to 40.

The Sea King HAS.Mk 5 is a much-upgraded ASW and SAR variant of the Sea King HAS.Mk 2 for the Royal Navy, with advanced sensors and data-processing capability in a cabin enlarged by the rearward movement of the aft bulkhead by 5ft 7.75in (1.72m). The variant's electronics include Thorn EMI ARI.5991 Sea Searcher surveillance radar, improved dunking sonar, mini-sonobuoys, and the AQS-902C LAPADS acoustic data processing and tactical display system. The Sea Searcher radar has a rotating antenna in a larger radome, and provides twice the range of the HAS.Mk 2's AW.391 type as well as better discrimination against ECM, while the LAPADS (updated in the late 1980s to AQS-902G-DS standard for improved operational capability) allows faster and more accurate processing of data from the dunking sonar and sonobuoys. Some 30 such helicopters were delivered between October 1980 and July 1986, and further helicopters of the same standard were provided by the update of 56 older machines (one Sea King HAS.Mk 1, 20 Sea King HAS.Mk 2 and 35 Sea King HAS.Mk 2A helicopters). In 1987 and 1988, four of the helicopters, with their anti-submarine electronics removed, were transferred to the RAF as Sea King HAR.Mk 5 SAR machines.

The Sea King AEW.Mk 5 designation is applied to three Sea King HAS.Mk 5 helicopters converted to the AEW role in a standard basically similar to that of the Sea King AEW.Mk 2 with Thomson Thorn Searchwater surveillance radar.

This view highlights the main features of the Westland Sea King with its boat-hulled fuselage, float-shaped stabilizing sponsons accommodating the retractable main units of the tailwheel landing gear, the carriage of homing torpedoes on the rear fuselage, the use of the main part of the fuselage for crew (flightcrew of two on the forward flightdeck and mission crew of two in the well-equipped central fuselage tactical compartment) and mission equipment including search radar and dunking sonar, and the powerplant of two Rolls-Royce Gnome turboshafts side-by-side ahead of the main rotor assembly.

Delivered between January and August 1990 to the extent of five helicopters, the Sea King HAS.Mk 6 is an improved version of the Sea King HAS.Mk 5 based on the Advanced Sea King concept. The variant has the AQS-902G-DS integrated acoustic data processing system (with inputs to cathode-ray tube displays from sonobuoys and GEC Ferranti Type 2069 dunking sonar, which is the older Plessey Type 195 with digital signal processing and the ability to operate at depths down to about 700ft/213m) in place of the original 'stand-alone' AQS-902C acoustic data processing system and analogue-processed Type 195 sonar able to operate to a depth of 245ft (75m), improved radar, an internal MAD system, enhanced ESM, provision for two Sea Eagle anti-ship missiles, a strengthened fuselage, a powerplant of two 1,660hp (1,238kW) Gnome H.1400-1T turboshafts transmission-limited to a combined maximum of 2,950hp (2,200kW), an uprated dynamic system including composite-structure blades on both the main and improved tail rotors, an unbraced stabilizer, and increased internal fuel capacity. The Royal Navy's force of Sea King HAS.Mk 6 helicopters is being enlarged by the conversion of older Sea King helicopters to this standard. The first step was the upgrade of 26 Sea King HAS.Mk 5s (one of them as a prototype for the new standard), and another 44 conversion kits have been ordered.

The designation Sea King AEW.Mk 7 is proposed for an upgrade of the Sea King AEW.Mk 2 for service from the year 2000, with improved surveillance radar (the Thomson Thorn Searchwater 2000 and GEC-Marconi Blue Vixen being the competing types), a joint tactical information distribution system (JTIDS) data link, and a new central tactical system with coloured displays.

Moderately large numbers of Sea King helicopters have been delivered to the air forces and navies of British allies, and the type has also been sold in modest numbers as a land-based tactical helicopter with the revised name Commando, with its payload/range and endurance capabilities optimised for the trooping, freighting, logistic support, and casevac primary roles, with air-to-surface attack and SAR as important secondary roles. The type's most obvious external differences are stub wings (in place of the Sea King's stabilizing sponson floats) and non-retractable tailwheel landing gear. The hold is 24ft 11in (7.59m) long, 6ft 6in (1.98m) wide and 6ft 3.5in (1.93m) high, and access to the hold is provided by a port-side airstair door at the front and a starboard-side cargo door at the rear.

The Commando first flew in September 1973 with a powerplant of two Gnome H.1400 turboshafts, and the designation Commando Mk 1 is used for five helicopters delivered from January 1974 to the Egyptian air force for the trooping role with accommodation for 21 troops. The Commando Mk 2 was first flown in January 1975 and built as the major version of the Commando series. It is an uprated version of the Commando Mk 1 with Gnome H.1400-1 turboshafts and a hold able to accommodate 28 men or 6,000lb (2,722kg) of freight. Saudi Arabia funded the purchase of 17 such troop transports for the Egyptian air force, and other deliveries included three Commando Mk 2A 15-passenger VIP transports for the Qatari air force, two Commando Mk 2B 15-passenger VIP transports for the Egyptian air force, one Commando Mk 2C improved 15-passenger VIP transport for the Qatari air force, and four Commando Mk 2E Elint and jamming helicopters for the Egyptian air force. The Commando Mk 3, of which eight were delivered to Qatar between December 1982 and January 1984, is an armed multi-role version with sponsons.

The Soviet counterpart to the Sea King, although built in considerably fewer numbers, is the Kamov Ka-25, which remains a classic example of the modern helicopter with co-axial contra-rotating main rotor units. The Ka-25 was designed to counter the American development of nuclear-powered

The version of the Sikorsky S-61 used by the US Coast Guard for the search-and-rescue mission is the HH-3F Pelican, which is in essence a version of the HH-3E 'Jolly Green Giant' without the features required for long-range penetration of hostile airspace.

The designation HH-3A was used for 12 Sikorsky SH-3A Sea King helicopters converted as interim combat search-and-rescue machines pending the arrival of the first HH-3E 'Jolly Green Giant' helicopters.

submarines carrying nuclear-tipped ballistic missiles (SSBNs) in the mid-1950s, which clearly threatened to upset the balance of power between the USA and the USSR in favour of the Americans. The USSR decided that the American SSBN capability would have to be counterbalanced by a Soviet SSBN force, but this was a longer-term solution to a problem that had to be addressed immediately. A factor working for the Soviets was the comparatively short range of the Lockheed UGM-27 Polaris first-generation submarine-launched ballistic missile (SLBM), which meant that American SSBNs had initially to operate in waters fairly close to the USSR's maritime frontiers if they were to strike at strategic targets deep in the Soviet heartlands.

This opened the possibility that Soviet submarines and surface warships could engage and destroy the SSBNs if they had the right sensors to detect their large targets. A far-ranging programme was therefore launched in 1957, and included the advanced anti-submarine helicopter fitted with modern sensors and weapons. Such a helicopter could operate from comparatively small and unsophisticated surface vessels, using its range and speed to extend the search and attack radius far beyond that of the parent vessel.

The resulting helicopter, introduced to service in 1965, was the Ka-25 (NATO reporting name 'Hormone') that was clearly derived from the Ka-20 'Harp' twin-turboshaft prototype revealed in 1961 and itself developed on the conceptual basis of the Ka-15 'Hen' and Ka-18 'Hog' piston-engined helicopters.

The Ka-25 is thus of typical Kamov configuration with superimposed co-axial rotors turning in opposite directions so that the torque reaction of each three-blade rotor cancels that of the other and thereby removes the need for an anti-torque rotor at the tail, which can thus be made shorter with consequent advantages in shipboard hangarage requirements. In other respects, the Ka-25PL 'Hormone-A' initial model has a large fuselage with a conventional tail unit carrying triple vertical surfaces, quadricycle landing gear, a powerplant of two 888hp (662kW) OMKB 'Mars' (Glushenkov) GTD-3F or, in later helicopters, two 896hp (735kW) GTD-3BM turboshafts located close to the main gearbox above the cabin roof, and the combination of the volume and weight-lifting capabilities for a mass of electronic equipment as well as weapons carried in an internal bay.

The Ka-25PL is the dedicated ASW version of the series with a cabin 12ft 11.5in (3.95m) long, 4ft 11in (1.50m) wide and 4ft 1.25in (1.25m) high accessed by a sliding door on the port side. The primary failing of this

variant is lack of any automatic hover capability, which prevents it from using its dunking sonar in night and adverse-weather operations. The Ka-25BShZ 'Hormone-A' is a derivative of the Ka-25PL designed to tow minesweeping equipment and therefore not fitted with sonar equipment.

The Ka-25T 'Hormone-B' is the missile support version of the Ka-25 family, fitted with data-link equipment for the provision of targeting data and the mid-course updating of long-range anti-ship missiles such as the SS-N-3 'Shaddock', SS-N-12 'Sandbox', SS-N-19 'Shipwreck' and SS-N-22 'Sunburn' weapons launched by major surface ships. This variant is distinguishable from the Ka-25PL by the domed undersurface of the nose radome for its 'Big Bulge' radar and the provision of a different radar with a cylindrical radome under the rear of the cabin. All four units of the landing gear can be retracted to reduce interference to the radar.

The Ka-25PS 'Hormone-C' is the utility and SAR variant of the Ka-25 family, without the offensive avionics and armament of the 'Hormone-A' but often carrying a rescue hoist and other specialist gear as well as equipment for mid-course update of ship-launched anti-ship missiles.

The Ka-25 series has now been supplanted on the more advanced warships of the Russian navy by the Ka-27 'Helix' series of helicopters. Designed from 1969 as successor to the Ka-25 'Hormone' series with improvements such as the ability to operate the dunking sonar at night and

One of the most important tactical transport helicopters in Western service, the Aérospatiale AS 332B Puma (now Eurocopter France AS 532 Cougar) carries a crew of up to three as well as a payload of 21 troops, or six litters and seven seated casualties, or 8,818lb (4,000kg) of freight in the cabin or 9,921lb (4,500kg) of freight as a slung load. Other details include a powerplant of two 1,877hp (1,400kW) Turbomeca Makila IA1 turboshafts, main rotor diameter of 51ft 2.2in (15.60m), fuselage length of 48ft 5in (14.76m), height of 16ft 1.75in (4.92m), maximum take-off weight of 20,613lb (9,350kg), maximum speed of 163mph (262km/h) at sea level, service ceiling of 13,450ft (4,100m) and range of 384 miles (618km).

in adverse weather, the Ka-27 retains the earlier type's configuration with superimposed co-axial rotors to obviate the need for a long tail carrying an anti-torque rotor. The 'Helix' first flew in prototype form during 1973. Compared with the Ka-25, the Ka-27 has considerably greater power from its two 2,205hp (1,645kW) Klimov (Isotov) TV3-117V turboshafts and slightly greater dimensions for much enhanced performance and payload within an airframe still able to fit into the same shipboard hangar as the Ka-25. The Ka-27PL 'Helix-A' is the dedicated ASW variant of the series, and was introduced to service in 1981, with a significant advantage over the Ka-25PL in that it possesses a hover coupler allowing the dunking sonar to be used at night and in adverse weather conditions. Curiously, given the fact that it has a substantial payload capability, the type is generally operated in tactically inefficient pairs, one helicopter acquiring and tracking the target submarine that is then attacked by the weapons carried by the partner helicopter. The Ka-28 'Helix-A' is the export version with a powerplant of two 2,173hp (1,620kW) TV3-117BK turboshafts, and presumably delivered with a different (probably lower) avionics standard.

The Ka-29TB 'Helix-B' is the dedicated Naval Infantry assault transport with accommodation for 16 fully-equipped troops and, perhaps more importantly, the ability to deliver precision-guided weapons in support of amphibious landings. The type has substantial armour protection for the

Helicopter Survivability

THE importance and cost of helicopter use over the battlefield are so great that in recent years considerable efforts have been made to enhance the ability of such machines not only to survive but also to retain an operational capability even in the course of sustained operations over the modern high-intensity battlefield. The approach to this capability has been undertaken along several lanes including the creation of an airframe (especially the main rotor and critical parts of the fuselage) with the basic strength and structural redundancy to absorb ground fire up to the destructive capability of 23mm cannon without suffering a major structural failure, the adoption of a measure of redundancy in key elements of the dynamic system, the introduction of armour protection for the crew and vital elements of the powerplant and fuel systems, the design and incorporation of seats and a fuel system that is 'crash-resistant' in that the seats attenuate the force of any high-speed impact with the ground and the fuel system resists any tendency to rupture in the same eventuality, and the use of equipment items to mitigate external threats. These last now include shrouds in the engine inlets to reduce the chance of metal fragment ingestion, a shrouded exhaust system to reduce the thermal signature of this part of the airframe and thereby reduce the target for missiles with infra-red guidance, an infra-red jammer and/or ejectable thermal flares that help to defeat the guidance of missiles with infra-red guidance, a laser warning system to alert the crew to the 'illumination' of their helicopter by a laser designation system, and a radar warning receiver and chaff launcher system to warn of the radar 'illumination' of the helicopter and then help to defeat the guidance package of any missile with radar guidance.

cockpit and engine bay, and the embarked troops are carried in a hold 14ft 10in (4.52m) long, 4ft 3in (1.30m) wide and 4ft 4in (1.32m) high. Rapid egress is facilitated by the provision on the port side of the fuselage, behind the main landing gear unit, of a door horizontally divided into upward- and downward-opening sections. The helicopter's fixed armament comprises one 0.3in (7.62mm) rotary four-barrel machine gun on a flexible mounting behind the downward-articulated door on the starboard side of the nose, and one optional 30mm 2A42 cannon on a fixed mounting on the port side of the fuselage; the disposable armament is carried on four hardpoints under braced outriggers, and comprises four-round launchers for AT-6 'Spiral' anti-tank missiles, or UV-32-57 multiple launchers each carrying thirty-two 2.17in (55mm) S-5 unguided rockets, or two pods each carrying two 23mm GSh-23L two-barrel cannon, or two 1,102lb (500kg) incendiary bombs. This variant's standard electronics include optronic and missile-guidance pods under the nose, an ESM system with its antenna above the rear part of the engine bay forward of the IR jammer, and an RWR.

Originally known as the Ka-29RLD 'Helix-B', the Ka-31 is the carrierborne AEW member of the family with surveillance radar whose antenna hinges down from the horizontal position under the fuselage to the vertical position before it starts to rotate in its search for fighter-sized echoes out to a maximum range of 93 miles (150km). The Ka-31 also has two equipment panniers on the starboard side of the cabin, an extended tail cone probably accommodating the antenna for an ESM/ECM system, a crew of two, and an endurance of 2 hours 30 minutes at an altitude of 11,480ft (3,500m). The NATO reporting name 'Helix-C' has been given to the Ka-32 civil helicopter.

The Ka-32S 'Helix-C' is the general-purpose member of the Ka-27 series that can be used in roles as diverse as SAR, planeguard and under-way replenishment of warships at sea. Although based on the 'Helix-A', the type has the two external fuel tanks of the 'Helix-C' and is fitted with a rescue hoist.

Reverting once more to the Western world, the S-61 was supported and then supplanted in its land-based military role by the 1961 Boeing Vertol CH-47 Chinook medium-lift helicopter, which is one of history's truly classic helicopters and was particularly valuable in Vietnam for moving vehicles and artillery to the weight of 12,000lb (5,443kg) into every combat area. The Chinook remains in production in the mid-1990s, the latest helicopters of this important type having greatly increased power and much-enhanced avionics.

The origins of the type can be traced back to the later years of the 1950s, when the US Army decided to procure a new helicopter for the battlefield mobility role, and initially ordered 10 examples of the Vertol Model 107 tandem-rotor design for evaluation under the designation YHC-1A. It was already becoming clear that the Model 107 was too small and lacking in power to meet the US Army's requirement, so the YHC-1A order was curtailed to just three helicopters as the service evaluated design submissions from

five manufacturers to meet a requirement that included all-weather capability and a payload including 40 fully equipped troops or freight varying between 4,000lb (1,814kg) carried internally or 16,000lb (7,257kg) carried externally. Other elements of the requirement were straight-in loading and unloading via a power-operated rear ramp/door arrangement, and provision for the hold to be configured for the transport of litters when the helicopter was used in the casevac role.

Vertol accordingly developed the Model 114 as an enlarged version of the Model 107 concept with considerably greater power from two turboshafts pod-mounted above and outside the rear fuselage and in line with the rear rotor pylon. Other obvious changes included fixed quadricycle landing gear and fuel tankage in the long side panniers that extended over three-quarters of the fuselage length and were sealed to provide additional waterborne buoyancy and stability.

The US Army ordered five examples of the Model 114 for evaluation under the designation YHC-1B (soon altered to YCH-47A). The first of these helicopters flew in September 1961 with a powerplant of two 2,200hp (1,641kW) Lycoming T55-L-5 turboshafts, and the CH-47A production model, of which 349 were built, entered service from December 1962 with a powerplant of two T55-L-5 turboshafts that were supplanted later in the production run by 2,650hp (1,976kW) T55-L-7 turboshafts.

Proved by a CH-47A conversion that first flew in October 1966, the CH-47B was an upgraded model with a powerplant of two 2,850hp (2,125kW)

Right: The Aérospatiale (now Eurocopter France) SA. 330 Puma in flight. This baseline model of the Puma, Super Puma and Cougar series was designed in the early 1960s and is still in widespread service. The tactical transport models carry a flightcrew of up to three, and a payload of 20 troops, or six litters and six seated casualties, or 6,614lb (3,000kg) of freight in the cabin or 7,055lb (3,200kg) of freight as a slung load.

Left: Infantrymen disembark from an Aérospatiale (now Eurocopter France) SA. 330 Puma of the French forces in a display of typical air-mobility tactics for the modern battlefield.

T55-L-7C turboshafts, modified rotor blades, and a number of detail improvements. The variant was delivered from May 1967, and production amounted to 108 helicopters.

The final new-build model of the Chinook was the much-improved CH-47C variant with 3,750hp (2,796kW) T55-L-11A turboshafts, an uprated transmission and greater internal fuel capacity. The first example flew in October 1967 for a service debut early in 1968, and production amounted to 270 helicopters. All surviving CH-47As and CH-47Bs were later upgraded to this same improved standard and, from the late 1970s, 182 survivors have been fitted with glassfibre rotor blades.

The CH-47D's extensively updated standard incorporates 13 major improvements such as more powerful engines, further strengthened transmission, rotor blades of composite construction, crash-resistant features, and more advanced avionics. The type has a three-point external attachment system to cater for heavy loads, and the first of a planned 472 older helicopters upgraded to this standard was redelivered in May 1982. The CH-47D's hold has a length of 30ft 6in (9.30m), a mean width of 7ft 6in (2.29m) increasing to 8ft 3in (2.51m) at floor level, and a height of 6ft 6in (1.98m), and this payload volume is accessed by a hydraulically powered rear ramp/door that can be left completely or partially open in flight, or even removed entirely to permit the loading of outsize freight items.

Pending deliveries of the MH-47E, 32 CH-47Ds have been revised as CH-47D Special Operations Aircraft with an inflight-refuelling probe some 24ft 0in (8.53m) long and located on the starboard side of the forward fuselage, an imaging FLIR system, weather radar, improved communication and navigation equipment, a navigator/commander station, and provision for two 0.3in (7.62mm) pintle-mounted machine guns.

CH-47D International Chinook is the basic designation of military Chinooks built by Boeing and licensed as the Model 414 for the export market with a triple external hook system for a load of 26,000lb (11,793kg) on the central unit, or 17,000lb (7,711kg) on the forward or rear units, or 23,000lb (10,433kg) on the forward and rear units combined. The type differs from the baseline CH-47D in its alternative powerplant of two T55-L-714 turboshafts each rated at 5,069hp (3,780kW) for take-off and 4,168hp (3,108kW) for continuous running, and driving a transmission rated at 7,500hp (5,593kW) on two engines and 4,600hp (3,430kW) on one engine. Other differences include a longer nose allowing the installation of weather radar.

The MH-47E is the US Special Forces version of the CH-47D under development from the later 1980s for service from 1994. Production of 51 such helicopters is schemed within the CH-47D total of 472 machines. The type was planned to carry a maximum of 44 troops, and its typical mission of 5 hours 30 minutes involves delivering 36 troops under adverse day/night conditions over a radius of 345 miles (560km) in temperate operating conditions, or 30 troops over the same radius under hot-and-high operating conditions.

The MH-47E has the lengthened fuselage of the CH-47D International Chinook with the forward wheels moved 3ft 4in (1.02m) closer to the nose to allow the use of longer side pannier tanks that increase fuel capacity in conjunction with two floor tanks, an inflight-refuelling capability via the retractable probe on the starboard side of the forward fuselage, and an advanced electronic suite based on two digital databuses for the integration of items such as terrain-avoidance/following, ground mapping and air-to-surface ranging radar, an inertial navigation system (INS) with inputs from the Doppler navigation and GPS receiver and terrain-referenced positioning navigation systems, digital moving map display, a 'glass' cockpit with four head-down displays compatible with night vision goggles, an FLIR sensor in

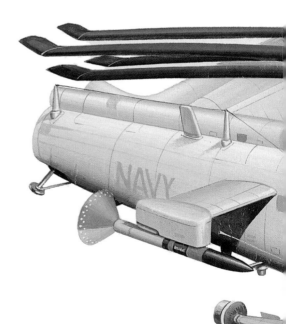

a chin turret, and a defensive subsystem incorporating a laser warning system, radar warning receiver, missile warning system, pulse radar jammer, continuous-wave radar jammer, and chaff/flare dispensers.

The type carries armament in the form of two 0.5in (12.7mm) Browning M2 heavy machine guns mounted in the port forward and starboard aft windows for the suppression of defensive fire, and can also carry defensive FIM-92 Stinger short-range air-to-air missiles (AAMs) aimed via the FLIR system.

The Chinook has also been built under licence in Italy and Japan as the Meridionali (Boeing) CH-47C and Kawasaki (Boeing) CH-47J.

The smaller counterpart of the CH-47, and indeed the type from which it was developed in conceptual terms, is the Boeing Vertol CH-46 Sea Knight. This type's origins can be discerned in the 1956 decision by Vertol, shortly after its creation, to design a medium helicopter optimised for civil use but possessing the features that would allow its evolution into a military type should such a demand materialise. The design team decided on a powerplant of two turboshaft engines as, despite its technical infancy, this type of engine offered an attractive combination of small installation volume, high power-to-weight ratio, low vibration and, in a twin-engined powerplant arrangement, good reliability and safety factors. The design team also opted for a twin-rotor design of the pattern established in the USA by Piasecki, for this avoided the technical demands associated with a single and inevitably much larger main rotor, and also reduced the need for careful weight

The Sikorsky S-70B is the naval version of the land-based S-70A series in service with the US Army as the H-60 Black Hawk in a number of missions for a variety of roles. The S-70B serves with the US Navy (as well as a number of other services) as the SH-60 Seahawk with features such as a folding tail and folding main rotor blades. The two main variants are the SH-60B Seahawk intended for the light airborne multi-purpose system Mk III (LAMPS III) role on destroyers and therefore fitted with search radar, magnetic-anomaly detection equipment, an electronic support measures system, sonobuoys used in association with an advanced acoustic data-processing system, and a data-link system, and the SH-60F Ocean Hawk carried by aircraft carriers for the battle group protection role with dunking sonar. Illustrated here is the SH-60B variant.

The LAMPS Concept

In 1967 the Israeli destroyer *Eilat* was sunk by a Soviet-supplied SS-N-2 'Styx' anti-ship missile fired by an Egyptian fast attack craft lying at anchor in Alexandria harbour, and this first operational success by a guided missile against a warship exerted considerable influence on naval thinking in the West, which had up to that time considered the anti-ship missile as a limited threat. It was now clear that the anti-ship missile was a major threat, and this was all the more dangerous as the USSR was clearly the world leader in the design and development of such weapons in the surface- as well as air-launched roles. Considerable effort was therefore expended in creating Western weapons of comparable lethality, resulting in the Aérospatiale Exocet and McDonnell Douglas Harpoon series to complement a few conceptually older weapons, and also in the rapid development of methods of defeating the anti-ship missile of the sea-skimming type that was deemed the greater threat than a missile flying at higher altitude. The defeat of such missiles was considered possible with fire from anti-aircraft guns, especially after the introduction of close-in weapon system mountings such as the Phalanx with its radar-controlled 20mm Vulcan six-barrel rotary cannon, but only if sufficient warning could be provided of the missile's arrival. This was the spur for the creation of the Light Airborne Multi-Purpose System helicopter that could be carried by smaller warships for its full range of operational requirements. The LAMPS helicopter had therefore to retain its current anti-submarine capability with dunking sonar and/or sonobuoys together with homing torpedoes, in combination with the new task of searching for, finding and reporting incoming anti-ship missiles. The task of searching for such missiles was entrusted to a combination of an active radar and a passive electronic support measures system, the former sending out its own radar pulses and the latter detecting the radar pulses of the missile radar guidance, and the timely relay of information about missile position, course and speed was made possible by the incorporation of a data-link system feeding information straight into the central computer of the parent ship's combat information centre, which then alerted and controlled the appropriate weapon in the interception and destruction of the incoming missile. The LAMPS I helicopter is the Kaman SH-2 Seasprite, now in the last stages of replacement on larger ships by the LAMPS III helicopter, namely the Sikorsky SH-60B Seahawk.

distribution of the payload to avoid centre of gravity problems. The engines were located above and behind the hold in the angles between the rear pylon and upper rear fuselage, and the transmission system ensured that, in the event of one engine failing, the other drove both rotors, which were carefully synchronised to avoid the possibility of blade tip clash in the area above the fuselage where the two rotors intermeshed.

The new design was designated Model 107, and in structural terms was based on a rectangular-section fuselage comprising the cockpit at the front, the hold in the centre, and a ramp/door arrangement in the lower side of the upswept tail unit. The landing gear was of the fixed tricycle type, with the main units carried under the large rear sponsons that also accommodated the fuel tanks, and the design of the fuselage as a compartmented and sealed unit opened the possibility of waterborne operation.

The Model 107 prototype first flew in April 1958, and in July the US Army ordered 10 (later reduced to three) examples for evaluation under the designation YHC-1A. The first of these helicopters flew in August 1959 with a powerplant of two 860hp (641kW) Lycoming T53 turboshafts, but by this time the US Army had decided that it needed a larger type to satisfy its battlefield mobility requirement, and no production order was placed.

Vertol had already reached the conclusion that the type lacked the performance and payload necessary to attract potential customers, and revised the third YHC-1A with larger-diameter rotors driven by two 1,050hp (783kW) General Electric T58-GE-6 turboshafts. In this form, the helicopter was the Model 107-II prototype that first flew in October 1960. The US Marine Corps had already seen the type as the basis of the assault helicopter it required as successor to its Sikorsky HUS-1 Seahorse, and Vertol developed the Model 107-II design as the militarised Model 107M which the US Marine Corps ordered as the HRB-1.

By March 1960, Vertol had become a division of the Boeing Company, and it was as a Boeing Vertol type that the first of these 164 helicopters flew in October 1962, by which time the designation had been altered to CH-46A within the new tri-service designation system. The type entered service from June 1964 with a powerplant of two 1,250hp (932kW) T58-GE-8B turboshafts for the carriage of a payload that could comprise 25 troops, or 15 litters plus two attendants, or 4,000lb (1,814kg) of freight carried over a range of 115 miles (185km) in a hold 24ft 2in (7.37m) long, 6ft 0in (1.83m) wide and 6ft 0in (1.83m) high, and accessed by the hydraulically operated rear ramp/door openable in flight and during water operations.

The HH-46A variant was developed as a base rescue model for the US Navy, and at least 23 were produced as CH-46A conversions with a rescue hoist and other specialised equipment. The RH-46A designation was applied to a few CH-46As converted for use by the US Navy in minesweeping, but the type lacked the power for this particularly exacting role.

The UH-46A was the US Navy's utility counterpart of the US Marine Corps' CH-46A helicopter, and 14 such helicopters were delivered from July 1964 for the primary task of vertical replenishment of under-way task groups and the secondary tasks of personnel transfer and SAR.

The CH-46D model was developed as an upgraded version of the CH-46A, with 1,400hp (1,044kW) T58-GE-10 turboshafts to drive improved rotors featuring cambered blades for greater lift. The type's considerably enhanced lifting power is evidenced by its ability to carry a maximum slung load of 10,000lb (4,536kg). Production amounted to 266 helicopters, and another 12 were produced as conversions from earlier helicopters.

The HH-46D is the US Navy's dedicated SAR version of the CH-46D, of which some 38 were delivered as conversions, while the UH-46D is the US

Navy's vertical replenishment counterpart of the CH-46D and was built to the extent of 10 helicopters supplemented by at least five CH-46As and UH-46As converted to this standard, which includes a powerplant of two 1,400hp (1,044kW) T58-GE-10 turboshafts.

The CH-46E is the standard to which 273 CH-46As, CH-46Ds and CH-46Fs have been upgraded with T58-GE-16 turboshafts, crash-attenuating crew seats, a crash-resistant fuel system, and glassfibre rotor blades. Further improvement was under way in the early 1990s to enhance range in a model unofficially called the CH-46E Bullfrog, featuring larger sponsons for a virtual doubling of the fuel capacity.

The last new-build model was the CH-46F, which was basically an improved CH-46D with updated avionics and equipment. Production amounted to 174 helicopters delivered between July 1968 and February 1971, and many have been revised to CH-46E standard. Five of the helicopters were completed as VIP transports with the designation VH-46F. A small number of export sales were made, and the licence-production rights (later increased to full rights) were sold to Kawasaki, which has produced the type as the Kawasaki KV-107.

In 1962 the Americans finally produced a proper heavy-lift helicopter in the Sikorsky S-64, which bears a close resemblance to the Soviet Mi-10 and entered service as the CH-54 Tarhe. This also proved useful in Vietnam, where it was tested to the limits of its structural strength and versatility. The S-64, for example, was used for naval minesweeping and even to lift light naval vessels.

The origins of the CH-54 can be found in 1958, when Sikorsky began work on its first flying crane helicopter, the S-60, to meet a West German requirement. The S-60 was a radical development of the S-56 that had entered service with the US Marine Corps and US Army (HR2S and H-37 Mojave respectively). The S-60 prototype first flew in March 1959 and, before its loss in a crash in 1961, demonstrated such capabilities that Sikorsky pressed ahead with the design of the larger S-64 that promised still greater capabilities. The type made its initial flight during May 1964 in the form of the first of three S-64A prototypes. The new helicopter was based on a long structural boom that supported, from front to rear, the cabin pod with fixed nosewheel unit, the side-by-side turboshaft engines, the transmission system and six-blade main rotor, the anhedraled outriggers that supported the landing gear's two fixed main units, and the tail pylon complete with four-blade anti-torque rotor.

The most impressive feature of the design was its combination of great ground clearance and a wheel track of 19ft 9in (6.02m), the latter allowing the helicopter to taxi over large loads for attachment to the cargo hook, which was rated at 20,000lb (9,072kg).

In June 1963 the US Army ordered six YCH-54A prototype and service test helicopters with a powerplant of two T73-P-1 turboshafts, and the first of these was delivered in 1964 for trials into the feasibility of using the flying crane helicopter for a host of applications including enhanced battlefield mobility. The YCH-54As were flown operationally in the Vietnam War and demonstrated a useful heavy-lift capability, including the ability to carry the specially designed Universal Pod that could accommodate 67 troops, or 48

Designed by Aérospatiale (now Eurocopter France) with the aid of Sikorsky, the SA. 321 Super Frelon (hornet) had a boat hull and float-type stabilizing sponsons for full amphibious capability, and is now used mainly for the protection of the French nuclear submarine base at Brest in north-west France, where the type uses its dunking sonar and/or search radar to detect underwater intruders that would then be attacked with depth charges or homing torpedoes. This SA. 321G variant has a flightcrew of two and a mission crew of three, the latter replaceable by 27 troops or 11,023lb (5,000kg) of freight for the alternative transport role, and its other details include a powerplant of three 1,609hp (1,200kW) Turbomeca Turmo III turboshafts, main rotor diameter of 62ft 0in (18.90m), fuselage length of 63ft 7.75in (19.40m), height of 22ft 2.1in (6.76m), maximum take-off weight of 28,660lb (13,000kg), maximum speed of 154mph (248km/h) at sea level, service ceiling of 10,170ft (3,100m) and range of 633 miles (1,020km) with a 7,716lb (3,500kg) payload.

litters, or a field hospital, or 22,890lb (10,383kg) of freight. The US Army then ordered 54 examples of the CH-54A production model that played an important part in the later stages of the Vietnam War for the recovery of downed aircraft and the movement of heavy equipment such as bulldozers.

The CH-54B is an improved version of the CH-54A, most readily identifiable by the twin wheels on its main landing gear units. The type also has a strengthened structure, greater power, higher-lift rotor blades and, as a retrofit on some helicopters, provision for two external tanks. The US Army ordered 37 of this version, which differs from the CH-54A in details such as its maximum payload of 25,000lb (11,340kg) and powerplant of two 4,800hp (3,579kW) T73-P-700 (JFTD12A-5A) turboshafts.

France's only heavy-lift helicopter, the Aérospatiale SA.321 Super Frelon, was adopted by several nations: the Israelis made good use of the type as a commando carrier, but the Super Frelon is very versatile and is currently operated by the French as a land-based heavy anti-submarine helicopter.

Developed as the production version of the SA.3210 prototype that flew in December 1962 as an evolution of the SA.3200 Frelon, the Super Frelon was designed with the aid of Sikorsky in the evolution of the dynamic system (powerplant, transmission and rotors). As a result, the type has a number of Sikorsky features reminiscent of the American company's S-61 (SH-3 Sea King), such as its watertight hull with a boat bottom, the tricycle landing gear with twin wheels on each unit, and the Sikorsky-designed dynamic system based on a six-blade main rotor and a five-blade tail rotor driven by three rather than two turboshafts, located as a side-by-side pair forward of the combining gearbox and the third engine to the rear of the gearbox.

The first prototype was representative of the planned assault transport version, and used a powerplant of three 1,250hp (932kW) Turbomeca Turmo IIIC2 turboshafts. The second prototype first flew in May 1963 and was representative of the naval version with stabilising sponsons on the main landing gear support structures to provide a genuine waterborne capability. The second prototype impressed the French naval air arm, which ordered three of the four pre-production prototypes with more powerful engines.

The first of the pre-production prototypes flew in November 1965, and their overall success led Sud-Aviation to expect a major commercial success for the Super Frelon in the civil as well as military markets. This success was not to be achieved, however, for few civil orders were placed and even the military orders were disappointingly low. The SA.321A land-based transport, SA.321B land-based troop transport, SA.321C land-based civil transport, SA.321D maritime ASW, and SA.321E maritime transport models were not built, and only one example of the SA.321F civil transport was produced, with a powerplant of three Turmo IIIC3 turboshafts.

The SA.321G naval demonstrator was powered by three Turmo IIIC6 turboshafts and was fitted with a folding main rotor and a hinged tail boom to reduce overall length for easier shipborne stowage. This paved the way for the French naval air arm's production version, which was delivered in the form of five SA.321Ga radarless transports with a powerplant of three Turmo IIIC3 turboshafts, and 19 SA.321Gb multi-role helicopters. Both models have a cabin 22ft 11.5in (11.00m) long, 6ft 2.75in (1.90m) wide and 6ft 0in (1.83m) high, and this is accessed by a starboard-side sliding door as well as a hydraulically powered ramp/door arrangement that allows straight in/out loading and unloading, and can be opened in flight for the dispatch of parachute-equipped men and loads.

The SA.321Gb helicopters were delivered with nose radar and provision for use in the anti-submarine role, most notably the protection of the sea approaches to the harbour of Brest, base for the French navy's nuclear-powered submarine force. The first 12 helicopters form a distinct subvariant with Sylphe nose-mounted radar and a powerplant of three Turmo IIIC3 turboshafts, while the last seven constitute a slightly different subvariant with Sylphe nose radar that was often replaced by ORB 31D radar and a powerplant of three Turmo IIIC7 turboshafts for an increased maximum take-off weight.

Export derivatives of the SA.321G were the SA.321GM for Libya (six helicopters delivered in 1980 and 1981 with a powerplant of three Turmo IIIC7 turboshafts, ORB 31WAS radar and dunking sonar), and the SA.321GV for Iraq (16 helicopters delivered between 1976 and 1981 in two batches with ORB 31D radar).

The SA.321Ja is the float-equipped transport and anti-submarine version sold to China and Zaire. The 16 helicopters for China were delivered between 1975 and 1977 with ORB 32AS radar and a powerplant of three 1,549hp (1,155kW) Turmo IIIC6 turboshafts. The single helicopter for Zaire was delivered as a presidential transport without radar.

The SA.321K is a simplified land-based transport helicopter that was developed as the SA.321H without stabilising floats. The type was placed in production in two differently designated variants for Israel and South Africa. The variant for Israel was the SA.321K, which was built in two subvariants as the SA.321Ka and SA.321Kb totalling 14 helicopters including replacements for two machines that crashed before delivery. The original order covered five SA.321Ka and seven SA.321Kb helicopters, and these were delivered from 1967 with a powerplant of three 1,475hp (1,100kW) Turmo IIIE3 turboshafts for the carriage of a payload that could comprise 30 troops, or 15 litters, or a freight load of 8,818 or 11,023lb (4,000 or 5,000kg) carried internally or externally. The helicopters were later revised with a powerplant of three 1,895hp (1,413kW) General Electric T58-GE-16 turboshafts. The variant for South Africa was the SA.321L, of which 16 were delivered between 1967 and 1969, without floats or radar but with a powerplant of three 1,569hp (1,170kW) turboshafts.

The SA.321M was the transport version for Libya, which received eight such helicopters in 1971 and 1972, without radar but with floats and a powerplant of three 1,569hp (1,170kW) turboshafts.

The influence of Sikorsky on the Aérospatiale (now Eurocopter France) SA.321 Super Frelon is evident in the design of the hull/float combination and of the dynamic system with its three engines powering a drive train that turns a six-blade main rotor and five-blade tail rotor.

The Gunship Helicopter

THE Bell Model 209 HueyCobra of 1965 was the first helicopter gunship to enter production and service. The type's advent heralded the split of helicopter design into more specialised types. Although it suffered heavy losses in Vietnam, the HueyCobra soon proved itself a valuable weapon incorporating considerable development potential. With its remotely controlled chin turret aimed by the co-pilot/gunner and its long, narrow fuselage, it showed clearly that armed helicopters could be used as close-support types for the accurate delivery of machine gun, cannon and grenade fire as well as unguided rockets and, in later variants, guided missiles such as the Hughes BGM-71 TOW wire-guided anti-tank missile; the HueyCobra can also carry a cannon pack. Although other helicopters had been fitted with armament (principally machine guns firing from the side doors and a number of different light ASM types) for use in the close-support role, it was with the HueyCobra that the concept came to maturity.

First flown in September 1965 as the private-venture Model 209 with a powerplant of one 1,100hp (820kW) Lycoming T53-L-11 turboshaft, the AH-1G HueyCobra evolved from the company's D-255 Iroquois Warrior design concept. This new type was required to meet an urgent demand by the US Army in the Vietnam War for a helicopter gunship able to escort its troop-carrying Bell UH-1 Iroquois helicopters, and to provide fire support for the troops landed from these tactical transport machines.

The Iroquois Warrior concept had been based on the D-245 design with small swept auxiliary wings, and resembled a hybrid rotary- and fixed-wing aeroplane in its combination of a slender fuselage (of small cross-section and very narrow profile) with vertically stepped tandem cockpits (which located the co-pilot/gunner below and forward of the pilot), retractable skid landing gear, stub wings, provision for extensive armament (including a streamlined cannon installation under the fuselage) and the dynamic system of the Model 204. The US Army examined the Iroquois Warrior mock-up in June 1962, but in August of the same year the Howze Board recommended the establishment of Air Cavalry Combat Brigades, and Bell decided to evolve an attack helicopter tailored specifically to the need of the new type of unit.

A first step was the conversion of a Model 47 into the Model 207 Sioux Scout prototype. This handled well and could carry a useful armament load, but Bell rightly appreciated that higher performance and maximum compatibility with current turbine-engined helicopters were essential factors, and therefore opted to develop a gunship variant of the Model 204. This was the D-262, in essence a scaled-down version of the D-255 for competition with Lockheed and Sikorsky designs in the advanced aerial fire-support system (AAFSS) competition.

Much to Bell's disappointment, the D-262 was the first casualty of the competition, which was won by the Lockheed design that was ordered in the form of 10 YAH-56A Cheyenne prototype and service test helicopters. The AAFSS requirement had called for a highly sophisticated helicopter, and the

The Bell AH-1 HueyCobra was developed with commendable speed as the Model 209 with the dynamic system of the UH-1C Iroquois or 'Huey' tactical transport helicopter married to a new and extremely slender fuselage carrying the crew of two, in vertically staggered seating that provided optimum fields of vision, and an armament scheme that was based on a trainable undernose turret carrying two 0.3in (7.62mm) Minigun machine guns, or two 40mm grenade launchers or one example of each weapon type, and rockets and/or gun pods on the four hardpoints under the stub wing.

order for 375 production examples of the Cheyenne was finally cancelled because of protracted development and financial problems.

Bell had realised that the development phase of the AAFSS programme would be so protracted that an interim type would be needed, and in December 1964 decided to proceed with the private-venture development of such a type as the Model 209 Cobra on the basis of the D-262. The company determined that the prototype should be completed in no more than one year and at a cost not exceeding $1 million; in the event, Bell bettered the time but missed the cost limit by a mere $40,000.

Work started in March 1965, and key elements in the design were a fuselage modelled on that of the D-262 with its width limited to 3ft 2in (0.97m), a powerplant of one 1,100hp (820kW) T53-L-11 turboshaft driving a UH-1C transmission system and a Model 540 rotor with blades of 2ft 3in (0.686m) chord, the traditional stabilizer bar replaced by a stability control augmentation system, the boom and tail unit (complete with anti-torque

Bell validated the concept of the helicopter gunship in its Model 208 Sioux Scout, which was a conversion from H-13 (Model 47) standard with the main features desired for a helicopter gunship. The type was too small and too poorly powered for any real consideration as a production type.

One of the most advanced helicopter gunships yet flown, the Lockheed AH-56 Cheyenne was designed to satisfy the US Army's extremely ambitious advanced aerial fire-support system (AAFSS) requirement, and was powered by two turboshafts, most of whose power was transferred to the large pusher propeller at the tail once the helicopter had translated into forward flight with much of its weight supported by the comparatively large stub wing. The Cheyenne was troubled by major development problems, however, and was cancelled in August 1972.

rotor but with a longer-span tailplane) of the UH-1C, small but unswept stub wings and, after considerable discussion, retractable twin-skid landing gear. The armament comprised a fixed element of one Emerson Electric chin turret carrying one 0.3in (7.62mm) General Electric GAU-2B/A Minigun rotary six-barrel machine gun with 4,000 rounds of ammunition, and a disposable element in the form of stores was carried on four hardpoints under the stub wings.

Construction of the prototype was well advanced when the US Army called for an interim gunship helicopter for service in South Vietnam within 24 months. Bell offered its Model 209 in August 1965, and other submissions were the Boeing Vertol H-47 Chinook, Kaman Tomahawk (H-2 Seasprite derivative with stub wings and a pair of twin-gun barbettes side-by-side under the nose), Piasecki Pathfinder and Sikorsky S-61.

The Model 209 prototype first flew in September 1965, three weeks ahead of Bell's own schedule. After a fairly intensive development effort, the Model 209 was evaluated against the H-2 and the S-61, and was declared winner of the competition in March 1966. The US Army's procurement of the resulting AH-1 began with just two pre-production helicopters based on the Model 209 but modified with fixed landing gear, a larger chin turret, and a stronger stub wing to cater for the heavier disposable loads anticipated by the operating service. The first of these two machines flew in October 1966, and

When the AAFSS requirement was superseded by the less demanding Advanced Attack Helicopter requirement, the winning contender was the Hughes Model 77 that was ordered as the AH-64A Apache and later became a McDonnell Douglas type after the latter's purchase of the Hughes helicopter operation. The Apache is the most advanced battlefield attack helicopter currently in large-scale service, and the AH-64A initial production model is notable for its somewhat angular but powerful appearance, excellent defensive features, powerful offensive armament, and highly capable flight and fire-control electronics. The armament is based on a 30mm trainable cannon under the fuselage and up to 3,880lb (1,760kg) of weapons including no fewer than 16 AGM-114 Hellfire anti-tank missiles carried on four hardpoints under the stub wings, and further capability is being added by the conversion of many surviving AH-64A helicopters to the AH-64D standard with the mast-mounted Longbow fire-control system that allows the helicopter to lurk behind cover but still see the target area electronically and control missiles fired into it.

the helicopters were then used in an accelerated development programme to qualify the weapons capability and stability control augmentation system.

The first AH-1G emerged from the production line in May 1967 and deliveries to the US Army began in June of the same year, with a powerplant of one 1,400hp (1,044kW) T53-L-13 turboshaft derated to 1,100hp (820kW), a Model 540 main rotor and, in all but the first helicopters, the anti-torque rotor relocated from the port to the starboard side of the tail pylon.

The turret was initially the Emerson Electric TAT-102A unit carrying a 0.3in (7.62mm) General Electric M134 Minigun rotary six-barrel machine gun with 8,000 rounds of ammunition, although this was later supplanted by the TAT-141 turret (part of the Emerson Electric M28 weapon system) carrying two Miniguns with 4,000 rounds per gun, or two 40mm Hughes (later McDonnell Douglas Helicopters) M129 grenade launchers with 300 rounds per weapon, or one example of each weapon type. Structural provision was also made for the TAT-141 to be replaced by the General Electric Universal Turret System carrying one 20mm General Electric M197 rotary three-barrel cannon. The chin turret was usually fired by the co-pilot/gunner using the hand-held pantograph M73 reflex sight to which the turret was slaved, and the disposable armament was usually controlled by the pilot, although either crew member could control the whole armament if necessary. The four hardpoints under the stub wing could lift up to 2,200lb (998kg) of ordnance such as four M159 multiple launchers each carrying nineteen 2.75in (70mm) unguided rockets, or four M157 multiple launchers each carrying seven 2.75in unguided rockets, or two General Electric M18 or M18E1 0.3in Minigun pods, or one General Electric M35 armament system with one 20mm General Electric M195 Vulcan rotary six-barrel cannon with 1,000 rounds; this last item was carried on the port inner hardpoint.

The HueyCobra's battlefield tasking was reflected in the provision of an armoured windscreen and Norton Company NOROC armour protection for the crew and vital areas such as the engine compressor.

The production total for the AH-1G was soon raised to 838 helicopters, and the first machines were deployed to South Vietnam by the autumn of 1967, only a few weeks after the type's service debut. The AH-1G proved very useful for the close-support and attack roles in the Vietnamese fighting, a fact recognised in the placement of additional contracts that raised the production total to an eventual 1,126 helicopters of which the last was delivered in February 1973, and some of these machines were later transferred to US allies as they became surplus to US Army requirements.

Some 38 of the helicopters were transferred in February 1969 to the US Marine Corps, whose commitment in the northern part of South Vietnam urgently required the support of fast and agile armed helicopters. A few other examples were converted into TH-1G dual-control trainers for the conversion of AH-1 pilots.

Developed in the early 1970s in the Improved Cobra Armament Program

The first production version of the Bell AH-1 HueyCobra series was the AH-1G whose details included a powerplant of one 1,400hp (1,044kW) Lycoming T53-L-13 turboshaft derated to 1,100hp (820kW), main rotor diameter of 44ft 0in (13.41m), fuselage length of 44ft 7in (13.59m), height of 13ft 6.25in (4.12m), maximum take-off weight of 9,500lb (4,309kg), maximum speed of 172mph (277km/h) at sea level, service ceiling of 11,400ft (3,475m) and range of 357 miles (574km). Late variants have retained the same basic layout with a considerably uprated powerplant whose additional power is used not for performance enhancement but rather for the ability to operate effectively with additional offensive and defensive equipment, the former now including heavyweight wire-guided anti-tank missiles.

(ICAP), the following AH-1Q was an interim anti-tank helicopter produced to fill the operational gap left by the failure of the AH-56. This gap lay in the US Army's ability to supplement the efforts of its ground forces with air-delivered weapons in the defeat of any tank-spearheaded Warsaw Pact invasion of Western Europe. The US Army therefore decided to re-equip its existing AH-1G force with BGM-71 TOW heavyweight anti-tank missiles and to procure additional helicopters of the same basic type.

The US Army placed its ICAP contract in March 1972, this specifying the conversion of eight AH-1Gs to YAH-1Q standard with TOW missiles and the Sperry-Univac helmet-directed fire-control subsystem (HDFCS). The first conversion was delivered in February 1973, and successful trials paved the way for the January 1974 contract ordering an initial 101 'production' conversions, supplemented in December 1974 by a contract for another 189 conversions to the same standard.

In the event, only 92 such conversions were completed with provision for eight TOW anti-tank missiles (four under each outer underwing hardpoint) controlled with the aid of a Hughes M65 sight system for the gunner in the front seat, who also had the HDFCS. The other 198 helicopters did not receive the conversion because the weight and drag of the TOW system seriously degraded manoeuvrability and performance.

As a consequence of the TOW system shortcomings, the US Army contracted with Bell for the Improved Cobra Agility and Maneuverability (ICAM) program involving two prototype conversions. Bell's response to the ICAM requirement was centred on the use of a much-uprated powerplant, a development of the T53-L-13 turboshaft known as the T53-L-703 and rated at 1,800hp (1,342kW), together with a revised transmission and the tail rotor of the Model 212.

The first prototype was the YAH-1R conversion of an AH-1G and the second was the YAH-1S conversion of an AH-1Q with full TOW capability. The two helicopters were evaluated from December 1974, and their performance confirmed the value of the uprated powerplant so emphatically that, in June 1975, the US Army ordered the completion of the AH-1Q programme and the conversion of existing AH-1Qs to this improved standard with the uprated dynamic system (as noted above), as well as fibreglass main rotor blades, a primary offensive armament of eight TOW anti-tank missiles, better defensive capabilities, and improved fire-control subsystems.

The helicopters were initially allocated the designation AH-1S (Mod) HueyCobra, but in 1987 the revised designation AH-1S HueyCobra was decreed. Some 15 of the helicopters were further converted with the designation TH-1S (Mod) Night Stalker for use by the Army National Guard as pilot's night vision system (PNVS) and integrated helmet and display sighting system (IHADSS) trainers for the McDonnell Douglas AH-64A Apache, and in 1987 these helicopters were also redesignated, in this instance to TH-1S Night Stalker.

In 1975 the US Army undertook the Priority Aircraft Subsystem Suitability (PASS) review, to fix ways in which the HueyCobra's capabilities could be extended beyond the limits of the ICAP and ICAM programmes. The review decided that the best course of action was to improve the basic helicopter's capabilities against the new generation of anti-aircraft weapons being developed and introduced by the USSR, through the incorporation of a new cockpit canopy, improved instrumentation, superior ECM equipment, and upgraded armament.

As a result of the review, Bell received orders for 305 (later reduced to 297) HueyCobras in three steadily-improving versions. The first of these was the AH-1S (Prod) HueyCobra with the same dynamic system

McDonnell Douglas AH-64 Apache Electronics

THE two most important groups of sensors carried by the McDonnell Douglas AH-64 Apache anti-tank and battlefield close-support helicopter are the target acquisition and designation system (TADS) and pilot's night vision sensor (PNVS). Northrop and Martin Marietta competed for these complex systems, Martin Marietta winning in April 1982. The two independent systems are both turret-mounted in the extreme nose and feed data to the two members of the crew via the monocle screen carried by the helmet of the integrated helmet and display sighting system (IHADDS). The TADS is based on a nose turret that can be traversed 120° left and right of the centreline and elevated in an arc between -60° and +30°. The turret accommodates daylight and night/all-weather sensors in its port and starboard halves respectively: the daylight sensors comprise a TV camera with wide- and narrow-angle fields of vision, direct-view optics with wide- and narrow-angle fields of vision, a laser spot tracker, and an International Laser Systems laser ranger and designator, while the night/adverse-weather sensor is an FLIR with wide-, medium- and narrow-angle fields of vision. In short, the TADS provides for the optronic, optical or thermal acquisition of targets that can then be laser-ranged and laser-designated to allow manual or automatic tracking for autonomous engagement with the cannon, missiles or rockets. It is worth noting, moreover, that while the TADS is designed primarily for the co-pilot/gunner, it provides back-up night vision capability for the pilot in the event of a failure in the PNVS. This latter is based on an FLIR in a separate turret located above the TADS turret, and this sensor's 20° and 40° fields of vision provide high-resolution thermal imaging for day/night nap-of-the-earth flight profiles under all weather conditions. The co-pilot/gunner is primarily responsible for the armament, which comprises disposable stores carried on the four underwing hardpoints and the 30mm cannon in an underfuselage installation designed to collapse upward between the two crew members in the event of a crash landing. The pilot can override the co-pilot/gunner in use of the weapons, but his principal task is flying the helicopter with the aid of the highly advanced all-weather systems that include the PNVS, Lear Siegler inertial

Continued on page 97

improvements as the AH-1S (Mod) but with a flat-plate canopy for reduced glint, an improved cockpit layout, better instrumentation for nap-of-the-earth operations, the APR-39 RWR, and (from the 67th helicopter) composite-structure rotor blades developed by Kaman. These 100 helicopters were redelivered between the summers of 1977 and 1978, and from 1987 the variant received the revised designation AH-1P HueyCobra.

Sometimes known as the Up-gun AH-1S HueyCobra, the AH-1S (ECAS) second version of the PASS improvement resulted in 98 new-build helicopters, identical to the AH-1S (Prod) machines apart from their provision with the enhanced cobra armament system (ECAS), including an undernose General Electric M79E1 Universal Turret (allowing installation of 20mm or 30mm cannon but used in American helicopters for the 20mm General Electric M197 Vulcan rotary three-barrel cannon) and the M138 underwing stores subsystem for multiple launchers carrying various numbers of unguided rockets. The helicopters were redelivered between September 1978 and October 1979, and in 1987 the variant was redesignated AH-1E HueyCobra.

The third and definitive production version of the HueyCobra resulting from the PASS review was the AH-1S (MC), the letter suffix standing for Modernized Cobra. This has all the features of the AH-1S (Prod) and AH-1S (ECAS) models plus Doppler navigation, an ALQ-144 IR jammer, a secure communications system, and a new fire-control system. This last uses a digital computer linked to a low-airspeed sensor and AAS-32 laser ranger for the solution of ballistic problems, and presents the results on the pilot's Kaiser head-up display (HUD). The initial 99 helicopters of this subvariant were delivered between November 1979 and April 1981, a supplementary batch of 50 helicopters was delivered from April 1981, and finally 337 AH-1Gs were rebuilt to the same standard between November 1979 and June 1982. In 1987 the variant was redesignated AH-1F HueyCobra, and a subvariant of this model is the TAH-1F dual-control trainer of which 41 were delivered as AH-1G conversions with the original designation TAH-1S.

In-service helicopters are being further modernised with the C-NITE system (50 helicopters only) for nocturnal and adverse-weather target detection, acquisition and engagement, the air-to-air Stinger (ATAS) system for FIM-92A Stinger lightweight AAMs, the AVR-2 laser warning system, and the Cobra fleet life extension (C-Flex) upgrade. Israeli helicopters are being fitted with the IAI Cobra Laser Night Attack System, which has a stabilized FLIR and laser ranger and designator to allow the firing of AGM-114A Hellfire missiles out to a range of 11,000yds (10,060m), an advanced mission computer with a moving map display, multi-function displays, a GPS receiver, a four-blade main rotor, a new transmission, and a lengthened tail boom.

The Fuji (Bell) AH-1S is the Japanese licence-built version of the AH-1F, with the 1,800hp (1,342kW) Kawasaki (Lycoming) T53-K-703 turboshaft transmission-limited to 1,290hp (962kW) for take-off and 1,134hp (845kW) for continuous running.

In the autumn of 1967 the US Marine Corps received an initial batch of 38 Bell AH-1G HueyCobra attack helicopters converted with naval avionics, a 20mm cannon in the

The US Marine Corps' counterpart to the US Army's AH-1 HueyCobra, a single-engined type intended only for land-based service, is the AH-1 SeaCobra with a twin-engined powerplant for improved performance and reliability in the type of amphibious operations that are the US Marine Corps *raison d'être*. The original model was the AH-1J SeaCobra, and further variants offering greater offensive and defensive capability have been the AH-1T Improved SeaCobra and the current AH-1W SuperCobra that is illustrated here. The SuperCobra switches from a powerplant of one 2,050hp (1,529kW) Pratt & Whitney Canada T400-WV-402 coupled turboshaft to two General Electric T700-GE-401 turboshafts driving a combining gearbox rated at 3,250hp (2,424kW), and the additional power allows a modest improvement in performance despite the fact that additional offensive and defensive electronics as well as additional weapons have increased the maximum take-off weight from the AH-1T's 14,000lb (6,350kg) to 14,750lb (6,691kg).

chin turret, and a rotor brake. These helicopters provided the marine aviators with an interim close-support capability for their ground forces in the northern part of South Vietnam during the Vietnam War, and also generated useful experience in the operation of attack helicopters. Although generally happy with the AH-1G, the US Marine Corps demanded a more specialised variant with the operational and flight safety advantages of a twin-engined powerplant, as well as a combination of avionics and weapons optimised for the Marine Corps' particular role. Ordered in May 1968, the resulting AH-1J SeaCobra first flew in October 1969, and all 69 production helicopters had been delivered to the Marine Corps by February 1975.

The AH-1J was a derivative of the AH-1G with the powerplant of the Bell UH-1N, namely the 1,800hp (1,342kW) Pratt & Whitney Canada T400-CP-400 coupled turboshaft but flat-rated at 1,250hp (932kW) for take-off and 1,100hp (820kW) for continuous running. Iran procured 202 examples of the AH-1J International derivative with a number of Model 309 KingCobra features and a powerplant of one 1,970hp (1,469kW) T400-WV-402 coupled turboshaft driving a larger-diameter main rotor. The first 140 helicopters were otherwise similar to the standard AH-1J, but the remaining 62 were completed to the more capable AH-1J (TOW) International anti-tank standard, with a revised fire-control system for a primary armament of eight BGM-71 TOW missiles.

In a programme that in many ways paralleled the US Army's development of the AH-1G into more capable variants with an uprated powerplant and a more capable combination of avionics and weapons, the AH-1T Improved SeaCobra variant was developed from the AH-1J but incorporated features of the Model 309 KingCobra and Model 214, including a larger-diameter main rotor as well as a higher-rated power train able to handle the full 1,970hp (1,469kW) delivered by the T400-WV-402 coupled-turboshaft powerplant.

The first of two AH-1J prototype conversions flew in May 1976, and the AH-1T entered service with an armament capability that includes the carriage of BGM-71 TOW or AGM-114 Hellfire anti-tank missiles on its outboard underwing hardpoints. The 57 AH-1Ts were delivered from October 1977, and 39 of the helicopters are being upgraded to AH-1W standard.

Developed as the AH-1T+ to remedy the performance shortfalls of the AH-1T under hot-and-high conditions, the AH-1W SuperCobra model first flew in April 1980 as a converted AH-1T, and entered service in 1987 with considerably improved capabilities resulting from the installation of a much uprated powerplant of two 3,250hp (2,423kW) General Electric T700-GE-401 turboshafts driving a combining gearbox derived from that of the Model 214ST and able to handle a maximum of 3,380hp (2,520kW). The variant's other features include a modified rotor head, a new vibration-suppression system, an upgraded avionics suite, and new subsystems such as a pilot's HUD that is compatible with night vision goggles. In combination with the latest weaponry, this provides the US Marine Corps with a highly advanced close-support and attack helicopter ideally suited to support of beach-head operations from forward airstrips or from assault ships lying just offshore. The primary armament comprises eight BGM-71 TOW or AGM-114 Hellfire anti-tank missiles, supported by a pair of AIM-9L Sidewinder short-range AAMs and AGM-122 SideARM anti-radar missiles for battlefield self-defence. The 84 helicopters were delivered from March 1986. The designation TAH-1W is applied to one dual-control trainer based on the AH-1W.

The AH-1(4B)W Viper is the latest SeaCobra version offered by Bell as a private-venture development of the AH-1W SuperCobra, with the considerably more advanced Model 680 four-blade bearingless main rotor, uprated transmission, an expanded manoeuvring envelope and greater

Continued from page 95

attitude/heading reference system, and Singer-Kearfott Doppler navigation system. This is only one part of the Apache's comprehensive electronics, which also include an RWR, active jammers, chaff/flare dispensers, an IR jammer, and a laser warning system. This core suite, as installed on the AH-64A, is augmented in the AH-64D by the Longbow fire-control system based on a Westinghouse millimetric-wavelength radar with its antenna in a mast-mounted radome above the main rotor. This radar is the primary sensor of the Longbow system (initially designated Airborne Adverse-Weather Weapon System) intended for rapid target-area search, automatic detection and classification of targets, and all-weather fire-and-forget engagement with a revised version of the Hellfire missile, namely the radar-homing Longbow Hellfire that carries, in addition to its semi-active laser seeker modified for improved resistance to optical countermeasures, a combined radio-frequency and IR seeker as well as a warhead optimised for the penetration of modern types of advanced tank protection.

An 'overhead' view of the McDonnell Douglas AH-64A Apache in a nose-down attitude reveals some of this impressive helicopter's most important features including, backward from the nose, the sensor platform for the TADS and IHADSS systems, the lateral panniers carrying most of the electronic equipment, the cockpit with its flat-panel canopy and vertically staggered seats, the stub wing with four hardpoints carrying two rocket-launcher pods outboard and two quadruplets of AGM-114 Hellfire missiles inboard, the four-blade main rotor above the two widely spaced engines, and the tail carrying the four-blade anti-torque rotor.

agility, a digital flight-control system, Doppler navigation, and night-targeting sights. In other respects, the AH-1(4B)W differs from the AH-1W in details such as its cranked stub wing with six hardpoints including overwing launchers for two AGM-122 SideARM anti-radar missiles, a total weapon load of 3,184lb (1,444kg) including 750 rounds of 20mm cannon ammunition and two chaff/flare dispensers, and greater internal fuel capacity.

The Hughes OH-6 Cayuse light utility helicopter, which appeared in 1966, also proved its qualities in Vietnam and has been adopted by several other countries in both its baseline and armed forms. Part of its success derives from its advanced structural design, giving the OH-6 great strength and rigidity at a low weight, and a sleekly streamlined fuselage. The combination of these factors made the OH-6 agile for its size, although not aerobatic. Further development of the type by Hughes and then by McDonnell Douglas after it had bought the company, resulted in the Model 500 intended mainly for the civil market but also developed into the Model 500 Defender series with provision for many types of armament.

The origins of the Kiowa can be found in the realisation by the US Army in the late 1950s that the fixed-wing aeroplane had been rendered obsolete for the battlefield reconnaissance and observation roles. In 1960, therefore, the US Army issued a light observation helicopter (LOH) requirement for a machine to replace not only its current force of Bell H-13 and Hiller H-23 light helicopters, but also its fleet of Cessna L-17 Bird Dog liaison and forward air control (FAC) aircraft. The requirement specified a turbine engine, cruising speed of 127mph (204km/h), endurance of 3 hours in the observation role, ability to hover at 6,000ft (1,830m) out of ground effect, and an exacting combination of low cost and easy maintenance.

The size of the order in prospect was very large, and the requirement elicited 22 design proposals from no fewer than 12 American helicopter manufacturers. In 1961 the US Army ordered five prototypes from each of three companies. The designs of the Bell YHO-4A (from 1962 YOH-4A) and Hiller YHO-5A (from 1962 YOH-5A) were clearly influenced by the two companies' considerable experience with piston-engined helicopters, but the Hughes YHO-6A (from 1962 YOH-6A) was of altogether more advanced concept; the company's sole successful helicopter to date, the Model 269, was just entering production.

The team that designed the Model 369, as the YOH-6A was known to Hughes at this time, had decided to concentrate on an advanced yet simple main rotor, high manoeuvrability and low drag. The main rotor was of an unusual part-hingeless four-blade configuration with conventional flapping and feathering hinges replaced by 15 flexible stainless steel straps connecting the two pairs of diametrically opposed blades set at 90 degrees to each other. This rotor core required no maintenance, lacked the complexity of conventional rotor cores, and offered advantages such as better control response, lower vibration and smaller diameter. The use of a four-blade rotor also allowed a more optimised blade design and thus better controllability, which in turn meant that the Model 369 could use a manual control system without hydraulic boost or any need for a stability-augmentation system. The use of a small main rotor also meant that the size of the tail rotor could be reduced and carried on a shorter and lighter tail boom. Low drag was provided by the teardrop shape of the main fuselage, which was sized to the width of two men, and fully enclosed the engine that was located at an angle of 45 degrees in the rear of the pod, with the drive shaft terminating in a bevel gear on the common shaft driving the main and tail rotors.

The structural core of the design was the payload compartment, a light alloy unit under the main rotor and accommodating folding seats for two passengers: the roof of this unit supported the fixed rotor mast, its front bulkhead supported the pilots' seats, its rear bulkhead supported the engine, the lower corners of the two bulkheads carried the legs for the twin-skid landing gear, and the floor carried the fuel tanks and batteries. Considerable care went into the streamlining of the fuselage pod, and even the short main rotor mast was nicely faired into the forward part of the boom that projected from the upper rear of the main pod to carry the tail unit, which comprised a small rotor on the port side of the boom, a vertical tail surface with large and small sections above and below the boom respectively, and a starboard-side stabilizer braced to the upper fin at an outward angle of 45 degrees.

First flown in February 1963, the YOH-6A was several hundreds of pounds lighter than either of its competitors but had the same maximum take-off weight, translating into greater payload with the same engine. The YOH-6A was also smaller, faster, longer-ranged, more manoeuvrable and easier to fly than the YOH-4A and YOH-5A, and after a seven-month competitive evaluation was declared winner of the LOH competition in May 1965, when the US Army placed an initial order for 714 OH-6A Cayuse helicopters out of an expected total of more than 4,000.

In the following month, Hughes announced a civil version as the Model 500 with the Allison 250-C18 version of the military helicopter's T63-A-5 turboshaft. These two engines were mechanically identical, but the civil model had a higher sea-level rating as the military model was derated by 20 per cent for constant power at higher altitudes and higher temperatures.

The OH-6A entered service in September 1966, and in the Vietnam War soon proved itself a superb operator in its designed role. All was not well with the production programme, however, as increased demand for fixed- and rotary-winged aircraft at this time was badly affecting the aerospace industry in the south-western part of the USA, where skilled manpower was soon in short supply, as were materials and many bought-in components. The result was a steep rise in production cost and a sharp decline in production tempo, and in 1967 the US Army was sufficiently unhappy with the situation to reopen the LOH competition.

This time, Bell won with the Model 206A JetRanger that it had evolved as an improved version of the YOH-4A (Model 206) for the civil market. The Bell helicopter was ordered into production as the OH-58A Kiowa, and

The McDonnell Douglas (originally Hughes) Model 500MD Defender is an export type offering capabilities similar to those of the OH-6D Kiowa Warrior with its mast-mounted sight and external provision for weapons including four BGM-71 TOW heavyweight wire-guided anti-tank missiles.

The light helicopters of the McDonnell Douglas Model 500 series originated as the Hughes Model 369 that was accepted for US Army service as the OH-6 Cayuse in the observation role, and are now notable for their excellent combination of performance, quietness and operating economy. This is a Model 500MD Defender for the export market with a mast-mounted sight allowing target surveillance, acquisition and designation as the helicopter hovers behind cover.

production of the OH-6A ended in August 1970 after the delivery of 1,434 helicopters. Even so, the type became the most popular helicopter of the Vietnam War, but was phased out of first-line service after the war so that regular army units could standardise on the OH-58A. Most of the OH-6As were passed to National Guard units, and many survive into the 1990s, a considerable number having been converted to alternative roles with the baseline designations AH-6 (armed support of Special Forces' operations), EH-6 (electronic reconnaissance), and MH-6 (infiltration/exfiltration of Special Forces as well as armed support).

The Model 500 was introduced in 1968 as the civil counterpart of the OH-6A, with a powerplant of one 317hp (236kW) Allison 250-C18A turboshaft derated to 278hp (207kW) for take-off and 243hp (181kW) for continuous running and, in the export version, for limited military applications such as casevac. The type has been developed in both American- and licence-built forms through a number of steadily more capable versions with uprated powerplants, and has also spawned dedicated military variants for the export market.

The first of these was the Model 500M that was the dedicated military export variant of the Model 500C, powered by the Allison 250-C18A turboshaft derated to 275hp (207kW). The type was built under licence in Argentina as the RACA (Hughes) 500M, in Italy as the BredaNardi NH-500M and also as the NH-500MC with hot-and-high features, and in Japan as the Kawasaki (Hughes) 500M (service designation OH-6J).

The Model 500MD Defender is an uprated military variant based on the Model 500D with the 420hp (313kW) Allison 250-C20B turboshaft, a five-blade main rotor, a T-tail and other improvements. The type was aimed at the market niche for light multi-role helicopters and first flew in 1976, and its success is attested not only by deliveries from the parent factory but also by licensed production in Italy as the BredaNardi (Hughes) NH-500MD and in South Korea as the Korean Air (Hughes) 500MD. The Defender can be used in a number of forms for virtually the whole gamut of battlefield and naval tasks, and was offered with options such as armoured seats, the Hughes 'Black Hole Ocarina' IR suppressor for the exhaust, self-sealing fuel tanks, a structural beam attached to the after side of the rear bulkhead and projecting upward and outward from each side of the fuselage for the carriage of disposable stores on two hardpoints, and port-side provision for armament ranging in calibre from the 0.3in (7.62mm) M134 Minigun in the McDonnell Douglas Helicopters (Hughes) HGS-5 package based on the OH-6A's M27 package, via the 30mm McDonnell Douglas Helicopters (Hughes) M230 Chain Gun, to the 40mm McDonnell Douglas (Hughes) M129 grenade-launcher in the McDonnell Douglas Helicopters (Hughes) M8 package; the HGS-5 package can be replaced by the HGS-55 package containing one 0.3in McDonnell Douglas Helicopters (Hughes) EX-34 Chain Gun with 2,000 rounds in a fuselage magazine.

The type was also developed in a number of specialised subvariants such as the Model 500MD Scout Defender for battlefield reconnaissance and light attack with 'Black Hole Ocarina' IR suppression, a nose-mounted stabilized sight, and provision for a wide assortment of light armament items including multiple launchers for unguided rockets and a gun up to 30mm calibre; the Model 500MD Quiet Advanced Scout Defender, similar to the Scout Defender but with noise reduction features and a mast-mounted sight for nap-of-the-earth flight profiles; the Model 500MD/TOW Defender dedicated anti-tank version with four BGM-71 TOW missiles and appropriate sight; the Model 500MD/MMS-TOW Defender, similar to the Model 500MD/TOW but with a mast-mounted sight on a pylon 2ft (0.61m) above the rotor head; the Model 500MD/ASW Defender dedicated ASW variant with search radar, MAD and two Mk 46 torpedoes; and the Model 500MD Defender II upgraded model with FIM-92 Stinger lightweight AAMs for self-defence, and fitted for items such as a mast-mounted sight, FLIR and an RWR.

The Model 500MG Defender is an improved multi-role military export version with a revised and sharper nose profile, advanced avionics, and the 420hp (313kW) Allison 250-C20B turboshaft driving a rotor system based on that of the Model 500E.

The Model 520N is the no tail rotor (NOTAR) version of the Model 500 – torque control is effected by the engine exhaust, which is ducted to the tail and ejected through the port side of the boom via Coanda slots and steering louvres. Overall, the system reduces complexity, vulnerability and power loss. A military variant of the Model 520N was developed in South Korea as the Korean Air (McDonnell Douglas) Model 520MK Black Tiger, but no details have been released.

The Model 530MG Defender is the military version of the Model 530F, with an advanced cockpit incorporating the Racal RAMS 3000 integrated display and control system (based on a digital databus to allow the use of the latest weapons), mast-mounted sight and a removable beam with provision for a wide assortment of weapons.

Top and above: One of the most important operational tasks that can be undertaken by the McDonnell Douglas Model 500MD Defender series is the battlefield anti-tank role. This is achieved in the Model 500MD/TOW Defender subvariant with a quartet of BGM-71 TOW heavyweight anti-tank missiles carried in external pairs and guided via wires using targeting information provided by means of the nose-mounted stabilized sight.

The type that replaced the OH-6A in production from 1968 was the Bell OH-58A Kiowa, derived ultimately from the D-250 design originally offered for the US Army's 1960 LOH requirement. The D-250 became the Model 206 in hardware and was evaluated as the YHO-4A, later YOH-4A, which was a trim all-metal type of orthodox pod-and-boom construction with twin-skid landing gear and a dynamic system of typical Bell design, including a two-blade main rotor (with stabilizing bar at right angles to the blades) powered by one 250hp (186kW) Allison T63-A-5 turboshaft. The first YOH-4A flew in December 1962, but the type was rejected in favour of the Hughes Model 369 (HO-6, later OH-6). This was a setback for Bell, but the company had already decided to prepare a civil version with a redesigned fuselage as the Model 206A. This had a more streamlined fuselage that replaced the Model 206's completely glazed and virtually hemispherical nose with a more conventional forward fuselage carrying a stepped windscreen, and faired the boom into the pod part in a less utilitarian manner. The Model 206A was launched with a powerplant of one 317hp (236kW) Allison 250-C18A turboshaft driving a revised semi-rigid rotor of increased diameter and not carrying a stabilizing bar. Construction of a prototype began in July 1965, and this machine first took to the air in December of the same year. Certification followed in October 1966, and deliveries began in January 1967. By this time, production of the OH-6A had run into cost and delivery difficulties, so the US Army reopened the LOH competition, in which Bell entered the Model 206A that was declared winner in March 1968. The US Army then placed orders for some 2,200 helicopters with the service designation OH-58A Kiowa. The type entered service from May 1969 with a powerplant of one 317hp (236kW) Allison T63-A-700 turboshaft and accommodation for two persons plus freight in the rear of the cabin.

Production lasted to 1974, and as a result of an improvement programme launched by the US Army in 1976, the OH-58C appeared as the OH-58A converted with flat-plate canopy for reduced glint, an uprated powerplant for better hot-and-high performance, and a 'black hole' IR reduction package to improve survivability against IR-homing missiles. Successful evaluation of three OH-58As modified to this standard resulted in the decision to convert another 435 helicopters, and this programme was completed by March 1985.

At the end of the 1970s the US Army became increasingly concerned about the continued viability of its scouting helicopter capability, and launched the Army helicopter improvement Program (AHIP) to provide a near-term scout helicopter (NTSH) that would bridge the operational gap until the advent of the planned light helicopter experimental (LHX) that was later ordered as the Boeing/Sikorsky RAH-66 Comanche. There were several suggestions for the required type, but in September 1981 the US Army announced that the Bell Model 406 Aeroscout proposal had been accepted and that five prototypes would be evaluated.

This proposal was based on a radical upgrade of the OH-58C Kiowa military version of the Model 206 light helicopter, with an updated avionics package and a considerably more powerful engine driving an advanced four-blade main rotor with composite-structure blades. The avionics package was based on two systems, namely the Honeywell Sperry cockpit control and display system, and the McDonnell Douglas/Northrop mast-mounted sight (MMS) system. The former is used in association with improved communication and navigation systems (including Doppler navigation and a strapdown INS), digital moving-map display, target hand-off system, and night vision goggles. The latter combines a magnifying TV camera, imaging FLIR sensor, boresight system, and a combined laser ranger and designator system for use in finding and designating targets to be engaged with laser-homing missiles fired by friendly air or ground forces.

The complete OH-58D package thus provides commanders with a real-time combat information, command and control, reconnaissance, aerial observation, and target acquisition/designation capability for operation with attack helicopters, air cavalry and field artillery units by day and night even under adverse weather conditions. A key feature in this important overall capability is the location of the sensor unit above the main rotor, as this increases the helicopter's survivability by allowing the machine to hover behind trees or masking terrain with only its MMS protruding.

The first of five prototype conversions flew in October 1983, and 376 (originally to have been 578, then reduced to 477 and finally to the figure quoted above) helicopters are being produced as OH-58A conversions and new-build machines to this AHIP standard, which includes the military version of the Allison 250-C30R turboshaft.

The MMS allows the OH-58D to scout for the McDonnell Douglas AH-64

The mast-mounted sight that can be fitted on the light helicopters of the McDonnell Douglas Model 500MD Defender series has a minimum effect on flight performance and agility, but provides the opportunity for considerably improved survivability by allowing the crew to operate effectively in the tactical sense without revealing the bulk of their helicopter for detection and engagement by the enemy's anti-aircraft defences.

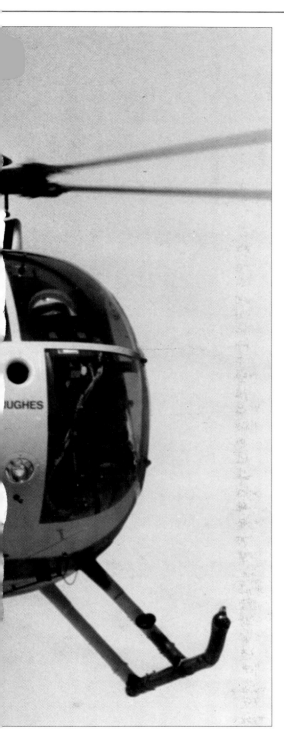

Apache, the typical teaming being three OH-58Ds leading five AH-64As, for whose AGM-114 Hellfire ASMs the OH-58Ds acquire and designate targets.

In December 1987 the US Army began to operate 15 examples of an upgraded version of the OH-58D in interim armed form as the OH-58D Kiowa Prime Chance or Armed OH-58D Kiowa. Created from September 1987, this configuration with clearance for the standard four types of Kiowa Warrior armament was designed to provide the US forces operating in the Persian Gulf with a capability against Iranian high-speed gunboats harassing shipping in this area in the closing stages of the Iraqi-Iranian Gulf War (1980-88).

The full production standard, as delivered from the 208th OH-58D, is now designated OH-58D Kiowa Warrior with the Allison 250-C30X turboshaft, ALQ-144(V)1 IR jammer and two lateral hardpoints able to carry four weapon types. These last are four AGM-114A Hellfire ASMs/anti-tank missiles, or four FIM-92A Stinger short-range AAMs, or two multiple launchers each carrying seven 2.75in (70mm) Hydra 70 unguided rockets, or two Global Helicopter Technology CFD-5000 pods each carrying one 0.5in (12.7mm) Colt-Browning M3 heavy machine gun or two 0.3in (7.62mm) machine guns, or a combination of these weapon types. The Stinger is used in conjunction with the Thomson-CSF/Hamilton Standard VH-100 ATAS (Air-To-Air Stinger) wide-angle HUD.

It is planned that all OH-58D Kiowas will eventually be upgraded to OH-58D Kiowa Warrior armed standard, 81 of them in an OH-58D Kiowa Warrior multi-purpose light helicopter (MPLH) configuration for special missions including casevac (with four externally carried litters), troop transport (with six externally carried outward-facing seats) and other roles in low-intensity warfare. Other features of the MPLH version are folding main rotor blades, a folding tailplane and a tilting fin to facilitate loading into tactical transport aircraft.

The two major trends in modern helicopter design both derive ultimately from American experience with rotorcraft in Vietnam. Firstly helicopters have become combat aircraft and therefore need heavy gun and missile armament. The only armed helicopters before this time were anti-submarine types operating from shore bases and warships, for which torpedo and depth charge weapons proved easy to install; and second, the use of helicopters in the combat zone made it clear that manoeuvrability and speed had to be improved.

To meet the need for heavier and better armament, helicopters sprouted a variety of stub wings and other protuberances to hold weapons. These additions had an adverse effect on performance, and stub wings are now designed more carefully to minimise drag and thus impede performance as little as possible. The increased use of advanced avionics has led to a revision of the basic fuselage shape, which, in modern combat helicopters such as the HueyCobra and later developments, resembles a conventional combat aeroplane more than typical examples of the older helicopter types.

Designed as the AAFSS, the Lockheed AH-56 Cheyenne mentioned above was a notable example of this trend. Speed was enhanced to a maximum of 244mph (393km/h) through the adoption of a retractable landing gear arrangement, a potent powerplant in the form of one 3,925hp (2,926kW) General Electric T64 turboshaft, and a novel lift/thrust concept: as the helicopter translated into forward flight, an increasing proportion of the lift burden was entrusted to the large stub wing, allowing power to be diverted from the main rotor to the large pusher propeller located at the extreme tail. Apart from a heavy load of avionics, the Cheyenne also carried a formidable array of guns, bombs, guided missiles and grenade-launchers. The model never entered production or service, being too costly and

complex, but it formed the conceptual basis from which was evolved the requirement for the advanced attack helicopter (AAH).

This requirement led to the Hughes Model 77 that first flew in 1975 and entered service as the AH-64 Apache, now a product of the McDonnell Douglas company since its purchase of the Hughes helicopter division. The Apache is a smaller, lighter and less powerful machine than the Cheyenne, but at the same time is fully effective as a result of its advanced design, thoroughly modern avionics and potent weapons. The type's main operator is the US Army, with which the Apache serves as a battlefield type specialising in the destruction of tanks with the Rockwell AGM-114 Hellfire missile, which has semi-active laser guidance and considerable stand-off range. First flown in September 1975, the Apache is thus the US Army's most important battlefield helicopter.

The concept of the armed helicopter was far from new when the Model 77 was schemed, for armament schemes had been planned for the first operational helicopters in World War II; the French had made extensive used of armed helicopters in the North African campaigns that ended in the early 1960s; and in 1965 the Bell AH-1 HueyCobra was about to enter service as the US Army's first rotary-wing warplane. What worried the planners of the US Army, however, was the fact that the HueyCobra resembled its predecessors in lacking all-weather flight and weapon-delivery capabilities, and in defensive terms was limited to light armour sufficient to provide protection only against small-arms fire.

The most important task faced by the US Army at that time, however, was spearheading the NATO defence of Western Europe against the threat of communist aggression by the Soviet-dominated forces of the Warsaw Pact. Such aggression would certainly exploit any tactical advantage offered at night or in poor weather conditions, and would use the very latest in heavily armoured battlefield vehicles. As adverse-weather operation and the defeat of heavy armour both lay beyond the HueyCobra's capabilities, it was clear that a more capable battlefield helicopter was needed. This had to possess the ability to fly and acquire targets under all weather and light conditions, to carry weapons

Above and right: With its size and aggressive appearance, the McDonnell Douglas AH-64A Apache offers little in the way of aesthetic appeal but is nonetheless a highly capable battlefield helicopter as proved in the 1991 UN-led campaign to expel the Iraqi aggressors from Kuwait. In this campaign the AH-64A revealed good reliability and devastating offensive capability, the latter resulting from the use of the underfuselage 30mm Hughes 'Chain Gun' cannon for the destruction of soft-skinned and lightly armoured vehicles as well as the elimination of air-defence elements, and of the Rockwell AGM-114A Hellfire semi-active laser-homing missile for the elimination of battle tanks.

capable of defeating the heaviest armour, and had to be fitted with the means of avoiding or surviving the attentions of modern battlefield anti-aircraft weapons.

The 1969 cancellation of the Cheyenne gave the US Army planners a chance to re-examine the requirement to which the AH-56 had been designed, and which was considered as having been too ambitious for the current state-of-the-art technologies. The planners' object was now to draw up a requirement for a more practical battlefield helicopter that would also be cheaper to buy and operate. Two early casualties of this simplification process were the need to escort other helicopters and provide them with protection against air as well as surface threats, and the need for very high speed. Elements of the requirement that were not relaxed, however, were agility (including rate of climb) and long endurance in fully armed configuration. The former was seen as the single most important factor in evading detection and consequent destruction through employment of nap-of-the-earth flight techniques and manoeuvres too tight to be followed by the tracking systems of missiles and anti-aircraft artillery.

In 1972 the US Army issued its resulting AAH requirement. Of the several companies that responded to the associated request for proposals, Bell and Hughes were each contracted to build two flying and one static-test prototypes as the YAH-63A and YAH-64A respectively, each powered by two examples of the turboshaft specially developed for this application as the General Electric GE.12 but later placed in production as the T700. Bell's Model 309 KingCobra clearly drew on the company's experience with the Model 209 (AH-1 HueyCobra), but adopted tricycle landing gear and reversed the positions of

The losing contender in the US Army's Advanced Attack Helicopter competition won by the Hughes YAH-64A was the Bell YAH-63A, designed as the Model 309 KingCobra with tricycle landing gear and the crew arranged with the gunner behind and above the pilot.

the crew so that the pilot was seated in the front seat ahead of and below the co-pilot/gunner. Hughes also drew on its own experience, in this instance with the diminutive Model 369 (OH-6 Cayuse), but added features from its own assessment of the AH-1 HueyCobra (including tandem seating with the pilot in the rear seat above and behind the co-pilot/gunner) and opted for fixed tailwheel landing gear. Hughes also teamed with Teledyne Ryan and Menasco: the former was responsible for the design and manufacture of the fuselage, tail unit and weapon-carrying stub wings, while the latter was entrusted with responsibility for the landing gear that was designed to absorb the stresses of a crash landing or a heavy landing on sloped surfaces, and was also intended to fold upward to reduce overall height when the helicopter was partially disassembled for transport in a cargo aeroplane.

As prime contractor and therefore responsible for the overall design, Hughes planned its Model 77 with a structure that was as conventional as possible in an effort to simplify construction and keep cost under tight rein. Thus most of the airframe was planned in light alloy semi-monocoque construction with redundant load-carrying paths to reduce the effect of damage from hits by projectiles in calibres up to 23mm. The crew seats were designed in Kevlar armour, and additional protection was afforded by boron armour under and around the cockpit section, and by an acrylic blast barrier between the two sections.

The advanced dynamic system drew heavily on the company's experience with the Model 369, and was based on a five-blade main rotor and a four-blade tail rotor, the latter with the blades set not at 90 degrees to each other but at 55 and 125 degrees for reduced noise.

The first of the two flight-test YAH-64A prototypes flew in September 1975 with a powerplant of two 1,536hp (1,145kW) T700-GE-701 turboshafts. It had been planned that competitive evaluation of the YAH-63A and YAH-64A would lead to a production decision in 1979, but in December 1976 the YAH-64A was declared winner and three more prototypes were ordered with a revised tail unit on which the fixed-incidence tailplane was moved to the top of the vertical tail surface in a T-tail arrangement. The vertical surface underwent considerable modification during the flight test programme, and the stabilizer eventually reverted to a low-set position, although it was now located behind the vertical surface and became an all-moving unit.

The real operational capabilities of the AH-64, which was named Apache in 1981, depend on its avionics, and Hughes decided that most of the electronic bays should be located externally in box fairings along the low sides of the forward fuselage. These fairings had to be enlarged several times, and eventually reached back under the stub wing, whose trailing edges were fitted with high-deflection flaps that were later deleted.

Another part of the design that underwent steady change was the nose, which accommodated the two most important groups of sensors, those for the target acquisition and designation system (TADS) and PNVS. Northrop and Martin Marietta competed for these complex systems, Martin Marietta winning in April 1982. The two independent systems are both turret-mounted in the extreme nose and feed data to the two members of the crew via the monocle screen carried by the helmet of the IHADSS.

The TADS is based on a nose turret that can be traversed 120 degrees left and right of the centreline and elevated in an arc between -60 and +30 degrees. The turret accommodates daylight and night/all-weather sensors in its port and starboard halves respectively. The daylight sensors comprise a TV camera with wide- and narrow-angle fields of vision, direct-view optics with wide- and narrow-angle fields of vision, a laser spot tracker, and an International Laser Systems laser ranger and designator, while the night/adverse-weather sensor is an FLIR with wide-, medium- and narrow-angle fields of vision. In short, the TADS provides for the optronic, optical or thermal acquisition of targets that can then be laser-ranged and laser-designated to allow manual or automatic tracking for autonomous engagement with the cannon, missiles or rockets.

It is worth noting, moreover, that while the TADS is designed primarily for the co-pilot/gunner, it provides back-up night vision capability for the pilot in the event of a failure in the PNVS. The latter is based on an FLIR in a separate turret located above the TADS turret, and this sensor's 20- and 40-degree field of vision provides high-resolution thermal imaging for day/night nap-of-the-earth flight profiles under all weather conditions.

The co-pilot/gunner is primarily responsible for the armament, which comprises disposable stores carried on the four underwing hardpoints and the 30mm cannon in an underfuselage installation designed to collapse upward between the two crew members in the event of a crash landing. The pilot can override the co-pilot/gunner in use of the weapons, but his principal task is flying the helicopter with the aid of the highly advanced all-weather systems. This is only one part of the Apache's comprehensive electronics, which also include an RWR, active jammers, chaff/flare dispensers, an IR jammer, and a laser warning system.

The development phase of the AH-64 programme was successfully completed in August 1981, and the first AH-64A production helicopters were delivered in February 1984 with a powerplant of two 1,696hp (1,265kW) T700-GE-701 turboshafts. Operational service has confirmed that while it is large, complex and costly, the AH-64A is a highly capable machine offering advanced sensors and useful performance for the very accurate delivery of a heavy ordnance load. The disposable load is optimised for the destruction of hard- and soft-skinned vehicles on the battlefield, while the underfuselage cannon is designed for the suppression of enemy ground defences. Particular advantages of the design are high survivability, good protection of the crew and primary systems, and sophisticated avionics such as the TADS and PNVS.

The manufacturer, which is now the McDonnell Douglas Helicopter Company after the McDonnell Douglas Corporation's January 1984 purchase of Hughes Helicopters Inc., has proposed that the type be retrofitted under a three-stage programme with the GPS, improved Doppler navigation, and enhanced versions of the TADS and PNVS. From the hundredth helicopter, the basic standard has been improved by the use of composite-construction main rotor blades, and since the late 1980s all

Tackling the Battlefield Helicopter

Such is the threat of the helicopter, within the context of operations on the modern high-intensity battlefield, that there has developed a see-saw technological competition between the helicopter and battlefield air-defence weapons. The object of the battlefield helicopter is to reach the battlefield, observe, acquire and/or designate the required target(s) and then, in the case of an attack helicopter, destroy the target(s) before exiting the scene. On the other side of the ground/air interface, the task of battlefield air-defence systems is to find, acquire, engage and destroy such helicopters before they can undertake their primary task. Helicopters and helicopter-launched weapons were developed with higher performance and with a sturdier structure better able to absorb combat damage, a measure of armour protection, crashworthy features such as impact-tolerant seats and fuel systems, countermeasures designed to reduce the efficiency of ground-fired weapons, mast-mounted sights so that the helicopter could both fly and operate in nap-of-the-earth mode, and improved weapons offering higher velocity and longer stand-off range as well as improved operational features such as a fire-and-forget capability or the ability to home on a target designated by a third party. All these factors helped to reduce the time the helicopter had to spend in the danger zone, extend the range from which the helicopter could tackle its target, and curtail the efficiency of the smaller number of weapons that could still be employed against the helicopter. The designers of anti-helicopter weapons then responded with improved, longer-range equipments such as fast-firing 40mm anti-aircraft guns firing specially designed ammunition with the aid of a more advanced fire-control system, and surface-to-air missiles with counter-countermeasures and/or un-jammable laser guidance. The balance between the helicopter and ground defences is now finely balanced with the tilt perhaps slightly in favour of the battlefield helicopter because of its low observability and ability to deliver fire-and-forget weapons at significant stand-off range.

Apaches have had upgraded self-protection capability in the form of four FIM-92A Stinger lightweight AAMs attached (two on each side) to the outboard underwing pylons.

The AH-64B Apache designation was first postulated for an improved version to be delivered in the mid-to-late 1990s with voice-actuated controls, a fly-by-light fibre-optical control system using a four-axis side-arm control stick, improved armament including a pair of AIM-9 Sidewinder AAMs, a GPS receiver, Doppler radar, improved night vision equipment, an advanced composite rotor hub, and a reinforced thermoplastic secondary structure.

The designation was then applied to 254 AH-64As, upgraded to reflect the lessons learned in the 1991 UN-led war with Iraq, and thus revised with GPS, improved radios, target hand-off capability, improved navigation, and greater reliability including new rotor blades. In the event, however, the revised designation was not applied to these upgraded machines.

The AH-64C Apache designation was reserved for an initial 308 AH-64As retrofitted to virtual AH-64D standard except for the omission of the Longbow radar (for which provision is nonetheless made) and the retention of the T700-GE-701 turboshafts. Late in 1993 the designation was abandoned, and all 562 upgraded AH-64A helicopters are now known by the designation AH-64D.

The AH-64D Longbow Apache is an improved version of the AH-64A/B with a powerplant of two 1,800hp (1,342kW) T700-GE-701C turboshafts and the Longbow fire-control system based on a Westinghouse millimetric-wavelength radar with its antenna in a mast-mounted radome above the main rotor. This radar is the primary sensor of the Longbow system (initially designated Airborne Adverse-Weather Weapon System), and is intended for rapid target-area search, automatic detection and classification of targets, and all-weather fire-and-forget engagement with a revised version of the Hellfire missile, namely the radar-homing Longbow Hellfire that carries – in addition to its semi-active laser seeker modified for improved resistance to optical countermeasures – a combined radio-frequency and IR seeker as well as a warhead optimised for the penetration of modern types of advanced tank protection.

The AH-64D will also carry lightweight AAMs (originally to have been FIM-92A Stinger weapons but now possibly to be Shorts Starstreak weapons) on the tips of its stub wings, and will have avionics based on a digital databus. It is also possible that the AH-64D will introduce features from the cancelled Apache Plus programme such as a redesigned cockpit, a larger forward avionics bay for improved electronics, and a digital fly-by-wire system developed by General Electric and Lucas.

Although it was the Americans who took an early lead in the development of manoeuvrable and heavily armed combat helicopters, the USSR began to whittle away this technical lead with the Mi-24 'Hind-D' gunship version of the Mi-24 'Hind' assault transport helicopter. Although large and relatively unmanoeuvrable by comparison with the American helicopters, the 'Hind-D' has the same type of narrow fuselage with a stepped cockpit arrangement, and among its virtues are good weapon-aiming systems and the ability to carry a heavy load of multiple weapon types.

In origin the Mi-24 is a multi-role helicopter, and has been the subject of contested evaluations in the West, in relation largely to the tactical capability of the gunship models. The type is based on the dynamic system of the Mi-14 and Mi-17, using two TV2-117 (later TV3-117) turboshafts, in this application married to a new fuselage of slender lines to enhance performance and battlefield survivability. The Mi-24A initial model, also known by the NATO reporting designation 'Hind-A', has a crew of three

The McDonnell Douglas AH-64A Apache is no longer in the first flush of its operational youth, but is still an extremely capable battlefield helicopter offering its operator high performance, high-quality flight and combat electronics and optronics, and a carefully balanced blend of short- and medium-range offensive weapons.

(pilot, co-pilot/gunner and ground engineer), and can carry an eight-man infantry squad in its hold. The 'Hind-A' was in fact the second production model, the initial Mi-24B 'Hind-B' having been a pre-production type built only in small numbers for service from 1973, and distinguishable from the 'Hind-A' by its straight wings with only four hardpoints, and by the location of the tail rotor on the starboard side of the fin.

The 'Hind-A' has an anhedraled wing with four underwing hardpoints and two overwing twin launchers for AT-3 'Swatter' anti-tank missiles, and a 0.5in (12.7mm) DShK heavy machine gun (slaved to the undernose sight system) is installed in the nose. It is unlikely that the survivors of the 'Hind-A' and 'Hind-B' variants are still used for the infantry assault role, a more likely task being the battlefield movement of anti-tank missile teams, and the Mi-24U 'Hind-C' is the dual-control trainer version of the 'Hind-A' without the nose gun and wing-tip missile launcher rails. Production of the Mi-24A and Mi-24U totalled about 250 helicopters between 1973 and 1977.

First seen by Western observers in 1977, the Mi-24 'Hind-D' helicopter is the much-altered version used in the dedicated gunship role, with a new upper forward fuselage featuring stepped cockpits for the gunner (nose) and pilot (behind and slightly above the gunner). The gunner controls a 0.5in (12.7mm) rotary four-barrel heavy machine gun in an undernose turret slaved to the adjacent KPS-53A optronic sighting pod for air-to-surface and air-to-air use, while the wing-mounted armament is similar to that of the 'Hind-A', although more extensive. The sensor fit for the accurate firing of air-to-surface ordnance includes an air data probe, low-light-level TV, radar and a laser tracker. Although the cabin can carry an eight-man infantry squad, it is likely that only one man and reload weapons are carried for battlefield replenishment of the underwing hardpoints.

The type clearly possesses considerable speed and offensive capability, but Western analysts point out that the 'Hind-D' is large and relatively lacking in manoeuvrability for the gunship role. Soviet experience with the type in Afghanistan led to the adoption under the tail boom of a dispenser loaded with 192 IR decoys for heat-seeking missiles, as well as an IR jammer and RWR. A training version of the Mi-24D is the Mi-24DU, which differs externally from the baseline gunship in its lack of the undernose machine gun turret. Production totalled about 350 helicopters between 1973 and 1977.

The Mi-24V 'Hind-E' is an improved Mi-24D version produced in two subvariants for service from 1976, with more specialised avionics and optronics including the ASP-17V automatic missile guidance pod under the nose with a searchlight in its rear section, and the pilot's reflector sight replaced by an HUD. The type also possesses upgraded systems, improved defensive features, and a modified combination of underwing and overwing hardpoints for up to eight AT-6 'Spiral' instead of AT-2 'Swatter' anti-tank missiles under the wings and AA-8 'Aphid' short-range AAMs on the overwing rails.

The Mi-24VP 'Hind-E' is a subvariant with the rotary four-barrel heavy machine gun replaced by a 23mm GSh-23L cannon with 450 rounds of ammunition. About 1,000 Mi-24V and Mi-24VP helicopters were built between 1976 and 1986.

The Mi-24P 'Hind-F' is a Mi-24V version that entered service in 1981 with a revised nose in which the undernose machine gun turret is removed, its space nicely faired so that primary emphasis is placed on the heavier capability provided by one two-barrel cannon (originally thought to be a 23mm GSh-23L but now known to be a 30mm GSh-30-2) with 750 rounds in a pack fixed on the starboard side of the nose. As a result of Soviet experience in Afghanistan during the 1980s, the type is also fitted with a number of measures to defeat heat-seeking SAMs; these measures include inlet and exhaust shrouds, a dorsally mounted 'hot brick' IR jammer and stub wing-mounted dispensers for IR decoy flares. Deliveries amounted to about 620 helicopters between 1981 and 1990.

The Mi-24RSh 'Hind-G1' is the specialised radiation-sampling variant, and about 150 such helicopters were built between 1983 and 1989. The Mi-24K 'Hind-G2' is a variant of the Mi-24RSh with a large starboard-facing camera in the cabin, and is believed to be used for the tactical reconnaissance and artillery-spotting roles. About 150 such helicopters were completed between 1983 and 1989. The Mi-24BMT 'Hind-?' was introduced in 1973 as a conversion of older helicopters for the minesweeping role. Other 'Hind' variants include the Mi-25 'Hind-D' export version of the Mi-24D with avionics of a reduced standard; the Mi-35 'Hind-E' export version of the Mi-24V with additional armour for the crew and vital dynamic system components, a heavier weapon load carried on six hardpoints, different avionics, and inbuilt chaff/flare launchers rather than the boom-mounted IR jammer of Soviet models; the Mi-35P 'Hind-F' export version of the Mi-24P; and the Mi-35M 'Hind-?' latest air mobility version for the Russian army, with the dynamic system of the Mil Mi-28 'Havoc' attack helicopter, a revised undernose turret carrying a 23mm GSh-23L two-barrel cannon, and a revised suite of avionics.

By the early 1980s the Soviets had evaluated the concept of combat helicopters and began to develop specialised types that were developed slowly throughout the decade for a possible service debut in the mid-to-late 1990s as the Kamov Ka-50 and Mil Mi-28.

The Ka-50, offered for sale with the name Werewolf and also known by the NATO reporting name 'Hokum-A', was designed with the co-axial twin rotors typical of Kamov practice and was initially known by the supposed designation Ka-41. The Ka-50 first flew in July 1982 in the form of the V-80 prototype for an advanced battlefield helicopter of which relatively few details are available. In combination with a slim fuselage and retractable landing gear, the rotor design offers a high degree of agility and speed, while the elimination of the tail rotor offers the advantages of a shorter fuselage for reduced battlefield visibility and vulnerability.

Although it was originally thought that the type was tasked with the anti-helicopter escort role over the land battlefield, in conjunction with offensive operations by Mi-24 'Hind' and Mi-28 'Havoc' helicopters, the Ka-50 was later assessed as a shipborne type designed to provide Naval Infantry amphibious assault forces with close air support over the beach-head. In 1992, however, the Russians finally revealed that the type had indeed been developed in competition with the Mi-28 and had been selected in preference to that type as successor to the Mi-24 'Hind-D'.

The Ka-50's cockpit, powerplant and transmission are protected by two layers of structural armour weighing some 772lb (330kg) and capable of withstanding the effects of 20mm cannon shells, and a notable feature is the installation of an ejector seat as the main component of an escape system that ensures explosive separation of the two rigid rotors' six blades at the moment of seat initiation. The Ka-50 is unique as the world's first single-seat attack/anti-tank helicopter to enter full production, and its electronics (including provision for third-party target acquisition) are optimised for the easing of the pilot's workload.

The cannon barbette on the port side of the nose can be elevated and depressed by a hydraulic system but has no traverse capability, so the complete helicopter is yawed to aim the weapon and then held on target by a tracking system that turns the helicopter on its vertical axis. The cannon

Accorded the Western reporting name 'Havoc', the Mil Mi-28 two-seat battlefield helicopter has been ordered by the air arm of the Commonwealth of Independent States after a complicated tussle with the Kamov Ka-50 'Hokum' single-seat combat helicopter that was also ordered, albeit at a slightly earlier date, and had also been offered on the export market with the name Werewolf. The Mi-28 is typical of modern battlefield helicopters in placing general operational utility above outright flight performance, and for this reason the helicopter is somewhat ungainly in appearance although clearly still a very formidable machine that has also been developed into a Mi-28N version with a mast-mounted sight and other enhancement for full operational capability at night and under adverse weather conditions.

is the same weapon as already used in the BMP infantry fighting vehicle, and is thus heavier than an equivalent weapon designed solely for aerial use, but is notably rugged under dusty and hot conditions and is a dual-feed weapon able to fire HE incendiary and armour-piercing ammunition.

The whole machine was designed for deployment away from base for at least two weeks without need of maintenance ground equipment, as all refuelling and servicing of the avionics and weapons can be undertaken from ground level.

The 'Hokum-B' is the two-seat conversion trainer derivative of the 'Hokum-A', retaining full combat capability and therefore accommodating a pilot and trainee or weapon operator side-by-side in a widened forward fuselage section.

First flown in November 1982 for service from the mid-1990s, the Mi-28 'Havoc' seems to have confirmed Western doubts about the battlefield viability of the Mi-24 'Hind' gunship models, for while this new machine is clearly derived from earlier Mil helicopters (including the dynamic system of the Mi-24 driving a new five-blade articulated main rotor), it adopted the US practice of a much slimmer and smaller fuselage for increased manoeuvrability and reduced vulnerability over the modern high-technology battlefield.

The Mi-28 thus bears a passing resemblance to the AH-64A Apache in US Army service, and among its operational features are IR suppression of the

249

The smallest of current battlefield helicopters, the Agusta A 129 Mangusta (mongoose) is fast and agile, but possesses no gun armament and carries the optronic sensors for its flight and fire-control systems on a steerable platform low on the nose. The weapons load is supported by the four hardpoints under the stub wing, and is here represented by two multi-tube launchers for unguided rockets, and two superimposed pairs of twin launchers for BGM-71 TOW heavyweight anti-tank missiles.

podded engines' exhausts, IR decoys, upgraded steel/titanium armour, optronic sighting and targeting systems for use in conjunction with the undernose 30mm cannon and disposable weapons (including AAMs) carried on the stub wing hardpoints, and millimetric-wavelength radar.

The type clearly possesses an air-combat capability against other battlefield helicopters, and other notable features include a far higher level of survivability and the provision of a small compartment on the left-hand side of the fuselage, probably for the rescue of downed aircrew.

In 1992 the Russians revealed that the type had been developed in competition with the Kamov V-80 (later Ka-50), and that the latter had been selected for Russian service as the Ka-50. Mil then offered the Mi-28 on the export market, with a view to placing the type in production should an order materialise, but in 1993 it was announced that the type is in fact to be procured for Russian service alongside the Ka-50, always providing that adequate financing can be assured.

Due to fly in 1996 for a possible service debut in the late 1990s, the Mi-28N 'Havoc-B' is a night and adverse-weather derivative of the baseline Mi-28, with a specialised nav/attack system including a mast-mounted sight incorporating the antenna for millimetric-wavelength radar, FLIR and a low-light-level TV.

The other three helicopter gunship types currently flying are the Agusta A 129 Mangusta from Italy, the Atlas CSH-2 Rooivalk from South Africa, and the Eurocopter Tigre/Tiger from France and Germany.

The first tandem-seat anti-tank helicopter developed in Europe, the A 129 Mangusta offers good performance, powerful anti-tank armament and associated sights, and a small fuselage profile featuring vertically staggered tandem seating for the gunner and pilot, the latter seated above and behind the former. The type was designed in response to a 1972 Italian army requirement, and the first of five prototype and development helicopters flew in September 1983, an exhaustive development programme then being undertaken before the Mangusta entered service in October 1990 with full day and night offensive capability. The Integrated Multiplex System monitors the helicopter and all its systems via two computers, leaving the two crew members to devote their attention to the mission. The standard A 129 has provision for the retrofit of a mast-mounted sight system, and the manufacturer has also proposed a shipborne model able to undertake the anti-ship or close-support roles, the former with an armament of two Sea Killer Mk 2 or four Sea Skua missiles supported by appropriate search/designation radar, and the latter with an armament of AGM-65 Maverick ASMs in addition to the A 129's standard TOW and rocket fit.

Revealed as the XH-2 prototype that first flew in February 1990, the CSH-2 Rooivalk was designed as South Africa's standard battlefield helicopter in light of its forces' combat experience in Namibia during the 1980s. The type was evolved from the Aérospatiale SA.330 Puma with a locally upgraded version of a French turboshaft, the Turbomeca Makila IA2, and represents the conclusion of South Africa's evolutionary programme of battlefield helicopter development via the Alpha XH-1 and Beta XTP-1. The XH-1 was a gunship demonstrator combining the dynamic system of the Aérospatiale Alouette III with a new fuselage and an advanced weapon system; the crew of two was seated in tandem in upward-staggered separate cockpits, and the gun armament comprised one 20mm GA1 cannon with 1,000 rounds in a servo-actuated mounting under the fuselage. The XTP-1 subsystems flight-test platform was evolved in similar fashion as a radical development of the SA.330 Puma. Designed from 1984, the CSH-2 has the Rattler cannon system (with a 20mm GA1 Cobra gun in a servo-operated chin turret fed from a magazine in the hold and operated in conjunction with a helmet sight worn by the co-pilot/gunner), and a variety of disposable loads on the six hardpoints under the two new stub wings (produced as a single unit passing through the erstwhile passenger cabin). The political situation in southern Africa has eased to the point at which the South African forces no longer need the Rooivalk in substantial numbers, although 16 of the type are being procured for the equipment of two squadrons from 1998, so the type's commercial success probably depends on export orders. In the early 1990s, Atlas was involved in discussions with possible co-production partners in the Middle East and South America. In 1995 it was announced that Malaysia is considering a purchase of the type.

The Tigre/Tiger single-rotor helicopter was planned to meet French and West German requirements for an advanced multi-role type for battlefield operations in the typical European scenario, and originated from a 1984 memorandum of understanding. The original development was halted in 1986 because of rapidly escalating costs, but was relaunched during 1987 in basically common French and West German anti-tank models and as a French escort model. The airframe is built largely of composite materials, and the first of five development helicopters flew in April 1991. The Tigre is planned in two forms for the French army. The first of these is the Hélicoptère Anti-Char (HAR), or anti-tank helicopter, of which 100 (originally 140) are required. The primary armament is planned as a maximum of eight anti-tank missiles (all HOT 2 or Trigat weapons or four of each type, all aimed via the Osiris mast-mounted sight) on the inner underwing hardpoints and four Matra Mistral short-range AAMs on the outer underwing hardpoints. The Osiris system combines a TV, FLIR and laser ranger for the weapon system operator, while the pilot uses a nose-mounted FLIR as his primary night vision sensor. The Hélicoptère d'Appui et de Protection (HAP), or attack and protection helicopter, is required to the extent of 115 (originally 75). This model carries a chin-mounted 30mm GIAT 30/781B cannon with between 150 and 450 rounds of ammunition and, on the underwing hardpoints, two multiple launchers each carrying twenty-two 2.68in (68mm) unguided rockets and either four Matra Mistral short-range AAMs or two multiple launchers each carrying twelve 2.68in unguided rockets. The sensors of this variant include a roof-mounted combination of TV and FLIR optics, direct optics and a laser ranger. Originally ordered as the PAC-2 second-generation anti-tank helicopter, the Tiger is now the UHU support for the German army, which requires 212 such machines. The model is basically similar to the HAC apart from its ability to carry Stinger 2 short-range AAMs on the outboard underwing hardpoints in place of the French variant's Mistral weapons. In common with France, Germany was reviewing the nature and extent of the programme during the early 1990s, the driving forces being rising development and procurement costs as well as the decline (or rather demise) of the Warsaw Pact threat that this battlefield helicopter was intended to tackle.

251

Multi-Role Versatility

THE cost of developing, building and operating aircraft as complex and advanced as modern helicopters has always placed a premium on helicopter versatility, so that any type can undertake as many roles as possible. This tendency has increased in recent years, especially with the collapse of the USSR and thus its end as a credible threat to the West, and as part of the resulting 'peace dividend' there has been further pressure for any new helicopter type to offer multiple capabilities on the basis of a common airframe/dynamic system combination.

Such a tendency had been obvious from the beginning of the helicopter's operational use, of course, as evidenced by the employment of the early Sikorsky and Bell helicopters for the observation, training, liaison, observation and casevac roles, and then taken to a more advanced level with the advent of more capable helicopters such as the Sikorsky S-58 that was delivered in general transport, assault landing and naval variants (the last in complementary anti-submarine hunter and killer pairs with specialised avionics and weapons respectively). The advent of the turboshaft further increased this tendency by improving the helicopter's all-round payload/range capabilities, and thus even small helicopters such as the Aérospatiale Alouette series could be configured for armed tasks (over both land and sea battlefields) as an alternative to its baseline transport and communications roles. Further development of the turboshaft-powered helicopter resulted in machines that were more fully optimised for their roles, especially in features such as

The Boeing CH-47 Chinook is the most important medium/heavy-lift transport helicopter available to Western-oriented nations, and has undergone a long programme of development as well as construction so that modern helicopters of the same basic type offer considerably more sophisticated capabilities as well as superior performance to the initial CH-47A helicopters that made their operational debut in the Vietnam War.

the mission package (avionics and weapons) and landing gear optimised for land and shipborne use (twin skid and wheeled tricycle respectively).

A classic example of this tendency is provided by a British type, the small but extremely versatile Westland Lynx that was planned from the beginning in closely related military and naval variants. The Lynx was designed from 1968 within the context of an Anglo-French agreement for the collaborative development of three tactical helicopters. Design leadership of two was allocated to France (the Aérospatiale SA.330 Puma and Aérospatiale SA.341 Gazelle) and of the third to the UK (the WG.13 design that matured as the Lynx multi-role type for land-based and shipborne use).

The WG.13 was designed as an all-metal type based on a pod-and-boom fuselage accommodating the flightcrew of one or two at the front, each crew member having his own jettisonable door. This left the major part of the pod section for the payload-carrying hold section, whose dimensions from the back of the pilots' seats include a length of 6ft 9in (2.06m), width of 5ft 10in (1.78m) and height of 4ft 8in (1.42m); the hold is accessed by two sliding and jettisonable doors. The boom extends rearward from the upper part of the pod section's rear face, and supports the anti-torque rotor. The helicopter was made as compact as possible to facilitate operations from small naval platforms such as frigates, but very careful design ensured that the hold was large enough to carry an infantry squad or other suitable load in the type's land-based variants. For full optimisation in the land-based and shipborne roles, provision was made for two types of landing gear, in the form of a fixed tricycle arrangement for the naval model and a twin-skid arrangement for the land-based model.

It was also decided from the start of the programme that high performance and great agility were essential prerequisites for naval and military success, and an advanced rotor system was designed. This was based on four-blade main and tail rotors, the main rotor being of the semi-rigid type with each blade attached to the rotor hub by titanium plates and a root arm. Power was provided by two 900hp (671kW) Rolls-Royce Gem Mk 2 turboshafts located side-by-side over the pod/boom junction and driving a gearbox between themselves and the main rotor.

The first of 13 prototypes flew in March 1971, and development centred on two streams for the land-optimised variant with skid landing gear and the

Top and above: The naval version of the Westland Lynx, identifiable by its tricycle rather than twin-skid landing gear, is a notably compact helicopter than can nonetheless carry a useful payload (men or equipment in its secondary transport role, or electronics and weapons in its primary anti-submarine and anti-ship role) and offers very high performance as well as considerable agility and excellent reliability.

ship-optimised variant with tricycle landing gear. The prototype of the baseline land-based Lynx AH.Mk 1 model first flew in April 1972, and the type entered service in 1977. Some 113 helicopters were built to this standard, which offers better performance than the naval Lynx as it has the same basic powerplant but a lower empty weight. Apart from the twin-skid landing gear, this model's major differences from the naval Lynx are a slightly longer fuselage and a different combination of avionics and weapons. The Lynx has been qualified for a wide assortment of weapons, but in its basic anti-tank role with the British army the Lynx AH.Mk 1 carries container-launchers for eight BGM-71 TOW heavyweight anti-tank missiles guided with the aid of an M65 stabilized roof-mounted sight. The cabin can accommodate reload TOW missiles, or up to 10 troops, or a Milan ground-launched anti-tank missile crew with launcher, missiles and other equipment, or casualties, or freight.

The Lynx AH.Mk 5 designation is applied to three examples of an improved version of the Lynx AH.Mk 1, with two 1,120hp (835kW) Gem Mk 41-1 turboshafts later upgraded to 1,135hp (846kW) Gem Mk 42-1 standard, and a maximum disposable ordnance load of about 1,210lb (549kg).

The Lynx AH.Mk 7 designation is applied to 11 examples of a further-improved model for the British army, with upgraded systems, Gem Mk 42-1 turboshafts, swept-tip BERP main rotor blades of composite construction (retrofitted as the original metal blades were withdrawn), and a tail rotor rotating in the opposite direction to that of the Lynx AH.Mk 1 for a greater maximum take-off weight. All surviving Lynx AH.Mk 1 helicopters are being upgraded via the Lynx AH.Mk 1GT interim standard (uprated engines and rotors) to this definitive standard, which also includes the thermal imaging TOW (TITOW) anti-tank missile sight system, which is the standard M65 unit fitted with a GEC Sensors thermal imaging sensor for improved nocturnal capability; the complete package offers better low-level hovering and manoeuvring capabilities, facilitating nap-of-the-earth anti-tank operations, and protection from IR-homing missiles is improved by the use of large hot gas/cool freestream air mixers fitted over the turboshaft exhausts.

The Lynx AH.Mk 9 designation is applied to 16 new-build examples and eight Lynx AH.Mk 7 conversions to an updated Lynx AH.Mk 7 unarmed mobile command post and tactical transport standard with upgraded avionics, BERP rotor blades of composite construction, an upgraded gearbox, Gem Mk 42-1 turboshafts, tricycle landing gear, secure radio equipment, an improved identification friend or foe (IFF) facility, a Decca Tactical Air Navigation System, a cockpit voice recorder, a tele-briefing system, and a maximum take-off weight increased by 550lb (249kg).

Developed as a private venture, the Battlefield Lynx is an armed version with a roof-mounted sight and provision for eight BGM-71 TOW anti-tank missiles. Westland is also offering a Battlefield Lynx 800 version of this helicopter with a powerplant of two 1,350hp (1,007kW) LHTEC

(Allison/Garrett) T800 turboshafts for improved hot-and-high performance. A variant that has yet to secure any production order, the Lynx-3 is a much improved dedicated anti-tank development with a powerplant of two 1,346hp (1,004kW) Gem Mk 60 turboshafts, an advanced-technology main rotor, and a slightly lengthened fuselage housing two pilots and a deployable anti-tank missile team, the missile team's reloads, and pylon-mounted weapons such as Hellfire, HOT or TOW anti-tank missiles, and provision for FIM-92A Stinger or Shorts Starstreak lightweight AAMs.

The Lynx HAS.Mk 2 is the baseline naval model of the Lynx family, and is an advanced anti-submarine and anti-ship helicopter suitable for deployment on small surface vessels. The Lynx HAS.Mk 2 prototype first flew in May 1972, and the variant entered service from December 1977. Production totalled 60 helicopters, and the type is distinguishable from its land-based counterpart by its fixed but castoring tricycle landing gear, its folding tail, and its combination of naval avionics and weapons. As alternatives to its primary roles, the Lynx HAS.Mk 2 can be used for transport (with a payload of 10 troops, or 2,000lb/907kg of freight carried internally or 3,000lb/1,361kg of freight carried externally), or underway replenishment of ships at sea, or SAR.

The Lynx Mk 2(FN) designation is applied to 26 of the Lynx HAS.Mk 2 version for the French navy, with a revised suite of electronics and operational equipment.

The Lynx HAS.Mk 3 designation is applied to 23 of an improved British naval model delivered between March 1982 and March 1985 with a powerplant of two 1,120hp (835kW) Gem Mk 41-1 turboshafts, and supplemented by 53 Lynx HAS.Mk 2s upgraded to the same higher-performance standard. Between November 1987 and November 1988, another seven

helicopters were delivered to the improved Lynx HAS.Mk 3S standard with secure radio and an upgraded ESM system, and this number was increased by 23 Lynx HAS.Mk 2 helicopters converted to the same standard. The latest subvariant is the Lynx HAS.Mk 3CTS, a designation applied to seven helicopters upgraded with the Lynx HAS.Mk 8's Racal RAMS 4000 Central Tactical System (CTS).

The Lynx Mk 4(FN) is the designation applied to 14 of the Lynx HAS.Mk 3 version for the French navy, with the same equipment as the Lynx Mk 2(FN).

The Lynx HAS.Mk 8 is the latest anti-ship and anti-submarine development in the naval Lynx series, a standard to which 65 helicopters of the Lynx HAS.Mk 3 series are being upgraded with improvements such as a better tail rotor turning in the opposite direction to that of earlier models, composite-structure BERP main rotor blades, and an electronic system featuring an upgraded ESM system (the Racal RNS252 'Super TANS' navigation system with GPS input, and the Racal RAMS 4000 CTS with all tactical data processed for display on a multi-function CRT). It had originally been planned to fit 360-degree scan radar (the GEC Ferranti Seaspray Mk 3 and Thorn EMI Super Searcher had been shortlisted) with its antenna in a

Top and above: The latest land-based version of the Westland Lynx has adopted the type of tricycle landing gear arrangement initially developed for the naval model. In its battlefield role the land-based Lynx can be fitted with an assortment of weapons including medium- and heavy-weight anti-tank missiles, and can also be used for the transport of specialised anti-tank teams with their ground-based firing unit plus a considerable number of reload missiles.

chin-mounted radome, but the installation of such a radar has been abandoned for financial reasons. The final electronic fit thus includes the original Seaspray Mk 1 radar, relocated to a chin radome, to leave the nose position clear for the GEC Sensors Sea Owl Passive Identification Device (PID), which is a long-range thermal imaging system. In other respects, the Lynx HAS.Mk 8 differs from the Lynx HAS.Mk 2 in details such as its powerplant of two 1,135hp (846kW) Rolls-Royce Gem Mk 42-1 turboshafts.

The naval version of the Lynx has also been widely exported in a number of Lynx Mk 20, Lynx Mk 80 and Lynx Mk 90 variants, and Westland is offering the Super Lynx version of the Lynx HAS.Mk 8 variant for export, with 360-degree scan GEC Ferranti Seaspray Mk 3 radar and a powerplant of two Gem Mk 42-1 turboshafts as standard, plus provision for customer options such as dunking sonar, Sea Skua or Penguin anti-ship missiles, Stingray torpedoes and the main and tail rotor developments of the Lynx AH.Mk 7/Lynx HAS.Mk 8 series.

Of the two French helicopters that were developed and placed in production within the context of the Anglo-French agreement mentioned above, the larger is the Aérospatiale Puma that has been extensively developed by the parent company (now Eurocopter France) through three main generations, and with a bewildering number of designation and name changes. Having made extensive use of helicopters in their Far Eastern and North African operations of the 1950s and early 1960s, the French were well placed to assess the capabilities of current tactical helicopters and thereby arrive at the right specification for an effective successor type. In the medium transport role, it was clear that helicopters such as the Sikorsky S-58 (CH-34 series) were limited in utility by their piston-engined powerplants, which were bulky, offered only a comparatively low power-to-weight ratio, and required the type of fuel and maintenance that would both become increasingly scarce as more operators switched to turbine engines. The low power-to-weight ratio of the powerplant meant that payload was fairly limited, and that it was impossible to outfit such tactical helicopters with the full instrumentation that would have provided them with an effective night and all-weather capability.

In 1962, therefore, the French army issued a requirement for a new tactical transport able to operate under all weather conditions, and in 1963 Sud-Aviation began work on the new type under the designation SA.330. The company already had extensive experience in turbine-powered helicopter design with its Alouette series, and its Super Frelon provided data on the design of large transport helicopters. What the company now planned was a helicopter mid-way between the Alouette and Super Frelon in size, with a pod-and-boom fuselage, retractable tricycle landing gear for higher speed, and a powerplant of two turboshafts located above the cabin roof as the core of a dynamic system also including a four-blade main rotor and a five-blade tail rotor.

The twin-engined powerplant offered great reliability and the turboshaft engines provided both a low vibration level and a high power-to-weight ratio, thereby reducing the fatigue experienced by the helicopter's occupants and maximising the helicopter's payload. The cabin was 15ft 4in (4.68m) long, 5ft 8in (1.73m) wide and 4ft 11in (1.50m) high, with access provided by a large sliding door on each side.

The first of two SA.330A prototypes flew in April 1965, and there followed six pre-production helicopters before the SA.330B initial production version entered service in March 1969, with a powerplant of two 1,328hp (990kW) Turmo IIIC4 turboshafts for the carriage of a 6,614lb (3,000kg) payload. The type was built to the extent of 145 helicopters for the French army, proving

256

Top: The Royal Navy's Westland Lynx HAS.Mk 8 is a development of the Super Lynx concept with the nose extensively modified for installation of the GEC-Marconi Sea Owl thermal imaging system in a trainable turret on a platform above the repositioned Ferranti Seaspray Mk I search radar that provides target data for the BAe Sea Skua missile that is the helicopter's primary weapon for use against light and medium surface vessels.

highly successful in its intended role and thus paving the way for substantial export orders for military and naval models. The SA.330C Puma was developed in parallel with the SA.330B as the baseline export version with a powerplant of two 1,402hp (1,045kW) Turmo IVC turboshafts.

The British had recognised the potential of the SA.330 from an early date, and in 1967 the type was selected as the last of the trio of helicopters for joint British and French manufacture (the other two being the Sud-Aviation SA.341 Gazelle and the Westland Lynx). The British saw the type as a supplement and replacement respectively for its Westland Wessex HC.Mk 2 and Westland Whirlwind helicopters. The resulting SA.330E made its maiden flight in November 1970, and the first of an eventual 48 helicopters (plus a number of attrition replacements) was delivered to the RAF during January 1971, for service with the British designation Puma HC.Mk 1.

The SA.330H is an uprated military version of the SA.330C, with a powerplant of two 1,576hp (1,175kW) Turmo IVC turboshafts for a higher maximum take-off weight. The SA.330L is a further improved export model with Turmo IVC turboshafts, inlet de-icing, and rotor blades of composite (fibreglass) rather than steel/light alloy structure. Among the operators of the type is South Africa, which during the early 1990s was evaluating a conversion for the battlefield role with a sensor/armament fit derived from that of the Atlas Rooivalk: a large stub wing carries two wingtip missile stations and four underwing hardpoints, the former for a pair of Armscor V3/Darter IR-homing AAMs and the latter for pods each containing four Atlas Swift laser-homing anti-tank missiles; the laser-designating equipment for the Swifts is carried in a substantial nose-mounted box.

The Puma has also been built under licence and further developed in countries such as Romania, with the local designation IAR-330, a powerplant of two 1,575hp (1,175kW) Turbomecanica (Turbomeca) Turmo IVC turboshafts and, in some helicopters, a considerably heavier armament; and South Africa, with the local designation Atlas Oryx (originally Gemsbok) as a hybrid combining the airframe of the SA.330 with the dynamic system of the AS.332 Super Puma for enhanced weight-lifting capability under hot-and-high conditions.

The AS.332 Super Puma is the second-generation derivative of the SA.330, designed to prolong the useful life of the basic SA.330 into the early part of the next century. In 1974, Aérospatiale began the process of developing the AS.332 as a much-redesigned and improved Puma with many detail changes (including revised landing gear able to absorb higher-rate landings and designed to 'kneel' for easier access to the larger cabin), in addition to an uprated powerplant of two 1,789hp (1,327kW) Turbomeca Makila IA turboshafts for greater performance even with a heavier payload (which could include 21 rather than 18 troops in a cabin 19ft 10.5in (6.05m) long, 5ft 10.75in (1.80m) wide and 5ft 1in (1.55m) high). Other changes were incorporated to reduce cabin noise, maintenance requirements and operational vulnerability.

The AS.331 prototype flew in September 1977 to test the revised dynamic system, and the first of six AS.332 prototypes made its initial flight during September 1978, a successful flight test and development programme allowing deliveries to begin in mid-1981. Since that time the helicopter has secured a useful rate of sales to operators who appreciate the type's low-maintenance but damage-resistant composite rotor blades and other tactically desirable features. The main subvariant is the AS.332B-1 with upgraded engines for better hot-and-high performance; since the January 1992 merger of Aérospatiale's and MBB's helicopter interests to create Eurocopter, the AS.332B has been designated as the AS.532UC Cougar.

Above: The Lynx AH.Mk 9 is the British army's version of the Battlefield Lynx, the land-based equivalent of the Super Lynx naval helicopter with an uprated powerplant, more advanced rotor blades, and more capable electronics. This machine is equipped with container launchers for eight HOT anti-tank missiles.

Offsetting Helicopter Development and Production Costs

THE cost of developing and producing any modern weapon, even before the type has entered full service and started to accrue operating and other life-cycle expenses, is very considerable. Moreover, the cost of developing and launching production of a modern weapon seems to increase geometrically whereas improvement in the weapons' capabilities seems to increase arithmetically. For this reason, therefore, there has been a tendency since the 1960s for the development of modern military aircraft, of both the fixed- and rotary-wing types, to be undertaken on a collaborative international basis. The additional administrative burden of such programmes certainly increases the overall cost to a certain degree, but the division of this cost and the promise of larger overall production totals is generally thought to yield an overall reduction in development and pro-duction cost even if, as is generally the case, there is a production line in each of the participating nations. Fixed-wing aircraft resulting from such programmes include the SEPECAT Jaguar, Panavia Tornado, Eurofighter EFA and SOKO J-22 Orao/CNIAR IAR-93, and rotary-wing machines now include the European Helicopter Industries EH.101 and Eurocopter Tiger/Tigre. There are many countries that lack the financial resources and technological skills to enter into such a collaborative programme except on terms of inequality with the major partner(s), and it suits such countries to become involved in a programme to build the warplane under licence, starting with assembly of machines delivered as kits of knocked-down major com-ponents and progressing to manufacture of the complete weapon with an increasingly large indigenous input. This keeps an increasingly large part of the production cost from moving to a foreign nation, and in the case of more advanced aircraft allows the licensee industry to develop its technological capabilities to the point at which it can begin to consider collaborative ventures in the future.

The AS.332F is the naval counterpart of the AS.332B with a folding tail, a deck landing-assistance device for enhanced ship compatibility under adverse weather and sea conditions, improved anti-corrosion protection, and provision for nose-mounted radar. The model is suitable for the SAR role with Bendix RDR-1400, RCA Primus 40/50 or Honeywell (RCA) Primus 500 radar; or the anti-submarine role with Thomson-CSF Varan radar, Alcatel HS 12 or Alcatel/Thomson-Sintra HS 312 dunking sonar and two Mk 46 torpedoes; or the anti-ship role with Omera-Segid Héraclès ORB 3214 radar and a missile armament of two heavyweight AM.39 Exocets, or six lightweight AS.15TTs, or one Exocet and three AS.15TTs; use of the AS.15TT requires the installation of Thomson-CSF Agrion-15 radar in place of the ORB 3214. The current variant is the AS.332F-1 with the improved powerplant of two Makila IA1 turboshafts and provision for two AM.39 Exocet anti-ship missiles, and since the creation of Eurocopter, the AS.332F-1 has been redesignated as the AS.532MC Cougar for the unarmed SAR role, or as the AS.532SC Cougar for the armed anti-submarine/ship role.

The AS.332M is the upgraded version of the AS.332B, with the cabin lengthened by 2ft 6in (0.76m) to 22ft 4in (6.81m) for the carriage of 25 troops, and more fuel for increased range despite the heavier payload. The current variant is the AS.332M-1 with a powerplant of two Makila IA1 turboshafts for unimpaired hot-and-high operations with 25 fully equipped troops, and since the creation of Eurocopter, this variant has been designated as the AS.532UL Cougar.

The AS.532UL Hélicoptère d'Observation Radar et d'Investigation sur Zone, or radar observation and zone surveillance helicopter (HORIZON) is the battlefield surveillance model of which France ordered four examples for delivery from 1995. The origins of the type can be traced to the evaluation from 1986 of an SA.330 with the small Orchée radar using an antenna arranged to fold down from the lower rear part of the fuselage's pod section, and success with this initial development model paved the way for the AS.532 with the larger Orchidée pulse-Doppler radar able to provide 360-degree coverage out to a radius of 93 miles (150km) from a hovering altitude of 9,845ft (3,000m). The radar antenna was located ventrally under the rear of the payload hold on a hinged arm that allowed it to be swung 90 degrees to the rear (under the boom) when not in use, and the radar was linked to its Mistrigri ground station by an Agatha data link. The type was also to be fitted with the Matra Saphir chaff/flare dispenser, a type capable of manual or semi-automatic operation, the latter requiring the installation of an RWR. In 1990 the type was cancelled for financial reasons, but the prototype's excellent performance during the 1991 Gulf War, when it was operated without a data link in the downgraded HORIZON form, led to a review of this decision, and as a result the French army has been permitted to place an initial order, scaled-down from the original requirement for 20 systems based on the larger AS.532 Cougar Mk II.

The IPTN NAS-322 is the version of the AS.332B-1 built under licence in Indonesia, and similar types have also been assembled in Singapore and Spain from kits of French-supplied components.

The AS.332 Super Puma Mk II is the third-generation development of the SA.300 family, and is a much improved Super Puma variant with upgraded electronics and systems, a higher-rated power train, an advanced main rotor with lengthened blades terminating in parabolic tips, and with the rear fuselage lengthened by 1ft 5.75in (0.45m) to provide clearance between the larger main rotor and the tail rotor. The first Super Puma Mk II flew in February 1987 and displayed improved performance and manoeuvrability as well as superior hot-and-high capability. The type entered service in 1993 and, since the establishment of Eurocopter, has been offered as the AS.532 Cougar Mk II whose two basic subvariants are the unarmed AS.532U2 Cougar Mk II and armed AS.532A2 Cougar Mk II.

The smaller of the two French helicopters included in the Anglo-French agreement mentioned above is the Aérospatiale Gazelle. The origins of this dainty type can be found in the realisation by Sud-Aviation that, although it had enjoyed great technical and commercial success with its Alouette II and Alouette III series of utility light helicopters, the decline in orders for these two types in the early 1960s indicated the onset of obsolescence, and that a successor type was needed to maintain the company's position as pre-eminent European manufacturer of light helicopters. The company used the proven capabilities of the Alouette III as a starting point, and decided that the new helicopter's most important improvements over the Alouette III should lie in the fields of speed and manoeuvrability. Additional speed should be made possible by the adoption of the Oredon engine, one of the new turboshaft engines then being designed by Turbomeca, and greater agility was promised by developments in the rotor head and rotor blade design.

A key factor was the company's July 1964 agreement with MBB of West Germany for the collaborative development of a glassfibre rotor blade and the semi-rigid rotor system to use this blade. In prospect, therefore, were greater speed, enhanced manoeuvrability, reduced weight and simplified maintenance. Another driving force was the British army's 1965 selection of the Sud-Aviation X-300 project as replacement for its fleet of Westland (Saro) Skeeter and Westland (Agusta-Bell) Sioux light helicopters, and in 1967 the British and French governments signed an agreement for the collaborative development and production of one British and two French helicopters, respectively the Westland Lynx and the Sud-Aviation SA.340 Gazelle and SA.330 Puma.

The SA.340 inherited the rigid rotor design of the X-300 project, but had to adopt a different engine as Turbomeca had abandoned development of the Oredon turboshaft. The selected engine was the same manufacturer's well-proved Astazou, and the first SA.340 prototype flew in April 1967 with a 362hp (270kW) Astazou II turboshaft driving conventional main and tail rotors. The second SA.340 prototype flew 12 months later and was typical of the planned production standard with a rigid main rotor and a *fenestron* shrouded anti-torque rotor set into the T-tail. Some directional instability was encountered as a result of distortion in the glassfibre fin, but this was cured by moving the tailplane to the low-set position and fitting it with small endplate fins. Efforts to cure the main rotor's tendency to stall, vibrate and pitch at high speed were less successful, and it was found that the problem lay with the use of rigid blades in a three-blade installation. The third helicopter was therefore completed to SA.341 standard with a semi-articulated rotor head, and this performed well. Another three SA.341 pre-production prototypes followed, and the SA.341's success seemed assured by several world records. The type was named Gazelle in July 1969, and the French manufacturer became Aérospatiale when Sud-Aviation and Nord-Aviation were amalgamated in January 1971.

The first SA.341 from the production line was completed in August 1971, but ran into severe transmission vibration and ground resonance problems on its first flight: the design team had successfully tested a number of improvements such as a longer cabin, an additional door, a larger tail unit, and the 590hp (440kW) Astazou IIIA turboshaft on an individual basis, but in concert they had created problems that took more than a year to solve.

The type entered production at much the same time in France and the UK, the latter's first model being the SA.341B (212 helicopters) that entered service as the British army's Gazelle AH.Mk 1 with a powerplant of one 590hp (440kW) Astazou IIIN turboshaft. The SA.341C is the Royal Navy's Gazelle HT.Mk 2 trainer of which 40 were delivered; the SA.341D is the RAF's Gazelle HT.Mk 3 trainer of which 29 were delivered; and the SA.341E is the RAF's Gazelle HCC.Mk 4 communications type of which just one was delivered but was later supplemented by three Gazelle HT.Mk 3 conversions.

The SA.341F is the initial French army version that entered service as partial replacement for the SA.318 Alouette II in the observation and liaison roles, and 170 were built with a powerplant of one Astazou IIIC turboshaft. Some 110 were later converted to SA.341M anti-tank standard with a roof-mounted sight and outrigger pylons for HOT missiles, redeliveries beginning in September 1978, and most of the others were adapted to SA.341F/Canon interim escort and gunship standard with a 20mm M621 cannon on the starboard side of the cabin. There is also a reconnaissance version with a simplified version of the Athos magnifying sight used on the HOT-armed SA.342M variant.

The SA.341H is the SA.341B/F export version with the Astazou IIIB turboshaft, and was built under licence in Yugoslavia as the SOKO SA.341H Partizan liaison and reconnaissance helicopter. In the armed reconnaissance role, the Yugoslav variant carries an armament of four AT-2 'Swatter' or AT-3 'Sagger' wire-guided anti-tank missiles and two examples of the air-to-air version of the SA-7 'Grail' shoulder-launched SAM.

The SA.342 is the variant of the SA.341, with an uprated powerplant of one 872hp (650kW) Turbomeca Astazou XIV turboshaft for greater performance and payload, especially under hot-and-high conditions. The type first flew in prototype form during May 1973, and entered production during 1976 as the SA.342J civil helicopter that was delivered from 1977, before being complemented for export by the SA.342K with the Astazou XIVH turboshaft fitted with momentum-separation shrouds over the inlet.

The SA.342L is the baseline military version of the SA. 342J civil helicopter, with an improved *fenestron* shrouded tail rotor and a number of detail modifications. The type has also been built under licence in Yugoslavia as the SOKO SA.342 HERA special-purpose and SA.342 GAMA gunship models. The current subvariant is the SA.342L-1 with a powerplant of one 858hp (640kW) Astazou XIVM turboshaft.

Although this looks like an S-61 that served with the US forces under the core designation H-3 and US Navy name Sea King, it is in fact a Sikorsky S-62 as indicated by the centrally located inlet for its single turboshaft engine. This was the company's first amphibious helicopter, and was first flown in May 1958 with the three-blade main rotor of the piston-engined S-55 helicopter. The type entered production as the S-62A and was later improved to S-62B standard with the four-blade main rotor of the piston-engined S-58 reduced to the same 53ft 0in (16.16m) diameter as the rotor of the S-62A. The example shown here is an HH-52A search-and-rescue version of the S-62B for the US Coast Guard.

The Sikorsky S-70 series, which serves the US forces with the core designation S-60, is a true multi-role type. The S-70 was planned in successful competition with a Boeing type as the Utility Tactical Transport Aircraft System replacement for the Bell Models 204 and 205 (UH-1 Iroquois or 'Huey'), and has since been built in large numbers for an apparently endless string of roles varying from combat-search-and-rescue to VIP transport via tactical transport, Special Forces infiltration and exfiltration, electronic warfare and casualty evacuation.

The SA.342M is the dedicated anti-tank version of the SA.342L-1 for the French army, with the SFIM APX-Bezu M397 Athos gyro-stabilized sight for the guidance of four or six HOT anti-tank missiles in two twin or triple installations, although the type can alternatively be armed with two 0.3in (7.62mm) machine gun pods or one 20mm M621 cannon (in the latter case being designated SA.342M/Canon Gazelle). Deliveries began in June 1980, and other modifications comprise an autopilot and an exhaust deflector for reduced vulnerability to IR-homing SAMs. All armed Gazelles are being fitted with the SFIM Divine night/adverse-weather thermal sight for HOT missiles to create the SA.342M Viviane Gazelle or, in the case of 70 helicopters, with the T2000 sight and provision for four Mistral short-range AAMs to create the SA.342M ATAM Gazelle for the escort role.

The French manufacturer, in either its original Aérospatiale or current Eurocopter France guises, has also produced a number of other light helicopters that have been adapted for the military roles, the most important being the Ecureuil and Dauphin series that are now known in their military forms as the Fennec and Panther. Of these, the larger and more capable is the Dauphin/Panther. Developed as successor to the SA.319 Alouette III series, the SA.360 Dauphin first flew in prototype form during June 1972 as a trim helicopter with a powerplant of one 1,050hp (783kW) Turbomeca Astazou XVIIIA turboshaft driving a four-blade main rotor and a *fenestron* shrouded tail rotor, and with accommodation for a crew of two plus up to 10 passengers, or four litters and a medical attendant, or freight. Only limited military sales were achieved, largely for use in the communications role, and although an SA.361H anti-tank/assault transport was developed as a private venture, Aérospatiale soon appreciated that both military and civil applications would be better served by a twin-engined powerplant.

The initial twin-engine version was the SA.365C Dauphin 2, flown in prototype form during January 1975 with a powerplant of two Turbomeca Arriel turboshafts. There was considerably greater sales interest in this model, which entered production later in the decade with a powerplant of two 660hp (492kW) Arriel IA turboshafts or, in the improved SA.365N Dauphin 2 version, two 710hp (529kW) Arriel IC turboshafts. The SA.365N introduced a large degree of composite construction as well as retractable

landing gear, and the SA.365F Dauphin 2 is the versatile naval development of the SA.365N intended primarily for the anti-ship role with Agrion-15 search radar, MAD with a towed 'bird', an armament of two or four AS.15TT short-range anti-ship missiles, and the avionics for mid-course targeting update of ship-launched Otomat long-range anti-ship missiles. The type is also available in SAR configuration with search radar, a rescue winch, an automatic navigation system, and a hover/transition coupler.

The manufacturer also offers a more advanced anti-submarine capability in a derivative with Thomson-Sintra (Alcatel) ASM HS 312 dunking sonar, Sextant Avionique (Crouzet) DHAX 3 MAD, and an armament of two lightweight homing torpedoes.

The creation of Eurocopter led to the redesignation of the military version of the SA.365 Dauphin 2 as the AS.565 Panther, which is now offered in the unarmed AS.565MA SAR and sea surveillance model, and the armed AS.565SA anti-ship and anti-submarine model.

First flown in February 1984, and now known as the AS.565 Panther, the AS.365M Dauphin 2 is the dedicated military version of the SA.365N series with greater use of composite materials, a longer fuselage fitted with armoured seats, cable cutters for safer low-altitude flight capability, a strengthened cabin floor and landing gear, sliding rather than hinged doors, crash-resistant fuel tanks, IR-reducing exhausts, and the use of composite materials and special paints to reduce electromagnetic and thermal signatures. The AS.565AA Panther is the armed subvariant with two lateral outriggers, each with a single hardpoint for the carriage of two multiple launchers for unguided rockets (either twenty-two 2.68in/68mm Thomson-Brandt or nineteen 2.75in/70mm Forges de

Zeebrugge weapons), or two pods each carrying one 20mm GIAT M621 cannon with 180 rounds, or four two-round packs of Matra Mistral short-range AAMs. The AS.565CA Panther is the anti-tank subvariant capable of carrying two quadruple launch units for HOT missiles, aimed via a Viviane day/night unit for an SFIM gyro-stabilized platform holding a TRT Hector IR camera and SAT deviation-measuring equipment. The AS. 565UA Panther is the unarmed utility subvariant designed to carry eight or 10 assault troops, or alternatively freight in the form of an internal or slung payload.

The manufacturer also offers an AS.565 Panther 800 derivative with a powerplant of two 1,322hp (986kW) LHTEC T800-LHT-800 turboshafts and an IBM suite of integrated avionics.

In the United States, the two most important types not already discussed are a pair of Sikorsky helicopters, namely the S-65 twin-engined and S-80 triple-engined variants of the Stallion family, and the Black Hawk land-based and Seahawk shipborne variants of the S-70 family. The larger of these types, by a considerable margin, is the helicopter that has been developed in S-65 and S-80 variants, which resulted from an exacting requirement issued in the early 1960s by the US Marine Corps for an assault helicopter. Sikorsky's work on the S-60 and derived S-64 flying crane helicopter designs stood the company in good stead, for the company responded with its S-65 design that drew on Sikorsky's experience with the S-64 (CH-54 Tarhe) and S-61R (CH-3) in the design of the dynamic system and watertight hull respectively. The US Marine Corps was impressed with the preliminary design, and in August 1962 ordered two YCH-65A prototype and service test helicopters. The first of these machines flew in October 1964 with a powerplant of two 2,850hp (2,125kW) General Electric T64-GE-3 turboshafts, and soon confirmed its ability to lift 38 troops or 24 litters as alternatives to a heavy freight load carried internally or externally.

The S-70B version of Sikorsky's current lightweight military helicopter is used by the US Navy in two forms as the SH-60B Seahawk for the LAMPS III role from smaller warships such as destroyers and cruisers, and as the SH-60F Ocean Hawk for the anti-submarine role from aircraft carriers. If funding permits, it is planned that the SH-60R will be produced as a converted type able to undertake either of these roles by changes in the embarked equipment.

Helicopter Armament

MOST modern military helicopters have provision for armament. Some of these rotary-wing machines are, of course, designed from the beginning for the carriage of specific weapons or types of weapon for the fulfilment of their intended task. Battlefield attack helicopters are generally fitted with a stub wing arrangement carrying four hardpoints for weapons such as multiple launchers for unguided rockets, clusters of air-to-surface missiles optimised for the anti-tank role, machine gun or cannon pods and, increasingly, two or four short-range air-to-air missiles for self-defence; most of these helicopters also carry a trainable cannon, usually between 20mm and 30mm in calibre of 20, for the suppression of ground threats and the engagement of targets of opportunity, the latter including threatening helicopters. Naval helicopters are generally tasked with the anti-submarine and/or anti-ship roles, and for these tasks carry lightweight homing torpedoes (or depth charges) or anti-ship missiles on hardpoints attached to the sides of the fuselage rather than under stub wings. This leaves the utility battlefield helicopter whose tasks are usually the provision of air mobility and the evacuation of the wounded. Such helicopters were initially unarmed, but since the time of the Vietnam War have gradually sprouted the capability for an increasingly wide assortment of weapons ranging from packs of rockets and/or fixed forward-firing cannon or multi-barrel machine guns on the sides of the fuselage under the control of the pilot or co-pilot, via trainable multi-barrel machine gun installations (fed with belted ammunition carried in large magazines installed on the cabin floor) on the sides of the central fuselage and controlled by gunners in a doorway, to trainable multi- or single-barrel machine guns pintle-mounted in a cabin door (or by the rear ramp/door of machines such as the Boeing CH-47 Chinook and Sikorsky CH-53 Sea Stallion/Super Stallion) also under control of gunners. The provision of such armament capability greatly enhances the tactical capabilities of the utility helicopter, for the gunner-operated trainable weapons can protect the helicopter from the attentions of attack helicopters and soften up the ground defences before the embarked troops are landed, and the provision of fixed forward-firing armament contributes to this latter capability as well as opening the possibility of limited close support for the troops after they have disembarked.

The US Marine Corps ordered an eventual 139 examples of the CH-53A initial production model, which entered service in the autumn of 1966. As delivered initially, the CH-53A was fitted with a powerplant of two 2,850hp (2,125kW) T64-GE-6 turboshafts, but later helicopters switched to two 3,080hp (2,297kW) T64-GE-1 turboshafts, and then to two 3,435hp (2,561kW) T64-GE-16 turboshafts for improved performance with a payload that could include one 4.13in (105mm) howitzer and ammunition, or 38 troops, or 24 litters plus four attendants, or more than 8,000lb (3,629kg) of freight carried in the hold, or alternatively more than 13,000lb (5,897kg) of freight carried as a slung load. The hold is 30ft 0in (9.14m) long, 7ft 6in (2.29m) wide and 6ft 6in (1.98m) high, and access is provided by a hydraulically operated ventral ramp/door and a door on the forward starboard side.

All but 32 of the helicopters were built with provision for the towing of a minesweeping sled. Israel operates 30 or more examples of the S-65 family (10 CH-53As supplemented by 20 or more S-65Cs), and is upgrading its fleet in a programme described under the CH-53D. The RH-53A designation was applied to 15 CH-53As transferred to the US Navy, and converted into dedicated minesweepers with a powerplant of two 3,925hp (2,926kW) T64-GE-413 turboshafts and the special winch/quick-release gear required to tow or release minesweeping sleds. The TH-53A designation was allocated to five CH-53As transferred to the USAF as basic qualification trainers.

The HH-53B Super Jolly is the USAF's combat SAR variant, first flown in March 1967 and fitted out with the same provisions as the Sikorsky HH-3E Jolly Green Giant (including a retractable inflight-refuelling probe and all-weather flight instrumentation), and powered by two 3,080hp (2,297kW) T64-GE-3 turboshafts supplied with fuel from an increased internal capacity including auxiliary tanks on external struts cantilevered out from the main fuel-carrying lateral sponsons.

The CH-53C was the pure transport counterpart of the HH-53C for the USAF, which received 20 such helicopters without inflight-refuelling capability, armour, armament or specialised avionics. The helicopters were initially operated for the insertion and extraction of Special Forces, but eight of them were later revised to provide battlefield mobility for the USAF's Mobile Tactical Air Control System. The HH-53C Super Jolly was an important type that was developed as an upgraded version of the HH-53B for the USAF, with greater performance and payload provided by an uprated powerplant comprising two 3,925hp (2,926kW) T64-GE-7 turboshafts for greater performance and payload. Procurement totalled 44 such helicopters with an advanced avionics suite, and these remained operational into the late 1980s.

The CH-53D Sea Stallion is an improved version of the CH-53A for the US Marine Corps, with greater power in the form of two 3,925hp (2,926kW) T64-GE-413 turboshafts for higher performance and increased payload (55 troops or a heavier load of freight) carried over short ranges. Delivery of 126 CH-53Cs was completed in the spring of 1972, and most of these helicopters have provision to tow a minesweeping sled. Two of the helicopters were later converted to VIP transport configuration under the designation VH-53D Sea Stallion. The export variant of the CH-53D is the S-65C, of which Israel operates 22. Israel cannot afford to replace its fleet with the more capable CH-53E model, and therefore in 1990 launched a programme for IAI's MATA subsidiary to upgrade the S-65Cs (together with the 10 CH-53As) to CH-53/2000 (otherwise Yasur 2000) standard. The first revised helicopter flew in June 1992 with structural revisions to the tail, extensive but not full rewiring, new electronic warfare warning systems

Seen here in the form of an MH-53J Super Dragon of the Japanese naval air arm, the Sikorsky S-80M is the dedicated minesweeping version of the S-80E (CH-53E Super Stallion) transport helicopter developed from the S-65 (H-53 Sea Stallion) with a three- rather than two-engined powerplant and large lateral sponsons for a considerably enlarged fuel capacity.

including an improved RWR, and an upgraded avionics suite including a new mission computer, a moving map display, two multi-function displays, an autopilot with added subsystems, and provision for the flightcrew to undertake nap-of-the-earth night flights with the aid of night vision goggles and an HUD.

First flown in October 1972 and built to the extent of 30 helicopters, the RH-53D is the US Navy's dedicated minesweeping version of the CH-53D, with a powerplant of two 4,380hp (3,266kW) T64-GE-415 turboshafts to provide adequate power for the type's exacting role with the AQS-14 minehunting sonar and the towed Mk 103 mechanical, Mk 104 acoustic, Mk 105 magnetic and Mk 106 magnetic/acoustic sweeps, as well as the SPU-1 'Magnetic Orange Pipe' for dealing with shallow-water magnetic mines. The type is also fitted with two 0.5in (12.7mm) Browning M2 heavy machine guns for the detonation of any mines brought to the surface.

The CH-53G is the version of the Sea Stallion series for West Germany, with a powerplant of two T64-GE-7 turboshafts. Sikorsky delivered the first two helicopters in 1969, and Dornier then license-built an additional 110 helicopters.

After evaluating the 'Pave Low II' avionics package for night/adverse-weather navigation and rescue capability in an HH-53B converted to YHH-53H standard, the USAF ordered a 'production' version of this improved HH-53C version as the HH-53H Super Jolly: this type comprises two CH-53Cs and eight HH-53B/Cs converted for the night/adverse-weather SAR role with the 'Pave Low III' sensor suite, which includes the APQ-158 terrain-following/avoidance radar, AAQ-10 IR sensor, provision for two sets of pilot's night vision goggles, and much improved navigational capability (including an INS working in concert with a colour moving-map display and Doppler navigation). In 1986 the helicopters were redesignated MH-53H when modified in the 'Concert Green' programme for the additional capability of inserting and extracting Special Forces teams.

The USAF was not altogether happy with the performance and capabilities of the HH-53H, and the RH-53D had revealed a number of failings when pressed into Special Forces service for the abortive April 1980 attempt to rescue American hostages held in Tehran. The service therefore decided to procure 31 of the improved MH-53J variant (24 HH-53B and

Opposite top: The CH-113 Labrador is the Canadian Armed Forces' search-and-rescue version of the Boeing CH-46A Sea Knight. Some 60 of the type were delivered during 1963-64 to what was then the Royal Canadian Air Force, and in the following year 12 generally similar CH-113A Voyageur helicopters were delivered to the Canadian army.

Opposite bottom: Seen in prototype form, the Bell/Boeing V-22 Osprey is a tilt-rotor aeroplane that has undergone a long development programme troubled by political and economical antipathies more than technical problems. Intended for large-scale service in a number of roles, especially in the assault transport task for the US Marine Corps, the Osprey combines fixed- and rotary-wing attributes, especially in the installation at the wing tips of two powerful turboshafts in nacelles that can be tilted between the vertical and the horizontal. Each of these engines drives a large-diameter 'proprotor' that with their axes vertical work as rotors for vertical take-off and landing, and with their axes horizontal as propellers for propulsion with the weight of the aeroplane supported by the fixed wing.

Right: The Sikorsky UH-60A Black Hawk is a highly versatile utility tactical helicopter for the movements of loads carried internally or externally, and can also be fitted with an external stores-support system for the carriage of additional fuel or weapons.

Below: Another type that has undergone a fairly tortured design and development process leading to a first flight in 1996, the Boeing/Sikorsky RAH-66 Comanche is an advanced helicopter of which much is expected. It was originally planned that production of 5,000 such helicopters would permit the Comanche to replace the Bell UH-1 Iroquois, Bell AH-1 HueyCobra, Bell OH-58 Kiowa and McDonnell Douglas (Hughes) OH-6 Cayuse in a host of light tactical roles, but the procurement total for this advanced 'stealthy' type, which has a structure largely of composite materials, has been steadily eroded to 1,292 machines for use mainly in the scouting role for the McDonnell Douglas AH-64 Apache.

seven HH-53C conversions) for use by the US Special Forces in clandestine and anti-insurgency missions. The converted helicopters were redelivered from July 1987 to a standard that includes a powerplant of two 4,380hp (3,266kW) T64-GE-415 turboshafts, so that performance is not degraded by the increase in maximum take-off weight through use of folding rotors and an additional 1,000lb (454kg) of titanium armour around vital points. Other changes include improvement of the terrain-avoidance/terrain-following radar and IR countermeasures, installation of a missile-warning receiver, retrofit of the original naval folding tail, and addition of new items such as a Texas Instruments AAQ-10 FLIR in a stabilized turret under the inflight-refuelling probe, secure voice communications, and a GPS receiver. The type has provision for two drop tanks and an armament of three 0.3in (7.62mm) Miniguns or three 0.5in (12.7mm) heavy machine guns

In the late 1960s, Sikorsky proposed a derivative of the S-65 (CH-53 Sea Stallion) in which much greater payload could be carried by the replacement of the original two-engined powerplant by a three-engined powerplant driving a larger main rotor. The US Navy was not interested at the time, but the demands of operations during the early 1970s in the Vietnam War persuaded the service to change its attitude, and in 1973 Sikorsky received an order for two YCH-53E prototype and service test helicopters based on its S-80 design. The first of these flew in March 1974, and deliveries of the CH-53E production version for the US Marine Corps began in June 1981. By comparison with the S-65 versions, the S-80 has a third engine (located in the port side of the dorsal fairing aft of the main rotor), a larger main rotor with seven rather than six blades, and a tail rotor of increased diameter. In conjunction with the considerably more powerful dynamic system, the CH-53E's improved payload capability results from its large hold.

The US Marine Corps has a requirement for 177 examples of the CH-53E, which are to be upgraded with more powerful 4,750hp (3,542kW) T64-GE-416 turboshafts and fitted with IR suppressors on their exhausts, composite tail rotor blades, Omega navigation, a ground-proximity warning system, an improved internal freight-handling system, a missile warning system,

The YUH-61A was a prototype of Boeings' (at the time Boeing Vertol) contender in the UTTAS competition won by the Sikorsky YUH-60A that was then placed in production as the UH-60A Black Hawk. The choice between the two helicopter types was difficult, but the Sikorsky machine was finally preferred for its greater versatility, easier partial disassembly for air transport, lower purchase and operating cost, and greater closeness to full production standard.

One of the major limitations of the helicopter had always been its range, resulting primarily from the fact that the engine or engines have to provide all the lifting and propulsive effort required to maintain the helicopter's flight capability. Additional range is an important factor in operations such as combat-search-and-rescue and the infiltration/exfiltration of Special Forces units, and helicopters used for those roles (this is a Sikorsky H-60 Black Hawk) are fitted with a long inflight-refuelling probe. This is installed low on the fuselage and is of the extending type designed to reach forward under the disc swept by the main rotor to make contact with the hose-and-drogue type of refuelling system used by tankers such as this Lockheed KC-130 Hercules, a propeller-driven type with performance that is better matched to that of the helicopter than is possible with any turbojet- or turbofan-powered type such as the Boeing KC-13 Stratotanker.

chaff/flare dispensers, a nitrogen fuel tank inerting system, AIM-9 Sidewinder short-range AAMs for self-defence, and the Northrop Helicopter Night Vision System.

The MH-53E Sea Dragon is the US Navy's mine-countermeasures version of the CH-53E that was developed as the S-80M, and first flew in September 1983 for service from June 1986 against a requirement for 56 such helicopters each able to tow a hydrofoil sled carrying mechanical, acoustic or magnetic sensors. The type has more internal fuel in larger composite-structure sponsons, provision for ferrying fuel in seven tanks carried in the hold, improved electrical and hydraulic systems, and enhanced navigation and automatic flight control systems (the last including capability for automatic towing, and automatic approach to and departure from the hover). In the influence sweeping role, the MH-53E has a maximum useful load of 26,000lb (11,793kg), and its equipment includes the Westinghouse AQS-14 towed sonar as well as options such as the AQS-17 mine neutralisation device, ALQ-141 electronic sweep, and EDO ALQ-166 towed hydrofoil sled (used for the detonation of magnetic mines). The same basic type is available for export as the S-80M, of which Japan has ordered 11.

Designed to meet the US Army's Utility Tactical Transport Aircraft System requirement for a Bell UH-1 Iroquois replacement, able to carry an 11-man infantry squad, the S-70 is of basically conventional configuration with its light alloy fuselage, fixed tailwheel landing gear with a single wheel on each unit, and a dynamic system that includes two turboshafts side-by-side behind the gearbox for the rotor system comprising four-blade main and tail rotors. In many of its features, however, the S-70 offers evidence of advanced aerodynamic, structural and operational thinking. The fuselage, for example, was designed to retain 85 per cent of the cockpit and hold intact after a vertical impact with the ground at 40ft (12.2m) per second; the cockpit provides armour protection for the two pilots; and a sliding door on each side provides access to the hold, which is comparatively large and well planned. The main rotor has blades of advanced aerodynamic design and composite construction (able to withstand cannon hits of up to 23mm calibre without loss of structural integrity) attached to the one-piece forged titanium rotor head by elastomeric (no-lubrication) bearings, and the tail rotor comprises two twin-blade units fastened in a crossbeam arrangement and tilted to port as a means of generating lift as well as anti-torque thrust.

269

The first of three YUH-60A prototype and service test helicopters flew in October 1974, and in December 1976 the type was declared winner over its Boeing Vertol YUH-61A competitor for selection as the UH-60A production model. The UH-60A entered service in 1979, and is a versatile helicopter able to carry a useful cargo payload (including a 4.13in/105mm howitzer and 50 rounds of ammunition) as an alternative to its standard load of embarked infantrymen. At first there were a number of in-service problems with the transmission, but a new gearbox has been developed to improve reliability and increase maximum take-off weight, which allows the carriage of a greater assortment of external loads as well as improved armament.

The UH-60A is also qualified for the carriage of AGM-114 Hellfire anti-tank missiles and the Honeywell Volcano dispenser system with 950 Gator anti-personnel and anti-vehicle minelets. From 1989 most helicopters have been upgraded in the aircraft survivability equipment (ASE) programme to UH-60A Enhanced Black Hawk standard with Omega navigation, satellite communications, a specific-threat RWR complementing the original general-threat RWR, and provision for the M60 machine gun to be replaced by the M134 Minigun.

The US Army plans a total procurement of 2,262 H-60 series helicopters,

By comparison with the US Army's UH-60 Black Hawk, the US Navy's SH-60 series (Seahawk for the LAMPS III role and Ocean Hawk for the 'CV helo' role from destroyers and aircraft carriers respectively) has a folding main rotor and a folding tail for reduced shipboard hangarage requirement.

and production of the UH-60A reached 985 helicopters before the improved UH-60L was introduced.

The EH-60A is the special electronics mission aircraft (SEMA) variant intended for the interception, monitoring, localisation, and jamming of battlefield communication nets with the 1,800lb (816kg) ALQ-151 'Quick Fix II' ECM system, which is a development of the system originally fitted on the Bell EH-1H Iroquois. The type first flew in YEH-60A prototype form during September 1981, and 66 production helicopters were delivered between 1987 and 1989 with a hover IR suppression subsystem and ASN-32 INS. The helicopters were to have received the revised designation EH-60C Black Hawk after the retrofit of the ASE defensive suite with the APR-39(V)3 RWR and two M130 chaff/flare dispensers as well as the ALQ-156 missile warning system, but the change of designation was not implemented, and the H-60C designation is currently reserved for an EH-60C command and control helicopter that has not yet received any funding.

The core designation H-60B was reserved for the first Seahawk naval version of the S-70 series, and the HH-60D Night Hawk was planned as the USAF's combat SAR variant of the UH-60A, with the dynamic system and rescue winch of the SH-60B. The avionics proposed for this important type included advanced radar, FLIR, Litton INS, and multi-function cockpit and helmet displays. Other equipment included stub wings for two external tanks, a retractable inflight-refuelling probe, and two side-mounted machine guns. The type was cancelled in 1989 after the completion of a single prototype, however, which placed emphasis on the MH-60A Credible Hawk interim version, of which some 30 examples were produced as UH-60A conversions (for the use of the 160th Special Operations Aviation Regiment) with features such as greater fuel capacity, inflight-refuelling capability, FLIR, IR jammer, chaff/flare dispensers, night vision equipment, multi-function cockpit displays, and provision for armament in the form of two door-mounted 0.3in (7.62mm) M134 Miniguns, but neither terrain-following radar nor FLIR. The conversions were effected pending the availability of the MH-60K (replaced by the MH-60L).

There is also an MH-60A Embassy Hawk version optimised for short-notice missions of a classified nature in Europe: this 'contingency mission' variant, of which four have been converted from UH-60A standard, has a number of special features including satellite communications and a GPS receiver. The core designation H-60F was reserved for the second Seahawk naval version of the S-70 series.

The MH-60G Pave Hawk is a considerably improved version of the MH-60A, and was designed for use by the Special Forces as well as combat SAR, and has the same operational features and additional fuel capacity as the MH-60A, plus an inflight-refuelling probe, secure voice communications, satellite communications, electronic map display, weather/mapping radar, Doppler navigation and Litton INS, auxiliary fuel, and various protective items all integrated by a digital databus. Some 103 such helicopters were delivered from 1982 to 1993, but from January 1992 some 82 of them were redesignated as HH-60G Pave Hawk helicopters (to indicate their revision for the combat SAR role), with a rescue hoist, the 'Pave Low III' night/adverse-weather navigation system's Hughes AAQ-16 FLIR, provision for two M134 Minigun door-mounted weapons, and provision for two external units for weapons and/or fuel. The core designations H-60H and H-60J were reserved for the SAR and special warfare versions of the Seahawk naval version of the S-70 series.

The MH-60K Black Hawk was derived from the UH-60L and first flown in August 1990, and is the US Army's special operations aircraft (SOA) version, of which 60 are required for the insertion and extraction of Special Forces' teams under adverse terrain and climatic conditions. The first helicopter was completed in February 1992, and the type has inflight-refuelling capability using an extending probe, weapons capability including provision for FIM-92 Stinger short-range AAMs and pintle mounts strengthened for 0.5in (12.7mm) heavy machine guns, a host of survivability features, a four-screen 'glass' cockpit, and an advanced avionics package. This last is a Boeing responsibility and is based on that of the Boeing Vertol MH-47E Chinook, with features such as Texas Instruments APQ-174A multi-mode terrain-following and terrain-avoidance radar, Hughes AAQ-16 FLIR, night vision equipment and secure communications gear.

First flown in March 1988 for delivery from October 1989, the UH-60L is the UH-60A's successor in the tactical assault transport role. The variant has an uprated transmission and a powerplant of two 1,800hp (1,342kW) T700-GE-701C turboshafts, and this combination restores the performance lost in the UH-60A by addition of 2,000lb (907kg) more payload.

The AH-60L is the direct action penetrator (DAP) conversion of the MH-60L, introduced in 1990 for the use of two platoons of the 160th Special Operations Aviation Regiment. The variant has radar, FLIR and the ESL for forward-firing weapons capability. The MH-60L, a standard to which a few basic transport Black Hawks were modified, is basically similar to the MH-60A, and is to be replaced by the MH-60K. The UH-60M had been proposed as an enhanced version for production from 1992 as a second-generation land-based version with T700-GE-701C turboshafts, the fuselage stretched by 1ft 0in (0.305m), new Sikorsky/Boeing composite-structure main rotor blades of revised section to provide 11 per cent more lift, digital avionics based on a digital databus, an integrated navigation/communications system, a new automatic flight-control system, and a 15 per cent increase in fuel capacity for a 10 per cent increase in range. The type was cancelled during 1989 in favour of the UH-60L.

The VH-60N designation is applied to nine examples of a VIP transport version procured by the US Marine Corps for the movement of the president and high-ranking officials of the US government. The airframe is that of the UH-60A, but the powerplant and some of the avionics are those of the SH-60B, and the rotor is fitted with the brake of the HH-60A. Other modifications include weather radar, additional fuel capacity, hardening against electromagnetic pulse, secure communications, and countermeasures such as exhaust suppression, IR jamming and an optional chaff/flare dispenser.

The UH-60P is the S-70A-18 version of the UH-60L for the South Korean army, with minimal modifications to the avionics. Sikorsky delivered three such helicopters in December 1990, and the remaining 90 are being assembled by Korean Air with an increasing proportion of South Korean components.

The UH-60Q is the casevac version of the UH-60L, of which the US Army

The Sikorsky SH-60B Seahawk is comprehensively equipped not only for the armed role (anti-submarine and anti-ship capabilities with sonobuoys and radar) but also for the detection of incoming threats with its radar and electronic support measures system, the presence of sea-skimming missiles and other such threats being relayed to the parent vessel in real time by a data-link system.

requires 120 conversions that have yet to be funded. The conversion, pioneered in a single prototype, includes an onboard oxygen generation system, patient monitoring equipment, cabin lighting and air-conditioning, personnel location system, rescue hoist, searchlight, FLIR, weather/mapping radar, and enhancements to the navigation, communications and survivability features of the basic helicopter.

The UH-60V is the command and control model with a Symetric Industries improved data modem, for digital communication with armoured fighting vehicles, troops and helicopters, and export helicopters are designated in the S-70A series, which includes the S-70A-12 combat SAR helicopter for Japan, which operates the type as the UH-60J in the hands of the Japanese Air Self-Defense Force (46) and Japanese Maritime Self-Defense force (18). Procurement started with one imported helicopter and two helicopters assembled from American-supplied kits (first flown in February 1990), and is now all-Japanese.

The naval version of the S-70 series is known to the manufacturer as the S-70B and to the US Navy as the Seahawk or, for more specialised roles, by other hawk names. This maritime S-70B version was produced to meet the US Navy's light airborne multi-purpose system (LAMPS) Mk III requirement for a helicopter to replace the Sikorsky SH-3 Sea King on destroyers and larger frigates, and to complement the lighter Kaman SH-2F Seasprite LAMPS Mk I helicopter on smaller surface vessels. Although the S-70B was derived from the land-based S-70A (UH-60 Black Hawk), extensive changes had to be effected in the airframe and systems to allow the incorporation of the shipborne variant's anti-submarine and anti-ship missile defence equipment, but the most obvious external difference

Opposite: One of the great tactical advantages of the helicopter is its ability to collect and/or deliver a slung load out of and/or into an area inaccessible to a fixed-wing aeroplane. This greatly enhances the overall capabilities of the helicopter for battlefield tasks such as the repositioning of equipment (such as this light assault gun carried by a Sikorsky CH-53E Super Stallion), and the delivery of supplies such as fuel and ammunition.

Below: With a triple-engined powerplant driving a seven-blade main rotor, heavily laden helicopters such as these Sikorsky S-80 (H-53E Super Stallion and Sea Dragon series) machines have a prodigious thirst for fuel that can be satisfied long-endurance or long-range missions only by use of drop tanks and/or inflight-refuelling from aircraft such as the Lockheed KC-130 Hercules.

between the UH-60 and SH-60 is the latter's modified landing gear, with its tail unit revised to twin-wheel layout and moved forward several feet to provide the shorter wheel base required for safe flight operations from the relatively modest flight platforms of the US Navy's smaller warships. Other changes include a folding main rotor with a rotor brake, a recovery assist and secure traverse (RAST) downhaul system providing the capability of landing on small naval vessels under adverse weather and sea conditions, a rescue hoist, and buoyancy devices.

The S-70B design was declared winner of the LAMPS Mk III competition in 1977, and the first of five YSH-60B prototype and service test helicopters flew in December 1979, paving the way for the first of a planned 260 SH-60B production helicopters to enter service in 1983: in 1994 procurement was ended after the delivery of 188 helicopters.

The SH-60F Ocean Hawk is the four-man SH-60B version designed to replace the Sikorsky SH-3 Sea King as the inner-zone anti-submarine helicopter carried by aircraft carriers. The concept was evaluated through a converted SH-60B that first flew in March 1987, and production helicopters entered service from March 1990: procurement was halted prematurely in 1994 after the delivery of 82 helicopters against a requirement for 150 such machines. The 'CV Helo' configuration differs from that of the SH-60B in its lack of LAMPS Mk III equipment (including the RAST downhaul system, cargo hook and radar for the detection of anti-ship missiles), but its construction with a digital databus allows the installation of a different avionics suite including the ASQ-13F dunking sonar, ASQ-81 MAD with a towed 'bird', ALQ-142 ESM system, and ARQ-44 data link to provide the data for the generation of a fire-control solution for a weapon fit that includes up to three lightweight anti-submarine torpedoes, two of them on the extended port hardpoint; these torpedoes can be either the obsolescent Mk 46 or advanced Mk 50 Barracuda.

The SH-60F can carry only eight sonobuoys compared with the SH-60B's figure of 25, but the ambient underwater noise levels of its inner-zone tasking make the dunking sonar altogether more important as the type's primary acoustic sensor. The sonar data are fed to the twin ASN-150 tactical navigation systems that drive two large multi-function displays (one on the instrument panel and the other at the sensor operator's station) and four central display units. Other elements of the tactical navigation system are the TACAN and Doppler Tactical Navigation systems, of which the latter has provision for GPS update.

The SH-60F is powered by two 1,900hp (1,417kW) T700-GE-401C turboshafts for a sustained high level of performance despite its higher maximum take-off weight.

Entering service from January 1990 after a first flight in August 1988, the HH-60H Rescue Hawk is the US Navy's helicopter combat support (combat SAR) and Special Forces variant of the SH-60B Seahawk, with the SH-60F Ocean Hawk's powerplant of two T700-GE-401C turboshafts. The US Navy plans a total of 18 helicopters of this type, which has the tasks of recovering a four-man crew at a radius of 288 miles (463km) and delivering an eight-man commando team to a point 3,000ft (915m) above their destination at a radius of 230 miles (370km). The variant's avionics include the APR-39A(XE)2 RWR, AVR-2 laser warning receiver and AAR-47 missile-approach warning system to trigger two ALE-39 chaff/flare launchers and/or one

Above: The Kamov Ka-32 'Helix' is the civil variant of the military helicopter in Russian service as the Ka-27, Ka-28, Ka-29 and Ka-31 series. The type is clearly a lineal successor to the Ka-25 series in its basic design with superimposed co-axial main rotors, but has more advanced systems, a larger cabin, and an uprated powerplant.

Right: The European Helicopter Industries EH.101 is a collaborative British and Italian type that was initially ordered in its shipborne version but which has since been contracted in its land-based utility military variant.

ALQ-144 'hot brick' IR jammer. The type's armament includes two 0.3in (7.62mm) M60D machine guns pintle-mounted in the cabin doors, but in October 1991 it was decided that the type should be qualified to carry, on its optional hardpoints, additional weapons such as the AGM-114 Hellfire ASM, multiple launcher for 2.75in (70mm) unguided rockets, and gun/cannon pods. The type has a crew of four (night vision goggles and associated equipment being carried for the two pilots) and can carry a commando team of up to 10 men.

First flown in August 1989 for a service debut in 1990 as partial replacement for the Sikorsky HH-3F Pelican, the HH-60J Jayhawk is the US Coast Guard's medium-range SAR helicopter, and as a counterpart to the HH-60H is also derived from the SH-60B. The type has a crew of four and has a radius of at least 345 miles (555km), with a loiter capability of 45 minutes at extreme range, where at least six persons can be recovered from the surface.

SH-60R is the standard to which surviving SH-60B Seahawk and SH-60F Ocean Hawk helicopters are to be rebuilt, assuming the availability of adequate financing, with provision for fully interchangeable equipment so that the helicopters can operate in the SH-60B or SH-60F roles as the tactical situation demands. Export helicopters of the Seahawk type are designated in the S-70B core system, and include the S-70B-3 for Japan, where it is known as the SH-60J.

The Soviets (now the Russians) did not need to emulate the assault transport capability provided to the US Marine Corps by the S-65 and S-80 series of Sea Stallion and Super Stallion helicopters for the amphibious role, but felt the need for a heavy transport type that could be built in utility form for civil and military use. The result is the Mil Mi-26 'Halo'. First flown in December 1977, the Mi-26 is the world's largest production helicopter, and is a highly capable heavy-lift machine scaled up from the Mi-6 but with proportionally more power, in the form of two 9,992hp (7,450kW) ZMDB 'Progress' (Lotarev) D-136 turboshafts, to drive an eight-blade main rotor. As with other such Soviet helicopters, the large hold is accessed by clamshell rear doors and a ramp for the loading of vehicles and pieces of

artillery. The hold is 39ft 4.25in (12.00m) long (increased to 49ft 2.5in (15.00m) if the ramp is kept open), the width is 10ft 6in (3.20m) and the height varies between 9ft 8in (2.95m) and 10ft 4.75in (3.17m). Up to 85 troops or 44,092lb (20,000kg) of freight can be carried in the hold, or alternatively the same amount of freight can be lifted as a slung load.

The Mi-26A is a development of the baseline Mi-26 with a PNK-90 integrated flight and navigation system; the Mi-26MS is the medevac/casevac version of the baseline Mi-26 with a life-support section for four litters and two medical personnel, a surgical section for one litter and three medical personnel, a pre-operation section with accommodation for two litters and two medical personnel, an ambulance section with accommodation for five litters, three seated casualties and two medical personnel, a laboratory section, and a utilities section with lavatory, washing facilities and galley; the Mi-26TM is the flying crane version of the baseline Mi-26 with an undernose gondola for the pilot and sling operator, and a rear gondola for a pilot and trainee; and the Mi-26TZ is the tanker version of the baseline Mi-26 with provision for the carriage of 3,088.4Imp gal (14,040 litres) of fuel, and 228.75Imp gal (1,040 litres) of lubricants that can be dispensed to waiting vehicles via four hoses.

The Mi-26M is an uprated version currently under development with a powerplant of two D-127 turboshafts, each rated at about 14,016hp (10,450kW) for improved hot-and-high capability with the same maximum payload as the baseline Mi-26, or with an increased 55,115lb (25,000kg) payload under standard operating conditions.

Such is the cost of helicopter development and procurement today that considerable efforts have been made to boost collaborative projects such as that for the Eurocopter Tigre/Tiger. The two most important of these, although neither type has yet entered service, are the European Helicopter Industries EH.101, involving Agusta of Italy and Westland of the UK for the creation of a utility helicopter with naval, military and civil applications; and the NH Industries NH-90, involving Agusta, Eurocopter Deutschland, Eurocopter France, and Fokker of the Netherlands for the creation of a utility helicopter with naval and military applications.

The naval model of the European Helicopter Industries EH.101 is called Merlin by the Royal Navy, which is currently the largest customer for the type.

Glossary

AERODYNAMIC LIFT type of lift created by the movement of an aerofoil-shaped body through the air (or vice versa), the more highly curved upper surface producing a low-pressure area that the higher-pressure air under the surface tries to fill, thereby generating lift

AFTERBURNING system to inject and burn additional fuel with the unburned oxygen in a turbine engine's exhaust and thereby generate additional thrust; also known as reheat

ANHEDRAL NEGATIVE angle at which a wing or tailplane section is installed relative to the lateral datum

ANTI-TORQUE ROTOR small vertically mounted rotor located at the tail to counterbalance the torque reaction of the main rotor

ARTICULATED ROTOR rotor system in which there are flapping hinges, drag hinges and pitch-change bearings between the rotor head and the root of each blade

AUTOGIRO type of rotary-wing aeroplane perfected by de la Cierva with an unpowered main rotor

AUTOGYRO Autogiro-type rotary-wing aeroplane designed by anyone other than de la Cierva and his licensees

BIPLANE aeroplane with two sets of flying surfaces one above the other

CANNON rapid-fire weapon firing ammunition with an explosive projectile

CO-AXIAL ROTORS two rotors turning on a common axis with one shaft rotating inside the other

COLLECTIVE PITCH control system to control the rise or descend of a helicopter by the simultaneous (collective) increase or decrease of the pitch angle of all the main rotor blades

CONTRA-ROTATING ROTORS two rotors turning on a common axis in opposite directions with one shaft rotating inside the other

COUNTER-ROTATING rotor two rotors turning on separate axes in opposite directions

CYCLIC PITCH CONTROL system to control the direction of a helicopter in level flight by consecutive (cyclic) altering of the pitch angle of each main rotor blade according to its geometric position during each revolution, thereby tilting the theoretical axis of rotation in the direction of flight desired

DIHEDRAL   positive angle at which a wing or tailplane section is installed relative to the lateral datum

DRAG HINGE   also known as a lag hinge, this is a hinge in the main rotor's vertical plane near the root of each blade permitting each blade to move freely backward and forward in the horizontal plane independently of the other blades and the rotor hub to eliminate bending moments

FLAP HINGE   hinge in the main rotor's horizontal plane near the root of each blade permitting each blade to flap (rise or fall) in the vertical plane independently of the other blades

GULL   type of wing with an angled joint at which the sharply dihedralled inboard section becomes less acutely dihedralled

INLINE   type of aero engine with the cylinders arranged in one or more longitudinal rows

INTERRUPTER   equipment to synchronise the firing of a machine-gun with the rotation of the propeller and thus prevent a blade being hit by a machine gun bullet

INVERTED GULL   type of wing with an angled joint at which the sharply anhedralled inboard section becomes a dihedralled outboard section

LAMINAR FLOW   type of wing specially designed to ensure a smooth flow of the boundary-layer air past the surface of the wing and so reduce drag and turbulence

MACHINE-GUN   rapid-fire weapon firing ammunition with a 'ball' (solid) projectile

MONOPLANE   aeroplane with a single set of flying surfaces
parasol type of monoplane in which the wing is carried above the fuselage

PISTON ENGINE   type of aero engine that develops its power by the reciprocating movement of pistons in cylinders as a result of the burning of a fuel/air mix in the cylinders, this reciprocating movement in the cylinders being turned into rotary power by the action of connecting rods on the crankshaft

PUSHER   with a propeller that pushes the aeroplane forward

RADIAL   type of aero engine with the cylinders arranged in one or two radial rows around the crankshaft

REHEAT   system to inject and burn additional fuel with the unburned oxygen in a turbine engine's exhaust and thereby generate additional thrust; also known as afterburning

RIGID ROTOR   type of main rotor lacking blade articulation or flexibility: the blades can therefore change pitch and the whole rotor disc can see-saw on the rotor shaft, but the individual blades are not fitted with drag or flap hinges

ROTARY type of aero engine similar in arrangement to the radial engine but with the crankshaft bolted to the airframe and remaining stationary as the rest of the engine, with the propeller attached, rotates

ROTOR HEAD unit connecting the rotor shaft and main rotor with provision for collective and cyclic pitch control mechanisms

SEMI-RIGID ROTOR type of main rotor without provision for blade articulation (no drag or flap hinges) but offering limited flexibility in the drag and flap planes and also free to see-saw about the rotor shaft

SESQUIPLANE biplane with the smaller wing considerably smaller than the upper wing

TORQUE REACTION tendency of the motor (and anything attached to it) to turn in the opposite direction to the rotor driven by this motor

TRACTOR with a propeller that pulls the aeroplane forward

TRIPLANE aeroplane with three sets of flying surfaces one above the other

TURBOFAN turbine engine combining turbojet and turboprop features in as much as the turbine stage powers a large-diameter forward fan whose central column of air is drawn into the compressor and whose outer cylinder of lower-velocity air passes round the core engine

TURBOJET type of aero engine that develops its power by the use of a system to compress air, which is then mixed with fuel and burned to create a powerful exhaust that drives the turbine system powering the compressor and generating thrust turboprop turbine engine in which the exhaust-powered turbine drives a propeller and produces only a small residual thrust

Index